A
Modern History
of Kenya

Evans

Published by Evans Brothers Limited
2A Portman Mansions
Chiltern Street
London W1M 1LE

Evans Brothers (Kenya) Limited
PO Box 44536
Nairobi

Evans Brothers (Nigeria Publishers) Limited
PMB 5164, Jericho Road
Ibadan

Acknowledgements
Editor — Margaret Sharman
Cover — Gay Galsworthy
Design — James Ralton

First published 1989

Typeset by TND Serif Ltd., Hadleigh, Suffolk

Printed in Hong Kong by Dah Hua Printing Press Co. Ltd

ISBN 0 237 51082 0

Contents

Contributors

JOHN LONSDALE: B.A., Ph.D.(Cambridge). He was born in 1939 in London. He was Lecturer at University College, Dar-es-Salaam between 1964 and 1966 and has since been Lecturer in History at Trinity College, Cambridge, where he is currently Chairman of the History Faculty. He is the author of 'Some origins of nationalism in East Africa', published in the *Journal of African History* of 1968; 'States and social processes in Africa', published in *African Studies Review* 24 (1981); 'The European Scramble and conquest in African history', published in R. Oliver and V.G. Sanderson, eds., *Cambridge History of Africa*, vol. VI: *1870-1905* (Cambridge, 1985); and Editor of *South Africa in Question* (London, 1987), among his numerous other publications.

TIYAMBE ZELEZA: B.A. (University of Malawi), M.A. (University of London), Ph.D.(Dalhousie University). He was born in 1955 in Harare, Zimbabwe. He has taught at the University of Malawi (1976-7), University of West Indies (1982-4) and is currently a Senior Lecturer in History at Kenyatta University. He is the author of *Night of Darkness and Other Stories* (Montfort Press, 1976); *The Emergence of Modern Societies* (London, 1988), 'African history: the rise and decline of academic tourism', in *Ufahamu* 13(1), (1983), and 'The political economy of British colonial development and welfare in Africa', in *Transafrican Journal of History* 14 (1985), among his other publications.

ROBERT M. MAXON: B.A. (Duke University), Ph.D. (Syracuse). He was born in 1939 at Oneonta, New York. He also attended Columbia University, University of London and Makerere University. He served as Education Officer in Kenya between 1961 and 1964, and has since taught at West Virginia University where he is currently Professor and Chairman of the Department of History. He is the author of *John Ainsworth and the Making of Kenya* (Washington, 1980); and *East Africa: an introductory history* (Morgantown, 1986), among his numerous publications.

TABITHA KANOGO: B.A., Ph.D. (University of Nairobi). She was born in 1952 in Nakuru, Kenya. She attended Alliance Girls' High School and Somerville College, Oxford. She is the author of *Squatters and the Roots of Mau Mau* (London, 1987); 'Politics of collaboration or domination? A case study of the Capricorn Africa Society', in *Kenya Historical Review* 2 (2), (1974); and 'Rift Valley squatters and Mau Mau', in *Kenya Historical Review* 5(2), (1977). She is currently a Senior Lecturer in History at Kenyatta University, Nairobi.

WILLIAM R. OCHIENG': B.A. (University of East Africa), Ph.D. (University of Nairobi). He was born in 1943 in Yimbo, Nyanza. He attended Alliance High School and taught at the University of Nairobi (1970-4), Kenyatta University (1975-87) and is currently teaching at Moi University where he is Professor and Head of the History Department. He has also taught at Stanford University (1976) and UCLA (1978-9). He is the Editor of *Kenya Historical Review* and the author of *A Pre-Colonial History of the Gusii of Western Kenya* (Nairobi, 1974); *A History of the Kadimo Chiefdom of Yimbo in Western Kenya* (Nairobi, 1975); *A History of Kenya* (London, 1985); 'Moralism and expropriation in a British colony: the search for a white dominion in Kenya: 1895-1923', in *Présence Africaine* 133/134 (1985); 'Autobiography in Kenyan history', in *UFAHAMU* XIV (2), (1985), among his numerous publications.

D. KATETE ORWA: B.A. (Hiram College, USA), M.A., Ph.D. (University of Akron, USA). He was born in 1950 on Rusinga Island, Kenya. He attended Kisii and Homa Bay High Schools. He was Lecturer in Political Science at Hiram (1977-8) before proceeding to the University of Nairobi, where he is currently a Senior Lecturer in the Department of Government. He is the author of *The Congo Betrayal: UN — US and Lumumba* (Nairobi, 1985), and 'National security: the African perspective', in Bruce E. Arlinghaus, ed., *African Security Issues* (Westview Press, 1984).

Introduction

William Ochieng'

It is fashionable in a tribute, such as this, to eulogize the distinguished scholar to whom the book is being dedicated. It is, certainly, not my intention to analyse in depth the distinguished academic career of Bethwell Allan Ogot. To have done so would have been a labour of romance, indeed an exercise in sanctimonious indulgence; for Ogot is my former teacher, mentor and a close and long-time friend. Bethwell Ogot is still robust of health and agile in mind and intellect, and has no intention of downing his pen in the near future. At the age of sixty his academic career is just beginning to flower. At some later date, after he has dismantled his reading glasses and laid down his pen, perhaps such an in-depth analysis will be necessary.

However, all the contributors to this book, who are either Ogot's friends or former students, got excited at the prospect of his sixtieth birthday, and decided to celebrate it with the publication of a Kenyan history text book, in his honour. This, we knew, would gladden his heart; for Ogot, more than any other historian, has spent more time researching, supervising, discussing, reading and writing Kenyan history. We salute his sixtieth birthday and dedicate this book to him not only because we recognize the profound influence which he has had on us all, but also because he is widely regarded as the father of Kenyan history. Indeed, the selection of the contributors to this book had to be an exercise in academic apartheid, for there are few historians of Kenya, in the world, who have not been influenced, personally and directly, by him. Many there are who wrote to complain that they were denied a chance to contribute to this book; to salute the academic *ruoth*; but as we have intimated, there will surely be another occasion, or pretext, to involve many of his friends, admirers and students in another and, hopefully, larger tribute.

Born at Luanda, Siaya District, on 3 August 1929, Ogot was educated at Luanda Primary School (1938-42), Ambira School (1943-5), Maseno Secondary School (1946-9), Makerere University College (1950-2), St Andrew's University, Scotland (1955-9) and the School of Oriental and African Studies, London University (1960-1), which awarded him the degree of Doctor of Philosophy in history in 1965.

In between his studies Ogot taught Mathematics at Alliance High School, Kikuyu (1953-5) and was a Lecturer in History at Makerere University College between 1959 and 1964. In 1964 Ogot transferred from Makerere to Nairobi

University College on promotion to Senior Lecturer in History. In 1966 he became a Reader and the following year he was appointed Professor and Head of the History Department.

Apart from his teaching responsibilities, Ogot has held a large number of prestigious academic and national responsibilities. He was the first Director of the Institute of African Studies, University of Nairobi (1965-75). In 1967 he was elected Dean of the Faculty of Arts, University of Nairobi – a post which he held until he was appointed Deputy Vice-Chancellor, University of Nairobi (1970-2).

Outside the university, Ogot was Secretary-General of the East African Institute of Social and Cultural Affairs (1964-9), founder and Chairman of the Board of Directors of the East African Publishing House (1964-74) and Secretary-General of the Jomo Kenyatta Foundation (1968-9). He has also served in various organizations. He was a member of the East African Examinations Council (1967-74); a member of the National Commission for Unesco from 1968; a trustee of the National Museums of Kenya (1969-77); a member of the Executive Committee of the Association of African Universities (1972-8); a member of the Executive Council of the British Institute in Eastern Africa (1969-78); a member of the East African Legislative Council (1974-7); a founder member and past Vice-President of the East African Academy; a founder member of the Historical Association of Kenya and its Chairman between 1966 and 1985; a member of the International Scientific Committee for the Preparation of the Unesco General History of Africa, and since 1977 he has been the President of the Committee. He has been a member of the Executive Council of the International African Institute, London, since 1978; President of the Pan-African Association for Prehistory and Related Studies since 1977, and Director of the International Louis Leakey Memorial Institute for African Prehistory in Nairobi. After about six years of service outside the university, Ogot was reappointed Professor of History in 1983, but this time at Kenyatta University, Nairobi.

While we appreciate and applaud these national and international responsibilities and contributions, for us fascination with Ogot lies in his brilliant academic contribution; in the broad sweep of his theoretical formulations; and in the poignancy of his faith in African oral traditions. He first burst into academic prominence when he insisted on using oral traditions to reconstruct the precolonial history of the Luo for his Ph.D. degree with London University. Although oral traditions had been used in the past by scholars such as Jan Vansina, Basil Davidson and K.M. Stahl to reconstruct the African past, nobody, until Ogot came forward, had the guts to use them to study for a professional degree, for African oral traditions were suspected by many Western historians to be inaccurate and mythical. Ogot, however, stuck to his conviction; proceeded to collect and analyse oral tradition, and succeeded. Soon after he had been awarded the degree he had the following to say in recollection:

> When I decided to study the precolonial history of East Africa, many of my friends and mentors ridiculed the decision on the ground that one cannot study what is non-existent. They reminded me that there are no documents on this period, and that without documents there cannot be any history. Documents to them had become, in the words of an eminent historian, 'the Ark of the Covenant in the temple of facts'. But I persisted because I did not personally find the fact that we have to rely to a considerable degree on oral traditions for certain periods of East African history at all perturbing. The problem of oral evidence is not peculiar to Africa. As historical evidence, neither oral traditions nor the written word can be an accurate and dispassionate record of the past.

To fortify his resolve, Ogot cited a large number of basic documents in English history which British historians have relied on a great deal for the reconstruction of early British history, but which were largely written from British oral traditions. Among these are Gilda's *Destruction of Britain*, written by a British priest more than a hundred years after the Romans left Britain, Bede's *Ecclesiastical History*, compiled in the early eighth century, Nennius's *History of the Britons*, a thoroughly unreliable book written in the ninth century, which glorifies the Britons and makes them win every battle in wars which they obviously lost; and *The Anglo-Saxon Chronicle*, the early part of which was probably written in the reign of Alfred the Great. According to Ogot, 'what the English historians have done with these documents is what African historians must do with ethnic chronicles'. Armed with this conviction Ogot settled down in the History Department, University of Nairobi, and began to train a new breed of African historians. So successful was Ogot's productivity that a number of universities in North America, Britain and Africa began to emulate his example and to train aspiring African historians in the methods of collecting and analysing African oral traditions as a tool for reconstructing Africa's precolonial history.

It is perhaps correct to say that most of the basic historical research which has been done in Kenya in the last two decades was either done by Ogot's students, or by foreign students who were advised by him. Thus, his influence looms large on Kenyan historiography. Apart from strictly academic supervision and introduction to appropriate authorities, he exercised an almost pastoral oversight on the affairs and progress of students committed to his charge; the tedious chores of mediation on their behalf with the dispensers of patronage in the forms of scholarships, research clearance, appointments and locating publishing facilities. Despite his huge national and international commitments, Ogot always created time to sit in every departmental seminar and in all the annual conferences of the Historical Association of Kenya, whose major *Hadith* publications he edited.

Ogot's wit, humour and sense of the ridiculous can at times be overwhelming, but those whose reaction to him is merely flippant simply do not understand the man and have failed to discern that beneath the somewhat remote exterior is a brilliant scholar whose contribution to learning is solid and distinguished. There must be thousands of African and European students whose interest in history he has awakened and informed by his pen, and who would gladly know what manner of man it was that has done them so great a service. Almost singlehandedly he has revolutionized the writing of East African history. While younger historians have experimented with Marxist or other approaches, he has stuck to the safely trodden pathways of liberal tradition, gradually 'reintroducing' the African at the centre stage of his country's history and relegating the European contribution, or interference, to the side lines. If today the content of Kenya's history is so very different from what colonial historians such as George Bennett, Kenneth Ingham, Elspeth Huxley and Reginald Coupland wrote some two decades back it is because of Ogot's persistent insistence to his protégés that African historical sources must command paramountcy over official colonial sources; after all Kenyan history must be the historical experience of the indigenous Kenyan peoples. Always avoiding the clangorous tumult of the unsophisticated radicals, he has ennobled African studies, purging them of their former unsavoury racist and colonial overtones, rechannelling them into the mainstream of world history; thus inspiring a whole generation in Africa, Europe and North America to see African history in a new way.

Although *A Modern History of Kenya* is a personal tribute, it was not conceived to point at all of Ogot's research interests, or to do justice to all the fields in which he has published. (The historical writings of Ogot are listed at the end of this book.) Indeed to have attempted to do so would have required a series, not just a single volume. What gives coherence to this book is its chronological consistency, its pro-African perspective, its liberal stance, and the fact that all the contributors are interested in aspects of modern Kenyan history, attempting, in their different ways, to demonstrate one of the virtues of Ogot's historical method – the ability, and broadness of mind, to set specialist study and professional expertise in its wider historical perspective and to use specialist evidence and techniques to illustrate more general problems.

I have already said enough in explaining why we are honouring a remarkable man and a great historian. I shall only affirm it. And with that affirmation I shall ask you to salute Professor Bethwell Allan Ogot's sixtieth birthday.

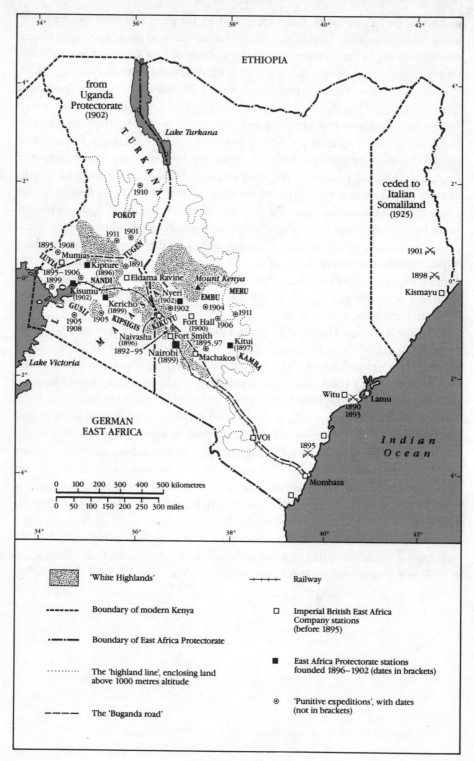

East Africa Protectorate

1 The conquest state, 1895-1904

John Lonsdale

In the ten years between 1895 and 1905, 'Kenya' – if such a retrospective concept may be permitted – was transformed from a footpath 600 miles long into a colonial administration. Territory which had taken up to three months to traverse could now be crossed in two or three days; and carriage by train cost a tiny fraction of the outlay which had been needed for a caravan of porters. And if one takes 'Kenya' to indicate a social formation rather than a level of power, then in 1895 it was an overlapping patchwork of hunting, cultivating and herding peoples. They exploited varied ecological arenas – forests, hills and plains – which were linked by the exchange of women, goods and trust. A decade later it had been wrenched into one, as yet very disjointed, field of competition between Africans to appropriate the power of colonial rule. Their former cultural identities, which had insured them against natural disaster with a non-sectarian elasticity, were being hardened into new 'tribes' by the factional politics of access to the narrow institutions of the young conquest state.

This transformation was the work of force. The British employed violence on a locally unprecedented scale, and with unprecedented singleness of mind. Their external force redefined internal power. Before the colonial conquest African power had been stored in unequal human relations which were under-written by an ideology of lineage seniority and kinship. Men's future capacity to produce meat, grain and milk was banked in their wives, in cattle loans, trading alliances and in grants of rights in land as payment for labour. Theirs was an intimately political capital, working face to face, not hidden in institutions. It demanded constant attention to its reciprocal undertakings if it was to yield returns. In normal times, therefore, its yields were marginal; Kenya's precolonial societies showed little stratification in their standards of living. Death could be a different matter. In hard times it visited the weak more than the strong. For the inequalities of power were most brutally revealed when, in some areas once in every generation, subsistence was threatened by prolonged drought – when the rains failed for more than just a couple of seasons – or by cattle plague. In such crises a strong man's dependants ceased to be his extra hands; they became extra mouths instead. Their claims for succour in return for service might have to be repudiated, if they failed to make good their patron's losses at the point of the spear. But at such times the weak could also beg for survival by pledging their labour or their children to other protectors less afflicted by drought or pestilence, often among

6

neighbouring peoples with a different language and an alien mode of subsistence. Kenya's peoples were like the American nation, made up of strangers, both adventurers and refugees.

After the conquest Kenya became a more harshly politicized economy. This was partly because power had been centralized in the state, which rested on force and the new imperial ideology of progress. It was also due to the new nature of productive capital. Modern capital has a dual character. It is partly subject, as productive power had previously been, to political protection and exclusion. But it is also a commodity in a global circulation that pays little respect to local privilege. It is amenable to political hierarchy and yet subversive of it. So it was in colonial Kenya. Capital seemed fixed in property and racial identity. Both preserves were demarcated and protected by the state. Exclusive property rights and bureaucratic power laid the ground for an acquisitive differentiation rather than a rough parity in the enjoyment of resources. For propertied capital was designed to recruit labour by seizing productive assets from workers rather than by allocating resources to dependants. And taxation, which was levied on all, made it possible for public expenditure to subsidize the few, to make them more attractive to outside investors. At times of economic crisis organized force enabled the strong to squeeze the weak harder, giving an entirely new meaning to the repudiation of their claims. 'From that time', the Kikuyu elder Kabetu wa Waweru remembered some thirty years later, 'the state of things began to change more and more rapidly, and ceased to be at all like it was in the olden days. The country became like a new country that was unknown to us.'[1]

But, despite appearances, it was not an entirely new country. Conquest enlarged African power as much as it redefined it as European. There was continuity as well as disruption. State-building could not be a wholly destructive process. The British conquerors had to create a new high politics, a hierarchy of self-interest, out of the existing networks of authority. African leaders may have been forced to carry unprecedented burdens, but they had also to be allowed new means to pursue old interests. Without obedient followers they were as useless to their new rulers as to their old communities. And it was not only African notables who found much that was familiar in the unknown. For the embryo state was not only *built*, as a deliberate means to contain and direct power for the benefit of the few. It was also *formed* out of the anonymous actions of many. In evading servitudes ancient and modern the weaker members of African society used novel forms of association to regain old personal freedoms. However unwillingly, the state protected these subversive young ways of common life and labour as much as it fostered fresh privilege. State-formation, the vulgarization of power, and state-building, its cultivation, were contradictory processes which complemented each other.

This was because conquest was not only a political process but an economic force. It made room for both the oppressive and the corrosive tendencies of propertied capitalism. Colonial rule entrenched power; it also enlarged markets. The African poor could exploit the new demands for their produce and their labour because there was also new competition for the prestige of their protection. They even found a market in land, despite its alienation to Europeans. As workers they were oppressed but as dependants they benefited from the rivalry for their service among a wider range of patrons. Their chiefs were fastened more securely over them with administrative sanctions but, as before, they were not the only masters. The power of the state had made room for others. Missionaries, produce-traders, officials and landlords, bid up the price of the productive allegiance of the poor, insisting that the state protect them from the inflationary consequences of their own competition.

The violence of conquest was thus never quite complete. It was to be repeatedly renewed in Kenya's subsequent history. Men of property and power would always demand new forms of protection whenever they discovered, yet again, that they could not appease the resentful ingenuity of the people, except by letting slip some of the existing privileges by which capitalism was sustained locally and made profitable to backers overseas.[2]

Conquest: the investment of force

The story of Britain's imperial interest in the East African interior and the subsequent colonial conquest has been often told and cannot be repeated here in any detail.[3] Until the mid-1880s Britain's position rested on the shaky fiction of the mainland sovereignty of her protected creature the sultan of Zanzibar and, more securely but at unwelcome expense, on the Royal Naval squadron which scoured the Indian Ocean coast for Arab slavers. Once the sultan had been pushed aside in the European scramble for Africa, the scarcely more substantial Imperial British East Africa Company was chartered to occupy the British sphere of influence. Then, in late 1889, Britain woke up to the prospect of a prolonged occupation of Egypt. Strategic panic over the control of the Nile headwaters overcame her determination to do nothing in East Africa that would antagonize Germany. But the Company was already sliding into bankruptcy, sunk by its efforts to hold Buganda rather than by improving the route to the interior, the future Kenya. By 1895 Britain had no option but to annexe what was then called the East Africa Protectorate, but showed how little she welcomed the Company's legacy by putting it in the care of her consul-general in Zanzibar.

The conquest of the territory proceeded in three distinct phases. First, an awkward paramountcy was established over the coastline, its sovereignty nominally shared with the sultan. Then, for six years, the British were preoccupied with the defence of the Buganda road, which was gradually strengthened into the line of the Uganda railway. This iron backbone of conquest reached Lake Victoria in 1901. In the following year the railway was brought under one administration by shifting the boundary between the East Africa and Uganda Protectorates 200 miles to the west, from the rim of the Rift Valley to the north-eastern corner of the lake. The foundation

8

of control had been laid. It had yet to be put to profitable use. The final and most violent phase of conquest followed, occupying the highland core of modern Kenya. In acknowledgement that diplomatic adventure had become administrative responsibility, the Foreign Office relinquished control to the Colonial Office in 1905, and peace, of a sort, came three years later.

Conquest is the proper term to use. The British forces were tiny and their armaments light; until the railway was complete they were less mobile than the forces of African resistance. Their supply was a constant nightmare, their intelligence often a farce. They depended on local African manpower for auxiliary troops and porters. They bought tons of food from African growers at prices that could not be dictated. They owed their political intuition to self-interested African informants. As in the rest of the continent, it was largely an African rather than an imperial conquest. But not entirely. The British were able to control the process and impose their own sense of direction because the disciplined, uniformed, core of the violence was unequivocally theirs. They employed strangers, recruited in distant labour markets, men whose home was a regiment rather than a district, who could be rewarded with pay instead of power. Many of these were Africans from elsewhere, but whenever the going got rough the British looked first to their Indians.[4]

Control over the coast did not mean storming the gates of Kenya but defending the ramshackle outposts of Zanzibar. The British feared that the abolition of coastal slavery might mean war with the Arab slave-masters. In the event, their extreme caution over this social revolution,[5] together with the openings provided by Arab dynastic rivalry and disputed successions, allowed the British to retain the alliance of Zanzibar's notables even while supplanting them. The decisive events came in the early 1890s. Two Arab dynasties were crushed, the Nabahani of Witu[6] and the Mazrui, formerly of Mombasa, both of whom contested the overlordship of the Al Bu Sai'di sultans of Zanzibar. These were the only campaigns of the conquest in which British units and heavy guns were employed, both loaned by the Royal Navy. The two further engagements at the coast, against the Somali, were also to protect the old Arab trade network rather than to establish a distinctively British presence. The expeditionary forces, again, reflected British supremacy in the Indian Ocean rather than over the mainland; they were composed of Zanzibaris, Sudanese, the Aden Camel Corps and, crucially, the foreign legionaries of the empire, Punjabis and Baluchis from India.

The two subsequent phases of conquest were quite different in character. The protectorate government inherited, it is true, the rag-tag troops of the Company, both the Sudanese of the upper Nile with their wives and children, and the sultan's guardsmen, the *viroboto* or dancing fleas, of whom some were Swahili coastmen, others Baluchi soldiers of fortune. They were renamed the East African Rifles, but the regiment was scarcely native to the protectorate. It recruited in India and in Egypt, where former Sudanese soldiers, some of them ex-Mahdists, could be picked up on the streets of Cairo. It also signed up men who had been the porters of the Zanzibari ivory and slave trades, Nyamwezi from what was now the German mainland to the south, and Manyema, ex-slaves from the still further interior, now King Leopold's Congo. The disruptions of the African hunting frontier, which had expanded in advance of the European scramble, had cast up many such homeless adventurers, ready to be enlisted in an imperial service that did not greatly differ from the employment they had already known.[7] By 1897 they numbered about 1,100 men, all strangers to the people they were ordered to fight. But they were products of African, not Indian Ocean history, and they would have been both blind and immobile without the assistance of barefoot warriors more local still.

The East African Rifles was not an impressive force. One of its companies bolted when charged by Somalis. Its white officers were said to be rejects from their home regiments; they kept their African mistresses in their quarters. As late as 1902 the troops were armed with single-shot rifles; these were rusted up for lack of a rifle range on which to fire.[8] But then the regiment's adversaries, the people of Kenya, were not very warlike either. They were stateless peoples, without standing armies. Having only recently met Zanzibari traders, few of them had learned the use of guns. Their young men, certainly, saw raiding as a legitimate means to acquire cattle, but most of Kenya's peoples valued livestock principally as the working capital of family formation, farming and trade. And household heads, the men of property and power, had good reason to curb the aggression of the young. War became destruction only in response to natural disaster, when social control crumbled and survival was at stake. Even then, war had a self-limiting quality. Land, cattle and manpower had to be kept in a rough equilibrium in societies with such simple working tools. There was no point in having more cows than one could herd, more land than one's wives could hoe or one's young men defend. Accumulation of resources was impossible without the accumulation of people. People could not be controlled without giving them a share not only in resources but also in esteem. Defeated peoples could not be kept in strict subjection. It would have entailed a literally unimaginable expense.[9]

This is where colonial warfare differed. In comparison with 'civilized warfare' it was ridiculously cheap, but its costs could still be calculated. It is estimated that her seventy million new African subjects cost Britain about 15 pence each; most of that paltry sum was spent not on armies but on the railways which followed them.[10] Even those who reject the concept of economic imperialism must concede that it had to be economical, and to the men who made this investment in European law and order the outlay was ruinous. It bankrupted the Imperial British East Africa Company, which found that export duties on ivory – the only local export that could bear the cost of porterage – were quite inadequate to sustain even its feeble pretence at control. The successor East Africa Protectorate did no better. In 1905 its treasurer was appalled to find that a decade of military effort had cost over £600,000, very nearly one-third of all public expenditure and rather more than total domestic revenues.[11] This was nothing when set beside the £5.5 million spent on the railway, itself a military necessity. It would have put another company out of business, and was not what the British taxpayer expected from Empire.

The British urgently needed to convert the external, costly and destructive force of conquest into internal, negotiable and productive power. They had to emulate their own Roman governor, Agricola, of whom the admiring Tacitus had said that 'when he had done enough to inspire fear, he returned to mercy and proffered the allurements of peace'.[12] Was Sir Arthur Hardinge, the protectorate's first commissioner, recalling his own schooldays in his echoed premise that, 'These people must learn submission by bullets – it's the only school; after that you may begin more modern and humane methods of education'?[13] But if Africans had to learn the European lesson of submission, the British had to learn the local African lesson, how to pacify their mastery.[14] 'Pacification', rightly, is no longer used to describe colonial conquest. What needed subjugation was not so much the disorder of Africa as the irruption of Europe. But pacification is still a proper term to describe what the British had to do *to* their conquest rather than *with* it. They had used African power in order to undermine it; now they had to make it profitable. They had to capitalize on the politics of conquest.

The highlanders of Kenya

Kenya is about as large as France, with an area of around 582,600 sq.km, or 225,000 sq. miles.[15] Most of it is arid steppe, in some places virtual desert, usable only for extensive pastoralism by sparse populations. Not more than about 14 per cent, or 80,000 sq.km, is suitable for agriculture or more intensive grazing. This high potential land is concentrated in the south-western corner of the country, 400 km (250 miles) and more from the coast. It is enclosed by the 1,000 m (3,300 feet) contour, above which one can expect rainfall of over 500 mm (20 inches) for at least seven years in every ten. This is the area of the Kenya highlands, split down the middle by the Rift Valley. It was the scene of the second and third phases of the colonial conquest.

The population of what became Kenya may have amounted to three million in 1890, of whom some three-quarters would have lived in the highlands. Three main groups of people were involved in the conquest. Inland from the coast the first to be met were the highland Bantu, primarily the Kamba and the Kikuyu, but also the Embu and Meru of Mount Kenya. They were peoples, not tribes, potential nations rather than actual dispersions of related lineages. There were boundaries between them, and they gave their neighbours different names, but these served to demarcate different environments and the different cultures that had grown up in their management, not absolute breaks in political allegiance and economic self-sufficiency. Trade, marriage and patronage knew no confines. The men of power within each group had dealings with their opposite numbers up in the hills or down in the plains.

11

Wandsworth Libraries

Opening Times

Wandsworth

**Wandsworth Libraries
Something for everyone**

Lending Libraries
▼ (Closed on Wednesday)

Balham Library
Ramsden Road
SW12 8QY &
0181 871 7195
Fax: 0181 675 4015

Balham Music Library
(as above)

Monday	10.00am - 8.00pm
Tuesday	10.00am - 8.00pm
Wednesday	Closed all day
Thursday	10.00am - 8.00pm
Friday	10.00am - 8.00pm
Saturday	10.00am - 6.00pm
Sunday	1.00pm - 5.00pm

Alvering Library
Allfarthing Lane
SW18 2PQ &
0181 871 6398
Fax: 0181 870 4599

Earlsfield Library
Magdalen Road
SW18 3NY &
0181 871 6389
Fax: 0181 944 6912

Northcote Library
Northcote Road
SW11 6QB &
0181 871 7469
Fax: 0171 228 6842

York Library
Wye Street
SW11 2SP &
0181 871 7471
Fax: 0171 223 0864

Monday	9.30am - 7.00pm
Tuesday	9.30am - 7.00pm
Wednesday	Closed all day
Thursday	9.30am - 7.00pm
Friday	9.30am - 5.00pm
Saturday	9.00am - 5.00pm

Tooting Library
Mitcham Road
SW17 9PD &
0181 871 7175
Fax: 0181 672 3099

Multicultural Library & Information Service
•Asian Section
Tooting Library
Mitcham Road
SW17 9PD
0181 871 7174
Fax: 0181 672 3099

Monday	9.30am - 7.00pm
Tuesday	9.30am - 7.00pm
Wednesday	Closed all day
Thursday	9.30am - 7.00pm
Friday	9.30am - 5.00pm
Saturday	9.00am - 5.00pm
Sunday	1.00pm - 5.00pm

Lending Libraries
▼ (Closed on Thursday)

Battersea Library
Lavender Hill
SW11 1JB &
0181 871 7466
Fax: 0171 978 4376

Multicultural Library & Information Service
•African Caribbean Section
•Children's Section
Battersea Library
Lavender Hill
SW11 1JB &
0181 871 7466
Fax: 0171 978 4376

Putney Library
Disraeli Road
SW15 2DR &
0181 871 7090
Fax: 0181 789 6175

Monday	10.00am - 8.00pm
Tuesday	10.00am - 8.00pm
Wednesday	10.00am - 8.00pm
Thursday	Closed all day
Friday	10.00am - 8.00pm
Saturday	9.00am - 5.00pm
Sunday	1.00pm - 5.00pm

Battersea Park Library
Battersea Park Road
SW11 4NF &
0181 871 7468
Fax: 0171 622 5459

Roehampton Library
Danebury Avenue
SW15 4HD &
0181 871 7091
Fax: 0181 780 2719

Southfields Library
Wimbledon Park Road
SW19 6NL &
0181 871 6388
Fax: 0181 780 9045

West Hill Library
West Hill
SW18 1RZ &
0181 871 6386
Fax: 0181 877 3476

Monday	9.30am - 7.00pm
Tuesday	9.30am - 7.00pm
Wednesday	9.30am - 7.00pm
Thursday	Closed all day
Friday	9.30am - 5.00pm
Saturday	9.00am - 5.00pm

Wandsworth on the web

- Access the Internet at all the libraries
- Set up your own E-mail account
- Browse the web

Minimum charge £1

Open on Sundays

- Balham Library
- Battersea Library
- Putney Library
- Tooting Library

All open every Sunday

1.00pm - 5.00pm

Reference Libraries

Battersea Reference Library
Altenburg Gardens
SW11 1JQ
0181 871 7467
Fax: 0171 978 4376
& via lending library

Monday 9.00am - 9.00pm
Tuesday 9.00am - 9.00pm
Wednesday 9.00am - 9.00pm
Thursday 9.00am - 9.00pm
Friday 9.00am - 9.00pm
Saturday 9.00am - 5.00pm
Sunday 1.00pm - 5.00pm

West Hill Reference Library
West Hill
SW18 1RZ &
0181 871 6387
Fax: 0181 877 3476

Monday 9.00am - 8.00pm
Tuesday 9.00am - 8.00pm
Wednesday 9.00am - 8.00pm
Thursday Closed all day
Friday 9.00am - 5.00pm
Saturday 9.00am - 5.00pm

Local History Library
Lavender Hill
SW11 1JB
0181 871 7753
Fax: 0171 978 4376

Monday Closed all day
Tuesday 10am - 1pm, 2pm - 8pm
Wednesday 10am -1pm, 2pm - 8pm
Thursday Closed all day
Friday 10am - 1pm, 2pm - 5pm
Saturday 9am - 1pm

Mobile Library
& Housebound Service

Mobile Library 0181 871 6350
Fax: 0181 870 4599

When and where a mobile library calls:

Battersea area
Monday	1.30 - 2.30	Battersea High Street
Monday	2.45 - 3.45	Wickersley Road
Monday	4.00 - 5.00	Thackeray Road
Monday	5.15 - 7.30	Condell Road
Thursday	3.45 - 5.00	Roseneath Road
Thursday	5.30 - 7.30	Petworth Street

Tooting Area
Wednesday	4.45 - 5.15	Mandrake Road
Wednesday	5.30 - 6.30	Smallwood Road
Wednesday	6.45 - 7.30	Strathdon Drive, Aboyne Estate
Saturday	3.45 - 4.30	Brudenell Road

Furzedown Area
Saturday	10.00 -12.30	Gracedale Road
Saturday	1.45 - 3.30	Abbotsleigh Road

Wandsworth Common Area
Thursday	1.45 - 2.15	Baskerville Road
Thursday	2.30 - 3.30	Ouseley Road

Roehampton Area
Tuesday	12.15 -12.45	Toland Square, Eastwood Estate
Tuesday	2.00 - 4.00	Putney Vale Estate
Friday	1.30 - 2.15	Aubyn Square, Eastwood Estate
Friday	3.15 - 5.15	Arabella Drive, Lennox Estate

Putney Area
Wednesday	12.30 -1.00	Westleigh Avenue
Friday	2.30 - 3.00	Carslake Road, Ashburton Estate
Friday	5.30 - 6.15	Clarendon Drive
Friday	6.30 - 7.30	Floss Street

Southfields Area
Tuesday	4.15 - 6.30	Inner Park Road
Tuesday	6.45 - 7.30	Victoria Drive

Please ring the number above for details of the
Housebound Readers Service

L-405 (rev.10.98)

All the highland Bantu were neighbours to the Maasai, the lords of the Rift. As the one purely pastoral people of the highlands, they could survive only in close connexion with the 'mixed farming' peoples who lived beyond their escarpments. The Maasai were the bankers of the highlands. Their capital, and their currency, was livestock.[16] The cultivators who surrounded them needed to invest any surplus harvest in stock, and much livestock in women. They had no other long-term means to store grain; vermin and humidity saw to that. So they traded grain for cattle and goats, using them to speculate in the future reproduction of manpower. Conversely, the Maasai had to reinsure their cattle. They fostered exchange friendships with their neighbours, married their daughters and took in the apprentice stockherd labour of their sons. When their livestock was next decimated by drought or disease they might then hope to reach accommodations that were not too unequal with near relatives across the agricultural border. At best, they might get by simply by selling off stock at famine prices. It was only on those rare occasions of real disaster, the famines that killed large numbers, that unequal exchange gave way to large movements of starving populations and really desperate raids.

Westwards still, beyond the Rift, lay the peoples who looked out on the Victoria Nyanza. The Kalenjin-speaking peoples, principally the Nandi, the Kipsigis and the Tugen, lived up on the watershed. Each controlled hill and plateau, farmland and pasture. It may be because they encompassed this marked dual economy within one culture that they seem to have had less intense relations with their neighbours than was typical of the highland peoples. Yet the more lowland peoples of the Nyanza basin, the Bantu-speaking Luyia and Gusii and the Nilotic Luo-speakers, had equally mixed economies and pursued trading strategies that linked them all, and the Maasai, in a regional system as busy as that which also joined the Maasai and the highland Bantu.[17]

In order to understand the politics of their British conquest one must first grasp some idea of their own. They were all colonizing peoples, for whom the control of scarce labour was paramount. Their basic unit of production and consumption was the extended family. But no family could survive in isolation. Each needed the cooperation of others in the seasonal chores of agriculture and in herding. The idiom of cooperation was patrilineal descent through the generations and the kinship of contemporaries. But the organization of work was less egalitarian than its ideology. It was focused on big men with large families who could exploit more than their families alone – impoverished dependent workers, immigrant families grateful for protection, marriage alliances with neighbouring settlements or herding sections, and mutual defence agreements with other big men. Small settlements could not prosper without wide networks.

This way of life had thrown up four different forms of authority, based on seniority, ambition, inspiration and organization. The pervading source of power was seniority. Age conferred superior knowledge of the environment, control over women and therefore control over young men. Its supportive ideology of lineage descent differentiated full citizens with prior entitlement to local resources from client outsiders who were most at risk when subsistence was squeezed by disaster, but whose descendants might earn full incorporation. Lineage was a court of claims rather than a family tree.

Lineage was matched by generation, both as a perceived division of society, and as a source of social control. Most highlanders dramatized in civic ritual the successive stages of life, from gallant youth to mature family headship and awesome old age. Youth was the time of ambition, an unruly phase which many peoples, the more pastoral especially, sought to discipline within the institution of the warrior age-group. But warriorhood was the moment to evade the elders' control by investing stolen stock in marriage. Youthful leadership paid off in later life in the ability to marry more wives, to enlist male dependants and to tend the alliances that protected trade in the products of home, pasture and field. The impatience of ambition was often relieved by the colonization of a fresh settlement, not so much by the single 'lineage founder' of oral tradition as by the families associated with him and their followers.

The inspiration which could divine and manipulate supernatural forces was the gift of few. It was inherited in prophetic lineages and fostered by apprenticeship. Its oracular power was most strongly developed among the Maasai as the sanction for internal alliance and external raids, but there was a wide regional market in the arcane knowledge believed necessary to cope with the unpredictable cruelties of climate, disease and personal misfortune.

All authorities were subject to the frailties of personality and chance. Their mutual competition was but rarely suppressed by organized hierarchies of precedence, consultation and control. The nearest approach to a power stable enough to be termed chiefship was found in the far west, over some of the Luo and Luyia settlements. Everywhere else chiefship was a figment of the ethnographic imagination of the early British officials.

These fragile powers had grown up to exploit and control the divisions of age, gender and natural environment. Never secure, their holders were always on the alert to buy fresh insurances against new threats. In the later nineteenth century they were faced with two challenges, one which could be turned to profit, the other which threatened disaster.

State-building 1: The politics of conquest

The Swahili trading frontier offered the challenge of profit. Backed by the Indian financiers of Zanzibar, it first advanced into the highlands in mid-century. The Swahili came for ivory; they captured or bought people only where they could most easily exploit social division or distress. Their caravans were well armed because they were also well capitalized. They traded rather than raided. They imported fashion items rather than productive goods, cloth, beads and iron and copper wire. Their external market intensified the regional highland traffic, linking more closely the domestic production of forest and plain, each with their elephant herds, and cultivated hills. Local circuits of influence and exchange opened out, making alliance with the coastal strangers a more reliable investment in power than anything previously available.

Internal leaders reinforced their role as external brokers. They could be elders, war-leaders or chiefs. Prophets flourished too, as successful men fretted over the rising stakes of power. Spirals of local accumulation developed. The caravan food market coupled the hire of outside firepower in local conflicts to the acquisition of the livestock needed to command more domestic labour, whether by increased polygyny or by funding young male clients.[18] There were new opportunities for conspicuous consumption, especially in dress. One or two gatekeepers with the wider world diversified their ideological standing with some outward show of Islam.

Much of the subsequent politics of conquest turned on the historical accident of whether the British advent reinforced or threatened these new commercial interests. The Company caravans resembled the Swahili parties in every way save for their avowed hostility to slaving. They employed the same leaders, recruited the same porters and guards, acted as wholesalers for some of the Swahili traders,[19] and had no stronger bargaining position with the local African food and ivory brokers. But while the Company men kept to the main track to Uganda, the Swahili fanned out more widely, as elephant were shot out nearer to hand and the Company tried to impose ivory duties at the established markets. By the early 1890s a series of concentric trading systems had begun to emerge, centred on the main food-buying areas on the Buganda road, in the southern Kamba and Kikuyu countries, at Baringo in the Rift valley, and in the Wanga chiefdom among the Luyia people.[20] The inner circle of contacts in each region traded with both the Swahili and the Company, the outer circle with the Swahili alone. In these frontier zones the guns which were used to shoot elephants seem to have been put more freely to political use. Swahili traders and ambitious young men joined in exploiting a new means of destruction over which there was no social control. Beyond the Company's reach a military revolution was stirring. In some places it overlaid a previous such revolution manned by hired Maasai spearmen.

It has been said that, in the context of the conquest, the Maasai were the hinge of Kenya.[21] If so, by the 1890s they were distinctly rusty. In the middle years of the century they had been engaged in recurring civil conflict, the Iloikop wars. These left the victorious sections, at the centre of the Rift's seasonal grazing system, with pastures too vast to defend. Conversely, the strong men of agricultural colonization on its margins rearmed themselves with the client warriors of defeated sections. Most notably, refugee prophets started to build a clannish ritual ascendancy among the Nandi. The Maasai world looked to be falling in on them.

14

Table 1.1. The disasters

	Nyanza Basin	Kalenjin	Turkana Basin	Maasai	Kikuyu Embu	Kamba	Coast
1870				Iloikop		famine	
		pleuro					
				civil			
1875				wars			
			pleuro				
1880							
	pleuro-pneumonia			pleuro			
						famine	
1885			smallpox				famine
	pleuro				✗ Teleki		
1890			r i n d e r p e s t				✗ Witu
			d r o u g h t				
	smallpox	locusts		s m a l l p o x			
	jiggers				jiggers & locusts		✗ Witu
					✗ Kabete		
1895	✗ Bukusu	✗ Nandi	smallpox	✗ Kedong	✗ Githunguri	✗ Mwala	✗ Mazrui
		✗ Tugen			locusts		
	pleuro	✗ Nandi		✗ Morijo	jiggers	Kilungu	famine
				war			
				r i n d e r p e s t			✗ Somali
	✗ Luo			famine — smallpox — locusts			
1900	smallpox	✗ Nandi	drought				✗ Somali
	sleeping —	✗ Pokot			✗ Maruka		
	sickness	✗ Nandi			✗ Tetu		
				1st move	✗ Mathira		
1905	✗ Gusii	✗ Sotik					
	drought	✗ Nandi			✗ Embu		
	✗ Gusii						
	smallpox		rinderpest				
1910			✗ Turkana	pleuro			
	rinderpest	✗ Marakwet	drought	2nd move	✗ Tharaka		

Note: smallpox (etc.) = natural disaster (pleuro = pleuro-pneumonia in cattle)

  ✗ Nandi (etc.) = official military action or government pressure, with the exceptions of
  (a) ✗ Teleki, which represents the fighting passage of Count Teleki's private expedition
      through Kikuyuland, and
  (b) ✗ Kedong, which represents the massacre of 650 Kikuyu and Swahili porters by
      the Maasai, followed by the massacre of 100 Maasai by a private British trader.

As if these man-made troubles were not enough, in the 1890s the Maasai were assailed by natural disasters which affected them more severely than the mixed farming peoples. The catastrophes were partly cyclical and predictable. There were droughts and locust infestations at the beginning of the decade and again, more viciously, at its end. As usual, famine gave rise to epidemic smallpox, as non-immune pastoralists searched for food among agriculturalists with whom the disease was endemic. The epidemic then raged among herders and farmers alike.[22] But these old scourges were reinforced by two calamities apparently new to Africa. The first was rinderpest or cattle plague. This also visited twice, in 1890-1 and in 1898. On the first occasion it swept down from the north, apparently imported in Russian cattle, the meat ration for the Italian invasion of Eritrea. The second rinderpest advanced from the coast along the line of railway construction, brought in by draught oxen from India.[23] Jiggers were the other newcomer, sandfleas from Brazil which arrived by ship on the Congo coast and spread across Africa. Burrowing into toes, they crippled cultivators or killed them off with gangrene.

It is difficult to quantify these disasters. European travellers penned a picture quite as harrowing as those seen by television audiences a century later. But it is not clear how widely the horror spread. Rinderpest can kill up to 90 per cent of affected herds, but it travels only along the lines of trade, raids and transhumant grazing, and Kenya's peoples knew the value of quarantine. Maasai herds were devastated, but not all of them. The same patchwork fate seems to have befallen virtually all their neighbours. The hill-dwelling Kalenjin, the Nandi included, were most able to preserve their herds from danger.[24] The scale of human suffering is just as uncertain. Death was best reported among the Maasai, the southern Kikuyu and the Kamba. Among some of their settlements anything up to 40 per cent may have perished; the mortality was heaviest among the old and the young, including the warriors. Death did not similarly ravage the populations of the Victoria lakeshore until the century's turn, when the sleeping-sickness epidemic advanced in parallel with the tsetse-infested bush which well-stocked pastures had previously kept at bay.[25]

The social consequences of demographic collapse were just as varied at both the societal and the individual levels. Among the Maasai civil strife was renewed in the Morijo war. Their pastoral sections regrouped and raided each other under the rival leadership of the brothers Olonana and Senteu, who competed for the prophetic mantle of their father, the great laibon Mbatiany. Thousands of Massai also sought refuge with their neighbours, principally the southern Kikuyu. The Kikuyu and Kamba mixed farmers profited from Maasai distress. They raided the shattered herdsmen, bought up their surviving stock at bargain prices, and used their refugee labour to expand their own cultivation, ready for the next rains. But the frontier of Kikuyu agriculture also receded northward, as colonist settlements fled from drought and smallpox to the better watered homes of the lineages they had left behind in central Kikuyuland.

Within these broad demographic struggles individual social differentiation seems to have become more marked. Big men were expected to organize the means of survival, offence and defence. Their large herds would have been prudentially scattered among dependants and allies, less vulnerable than concentrated small herds to the caprice of calamity. Their warrior sons could enforce the repayment of livestock loans. They could protect their closest followers by rejecting those with lesser claims. With their famished refugee workers they could exploit soaring food demand with increased production. Between 1890 and 1899 grain prices on the Kikuyu caravan market rose at least thirty-fold. It is no wonder that elderly Kikuyu sixty years later, when asked who died in the famine, answered simply, 'the poor'.[26] How much of the price inflation should be blamed on the increased food purchases of the British, now feeding railway navvies as well as troops and porters, is a matter for dispute.[27] But it is scarcely open to doubt that many more of the poor would have died had they not been able to find a new refuge in the civil and military labour markets of conquest.

The politics of conquest was an integral part of the crisis. The conquest itself, not of Kenya alone but of the rest of Africa, bore a heavy responsibility for the disasters. Rinderpest, jiggers and the tsetse fly would not otherwise have wreaked their havoc. But conquest also provided outdoor famine relief. Many Africans reconstructed their resources, if often at the expense of their fellows, by drawing in an auxiliary role on the British investment in force. The politics of conquest was 'intensely local'.[28] But one can discern four broad patterns, each related to the double trading frontier and to the disasters.

Until 1901 the chief British interests remained the security and supply of the Buganda road. By the mid-1890s there were three main food-buying stations, each with a small garrison, Machakos in southern Kamba country, Fort Smith at the southern end of Kikuyu, just above the swamp that became Nairobi, and Mumias, a village named after its Luyia Wanga chief.[29] These became the forward bases of conquest. In each area the British attracted market brokers from the nearest settlements. There was nothing new in their mutual confidences. But in each of the three areas a rift developed between an inner circle of those whom the British saw as 'friendlies' and an outer circle of recalcitrants. These rifts became the fault-lines of violence.

Local economic differences became the frontiers of British security. Among the Kamba, John Ainsworth, a Company man who became the senior protectorate official in the interior, trained firearmed militias from among his food-suppliers, so that they could defend themselves against the Maasai. But they soon became his tactical reserve against the more pastoral northern Kamba settlements, amongst whom the displaced Swahili found auxiliaries for ivory and slave hunting further afield.[30] A similar patchwork of alliances and hostility evolved among the southern Kikuyu. Their cultivation may have expanded as early as the 1860s, in response to the caravan market.[31] And although the evidence is slender, it appears that senior members of Kikuyu settlements, who controlled the core arable land, became increasingly incensed

17

with their junior members who were more interested in cattle, and with the warrior age-grades. Both the latter pursued ambitions which disrupted trade. The Fort Smith 'punitive expeditions' of the middle 1890s can well be interpreted as defending Kikuyu grain suppliers against their more pastoral relations, impoverished by rinderpest, lower down the hills. Swahili adventurers do not seem to have provided an additional irritant here. Indeed, the Kikuyu leaders on whom the British most relied, Waiyaki and, after him, Kinyanjui in the south, Karuri in the centre and Wang'ombe to the north, had all risen to prominence as brokers for the Swahili trade, the last three by virtue of their close ties with the Athi forest people, the elephant hunters.[32]

The politics of conquest among the Luyia, finally, combined elements of both the Kamba and the Kikuyu patterns. Until 1902 this arena of conquest came under the Uganda Protectorate, a sideshow to the drama of royal resistance and rebellion in the kingdoms of Bunyoro and Buganda. Mumias was like Machakos, its storekeeper Charles Hobley not unlike Ainsworth. He too armed a local militia, struggling to survive in a fragmented regional economy set on edge by rinderpest and famine. Its conflicts profited long-established Maasai military colonies and Swahili traders, who tried to retain their local alliances while evading British censure. Hobley's forces gradually supplanted both. Mumia, at the centre of the British supply network, had the same interest as the Kikuyu grain sellers in shuffling off his pastoral spearmen, in this case his Maasai. And the Swahili cut their losses by shifting their attentions to the Luyia periphery, as their colleagues had done among the Kamba. It was not until 1908 that the Bukusu, the northernmost Luyia people, were forced to give up their Swahili-supplied guns.[33]

That was the first pattern of conquest. It enlarged the power of the agricultural authorities along the road, at the expense of their more pastoral interests. But the British would have been unable to engineer these accommodations with such comparative ease had they not enjoyed the alliance of the Rift Valley Maasai, the former victors of the Iloikop wars as distinct from the losers who had settled among the Luyia. So the second pattern of conquest entailed the reconstruction of the pastoral system at the heart of the highlands. The Maasai found the British military labour market more rewarding and culturally more congenial than Kikuyu farmworking.

In virtually all the minor campaigns which stitched together the defence agreements of the Buganda road, a company or two of the East African Rifles was supported by Maasai auxiliaries, often many hundreds of them. These volunteered to raid people they may now have been too weak to attack without British help, often in support of British 'friendlies' with whom the Maasai had previous understandings. The conduct of warfare did not change greatly in the 1890s; enemy African casualties were not so large as they later became. The British aimed to destroy huts and crops, and to capture livestock, so as to enforce submission. And their peace terms were not, at first, particularly onerous – the surrender of both guns and the deserter Swahili porters who

18

knew how to use them, promises to give free passage to official caravans and readiness to sell food.[34]

On the early expeditions the Maasai were awarded most of the stock which they themselves had looted. British power was still questionable enough to need sharing out. Indeed the Maasai were only doubtfully under British control. Their misinformation was distrusted, especially with respect to their old rivals the Nandi. In one early skirmish the Maasai word for 'enemy', *mangati*, was taken to be the proper name of a Luyia settlement.[35] But to the Maasai the significance of their British alliance lay in its domestic ramifications. The patronage of providing opportunities for military adventure accrued to Olonana and helped his clientele to win the Morijo civil war. But the threads of patronage then slipped through Olonana's fingers into the hands of the separate warrior leaders, the *il aigwanak*. As the political capital of cattle accumulated once more, providing fresh breeding stock for family herds, so Olonana's prophetic assets declined. The chief support of the British, he became the main loser in the final reckoning of conquest. Maasai herdsmen were well on the way to recovery from the disasters and could afford to disengage from the British connexion. Nor did the British stand in such need of the Maasai. Without bargains to negotiate, Olonana was no longer broker but broken. The politics of conquest had certainly enlarged pastoral power, but it was not clear how it could be used in the new dispensation.[36]

The Maasai lever of conquest lay ready to hand because of the disasters. And openings for its insertion along the road were available in the divisions of self-interest between those settlements that were involved in the caravan market and those which were not. It was the people who had suffered least in the disasters who offered most resistance to conquest. These were the Kalenjin highlanders, with the Nandi at their centre. They furnished the third pattern of conquest. The Nandi had lost many cattle from pleuro-pneumonia in the 1880s, and their people did not escape the drought of the early 90s. In 1890 some Nandi groups killed their ritual expert, the *orkoiyot* Kimnyolei, for his self-evident failings, the last of which was an abortive Nandi raid which may or may not have introduced rinderpest from elsewhere. The evidence on this point is conflicting, but it does seem that the Nandi avoided the second rinderpest later in the decade.[37] Not only did the Nandi suffer less grievously than others but, despite their central position, they also lay beyond the outer circle of contacts discerned in the first pattern of conquest. For the Swahili avoided them after some pioneer traders had been roughly handled, giving them the nickname that everybody else adopted, *mnandi*, the greedy cormorant. So there was no external trading alliance for the British to pick up, nor any political intelligence to use. Nor were Nandi cultivators and pastoralists at odds over their external relations.

British ignorance was as much a cause of conflict as Nandi obduracy. The British turned more readily to violence for want of any known broker with whom to remonstrate, nor could they find any guarantor of peace. The two

Table 1.2. British military operations in the Kenya highlands 1893-1911

Date	Enemy	Auxiliaries	Numbers killed		Livestock confiscated	
			'British'	'enemy'	cattle	small-stock
Nov 1893	Kabete Kikuyu	87 Maasai	?	many	6	922
June 1894	Githunguri	124 Maasai	2	90	10	847
July 1894	Kikuyu	220 Maasai			—	1,100
Nov 1894	Bakusu Luyia	—	70	—	—	—
Jan 1895	Bukusu Luyia	Maasai Luyia Ganda	2	?	450	?
Aug 1895	Bukusu and other Luyia	900 Maasai Luyia	70	420	1,900	?
Nov 1895	1st Nandi	25 Ganda	28	190	230	2,400
Dec 1895	Mwala Kamba	800 Maasai	?	?	560	1,300
Mar 1896	northern Kamba	300 Kikuyu 900 Maasai	?	many	many	
Aug 1896	southern Luyia	Luyia Massai	2	?	273	?
Feb 1897	Kilungu Kamba	Maasai Kamba	3	100	700	1,000
May 1897	Tugen (Kamasia)	200 Maasai	?	100	300	8,000
June 1897	2nd Nandi	400 Maasai	6	few	140	1,500
Nov 1899	Kamelilo Nandi	75 Maasai	?	?	58	1,072
Dec 1899	central Luo	Luo Luyia Maasai	1	250	2,620	many
July 1900	3rd Nandi	1,000 Maasai Tugen Luo	127	350	3,470	29,370
Jan 1901	Pokot (Ribo Post)	500 Maasai 100 Il Chamus	43	300	520	10,000
Sept and Dec 1902	Maruka & Tetu Kikuyu	300 Maasai	12	310	1,300	10,000
Mar 1903	4th Nandi	700 Nandi	4	40	300	4,500
Feb 1904	Mathira Kikuyu	450 Maasai	?	1,500	1,087	8,150
Apr 1905	Sotik (Kipsigis)	900 Maasai	2	92	2,000	3,000
Sept 1905	Gusii	150 Maasai	—	120	3,000	?
Nov 1905-Jan 1906	5th Nandi	1,500 Maasai Somali Tugen	97	1,117	16,210	36,200
June 1906	Embu	—	2	407	3,180	7,150
Jan 1908	Gusii	Nandi	—	240	7,000	?
Dec 1911	Marakwet (Kalenjin)	—	—	22	8	350

Note: Operations are grouped together where they were directed against the same or closely related peoples, or where they comprised part of a regional campaign.

Only the larger operations are listed. There were at least as many more smaller skirmishes. But those listed probably accounted for 90 per cent of all casualties and livestock confiscations.

All forces included regular Company or protectorate forces, as well as the local African auxiliaries. 'British' casualties numbered less than half-a-dozen Englishmen.

Sources are to be found in the references cited in the footnotes, save for the Appendix in A.T. Matson, The Nandi campaign against the British 1895-1906 (Nairobi, 1974).

expeditions of the 1890s, both in revenge for Nandi attacks on caravans or food suppliers, achieved nothing. The three campaigns of the new century marked a turn in the tide of conquest. They were still in defence of the route, but by this time it was the railway, not only a means of swift transport for large bodies of troops but also the startline for concerted attacks. And it was at this point, when conquest started to hurt, that the Nandi began to split in similar fashion to those peoples who had had longer experience of the trading frontier. Some of the men of their core agricultural settlements were persuaded to take the field in support of the British against the younger, more pastoral sections.

Time had caught up with the Nandi, and it is time which provides the fourth and final pattern of conquest. As the 1890s came to their wretched end, so peoples whose previous experience had differed now underwent ordeals that were much the same. The common factor was labour. Many African men were anxious to sell their labour in return for survival, but in some areas the British needed more labour than Africans were ready to sell. In either case, the established Anglo-African alliances were brought to the point of collapse. In the early 1890s African brokers had profited from their control over the fruits of agricultural and military labour, but had provided little of what has been called 'tribute labour' for porterage, path-clearing or fort-building.[38] But any discretion they may have had to negotiate the terms of the labour market was now overwhelmed by the desperation of both parties, in the double crisis of African famine and British military collapse in Uganda.

There were three patterns in the dissolution of authority over labour among, respectively, the Kamba, the Kikuyu and the peoples of the Nyanza basin. Famine was the press-gang among the Kamba. They were thrown into a turmoil which was reduced to order less by their own patrons than by the railway contractors who employed them in large numbers.[39] In southern Kikuyuland, by contrast, young men took collective responsibility for their own survival. With a violence which some Kikuyu have compared with the behaviour of both sides in the Mau Mau war fifty years later, warrior bands 'terrorized all and sundry'; they were called *thaberi,* after the Swahili caravan *safari,* a term also applied to British raiding parties.[40] The Nyanza story was different again. In 1898 its British officials became little more than recruiting sergeants for the hundreds of porters needed to support the Indian battalion that was rushed across the sea to put down the Sudanese mutiny, away in Uganda. Hobley faced a crisis of collaboration. His broker allies were unable to meet his demands; they could channel food but could not drag out men. So he cast aside his 'tribal chiefs' and dealt directly with the myriad 'clan heads' beneath them. A refusal to turn out labour became, for the first time, a reason for punishment, and its supply a condition of peace.[41] Conquest had begun by building up African power; now it was breaking it down.

It must be that the crucial work of recovery from famine lay in the productive and reproductive labour of women, yet for this vital period we know little about them.[42] We know that in some places bridewealth was reduced or even suspended for lack of livestock, which might suggest that marriage was made easier for all men, including the poor. But we can also guess, from studies of comparable periods of disruption elsewhere, that many men abandoned their women to fend for themselves, and that women therefore swelled the followings of any strong man who could protect them.[43] It may also be, but one cannot be certain, that young men went out to work in obedience to the same patrons, performing what was in effect the poor man's traditional labour service for his father-in-law, in place of bridewealth. It is significant that the three men of the 1890s best known for mobilizing large numbers of porters despite the general collapse of authority, Kinyanjui and Karuri among the Kikuyu and Odera Ulalo among the Luo of Nyanza, were shortly afterwards recognized as 'paramount chiefs' over their areas. The British would have granted such a status only to big men with large numbers of settled dependants, families whose formation they had perhaps sponsored. The political economy of conquest, even at its most oppressive, could apparently still provide for the customary enlargement of African power.[44] This was to be the central paradox of the politics of control.

State-building 2: The politics of control

In the politics of conquest, before 1901, public power (an innocuous term for British force) was shared in private African hands. It was the only way in which external force could become socially engaged. Officials had to come to terms with the local contractors of military intelligence, manpower and supply. The initial phase of state-building required alliances which were not too unequal. But usable state power was a different matter. The labour crisis in the late 1890s had already shown that. Somehow, public power had to be concentrated in official hands, above society and yet socially influential rather than merely forceful. Allies had to be made agents, wielding a locally legitimate authority that was nonetheless, in the last instance, delegated from the centre. The British never mastered this alchemy of rule, as rulers never do, but it was not for want of trying.

The official monopoly on public power had begun to emerge in the process of conquest. Backed by the ever-present threat, and frequent use, of external force, the British multiplied their allies along the Buganda road. As they grew in number, so each African broker became less indispensable, more vulnerable therefore to British displeasure. As individually they declined in value, so too the British lowered the collective price of their support. This can clearly be seen in the conquest of Nyanza. On the first sally against the Luyia in 1895, the hundreds of African levies were rewarded with nearly three-quarters of the captured cattle. On the last, in 1908, there were no auxiliaries, and local African friendlies were fobbed off with 3 per cent of the loot. This example makes a second vital point, that force became bureaucratized. There were no spearmen on this last expedition, and thus no African power-brokers.

22

Instead, the African troops and policemen were under direct British command, they were paid in cash rather than endowed with livestock, and were beginning to be locally recruited.[45] The two processes together, the accumulation of allies and the bureaucratization of force, were the necessary second stage of state-building. Together they obliged any pretender to power to pay close heed to his standing in the high politics of the state, if he were to enhance his local patronage.

The British increasingly imposed on their allies a discipline more appropriate to agents. By 1900 Olonana was no longer allowed to act as if his enemies were also the enemies of the British.[46] And while some 'punitive expeditions' in the 1890s marched out to avenge rapacious African soldiery killed by a justifiably angry local population, in 1904 a British officer shot five of his own men, both soldiers and auxiliaries, for killing women and children once the battle was done.[47] But British officials found themselves under new disciplines too, especially after the Colonial Office took over in 1905.

British self-discipline became the more necessary as they freed themselves from their prudential dependence on Africans. The third phase of conquest, between the completion of the railway and 1908, was the most ruthless. All African peoples who were not yet submissive were treated like the Nandi. As more obedience was expected of those under control, in particular the payment of hut tax, so African freedom beyond the administrative frontier became less tolerable. Besides the Nandi themselves, the Gusii of Nyanza, the most northerly Kikuyu, and the Embu beyond them were subjected to an organized ferocity quite beyond any British capacity a decade earlier. 'Enemy' mortality rose from scores into hundreds, livestock confiscations from hundreds to thousands. An official sense of shame began to stir. Early in 1904 the report on the expedition against the Mathira (or Iraini) Kikuyu suppressed the true casualty list. Some 1,500 had been killed; the governor admitted to 400 only.[48]

More was at stake than the conscience of local officials. At home, the Treasury was increasingly impatient of African military adventure. The Foreign Office feared embarrassment at a time when international outrage was growing over the savagery of King Leopold's Congo. The Colonial Office was torn between faith in the imperial civilizing mission and donnish pessimism lest the Empire be destroyed by local conflicts between pushy white capitalists and resentful natives. Punitive expeditions were doubtless a painful necessity, but their conduct ought to foster grateful prosperity rather than rebellion.[49]

The protectorate government was similarly divided. It closed frontier areas to white and Indian traders, lest African anger at private extortion cause more public expense and endanger new public income.[50] At London's request, district officials were also deprived of their armies, the African levies, who could in future be used only on the orders of the governor.[51] An army officer, the same who had shot his own men for murder, was sent home for overzealously killing the Nandi *orkoiyot*.[52] Officials were forbidden their common practice of keeping African mistresses; it was thought bad for prestige, the social distance that was the cheapest form of security.[53] Above all, the Colonial Office centralized recruitment and improved service conditions, to attract graduate officials in place of footloose adventurers. It selected governors thought to be sympathetic to African interests, and sacked or demoted those who nonetheless put private white interests first.[54] The Oxford classicists of Whitehall were, again, following Agricola, who had earlier learned 'that arms can effect little if injustice follows in their train. He resolved to root out the causes of war. Beginning with himself and his household, he enforced discipline. He preferred to appoint to official positions and duties those whom he could trust not to transgress, rather than punish the transgressor.'[55]

But all this was a necessary curb on the engine of rule rather than a source of productive energy. If the spoils of war were no longer permissible, how were the Africans to be pacified? On the other side of the continent, in Nigeria, Governor Lugard put his finger on the problem. The British needed a 'class who in a crisis can be relied on to stand by us, and whose interests are wholly identified with ours'.[56] And the British knew what they meant by 'class'. Winston Churchill, Under-Secretary for the Colonies, devoted a chapter to the question when recounting his visit in 1907 to East Africa.[57] He could imagine no development without the ambitions of capitalists, employers and professional men who, with discipline, education and justice, stir 'the African aboriginal' out of his 'contented degradation' into 'peaceful industry'.[58]

The local prospects for such a class were not promising. Hardinge had had ideas of enlisting 'the rising generation of Arabs and Swahilis (of the better class) in the service of Government, and whose interests with theirs would thus become identified',[59] but that was before the focus of British interest shifted inland to the highlands. The footsoldiers and porters of conquest had been the polyglot Zanzibari, 'not a tribe but a class'[60] (and not of the better sort), whose services were civilianized as messengers, hut-counters and policemen, and whose campfire lingua franca, Swahili, became the universal language of command. But, like the Sierra Leoneans of West Africa, they did not long survive as the executive agents of colonial rule. They were kin neither to rulers nor to subjects and jarred on the sensitivities of both. Yet the British had little confidence that the local 'native chiefs' had any of the qualities of a productive ruling class. How could they organize increased production and yet remain socially legitimate?

The British seemed to meet in Africa the two conflicting mirrors of their own mythical past, the Norman yoke of conquest kingdoms, and the Anglo-Saxon democracy of tribes.[61] They did not scruple to use African aristocrats, who they assumed must be immigrant rulers like themselves, as the agents of economic change. But they did not see how tribal leaders could be similarly used without tearing apart the consensual fabric of 'tribal control', throwing the common people into potentially dangerous disorder.[62] If free tribesmen did not have the habit of obedience, neither could their chiefs be trusted

24

to possess the self-discipline of command. This was the dilemma the early officials believed themselves to face in Kenya. They needed tax, labour and exportable produce from people whom they had just seen die in thousands from famine and disease. London doubted whether any resources could, or should, be derived from a 'poverty stricken peasantry with a backward agriculture'.[63] And when production did nonetheless increase, district commissioners complained that their officially recognized chiefs used their authority 'to enrich themselves at the expense of their people'. They ignored their 'tribal elders', enforced public and private demands with armed retainers whom officials were now debarred from using themselves, and then trusted to the state to rescue them from popular anger.[64] Without established class differences in the relative enjoyment of wealth, increased prosperity, in any case doubtful, seemed to presage not peace but uproar.

The government never resolved this contradiction between legitimate authority and the labour of increased production. It first attempted to do so by the complete separation of export production from authority over Africans. It looked for Punjabi peasants, Finnish homesteaders, even Zionist pioneers, all small farmers, reliant on their own labour. Only the first of these experiments in productive classlessness took any root. And Indian settlement was soon fettered by white immigration. Kenya's white settlement was almost an accident, a private bargain between the second commissioner, Sir Charles Eliot, and the first white frontiersmen who took Lord Delamere for their leader. But it turned Kenya into a proper conquest state, with alien barons impatient of legal discipline and contemptuous of the native population.[65]

White settlement was both the baronial consolidation of conquest and the chief threat to the politics of control. If it could not have politically dependent but independently productive small farmers, the Colonial Office came round to the view that it must have big capitalists instead. Big capital would provide the state with a different but equally controllable answer to the nervous 'rhinoceros questions' of African rights in expanded production. It was 'no good trying to lay hold of Tropical Africa with naked fingers'. What was wanted was 'tireless engines, not weary men; cheap power, not cheap labour'. Capital was the axe with which to cut a path through political jungles as well as nature's. If only it could be given room to exploit African land, then the state could 'regulate in full and intricate detail' the relations between capitalists and the few skilled workers they would need. And the colonial state was indeed a cartographer; maps were its images of order. They showed strategic bases and frontier zones, they marked property and the absence of it.[66] White settlement filled in dangerous spaces with roads, fields and boundary beacons. The imagery should not be underestimated, and the reality hoped for, contented black labour on quiet farms with mortgages, producing payloads for a railway with a sinking fund, was itself the image of the civilizing mission, the self-justifying myth of the state as well as its mirage of calm.

White settlement marked and maintained boundaries, the very essence of state-building, in three distinct dimensions. Settlers, first, were marcher lords; they held 'buffer zones' between warring tribes. They would curb the Kalenjin and divide the Maasai from their neighbours. The final phase of highland conquest owed some of its violence to a government desire so to crush resistance that white settlers on the border would be safe.[67] Second, land alienation would separate the thorny opposites of export production and African authority, capital and classlessness. There was a vital proviso. It must be effected by state confiscation and reallocation, not by private sales between Africans and Europeans. The first few settlers had bought privately, at prices much higher than their successors bought from government.[68] But to the state, if not to settlers, the price of land was secondary to its politics. The land frontier must be 'closed', not 'open'.[69] A free market would invite conflicting claims between the races. It would also raise storms of internal African controversy over whether their rights in land were such as to allow private sale. Official alienation, on the other hand, would literally fence capital into a European preserve. Inside the fence a productive class would form. From outside it, classless Africans would be controlled and temporary immigrant workers. Tribal seigniories would be defended against subversion by possessive individualism.[70]

Finally, white settlement would pin down pastoralism, the way of life which kept Africans idle, unnervingly on the move, and impervious to the benefits and constraints of civilization.[71] The politics of conquest was brought symbolically to an end with the Maasai moves of 1904 and 1911. These fenced pastoralism out of the best grazing in the Rift while fencing capitalist ranching in. Three-quarters of the 'White Highlands' was once Maasailand. Conquest had earlier helped to replenish the highlands' livestock banking system. But from 1905 government started to sell looted stock to settlers, having withheld it from African auxiliaries. Maasai were even banned from bidding against settlers in auctions of imported breeding stock.[72] Allies of conquest were never more fully discarded.

State-formation: the vulgarization of power

None of these strategic hopes was fulfilled. The building of power was subverted by the power of markets, in capital, labour and commodities. The white barons were the first to slip the leash of state control. They had to. The state tried to tie their rights in land to strict conditions of improvement, so as to force them to invest in intensifying production rather than rest content with the extensive use of cheap labour or, worse still, idle speculation on the rising land values which could be expected from the state's own continuing investments in roads and peace. But the capital market was nervous of untried land in tropical climes. No settler, large or small, could borrow much without first winning a free market, and secure tenure, in the government's stolen lands. By 1915 they had got it.[73]

This first defeat to state control confirmed a second. Settlers who could not afford to put more than a few acres under the plough could neither afford to let their square miles lie empty. They had to keep the hostile bush at bay. Both their small labour wants and their large land-cleansing needs were met by the South African remedy of 'kaffir farming', inviting in African tenants where these were not already in prior residence on what had been their own land. The buffer zones of white settlement became frontiers of opportunity for African mixed farmers, the 'squatters'. Africans had not been allowed to sell land but, in effect, they were allowed to buy in return for labour service. By the Second World War more than one in ten of the Kikuyu had colonized Maasailand as dependants of big men who happened to be white. The Kalenjin similarly reconquered their confiscated frontiers. Capitalist production and authority over Africans became inextricably mixed. The strategic white marches on the Land Office's maps were riddled with black lines of cultivation, grazing, trade and cattle theft. Pastoralism was not pinned down, it merely became subversive.[74]

It was the same with labour and authority in the African reserves, beyond the broken boundary fence of capital. By 1910 up to one-third of all adult men in the Kikuyu districts and in lowland Nyanza were out of work at any given time, generally for only a few months. Perhaps half of these were employed on public works and in porterage for government officials. They were recruited through an intensification of state-building, an implosion of raiding. Officials and chiefs colluded in the methods of the 1890s, providing tribute labour, whether public or private. Chiefs were chosen for their ability to get things done without questions asked. Ritual authority was useless for the task; the story of Olonana and the *il aigwanak* was a parable for the times. The ambitious young entrepreneurs of the conquest remained to the fore, men with followers and well-tried connexions. The expansion of state power and state demand allowed them to widen the gap between the factional benefits of patronage and the penalties of exclusion from favour. Their armed retainers were press-gangs and tax-collectors, bullying some and exempting others. White officials could scarcely complain at this flouting of 'tribal control', this enrichment of chiefs at their people's expense. It was the consequence of their own demands. Social division and the corruption of authority were the essential foundations of state power.[75]

But power over people was always slipping from chiefs, just as power over capital escaped the state. Peace drew cultivators out of their defended villages, out of chiefs' sight and close to their crops.[76] Indian traders went everywhere with their ox-carts and donkeys. Thousands of African households sold them penny-packets of grain and vegetables, so much so that by 1912 the white settlers, undersold in the domestic market for workers' rations, were forced to take steps to export their maize.[77] African women toiled harder with their hoes.[78] And large numbers of unmarried young men voluntarily earned the means to invest in marriage, the essential starting capital for market production. To the disgust of their seniors they were reshaping old warrior freedoms.[79]

They protected them with novel forms of association. Squatters and migrant workers pioneered the land and labour markets in chain-migrations of friends and neighbours. Squatter families rebuffed unwelcome competitors for white settler land by excluding them from community rituals.[80] Migrants increasingly went out without waiting for their chief's compulsion, not singly but in groups, to bargain as a team with known employers rather than face assignment to unknown ones. In this way they broke the employers' hold on market intelligence, gained the initiative in wage-bargaining and softened the rigours of travel.[81] Mission schools and congregations provided the most noticeable new bonds of allegiance. The numbers of professional Christians increased rapidly from about 1912.[82] Missionaries attracted two very different streams of clients, both the young relatives of chiefs who had an eye to another source of advantage and the poor, including a striking number of orphans, who had no other protector.[83] 'Mission boys' soon became an essential evil for district officials. They were useful as hut-counters and clerks, but they highlighted the factional ills of state-building. Some added intellectual arrogance to a canny chief's retinue; others opposed chiefs who did not befriend them, secure in the support of missionary patrons who could be very naive about the inescapable harshness of chiefs' rule.[84]

Government tried to rescue state control from these vulgarizations of power, conceding representation where no sterner discipline was feasible and bringing oppression under the law. It continually rebuilt institutional power to bridge the social rifts and regulate the oppositions that opened up as people formed the state for themselves, using its public power for their private ends. It was an unending task. The settlers were represented in a Legislative Council in 1907, but refused to be tamed by it. A Native Affairs Department was created at the same time, to meet settler demands to discipline labour. Its officials suggested a greater self-discipline in employers and the settlers marched in a mob on Government House. 'Tribal elders' were then represented in local councils in 1911, but they too could do nothing to tame the demands that the state imposed on chiefs. African evangelists were compelled to get preaching permits from chiefs under the Native Catechists Regulations, but the potentially subversive skill of typing was encouraged by the state and even certified by the governor in person.[85]

African society increasingly conformed to the rules of power. The conquest state appeared to be bending African ambition to its own needs. Africans adopted ethnic identities as novel as any missionary denomination. As early as 1910 they joined themselves together in 'clans' out of previously scattered allegiances, the better to claim or repudiate the rights of chiefship. At a wider level, district boundaries, lines on the map rather than shifting margins of subsistence and trade, began in the same way to mark out 'tribes' which claimed the ethnographic purity that the British expected of them, quite unlike the hospitable eclecticism that had existed before.[86] On a still larger scale, agriculturalists and pasturalists began to specialize in one form of production or the other, and lost their previous understandings. Their trade became channelled within ethnic diaspora. Somali stocktraders and Indian produce dealers used the peace of the state in place of the narrower peace of the market, which had nonetheless direct producers of different livelihoods face to face. People and goods had once crossed cultural boundaries, now it was increasingly a traffic in goods alone.[87]

But boundary-building, whether in pursuit of government policy or in response to anonymous African action, was a two-edged weapon of security. As settlers separated African herdsmen and cultivators so also the state replaced the Maasai as the highland bank, a depository of forced savings rather than calculating investment. It was easier to tax settled cultivators than wandering herdsmen. In 1907 the Maasai paid less than 2 per cent of African direct taxation, the Kikuyu and the Nyanza lowlanders more than 30 per cent each.[88] The Maasai did not have to recoup their capital from the state, the agriculturalists did. These invested their earnings from employment and produce sales in education, winning a footing in the skilled labour market of government, the railway and business. Pastoralism became conservative, agriculture progressive. Where once there had been ecological arenas of exchange, regional inequalities of wealth and power were on the way. These divisions of interest were a form of political control, but they also became ethnic constituencies for political mobilization. The Maasai replied to their second move not with spears but with a lawsuit, a decade before the Luo and Kikuyu, with men who could type, created their political associations. Tacitus seems to have despised those Roman Britons who described, and in Latin, their temples, togas, baths and banquets as civilization, 'when really they were only a feature of enslavement'.[89] But if conquest shapes societies, even conquered peoples can force changes in the forms that states take, so leading, to some extent, their captors captive.

Notes

1 L.S.B. Leakey, *The Southern Kikuyu before 1903* (3 vols, London and New York, 1977), i, 33.

2 The arguments of this chapter have been developed in close consultation with my colleagues David Anderson, Bruce Berman and, especially, Greet Kershaw and Richard Waller. None is responsible for its conclusions. Some of its ideas were first developed in J. Lonsdale and B. Berman, 'Coping with the contradictions: the development of the colonial state in Kenya 1895-1914', *Journal of African History* 20 (1979), 487-505; others have been more widely deployed in my two essays, 'The European scramble and conquest in African history', ch.12 in R. Oliver and G.N. Sanderson, eds., *The Cambridge History of Africa*, vol.VI (Cambridge, 1985), and 'Political accountability in African history', in P. Chabal, ed., *Political Domination in Africa* (Cambridge, 1986). The present chapter is concerned with the social rather than the military history of the conquest of Kenya. Its main thesis, that there was much African continuity within the European disruption, represents a revision of the standard accounts listed below in n.3. This revision took its point of origin in R.D. Waller, 'The Maasai and the British 1895-1905: the origins of an alliance', *Journal of African History* 17 (1976), 529-53.

3 See, especially, R. Robinson and J. Gallagher, with A. Denny, *Africa and the Victorians*

(London, 1961); J.S. Galbraith, *Mackinnon and East Africa 1878-1895* (Cambridge, 1972); G.H. Mungeam, *British Rule in Kenya 1895-1912* (Oxford, 1966); D.A. Low, 'British East Africa: the establishment of British rule 1895-1912', ch.1 in V. Harlow and E.M. Chilver, with A. Smith, *History of East Africa,* vol.II (Oxford, 1965).

4 See Sir Harry Johnston's appreciation of his Indian troops in Uganda, 1900, quoted in J.S. Mangat, *A History of the Asians in East Africa c.1886 to 1945* (Oxford, 1969), 43n; and, for labour markets, Winston Churchill, *My African Journey* (London, 1908), 33ff, and S. Stichter, *Migrant Labour in Kenya* (Harlow, 1982), 3ff.

5 R.W. Beachey, *The Slave Trade of Eastern Africa* (London, 1976), ch.10; F. Cooper, *From Slaves to Squatters* (New Haven and London, 1980).

6 M. Ylvisaker, *Lamu in the Nineteenth Century* (Boston, 1979).

7 For military recruitment, see H. Moyse-Bartlett, *The King's African Rifles* (Aldershot, 1956), chs.4 and 6. For porters, J.W. Gregory, *The Great Rift Valley* (London, 1896), ch.16; R. Cummings, 'A note on the history of caravan porters in East Africa', *Kenya Historical Review* 1(2) (1973), 109-38; J. Iliffe, *A Modern History of Tanganyika* (Cambridge, 1979), 44ff.

8 R. Meinertzhagen, *Kenya Diary 1902-1906* (Edinburgh, 1957), 9ff. The EAR was not armed with repeating rifles until 1905.

9 J. Fadiman, *Mountain Warriors: the pre-colonial Meru of Mt Kenya* (Athens, Ohio, 1976); R.D. Waller, ' "The Lords of East Africa": the Maasai in the mid-nineteenth century', Ph.D. Dissertation, Cambridge University, 1978; *idem.,* 'Ecology, migration and expansion in East Africa' (University of Malawi seminar paper, May 1984). R.R. Kuczynski (*Demographic Survey of the British Empire,* Vol.II (London 1949), 194) was one of the first scholars to doubt that indigenous warfare was responsible for heavy mortality. And see *The Diaries of Lord Lugard,* ed. M. Perham and M. Bull (3 vols, London, 1959), I, 344 (31 Oct. 1890). When some Kikuyu asked Lugard to help them against Kikuyu cattle-thieves he asked 'what had happened in the scrimmage, and was told one of their men had been badly hit in the foot with a knob-kerry. "Just so," I said. "When Wakikuyu fight, a man gets his skull cracked perhaps at worst. If the British fight, and bring guns, many many men *die*" ' (original emphasis). But local war was not always a game. The British commander of an expedition against the Tetu Kikuyu in 1902, himself 'surprised at the ease with which a bayonet goes into a man's body', observed the killing methods of his Maasai auxiliaries: 'Once their man is down they use their short sword, inserting it on the shoulder near the collar bone and thrusting it down...through the heart and down to the bladder': Meinertzhagen, *Kenya Diary,* 74.

10 T. Lloyd, 'Africa and Hobson's Imperialism', *Past and Present* 55 (1972), 143.

11 Mungeam, *British Rule,* 132.

12 *Tacitus on Britain and Germany,* trans. by H. Mattingly (West Drayton, 1948), 71.

13 Mungeam, *British Rule,* 30.

14 The 'local African lesson' because, unlike stateless societies, African kingdoms elsewhere were not very good at organizing productive peace.

15 This is the area within Kenya's present boundaries, after the inclusion of eastern Uganda in 1902, and after the cession of Jubaland to Italian Somaliland in 1925.

16 This stage of the argument is heavily indebted to Richard Waller, see n.9 above.

17 My main sources for nineteenth-century social history are, for the highland Bantu: Godfrey Muriuki, *A History of the Kikuyu 1500-1900* (Nairobi, 1974); Leakey, *Southern Kikuyu;* G. Kershaw, 'The land is the people', Ph.D. Dissertation, Chicago University, 1972; J.F. Munro, *Colonial Rule and the Kamba* (Oxford, 1975). For the Maasai and other pastoralists: Waller (above, n.9); D.M. Anderson, 'Herder, settler, and colonial rule; a history of the peoples of the Baringo plains, Kenya, c.1890-1940', Ph.D. Dissertation, Cambridge University, 1983; N.W. Sobania, 'The historical tradition of the peoples of the eastern Lake Turkana basin c.1840-1925; Ph.D. Dissertation, London University, 1980. For the Nandi: A.T. Matson, *Nandi Resistance to British rule 1890-1906* (Nairobi, 1972); A. Gold,

'The Nandi in transition: background to the Nandi resistance to the British 1895-1906', *Kenya Historical Review* 6 (1978), 84-104. For the Nyanza peoples: G.S. Were, *A History of the Abaluyia of Western Kenya c.1500-1930* (London, 1967); J. Dealing, 'Politics in Wanga, Kenya, c.1650-1914', Ph.D. Dissertation, Northwestern University, 1974; B.A. Ogot, *History of the Southern Luo* (Nairobi, 1967); J.M. Butterman, 'Luo social formations in change: Karachuonyo and Kanyamkago c.1800-1945', Ph.D.Dissertation, Syracuse University, 1979; W.R. Ochieng', *A Pre-colonial History of the Gusii of Western Kenya* (Nairobi, 1974); D.W. Cohen, 'Food production and food exchange in the precolonial lakes plateau region', ch.1 in R.I. Rotberg, ed., *Imperialism, Colonialism and Hunger: East and Central Africa* (Lexington, 1983).

18 M.P. Cowen, 'Differentiation in a Kenya location' (University of East Africa Social Sciences Council annual conference paper, Nairobi, 1972).

19 *Lugard Diaries*, vol.I, 369f (14 Nov.1890).

20 P. Rogers, 'The British and the Kikuyu 1890-1905: a reassessment', *Journal of African History* 20 (1979), 255-69; D. Anderson, 'Expansion and expediency on the colonial frontier: the British in Baringo before 1914' (Institute of Commonwealth Studies seminar paper, London, 1982); Dealing, 'Politics in Wanga'.

21 By Low, 'British East Africa', 1.

22 M.H. Dawson, 'Smallpox in Kenya 1880-1920', *Social Science and Medicine* 13B(4) (1979), 245-50; the best summary of the disasters is in Swartz, 'Disease and population decline of the Kikuyu of Kenya 1895-1920', 121-38 in *African Historical Demography* 2 (Centre of African Studies, Edinburgh, 1981).

23 J. Ford (*The Role of the Trypanosomiases in African Ecology: a study of the tsetse-fly problem* (Oxford, 1971)) was the first to emphasize the historical importance of rinderpest. For a summary of its continental effects during the late nineteenth century see Lonsdale, 'European scramble', 689ff.

24 There appears to be a conflict of evidence on this point between relatively optimistic contemporary accounts and gloomy oral tradition. Compare Matson, *Nandi Resistance*, 68, 313, and R.J. Stordy's observations in *Kenya Land Commission Evidence* (3 vols, Nairobi, 1934), III, 3338, 3341, with Nandi traditions in Gold, 'Nandi in transition'.

25 Kuczynski, *Demographic Survey*, vol.II, 190-9; Swartz, 'Disease and population decline'; H.G. Soff, 'Sleeping sickness in the Lake Victoria region of British East Africa 1900-15', *African Historical Studies* 2 (1969), 255-68.

26 From the field notes of Professor G. Kershaw, generously shared.

27 British responsibility was first suggested by Kuczynski, *Demographic Survey*, vol.II, 199; he is followed by Muriuki, *History of the Kikuyu*, 155; but Rogers, 'British and Kikuyu', 263f questions this thesis.

28 Munro, *Kamba*, 49.

29 By this time the Baringo food market had been by-passed by a shorter route. The new half-way house between Kikuyu and Nyanza was Eldama Ravine, in an area where the British could not buy food locally. It was rationed by headload from Kikuyu and Mumias, about 160 km (100 miles) distant in each direction.

30 Munro, *Kamba*, 38, 41. These early militia perhaps gave the Kamba their taste for service in the police and army, for which they supplied a disproportionate number of recruits throughout the colonial period.

31 Kershaw, 'Land is people', 148 n.

32 Muriuki, *History of the Kikuyu*, passim; Rogers, 'British and Kikuyu'.

33 J.M. Lonsdale, 'The politics of conquest: the British in western Kenya 1894-1908', *Historical Journal* 20 (1977), 841-70; R.D. Waller, 'Interaction and identity on the periphery: the Trans-Mara Maasai', *International Journal of African Historical Studies* 17 (1984), esp. 258f.

34 Lonsdale, 'Politics of conquest', table on p.858.

35 The European involved was in fact the German traveller, Karl Peters, but that does not

alter the point. See his *New Light on Dark Africa* (London, 1891), 301-10.

36 Waller, 'Maasai and British'; Waller, 'Interaction and identity'.

37 For differing accounts of Kimnyolei's death see A.T. Matson, 'Nandi traditions on raiding', in *Hadith* 2, ed. B.A. Ogot (Nairobi, 1970), 78; S.K. arap Ng'eny, 'Nandi resistance to the establishment of British administration 1893-1906', 106f in *ibid*; Gold, 'Nandi in transition', 94f. See also n.24 above.

38 Stichter, *Migrant Labour*, 5-14.

39 Munro, *Kamba*, 47f.

40 Muriuki, *History of Kikuyu*, 94f; for central Kikuyu, D.M. Feldman, 'Christians and politics: the origins of the Kikuyu Central Association in northern Murang'a 1890-1930', Ph.D. Dissertation, Cambridge University, 1978, 45f.

41 Lonsdale, 'Politics of conquest'; Stichter, *Migrant Labour,* 12ff.

42 M.J. Hay, 'Economic change in Luoland: Kowe 1890-1945', Ph.D. Dissertation, University of Wisconsin, 1972, ch.4 and Hay, 'Luo women and economic change during the colonial period', 87-109 in *Women in Africa,* ed. N.J. Hafkin and E.G. Bay (Stanford, 1976) are the most helpful for this period, but deal with an area much less disrupted than central Kenya. For the Kikuyu two otherwise valuable studies have nothing to say specifically about the 1890s: G. Kershaw, 'The changing roles of men and women in the Kikuyu family by socioeconomic strata', *Rural Africana* 29 (1975-6), 173-93, and C.M. Clark, 'Land and food, women and power, in nineteenth century Kikuyu', *Africa* 50 (1980), 357-70. Neither Leakey, *Southern Kikuyu* nor W.S. and K. Routledge, *With a Prehistoric People* (London, 1910) are helpful. L. White ('Women in the changing African family', ch.4 in *African Women South of the Sahara*, ed. M.J. Hay and S. Stichter (London, 1984)) makes some interesting suggestions which could serve as research hypotheses.

43 For example, M. Wright, *Women in Peril: Life stories of four captives* (University of Zambia, Lusaka, 1984); Wright, 'Bwanikwa: consciousness and protest among slave women in Central Africa 1886-1911', ch.13 in C.C. Robertson and M.A. Klein, eds., *Women and Slavery in Africa* (Madison, 1983); E.A. Alpers, 'The story of Swena: female vulnerability in nineteenth-century East Africa', ch.11 in *ibid.*; M. Vaughan, 'Famine analysis and family relations: 1949 in Nyasaland', paper presented to the African Studies Association annual meeting, Boston, 1983. For an overall thesis, see A. Sen, *Poverty and Famines: an essay on entitlement and deprivation* (Oxford, 1981).

44 Rogers, 'British and Kikuyu', 264f; Feldman, 'Christians and politics', 49f; Lonsdale, 'Politics of conquest', 869; Stichter, *Migrant Labour,* 9-17. The inclusion of Kinyanjui in this list revises the received view, before 1976, that he was merely an upstart camp follower of conquest.

45 Lonsdale, 'Politics of conquest', table on p.858. The first highlanders, Maasai, were recruited into the East African rifles in 1901; but the Maasai company was disbanded in 1907, as incorrigibly undisciplined. In 1908 a Nandi company was recruited into what was now the 3rd King's African Rifles, but it remained a largely Sudanese force until 1914. The Protectorate's police force, on the other hand, was 40 per cent 'highlander' in composition by 1912 (mainly Luo, Kamba, Maasai and Kikuyu): T.H.R. Cashmore, 'Studies in district administration in the East Africa Protectorate 1895-1918', Ph.D. Dissertation, Cambridge University, 1965, 128f.

46 Waller, 'Maasai and British', 544.

47 Meinertzhagen, *Kenya Diary,* 144 (29 Feb. 1904).

48 Mungeam, *British Rule,* 84; Muriuki, *History of Kikuyu,* 165.

49 R. Hyam, *Elgin and Churchill at the Colonial Office 1905-1908* (London, 1968), 207-17; idem., 'The Colonial Office mind 1900-1914', *Journal of Imperial and Commonwealth History* 8 (1979), 30-55.

50 Meinertzhagen, *Kenya Diary,* 119-22 (Nov.1903) tells how one white freebooter was brought to book.

51 Mungeam, *British Rule*, 171-80, 238f; Governor Sir Percy Girouard, *Memoranda for Provincial and District Commissioners* (Nairobi, 1910), 'Instructions for the control of expeditions and patrols'.

52 Meinertzhagen, *Kenya Diary*, 327 (5 May 1906).

53 Cashmore, 'District administration', 40; we look forward to Ronald Hyam's forthcoming study of the subject.

54 Cashmore, 'District administration', 24ff. The two governors sacked were Eliot in 1904 and Girouard in 1912 (although both were in fact allowed to resign), both in relation to the Maasai moves (below). Hayes Sadler was demoted to the governorship of the Windward Islands in 1909 for being too weak both with white settlers and the military.

55 *Tacitus*, 70.

56 Writing to the Secretary of State, Jan.1904. Quoted in R. Robinson, 'European imperialism and indigenous reactions in British West Africa 1880-1914', ch.8 in H.L. Wesseling, ed., *Expansion and Reaction: essays on European expansion and reactions in Asia and Africa* (Leiden, 1978), 159f.

57 Churchill, *My African Journey*, ch.3.

58 *Ibid.*, 42f.

59 April 1896; quoted in Mungeam, *British Rule*, 26.

60 Gregory, *Rift Valley*, 304.

61 Henrika Kuclik, 'Tribal exemplars: images of political authority in British anthropology 1885-1945', 59-82 in George W. Stocking, ed., *Functionalism Historicized: essays in British social anthropology* (Madison, 1984).

62 Girouard, *Memoranda*, 'Native policy'.

63 Lord Lansdowne to Commissioner Eliot, June 1901, quoted in Rogers, 'British and Kikuyu', 266. See also, C.C. Wrigley, 'Kenya: the patterns of economic life, 1902-1945', ch.5 in V. Harlow and E.M. Chilver, eds., *History of East Africa*, vol.II, esp. pp.211-14.

64 R.W. Hemsted, *South Kavirondo Annual Report 1910-11*, Kenya National Archives, Nairobi.

65 M.P.K. Sorrenson, *Origins of European Settlement in Kenya* (Nairobi, 1968) is still the essential authority.

66 Churchill, *My African Journey*; 41, 53, 36; J.D. Overton, 'Spatial differentiation in the colonial economy of Kenya: Africans, settlers and the state 1900-1920; Ph.D. Dissertation, Cambridge University, 1983.

67 For the relationship between expeditions and alienation: *ibid.*, 23; and Mungeam, *British Rule*, 141-5, 155-60, 161-4. The later rationalizations for buffer zones are summarized in E.W. Soja, *The Geography of Modernization in Kenya* (Syracuse, NY, 1968), 20f.

68 P. Mosley, *The Settler Economies: studies in the economic history of Kenya and Southern Rhodesia 1900-1963* (Cambridge, 1983), 15f.

69 For the distinction, see H. Giliomee, 'Processes in development of the Southern African frontier', ch.4 in H. Lamar and L. Thompson, eds., *The Frontier in History: North America and Southern Africa compared* (New Haven, 1981).

70 *Report of Commission on Native Land Tenure in the Kikuyu Province* (Nairobi, 1929) is the best early source for official thinking on the matter. For an official view on the contradiction between what I have called state-building and state-formation with reference to land tenure, see J. Ainsworth's memorandum to the Kenya Land Commission (*Evidence iii*, 3451): 'I think that the introduction of individual tenure to land through title issued by the Government will tend to break down tribal authority but it should help in time in building up the native state... (By the term "native state" I mean each individual adult being responsible to the authorities as opposed to the custom of tribal responsibility.)'

71 The most pungent early official opinions on 'pernicious pastoral proclivities' are conveniently reproduced in *ibid.*, 3438-49, memorandum by C.M. Dobbs. For good studies of official pastoral policy: I.R.G. Spencer, 'Pastoralism and colonial policy in Kenya 1895-1929', ch.5 in *Imperialism, Colonialism and Hunger*; and R.L. Tignor, *The Colonial*

Transformation of Kenya: the Kamba, Kikuyu and Maasai from 1900 to 1939 (Princeton, 1976), ch.14.

72 For the auction ban, R.J. Stordy's evidence, *ibid.*, 3342; for the moves, Mungeam, *British Rule*, 119-23, 259-69; Sorrenson, *European Settlement*, ch.12.

73 *Ibid.*, chs.2-9 for land policy and its changes.

74 There is a growing literature on squatters. See, especially, R.M.A. van Zwanenberg, *Colonial Capitalism and Labour in Kenya 1919-1939* (Nairobi, 1975), ch.8 – which has much on stocktheft too; T. Kanogo, 'The political economy of Kikuyu movement into the Rift Valley 1900-1963: the case of Nakuru district', Ph.D. Dissertation, Nairobi Univertsity, 1980. It was not until the 1940s that squatter security was seriously threatened by their lack of legal standing in the White Highlands; the Mau Mau rebellion was in part their struggle for security.

75 The best published source for all this is *Native Labour Commission 1912-13: evidence and report* (Nairobi, 1913). For discussions of early colonial chiefs, see: B.A. Ogot, 'British administration in the Central Nyanza district of Kenya 1900-60', *Journal of African History* 4 (1963), esp. pp. 252ff; E. Atieno-Odhiambo, 'Some reflections on African initiative in early colonial Kenya', *East Africa Journal* 8 (1971), 30-6; W.R. Ochieng', 'Colonial African chiefs: were they primarily self-seeking scoundrels?', ch.3 in B.A. Ogot, ed., *Hadith 4: Politics and Nationalism in Colonial Kenya* (Nairobi, 1972); Tignor, *Colonial Transformation*, ch.3.

76 Low, 'British East Africa', 33f; Hay, 'Economic change', 99.

77 E. Huxley, *The Easy Way: a history of the Kenya Farmers' Association and Unga Ltd.* (Nairobi, 1957), 4.

78 For women's labour, see works referred to in n.42 above; also, importantly, G. Kitching, *Class and Economic Change in Kenya* (New Haven and London, 1980).

79 M. Beech, 'The Kikuyu point of view', Dec.1912, repr. in G.H. Mungeam, ed., *Kenya: select historical documents 1884-1923* (Nairobi, 1979), 477ff. For a pioneering discussion of how African seniors and colonial officials together disciplined juniors, both men and women, through the construction of 'customary law', see M. Chanock, *Law, Custom and Social Order: the colonial experience in Malawi and Zambia* (Cambridge, 1985); the same exercises in social control were undoubtedly attempted in Kenya, but the research that would confirm this impression has yet to be done.

80 Information from Professor Kershaw, who has unrivalled data on Kikuyu social history.

81 *Native Labour Commission*, 150, 159, 162, 203, 234f (evidence from chiefs and workers).

82 D.B. Barrett *et al.*, eds., *Kenya Churches Handbook* (Kisumu, 1973), 158, fig.1.

83 K. Ward, 'The development of protestant Christianity in Kenya 1910-40', Ph.D. Dissertation, Cambridge University, 1976, ch.4; Feldman, 'Christians and politics', ch.3; R.W. Strayer, *The Making of Mission Communities in East Africa* (London, 1978).

84 J.M. Lonsdale, 'A political history of Nyanza 1883-1945', Ph.D. Dissertation, Cambridge University, 1964, chs.4 and 5.

85 A. Clayton and D.C. Savage, *Government and Labour in Kenya 1895-1963* (London, 1974), 31-40 for Native Affairs Department; Cashmore, 'District administration', 97-100 for elders' councils; J. Spencer, *James Beauttah: freedom fighter* (Nairobi, 1983), 10 for the typist and the Governor.

86 J.M. Lonsdale, 'When did the Gusii (or any other group) become a tribe?' *Kenya Historical Review* 5 (1977), 123-33; Waller, 'Interaction and identity'; compare Iliffe, *Tanganyika*, ch.10.

87 M.J. Hay, 'Local trade and ethnicity in western Kenya', *African Economic History Review* II(1) (1975), 7-12; I.R.G. Spencer, 'The first assault on Indian ascendancy: Indian traders in the Kenyan reserves 1895-1929', *African Affairs* 80 (1981), 327-44.

88 Calculated from taxation figures in Cashmore, 'District administration', 136 n.

89 *Tacitus*, 72.

2 The establishment of colonial rule, 1905-1920

Tiyambe Zeleza

In 1905 the East African Protectorate, as Kenya was then known, was transferred from the British Foreign Office to the Colonial Office. In practical terms of course this meant little change, although the settlers welcomed the move, hoping the new administration would be more sympathetic to them and less miserly.[1] By then some of the basic colonial state institutions were in place, and 'the question of who would play the key role in economic development had been decided [and only] how development proceeded remained the great question'.[2] But African resistance was then far from over, and already new patterns of protest were discernible over the murky horizons of a fledgling colonial capitalism.

The period between 1905 and 1920 witnessed the consolidation of colonial administration, the unsteady beginnings of settler agriculture and the spasmodic development and underdevelopment of Kenya's peasantries.[3] A coercive labour system was instituted. Colonial patterns of class formation began to take root. And the effects of incorporation into the British colonial empire began to be felt, most brutally through the pulverizations of the First World War, and more subtly through the agencies of colonial socialization: the mission church and school, the colonial town and market. In the meantime, working-class, peasant and petty-bourgeois nationalist struggles began taking their incipient forms.

This chapter is divided into six parts. First, it presents a theoretical analysis of the penetration of capitalism in the colonial world and the role of the colonial state in this process. Second, it examines the growth of settler power and production. Third, it focuses on the development of peasant commodity production and rural class formation. Fourth, it looks at the emergence of the coercive labour control system. Fifth, it analyses the role of merchant capital and the patterns of African petty-bourgeois accumulation. Finally, an attempt is made to outline more specifically the broad contours of social change during this formative and critical period in Kenya's colonial history.

Primitive accumulation of capital and the colonial state

First and foremost, the imposition of colonial rule entailed the process of capitalist penetration of African economies. Colonialism, then, effected the articulation of indigenous modes of production with the capitalist mode of production (CMP) and the integration of African economies into the Western capitalist system. The CMP is characterized by, first, the exclusive appropriation

35

by one class of means of production that are themselves the product of social labour; second, the whole of social production takes the form of commodities; and third, labour power itself becomes a commodity, which means that the producer, having been separated from the means of production, becomes a proletariat.[4]

According to Marx, capitalism arose from the womb of feudal society and the pillage of the rest of the world. This period, when the capitalist mode of production is being born, is termed 'primitive accumulation'. Thus primitive accumulation of capital (pac) in Europe evolved out of a two-fold process. It involved the violent restructuring of feudalism and proletarianization of the peasantry.

> So-called primitive accumulation . . . is nothing else than the historical process of divorcing the producers from the means of production. It appears as 'primitive' because it forms the pre-history of capital and of the mode of production corresponding to capital . . . And this history, the history of their expropriation, is written in the annals of mankind in letters of blood and fire.[5]

Alongside these violent transformations of the agricultural economy of feudalism, means no less violent were used to acquire monetary capital and other forms of wealth from the rest of the world.

> The discovery of gold and silver in America, the extirpation, enslavement, and entombment in mines of the aboriginal population, the beginning of the conquest and looting of the East Indies, the turning of Africa into a warren for the commercial hunting of black-skins, signalled the rosy dawn of the era of capitalist production.[6]

At the beginning of colonial rule Europe was capitalist, Africa was not. The question is: how was capitalism introduced in Africa? A process of primitive accumulation was launched. In *Talking of Kenya*, van Zwanenberg (1975: 288-9) argues:

> There are *some* similarities between the *national* capitalist accumulation which occurred in Britain and the *colonial* accumulation which was being attempted in Kenya. In both situations the extraction of a labour surplus was of very considerable importance, and in both the state was used to facilitate the process . . . However, here the similarities end. In Britain the new mode of production was introduced relatively slowly, while in Kenya it occurred much faster and from the invaders. Also, the precapitalist producers were not robbed of all their means of production, a large proportion of their land was left to them, and as a consequence the process towards proletarianization was of a different character . . . [and] agricultural capitalism as the dominant mode of production was never fully developed in Kenya right up to the period of political independence.

In extending the concept of the pac to colonial accumulation is to recognize, in Samir Amin's words, that 'primitive accumulation is not something that belongs to the prehistory of capital, it is something permanent, contemporary'.[7] In other words, the pac was not a once-and-for-all process that ended with the emergence of industrial capitalism. Indeed, Marx himself acknowledged that in different countries primitive accumulation 'assumes different aspects and runs through its various phases in different orders of succession'.[8]

The concept of pac can be applied to the colonial epoch in two related senses. First, as a theoretical construct of imperial–colonial relations. Insofar as the objective of imperialist penetration was to render the colonies even more effective as a principal source of monetary capital, the penetration of the CMP led to an unparalleled rise in the rate of primitive accumulation.[9] Second, the concept can be used to describe the historic process of expropriation of sections of the peasantry, that is, their proletarianization and the commoditization of production in the colonies.

Unlike classical pac in Europe, primitive accumulation in the colonies neither arose organically out of feudalism, nor was it fed by the booty of external pillage. Instead, it arose out of a violent restructuring of modes of production which were not pre-capitalist in the sense that feudalism was pre-capitalist, and the accumulation of monetary capital depended upon exclusively internal sources. This accounts for the exceptional violence and incompleteness of pac in these territories.

Banaji is correct to argue that any process of primitive accumulation in colonial societies 'implies an articulation of modes of production', in which the indigenous modes are progressively subordinated to the capitalist mode through a process of dissolution, conservation and transformation.[10] According to Berman and Lonsdale:

> Concretely, articulation involved extracting surplus product from and/or forcing labour into capitalist or quasi-capitalist formation, thereby partially transforming them and making their self-reproduction increasingly impossible. The form of articulation varied according to the particular character of capitalist penetration, the nature of the indigenous modes of production, and the local ecology and resource endowment. The resulting variations in the subjugation and transformation of local societies and the degree to which capitalist forms of production were introduced also determined the differing patterns of class formation within and between colonies.[11]

Modes of production are of course not actors in themselves endowed with their own inexorable logic; a mode of production is simply an abstraction of the conjunction of production relations and processes and social struggles. So articulation of modes of production essentially involves a struggle between 'peoples' and 'classes', which these modes define.[12] In short, articulation is always accompanied by violence, at least in its early stages. Since conquest paved the way for the penetration of the CMP, 'the colonial state was necessarily instrumental with regard to metropolitan capital's "opening up" Africa's modes of production'.[13]

The nature of the state has of course been a subject of intense theoretical debate. It is readily agreed that the state is distinguished by domination over a territory, that its domination is enshrined in a legal system, and that this domination is buttressed by a monopoly over the means of violence. What is contentious is the ultimate rationality of this domination. For liberal theorists the state is a relatively benign neutral arbitrator of contending group interests.[14] Classical Marxists see the state as the direct agency of capitalism, as the executive committee of the bourgeoisie.[15] For neo-Marxists with their instrumentalist and structuralist perspectives, the state provides relatively autonomous protection of the long-term interests of the capitalist system as a whole.[16] Dependency theorists simply see the state as the engine of under-development in the service of international capitalism.[17]

The colonial state was a dependent appendage of the set of European states that conquered Africa. But, as Young has noted, the colonial state had its own peculiarities. Its territoriality was ambiguous. Sovereignty ultimately resided in the imperial metropole. Its derivative territorial personality was empty of nationality. Its membership as an autonomous player in the anarchical world system of states was hardly recognized. And its institutions of rule, legal order, and ideological representation were all extraverted and embedded in metropolitan practices and traditions.[18]

These peculiarities were derived from the manner of colonial state construction in Africa. The scramble in Africa, Young contends, was far more concentrated, intense and competitive than in other regions. Moreover, the colonial state-building venture in Africa included a far more comprehensive cultural project than was the case in Asia. Finally, colonial expansion in Africa occurred when European states were fully developed and consolidated, and therefore less likely to experiment with indigenous political structures. In other words, the problems of hegemony, security, autonomy, legitimation and revenue, the five reasons of state, were more pressing and required constant application of brute force, certainly during the first phase of colonial state construction.

The colonial state, then, was fundamentally a direct agency of imperialism and an engine of underdevelopment. Its task was far more complex than that of the state in the imperial heartlands themselves. The colonial state...

> had to organize the reproductive conditions not of one dominant mode of production, but of a capitalist mode not yet dominant whose social integument included the other modes to which capital was articulated and whose own social relations and ideological charters it therefore threatened ... The colonial state indeed straddled not one but two levels of articulation: between the metropole and the colony as a whole as well as within the colony itself. It was at once a subordinate agent in its restructuring of local production to meet metropolitan demand, yet also as the local factor of cohesion over the heterogeneous fragmented and contradictory social forces jostling within. This very Dual Mandate defined the dilemmas of the colonial state.[19]

In grappling with these dilemmas the colonial state was, unsurprisingly, more interventionist in the economy than contemporary capitalist states, and its institutional reflexes were conditioned to authoritarianism like Pavlov's dog was conditioned to food.

The colonial state in Kenya was faced by the same dilemmas and its institutional responses were also characterized by extreme economic interventionism and political authoritarianism. After conquest, it had to facilitate the penetration of capitalism and the growth of capitalist social relations and mediate the new colony's external dependency. In short, Kenya's colonial state, as in all other colonies, was the midwife of primitive accumulation. Indigenous modes were retained in some form, but as complementary and no longer as self-sustaining and self-perpetuating structures. Thus the peculiar forms that colonial labour took during this period, namely, the squatter system and labour migrancy, developed because the capitalist mode of production was as yet incapable of paying for the maintenance and reproduction of the nascent working class. These costs were borne in the spheres of peasant production.

The following, then, are the salient features of the process of primitive accumulation in Kenya. First, the colonial state played a fundamental role in this process. It acted as an instrument of primitive accumulation on the settlers' behalf by appropriating African land, confiscating livestock, introducing taxation, building rail and transport networks and creating marketing and financial structures highly favourable to settlers, and, finally, through the imposition and institutionalization of forced labour. But it needs to be emphasized, secondly, that despite this imposed dominance of settler production, peasant commodity production was not 'destroyed'. On the contrary, many Africans responded effectively to opportunities offered by expanding local and external markets. The conflict and uneasy coexistence between the settler and peasant sectors were the warp from which the fabric of primitive accumulation in Kenya was made.

Settler power and production

Settler estate production in Kenya was introduced as a result of a specific conjunction of economic, political and geographical factors. By the turn of the century the Foreign Office, then in charge of the protectorate, was already complaining about the imperial grants-in-aid being sent to Kenya for running the administration and executing punitive military expeditions. It urged the protectorate to become self-sufficient and pay for itself. Meanwhile, the Treasury was getting concerned about recovering the £5½ million sunk into the Uganda Railway, and the means by which the railway would continue to be maintained, since 'at that time there was virtually no freight for the Uganda Railway to carry'.[20] Thus the British government faced the problem of how to develop local export production to make 'both the Protectorate and the railway pay'.[21]

In the meantime, the few hundreds of European settlers already in the colony were vocally agitating for a policy of settler colonization. In 1902 they founded a Society to Promote European Immigration and they appealed successfully to Sir Charles Eliot, the first Commissioner, to stop encouraging Indian settlement and support European immigration. London was initially wary of the settlers' ability to develop the new colony without immense support from the colonial state. But these reservations were soon thrown aside. It was in the hope of attracting private capital for development and investment in the colony that 'London supported Eliot's policy of encouraging small, European settler immigration, including the settlers who came from South Africa. For the same reason large European syndicates were given grants'.[22]

The number of resident settlers rose from 600 in 1905 to 2,000 in 1907.[23] In the years that followed there was a steady influx of new settlers,[24] a trend which was temporarily slowed down during the First World War, but which accelerated after the war with the launching of the Soldier Settlement Scheme. By 1920 the number of settlers was still ridiculously small; certainly it was out of all proportion with their political power.

The settlers were keen to have some control over land and labour policy and to achieve elective representation, which was seen as a prelude to the attainment of Crown Colony status. Settlers' demands were articulated through the Colonists Association, formed in 1902. These demands became more insistent, especially from 1905 when the Association increasingly came under the influence of new settlers from South Africa. A number of local associations were also formed, but the Colonists Association remained pre-eminent. In 1907 it succeeded in forcing the government to appoint a Land Board with five unofficial members. In the following year it made considerable progress in pressing its views on labour on government policy. It was not until 1911 that all the colony's settler associations came together under the umbrella of the Convention of Associations. The Convention was soon dubbed 'the Settlers Parliament'.

In 1915 the Crown Lands Ordinance and the Native Registration Ordinance were passed. This marked considerable settler achievements in respect of both land and labour policy. The question of exclusive settler elective representation took longer to settle. Although as early as 1906 the government had yielded to the Colonists Association's pressure to introduce a Legislative Council, the principle of elective representation was not won until 1917. Its implementation came after the war. These victories were won in the face of concerted Indian opposition and opposition from the liberal lobby in Kenya itself and Britain, and of course in the midst of spirited African resistance.

The rise in settler political influence and power can partly be attributed to their aggressive tactics, and partly to governors who were either too weak to resist settler pressure or too sympathetic to their cause. Exigencies of war simply reinforced these tendencies. For example, the settlers were well represented on the War Council, and they fully exploited the Council's powers, which were quite considerable, to advance their own cause. At the root of it all lay the fact that the colonial state, as an alien transplant, derived its *raison d'être* from the imperial state and society, not from African society, hence its greater responsiveness to European settlers who, after all, were children of the imperial motherland. Colonialism was ideologically represented as a 'civilizing mission'. The settlers saw themselves as the 'civilizing missionaries'. This could only be challenged at the risk of undermining the very basis of colonialism in Kenya. That is why even the harshest critics of the settlers questioned their methods and excesses, but not the Europeans' mission to bring light to a 'Dark Continent'.

With the exception of the large 'aristocratic' landowners like the Delameres, Scotts and Grogans, the vast majority of settlers who came to Kenya consisted of small-scale farmers who were not only grossly undercapitalized but 'usually they lacked even the elementary skills of farming'.[25] It was this very weakness of settler capital which forced the colonial state to intervene actively on their behalf. This should put the lie to the thesis of settler investment, at least in the case of Kenya. In Kenya, settler accumulation was effected through a process of primitive accumulation, with all its violence and pillage.

Colonial state support for settler production was varied and incremental. Conquest was of course the necessary precondition for establishing any form of settler export production. In addition, the military campaigns 'often made new lands available for alienation . . . [they] also involved sizable transfer of livestock from Africans to Europeans . . . importing livestock was always an extremely expensive and risky transaction'.[26] Thus, through the wars of conquest, the colonial state expropriated the means of indigenous production on behalf of the settlers, which could not have been obtained in any other way, since economic necessity overlaid by social customs prevented most Africans from selling their land and livestock to settlers in the quantities the latter wanted.

The number of settler landholdings increased from 263 in 1905 to 312 in 1914. This represented an increase from 368,165 acres to 639,640 acres. Under the Soldier Settlement Scheme launched in 1919 an additional 2.5 million acres 'were parceled out into essentially free farms. Ultimately a group of 545 families, mostly families of low-ranking commissioned officers, occupied lands made available under the scheme'.[27] Very little of this land was put to actual use. It would seem many settlers acquired land for speculation. No wonder land prices shot up from 6d per acre in 1908 to £1 per acre in 1914. Land speculation went hand in hand with land concentration. 'By 1912 five owners together held over 20 per cent of all land alienated to Europeans in the protectorate. In the most fertile, centrally located Rift Valley of East Africa, over 50 per cent of all alienated land was owned by two syndicates and four individuals'.[28]

Needless to say, the land alienated to the settlers was carved out of the most fertile regions and was located in the vicinity of the railway. In fact, the state sought to boost settler agriculture by providing it with good infrastructural services. This was particularly so in the 1920s when railway branch lines were built to serve and open up areas of actual and potential European settlement.[29] But even before this, a graduated rating structure was used by the railway administration to force African producers and producers from Uganda to subsidize the railway system as a whole on behalf of settler production. Railway rates on the exports of maize and wheat, almost exclusively exported by settlers, were low, and items geared for settler production, such as agricultural implements, breeding stock, and commercial seeds were exempted from customs duties. Meanwhile, railway rates on exports of raw cotton, which was almost entirely produced by African peasants, especially in Uganda, were very high, and so were customs duties on the import of cheap textiles, largely geared for African consumption.[30] Colonial state policy on road building was no different. In the European settled areas roads were built and maintained by the settler-controlled Rural District Councils, which were entirely and generously financed by the state, whereas in the reserves it was the responsibility of Local Native Councils, whose only source of funds came from extra taxation.

In addition to land alienation and the inequitable allocation of infrastructural services, the colonial state, through the Department of Agriculture, provided extension services almost exclusively to the settlers during this period. The department provided settler farmers with equipment, seeds, seedlings and stud animals. It published many articles and disseminated information on agricultural research to help them improve their farming. The department also established demonstration farms and supervised, graded, and certified settler crops for export. 'It is no exaggeration to conclude that the quantity and quality of official assistance to European agriculture in Kenya were among the highest in any colonial experience'.[31]

The department, in conjunction with the settlers and imperial authorities in London, decided on what crops were to be grown. The clearest example of this was coffee. At the turn of the century blight destroyed Ceylon's coffee plantations. That left Latin America as the main source of coffee. Since the United States controlled the Latin American coffee trade, this gave her a virtual monopoly in the world coffee trade which was resented by British merchants. They persuaded the British government to encourage coffee production elsewhere in the British colonial empire. Britain hoped that coffee re-exports to continental Europe would also help reduce her growing balance-of-payments deficits with Europe. From 1905 to 1907 the Department of Agriculture in Kenya conducted research on the feasibility of large-scale coffee production. The results were encouraging. Coffee exports increased from 8.5 tons in 1909 to 5,329 tons in 1920. In value the rise was from £236 to £392,507.[32] The settlers had discovered their golden beans. They jealously guarded them. Peasants were not allowed to grow coffee until 1933 when its cultivation was permitted in a few African areas experimentally. The case of coffee clearly demonstrates that settler production, and colonial production in general, was conditioned by, and subordinated to metropolitan needs and demands.

42

Settler farming was also able to expand because the settlers were able to get credit from British commercial and merchant banks established in the country, and from private money-lenders, some of whom were Indian.[33] Initially these banks had been established to finance external trade, but as capitalism expanded in the colony they began to provide credit to private farmers. The credit provided was mostly short-term, high-interest finance. But as long as land prices kept rising this did not matter too much. The Great Depression brought an end to the speculative spree. Many settler farmers sank into bankruptcy. In the aftermath of the depression the financial structure in Kenya was drastically overhauled. It was only then that the colonial state directly intervened in the provision of credit to settler farmers through the creation of the Land Bank in 1931.

The formation of the Kenya Farmers Association in 1919 presaged a movement that became only too apparent in the 1920s and 1930s, namely, the settler drive, supported by the state, to control the internal market of key commodities and cushion themselves against the vagaries of international commodity fluctuations. The KFA was set up to handle maize and wheat. Later in the mid-1920s the Kenya Creameries Cooperative was set up to handle butter and milk. These organizations succeeded in pushing the state to erect tariff barriers against imports of commodities they handled. The KFA did not have it all its own way, however. Maize was also grown by peasants. So the two were locked in fierce competition over the internal distribution of maize.

By 1920, therefore, the settler estate sector had emerged as an important pillar of Kenya's economy by virtue of the enormous resources allocated to it. But it would not be far-fetched to argue that despite this immense and, indeed, over-generous support from the colonial state, settler agriculture was a text-book case of terminal inefficiency. Perhaps the most telling commentary of the wastefulness and unproductivity of settler production lies in the fact that, of the nearly 3,157,440 acres occupied by settlers in 1920, only 176,290 acres, or 5.6 per cent of the total, was under cultivation.[34] Thus by 1920 Kenya was only a settler colony in name, in reality it was an economy sustained by peasant production which generated a surplus to provide revenue for the state so that it could pay for the running of the administration, subsidize settler production, and bear the costs for the maintenance and reproduction of the labour force. The weakness of settler agriculture made it possible and necessary for peasant production to continue, and indeed expand in some areas in the period leading to, during, and immediately after the First World War.

Peasant commodity production and rural class formation
Some writers have been so overwhelmed by the evidence of colonial state support for settler agriculture that they were blinded to the reality not only of peasants' continued existence, but their vigorous growth.[35] Kenya's colonial history was frozen into a static conflict between the 'colonized' and the 'colonizers' so beloved in nationalist historiography and folklore. The fact

of African subjugation was trumpeted so loudly that the distinctive regional forms of that subjugation, the various levels of resistance and incorporation into the colonial capitalist economy, and the emerging multiple contradictions in the colonial social formation, were obscured.

Research done in the last decade or so has revealed that, despite land alienation and discriminatory state policies which favoured settler agriculture, peasant commodity production was not 'destroyed'. On the contrary, it expanded. Indeed, the trend toward African agrarian capital accumulation was discernible even in these early decades of colonial rule, although of course it was accelerated from the 1950s as decolonization gathered momentum, and in the 1960s once the nationalists captured control of state power.[36] There is a danger of the new approach romanticizing peasant accumulation. It can never be overemphasized that peasant accumulation has always been accompanied by its ugly twin, peasant pauperization. In short, peasant commodity production led to, and was affected by, rural class formation.

In analysing the development of peasant commodity production it has to be stressed that there were important regional differences within Kenya which were dependent on many factors, like the potential for local cash-crop production and proximity to settler-occupied areas and colonial towns. Also, there emerged regional patterns of class formation, since there were different precolonial social formations which were incorporated on different terms into the local and international capitalist system. For example, pastoral peoples like the Maasai, and agricultural peoples like the Kikuyu, were affected and responded differently to the encroachment of colonial capitalism.[37]

Broadly speaking, colonial capitalism led to the marginalization of pastoralism and expansion of agriculture. While both groups lost land to European settlement, the impact of land alienation was more immediate for pastoral than agricultural peoples. In the early years of colonial rule more than one-third of the old Maasai grazing areas were alienated to European settlement. In 1904 the Maasai were moved out of large tracts of the Rift Valley onto the Laikipia plateau. They were promised that they would not be moved out again. But the agreement was soon broken as the settlers turned their covetous eyes on the Laikipia settlement. In 1911 the Maasai were moved again, this time to semi-arid lands far to the south of the Uganda Railway. With the Maasai moves, the principle of exclusive settler 'areas' and African 'reserves' was established. Thus enclosed, the old Maasai patterns of transhumance were broken. Large concentrations of livestock and overgrazing were the result. To make matters worse, in 1912 the Maasai were prevented from using their old trading routes, through which they previously exchanged breeding stock with the Somali and Oromo. So the Maasai could no longer improve the quality of their cattle. In 1917 quarantine regulations 'were imposed mainly to separate Maasai and European stock. This further limited access to markets. The few markets that existed within Maasailand offered low prices and the Maasai were discouraged from selling stock . . . Lack of markets contributed to a build-up of stock populations'.[38] The introduction of livestock taxation and the establishment of national parks, where Maasai were discouraged from grazing their herds, only added more salt to their already deep injuries. Thus, incorporation of the Maasai into the colonial-capitalist system not only underdeveloped the Maasai economy, but was in fact accompanied by an actual deterioration in the forces of production.[39]

But not all pastoral peoples were affected by the imposition of colonial rule in the same way as the Maasai. During the period under review, Somali pastoralism, for one, continued to expand as increasing numbers of Somali people entered north-eastern Kenya from southern Ethiopia and eastern Somalia in search of the scarce resources of water, pasture and salt. The spread of British administration in Somali territory occurred over a thirty-year period.[40] First to be occupied was the Indian Ocean port of Kisimayu. Then in 1912 the British established a station at Wajir in the heart of Somali territory. A post among the Aba Wak on the Tana was set up in 1917. Only in the 1920s was British administration extended to the whole of northern Kenya.

Until the 1930s the Somali effectively evaded British attempts to control their movements across the so-called 'Somali-Oromo line' and the Kenya–Italian Somaliland border. The Somali continued moving their livestock according to seasonal needs. The British were only too aware of the potential costs of challenging the Somali too directly. Since northern Kenya was not coveted by settlers, it made little sense to deploy already meagre resources to try to bring the Somali to heel. Attempts by some provincial officials to restrict Somali movement in the region were not only met with successful Somali resistance, but also received little support from Nairobi.[41] So up to 1920 the impact of the new colonial economy on Somali pastoralism was limited. The British were more successful in imposing early effective control over the Somali caravan trade.

The pressures of colonial capitalism turned other predominantly pastoral groups into agricultural peasants. The Nandi and Kipsigis, for example, lost some of their best pasture lands to European settlement, especially after the First World War. 'Throughout the period the Nandi and Kipsigis came to depend as much on farming as on herding for sustenance, and, indeed, after the Second World War the Kipsigis were to become perhaps the most "progressive" of all African farmers in Kenya.'[42]

Among the agricultural peoples themselves there also emerged regional and local patterns of socio-economic differentiation, depending on the extent of land alienation, each area's accessibility to suitable land for the production of cash crops, markets, and the manner in which the pre-existing economic system was articulated with colonial capitalism. Peasant commodity production was partly encouraged by the need to pay colonial taxes. Taxes rose from Rs1 in 1901 to Rs8 in 1920. Unlike settlers, Africans spent an increasing proportion of their incomes on taxation. Thus, while taxation stimulated peasant commodity production, it also delimited peasant accumulation. In

45

the early decades of colonial rule peasant commodity production was tolerated also partly because peasant marketable produce helped fill the empty rail wagons returning to Mombasa. As we have already shown, settler production was only limited at this time.

On the whole, the peoples of Central Province lost more land to European settlement than peoples of other regions in the country. It was the Kikuyu, especially the Kiambu Kikuyu, who were most seriously affected by land settlement. Other agricultural groups who lost their open land frontiers to settlers included the Machakos Kamba. A good deal of land in the coastal belt was also alienated to Europeans, who used it for sisal and rubber plantations and grazing. There was comparatively little land alienation in Nyanza, except in the north and east of the area.[43]

The expansion of peasant commodity production in the Central Province was first evident in southern Kiambu, where food-crop surpluses were being produced for the burgeoning town of Nairobi. Potatoes for the Nairobi market were being grown as early as 1900. From 1905 to 1918 the output of maize and beans increased massively, although, due to the 'informal' marketing channels used, there are no reliable production statistics. Peasant production also expanded in Nyeri and Murang'a districts 'in response to the demand of settlers to the north and west for maize flour to feed the resident labour'.[44] Thus, peasant production in these districts was stimulated by growing markets for food crops on settler farms and in colonial towns, especially Nairobi. The greatly swollen population of Nairobi during the First World War led to increased demand for peasant production. Cash-crop production in Embu and Meru developed much later because of their remoteness and their rugged terrain.[45]

By 1920 the problems of land shortage in the Kikuyu reserves were already becoming evident. This resulted from the twin pressures of settler land expropriation and peasant commodity production. Increased commodity production was accompanied by the breakdown of precolonial land tenancy relationships and the concentration of land. The independent landowners (githaka owners) began limiting the rights of tenant farmers (ahoi). The latter were therefore the first to lose access to land and seek wage employment. Also, some lineage heads began appropriating land privately. In such circumstances it was mostly the youth who lost out, and many drifted to settler farms and colonial towns in search of work. Then there were the predatory colonial chiefs. They often looted livestock from their subjects, collected more taxation than was officially required, exacted bribes from people who wanted to avoid conscription for communal work and military service, and registered some of the best lands in the reserves in their names. Another group of land accumulators consisted of the educated elite who were employed as teachers, preachers, clerks, court interpreters and so on. They sometimes used the cash they obtained from wages and their official positions to buy land and employ wage labour.[46]

This process of rural class formation was of course still in its embryonic stages up to 1920. But the basis of rural land accumulation had been set. It depended upon the ability to use the government and its legal machinery, and access to wage income. It was only the chiefs and other colonial functionaries as well as the emerging petty-bourgeoisie who were in such a position. This new class of African capitalists had a fundamental conflict with the class of settler estate producers. It was from their ranks that the earliest nationalist organizations emerged. Needless to say, all these changes generated changes in all social relationships; kinship and family patterns and obligations were reshaped by shifts in land tenurial arrangements and the changes in the organization and division of labour that were taking place.

Like Kikuyuland, there was increased peasant commodity production in Nyanza during this period. But here a different pattern of class formation emerged. In Nyanza Province, as stated above, there was little land alienation to European settlers. This meant that the extension of commodity relations was not as spatially confined as in the Central Province. The problems of land shortage were, therefore, less acute in Nyanza than in the Central Province. Thus pressures for land privatization and concentration were less manifest as well. This helped delay the development of agrarian capitalism. It is not that peasant commodity production did not develop at all, as Anyang' Nyong' asserts.[47] Rather, it took capitalist forms comparatively slowly.

At first the administration tried to encourage peasant production in Nyanza simply to generate cash income for Africans from which they could pay their taxes. 'Initially almost everything was tried, including industrial crops such as sesame, improved varieties of food crops such as maize, beans and peas, and crops with both industrial and domestic uses such as groundnuts and wattle.'[48] Cotton was also introduced from 1908, but it had little success during this period, because it demanded too much labour and fetched low prices.[49] The initial failure of cotton production also reflected a deliberate strategy by rural households, now increasingly 'headed' by women as more men joined the trails of labour migrancy, to earn cash without compromising on subsistence consumption. Cotton was an 'inedible or "pure" cash crop, and thus commitment of land and labour power to it did not carry the element of built-in security inherent in the production of increased food crop surpluses'.[50] Thus, the lack of production of 'pure' cash crops by peasants in the first decades of colonial rule was not always a product of colonial state opposition to peasant production of such crops as is so often asserted. Rather, cultivation of surplus food crops was a rational response by peasants to meet their needs for self-reproduction and the integrative demands of a fledgling colonial capitalism.

Crops other than cotton made modest progress. According to available figures in 1919-20, the South Nyanza district exported some 259 tons of sesame seed, 47 tons of groundnuts, 21 tons of maize and 15 tons of wheat. North Nyanza district exported 305 tons of sesame seed in 1917-18. The expansion in maize production was most impressive of all. Kisumu district produced between 4,500 and 5,000 tons of maize and maize flour in 1917-18. Kisumu in fact produced the bulk of the maize and maize flour leaving the district during this period.[51] If produce for sale within and between districts were included, one cannot escape the conclusion that expansion of peasant commodity production in Nyanza during this period was quite considerable.

In the coastal region, colonial capitalism was superimposed on a declining plantation economy. Slavery, on which the plantation system had been based in the nineteenth century, was abolished in 1907. Some ex-slaves moved further into the interior, others sought employment in Mombasa. A few settled in a small reserve for ex-slaves. The majority stayed with their old masters, now as squatters. Many members of the old planter class received land titles from the new colonial government. These titles were issued over land that included their former plantations and lands fraudulently acquired from the Mijikenda. By 1922 the Land Office had issued 9,190 titles in Mombasa, Malindi, Mambwi and Takaungu.[52] A good number of these titles were issued to Indians and Europeans. The Indian landowners were mostly interested in urban real estate development. Not surprisingly, 60 per cent of them left their land idle. The European landowners set up rubber and sisal estates. With the dramatic fall in world rubber prices in the early 1910s almost all the rubber estates were sold or abandoned to squatters. In short, while the old Arab-Swahili plantocracy retained their ownership of the land, they lost the ability to use that land through control of a labour force. 'They remained landlords but ceased to be planters.'[53] For their part, the new Indian and European landowners also failed to develop estate agriculture, although they retained legal ownership over vast tracts of land.

In the meantime, the Mijikenda were spreading from the hinterland. They became squatters on coastal plantations and estates. The ex-slaves and Mijikenda brought about a modest revival in grain production. It was the Mijikenda, in fact, who supplied the grain that kept Malindi as a grain-exporting port. The town-dwellers of Malindi and Mambwi themselves lived off Mijikenda grain. The Mijikenda also provided Mombasa with most of its grain. In 1910-11 445,000 lbs were sent from Rabai alone.[54] This, however, did not impress the colonial government. To the government the ex-slaves were a feckless and diminishing people hardly worth bothering about, and the Mijikenda were seen as hopelessly lazy and degenerate. These prejudices masked government intentions to smash squatter agriculture by ex-slaves and the Mijikenda in an effort to turn them into a pool of cheap labour for Mombasa and the European estates at the coast.

The state tried to frustrate peasant production by creating marketing, licensing, taxation and transport conditions which presented obstacles to peasants' capital accumulation. This directly led to the Giriama Rebellion in 1914 in which 250 Giriama were killed, 70 per cent of all Giriama houses were burned, and 6,000 goats were captured. Also a fine of 33,000 goats was levied, and the Giriama were made to supply porters for the First World War.[55] After the rebellion, however, the government abandoned its dream of turning the Mijikenda into a working class.

> Caught between the commercialization of land and the resistance of ex-slaves and Mijikenda to the commercialization of labour, the coastal economy inhibited investment and change. Landlords lacked the labour to cultivate intensively or make improvements on their land. Squatters could neither innovate nor develop the most important form of productive capital on the coast – coconut trees – for fear of expropriation and eviction. Neither landlords nor tenants could accumulate capital.[56]

Thus, the economic structure that emerged at the coast during this period stifled increased productivity, investment, innovation and capital formation. The making of a backward region, to use Cooper's phrase, had begun. In 1920 the volume of exports was lower than it had been a decade earlier. For example, grain exports from Malindi dropped from 49,000 cwt in 1910-11 to 18,000 cwt in 1919-20, millet from 6,000 cwt in 1910-11 to 5,000 cwt in 1919-20. Sesame remained steady at 3,000 cwt.[57] Kenya's copra exports, almost entirely from the coast, dropped from 37,068 cwt in 1910 to 33,219 cwt in 1920.[58] The variety of marketable crops being grown on the coast also diminished during the early colonial period. Colonial officials blamed this decline on the laziness of the peasants and managerial incompetence of the landlords, an explanation that was as incorrect as it was self-serving in that it absolved colonial policy in bringing this state of affairs about. But it became a widely accepted myth.

By 1920, therefore, the patterns of uneven regional development had begun to take shape. The basis for the marginalization of pastoralism and expansion of agriculture had been set. Despite the state's propensity to resolve the conflict between peasant agriculture and settler agriculture in favour of the latter, generally peasant production was expanding, even if in fits and starts. Certainly by 1920 the rural areas did not consist of undifferentiated and poverty-stricken peasants. These were groups of Africans who had begun concentrating wealth in their hands at the expense of others. This new class had its basis in links between commodity production in the reserves, trade and salaried positions in the state apparatus. It was composed of those who had collaborated with the British during and after the conquest of Kenya, and others who were straddled between permanent employment as teachers, for example, and private accumulation as traders. To some extent, therefore, 'the legitimacy of the colonial state was hitched to the ox-cart of African accumulation'.[59]

Establishment of the coercive labour control system

Through the initial act of alienating land to settlers, the colonial state deprived some Africans of their means of production and laid the basis of the entry of Africans in ever-increasing numbers into the wage labour force. Taxation was also used for the same purpose to force Africans to enter into wage employment. Taxation was, of course, a double-edged sword: it encouraged wage employment as much as peasant commodity production. Peasant commodity production increased precisely in those areas whence settlers hoped to draw labour, namely, the Central and Nyanza Provinces. Therefore, over and above mechanisms like land alienation and taxation, it became necessary to resort to direct use of forced labour.

Forced or compulsory labour was widely used and became institutionalized during the first few decades of colonial rule in Kenya. This was a period when massive supplies of labour were required to lay the very foundations of the colonial economy: rail lines and roads had to be built, dams and bridges constructed, administrative centres erected, and settler farms established. Undercapitalized as the colonial state and the settlers were during this period, they could not provide wages and conditions of service that could attract and retain labour. Also, the need for Africans to sell their labour power in order to survive was not yet compelling. Consequently forced labour became the most reliable means of securing labour. In the warped rationalization of colonialism, forced labour was even seen as an act of benevolence, a necessary 'shock therapy' for a people mired in idleness and indolence. Even the humanitarian critics of forced labour, like Leys[60] and Ross[61] and the missionaries did not question the need to inculcate a steady and disciplined 'work ethic' among Africans as a precondition for their advancement.

Before the First World War many settlers, especially those of South African origin, urged and used corporal punishment in order to force Africans to work. Legislation was passed which included penal clauses for breach of contract on the part of workers, since dismissal was not deemed effective either as an economic or moral threat. Professional labour recruiters were given a free rein and they used dubious and cruel methods in order to get labour. Chiefs were expected to recruit labour on behalf of the settlers and government. They were also supposed to provide communal labour for public works programmes, and many of them were only too glad to do it. After all, it paid to be a 'colonial bully-boy'.

The deplorable working conditions during this period cannot be overemphasized. Wages, if paid at all, were extremely low. They actually fell between 1910 and 1920.[62] It became conventional wisdom that raising wages would only succeed in 'corrupting' the African and making him lazier. The lot of workers employed by contractors consisted of 'frequent beating, poor feeding and housing, and ill-treatment generally leading to many deaths'.[63] The record of the railway, the Public Works Department, the municipalities, and even some Christian missions, was equally appalling.

The pressures of the First World War only made matters worse, for additional labour had to be secured for the military forces and Carrier Corps. Conditions for *askaris* and carriers were so bad that more died from them than from actual combat. In 1917 the government resorted to recruitment through armed raids in order to increase the diminishing ranks of the Carrier Corps. Adding grievous insult to irreparable injury the British government refused to pay unclaimed carriers' pay despite repeated requests by the Kenyan government and promises that the latter would use this money to improve African welfare.[64] In the meantime, settler demands for labour were unabated. More repressive labour legislation was passed. In 1915, for instance, came the Native Registration Ordinance, which had been recommended by the Native Labour Commission. It introduced the infamous *kipande* registration system that was implemented from 1920 onwards.

Settlers came from the war more assertive than ever before. New European immigrants arrived. They came in the midst of a financial crisis that was provoked by the depression in international commodity prices and the change in local currency from rupees to shillings.[65] As a result wages were reduced by a third. All these factors reinforced old pressures for labour coercion. The government itself wanted large supplies of labour for its infrastructural and public works programmes. But labour was in short supply as never before, thus fuelling the pressure for forced labour. The war, following hard on the heels of a violent colonization process, accompanied by outbreaks of epidemics and famine, had accentuated the demographic haemorrhage, especially of able-bodied males. The hen of primitive accumulation was coming home to roost.

Some coastal planters even toyed with the idea of importing indentured Indian labour and labour from Malawi. Upcountry settler opinion was strongly opposed to Indian immigration. Malawi labour was objected to because it was accustomed to high wages which would 'tend to raise the price of other native labour'.[66] Forced labour within the colony was seen as the only solution. In 1919 Governor Northey issued his notorious circulars. The old policy of labour coercion was given a new baptismal name, 'encouragement'. The government liberally defined services for which compulsory labour was legal. They included public services and private contractors working for the state, which under the circumstances could mean anybody. It was in fact quite common for men signed under the compulsory labour procedure to be forced to sign labour contracts with settlers.[67]

Probably the worst abuses of forced labour and certainly the most widely publicized occurred in the reserves under the disguise of communal labour. Originally communal labour was supposed to be undertaken voluntarily by people to build and improve services in their community. But, as with everything else under colonial capitalism, African institutions were distorted in order to serve wider colonial objectives. They were emptied of their social and cultural meaning and remoulded into vehicles of naked extortion and exploitation. Communal labour was compulsory for everybody, including men past working age, women and children, as stipulated in the Native Authority Ordinance of 1912 which, in effect, amounted to forced labour for government purposes in the reserves.

Accurate statistics for the number of people involved in forced labour are hard to come by. According to official estimates about 1,500 people were being called upon each year from 1920 under the compulsory labour programme. But the official figures are a gross underestimate. For one thing, those conscripted for railway construction were excluded from the count. So were those engaged in communal labour. The correct figures were certainly much higher than the official estimates.[68]

The introduction of *kipande* in 1920 represented an attempt to systematize the labour control system. Since once registered a worker could not be deregistered, *kipande* was designed to be used as an instrument with which to keep track of labour supply. It facilitated the enforcement of labour contracts in that it enabled penal sanctions to be returned to their erstwhile employers. For example, of the 2,790 reported desertions in 1921, 2,364 were traced and large-scale prosecutions took place.[69] Chiefs played a key role in tracing deserters in their communities. *Kipande* also restricted workers' freedom to leave their work and change employers. Finally, the *kipande* system led to standardization of low wages because it made it virtually impossible for a worker to bargain with a new employer for a wage that was higher and unrelated to his former wage as recorded on his *kipande.* It is significant to note that the emerging African petty-bourgeoisie could be granted exemption from *kipande,* and compulsory labour, at a fee of £4. This 'concretised the privileged position of the petty-bourgeoisie from the mass of the African peasants and workers'.[70]

Overt coercion was, however, not an entirely reliable system of labour supply and control. Consequently, settler farms and corporate plantations also came to rely heavily on resident, or what was popularly termed 'squatter' labour. From as early as 1911 settler farmers had realized that the squatter system was one way of keeping a 'free' cheap labour force and countering the problem of perennial labour shortages. The trend toward the resident labour system was intensified by the war, as shown by the passage of the Resident Natives Bill in 1916, the first in a series of such bills. Increased post-war demands for labour only served to reinforce pressures to expand and legalize the squatter system.

The growth of squatting underscores the fact that undercapitalized settler production could not operate fully capitalist relations of production and, short of direct compulsion, developed semi-feudal relations. It was already apparent during the war that squatters were challenging settler production. Many switched their rent payments from labour into money. This led the government to pass the Resident Native Ordinance in 1918, which required future payments to be made in labour and not in cash. The relationship of the African squatters with the European settlers was effectively turned from tenancy into serfdom. The basis of squatter-settler conflict had been laid, and the seeds of the Mau Mau rebellion had been sown.

The early squatters were in many cases original inhabitants of the alienated settler lands. Others became squatters when they lost access to land in the reserves, for example, the *ahoi.* Some people left the reserves for squatter life in order to escape the restrictions of reserve life, especially conscription during the war, and the rigours and abuses of communal and forced labour after the war. Food shortages in the reserves also pushed many to settler farms. So did the desire to escape the creeping western cultural influences such as education and missionary activities which, paradoxically, were becoming more pervasive in the reserves than on the settler farms.[71] Up to 1920 conditions for squatters were favourable. They began to deteriorate, at first imperceptibly from the mid-1920s, then dramatically from the 1930s.[72]

While the dominant patterns of labour relations were set on settler estates, there was a gradual growth of urban wage employment. Rural–urban migration during this period was more a result of push than pull factors. Wages in the urban centres were extremely low and the working and living conditions depressing. To enter urban wage employment was, in fact, 'to choose between celibacy and syphilis', a most unpleasant choice to have to make.[73] During this period urban wage labour was mostly restricted to men and was migrant in nature. Through the migrant labour system, women's production in the peasant sectors subsidized colonial capital accumulation.

The majority of urban workers were engaged in administrative and service occupations. There were as yet hardly any manufacturing industry jobs. Urban employment was concentrated in Nairobi and Mombasa. The skilled jobs were generally monopolized by Indian workers, while Africans were relegated to semi-skilled and unskilled jobs. Workers from the Central and Nyanza provinces dominated the labour market in both Nairobi and Mombasa. For example, by 1925 workers from Nyanza and Kikuyuland each outnumbered coastal – both Swahili and Mijikenda – among the 7,555 registered labourers in Mombasa. Only 17 per cent of the city's registered work force were from the coast.[74]

Through the use of brute force, coercive administrative and legal mechanisms, adoption of a system of labour tenancy and labour migrancy, the colonial state, on behalf of the settlers, corporate plantations and other employers, had managed to create a fairly large and cheap labour force. It was a labour force subjected to paltry wages, depressing working conditions, and semi-servile labour relations. Its chief means of skill acquisition were 'the prison industries carried on in Nairobi and Mombasa'.[75] A contemporary South African observer was moved to say that the Kenyan labour force was 'probably the cheapest in the world'.[76]

This labour force, however, was anything but quiescent. Labour protests in Kenya can be traced back to the very first few years of colonial rule. As Cohen has reminded us, 'there was a high element of labour protest in events that have been interpreted by colonial historians as wars of pacification and by post-1950s Africanist historians as proto-nationalism'.[77] The Giriama Rebellion of 1913-14, for instance, was a direct result of the Kenyan government's attempts to use Giriama labour on the European and Arab-Swahili plantations. The communal revolts were, therefore, among the earliest forms of labour protest in Kenya. Over the years various patterns of labour protest and organization emerged encompassing the whole spectrum from the spontaneous to the organized, from the individual to collective forms of action, depending on the nature of labour recruitment, utilization and composition, which, in turn, effected changes in the subsequent relationship between labour and colonial capitalism.

During this period desertions were the dominant form of labour protest. In the 1900s people sometimes ran away from their villages and went into hiding to avoid being pressed into forced labour by labour recruitment gangs. During the First World War some went as far as Uganda so as to escape enlistment into the notorious carrier corps.[78] These desertions represented an attempt to avoid conscription into the colonial labour system. Many workers also deserted when already at work whenever they got a chance. This represented permanent withdrawal of labour from the capitalist sectors. For their effectiveness desertions depended upon the continued ability of the peasant economy to reabsorb the deserters.

As colonial capitalism became entrenched from the 1920s and 1930s desertions became a declining form of labour protest. From then on struggles between labour and capital took place within the capitalist sphere. Hence the growing importance of strike action as an instrument of labour protest from the 1920s. Strikes had of course taken place before 1920. There is evidence to show that there was a strike, for instance, in 1900 involving railway workers. Other strikes took place in Mombasa in 1902 among policemen, in 1908 among dockworkers, also in Mombasa, and in the same year too, among African workers employed at a government farm at Mazeras near Mombasa. Later, in 1908, Indian railway workers also went on strike at Kilindini harbour works, and in 1912 African boat workers struck in Mombasa as well. In July 1914 most of the Indian railway and Public Works Department (PWD) workers 'went on strike in order to oppose the introduction of poll tax and for the removal of other grievances regarding housing, rations, medical facilities and low wages'.[79]

It can be seen that strikes tended to break out among the well-established pillars of the colonial economy – the railway, Mombasa port and harbour, the PWD and other government departments. Perhaps this was because it was in these establishments that the first attempts at labour stabilization were made. Also, it is notable that Indian workers took a leading role in strike action. This is because they were more proletarianized than African workers. Unlike the latter, Indian workers were immigrants who did not have one foot in the peasant sector and another in the capitalist sector; both their feet were firmly stuck in the latter. Not surprisingly, Indian workers pioneered trade unionism in the country. In March 1914 there was formed the short-lived Indian Trade Union in Mombasa. At the end of the First World War the first staff or civil servants' associations were formed. They were almost exclusively confined to separate European and Asian clerical staffs of the railways and government departments. These associations were not open to artisans and other workers, so that they were more welfare associations than trade unions. Trade unions did not really begin to grow in earnest until the late 1930s and early 1940s. But the seeds had been sown in the 1910s and 1920s.

Development of merchant capital

Colonization altered precolonial patterns of trade and marketing and introduced new ones. Old caravan routes gave way to new rail and road networks. Old market places were either expanded or abandoned, and new ones grew at colonial military posts and administrative centres. Imports of new wares changed the commodity composition of internal trade. Local trade now became an extension of a complex international trade network. The colonial state imposed its singular control over numerous trading suzerainties. And in this new and fragile but growing 'national' market the racially structured merchant capital of Africans, Asians and Europeans struggled for survival and dominance.

The odds were heavily struck against African traders. The old caravan trade collapsed in the face of a new transport network, currency and political authority. Two examples will suffice. From the 1880s the Imperial British East African Company tried to supplant Swahili caravans into the interior. The Kamba traders were initially hostile to the company and carried acts of overt warfare against it. These irruptions were quickly put down. Soon Kamba traders were supplying the company's caravans with foodstuffs. Some former porters even joined the company's caravans as porters. The colonial government in fact was keen to undermine Kamba trade and economy in order to turn the traders into a supply of labour. Before long, Kamba caravan trade was no more. The former 'caravan porters actually became the first interpreters, house servants, clerks, lorry drivers, and local chiefs among others, and thus they were the primary pool from which the local level administrators were recruited'.[80]

Colonization also eventually led to the decline of the Somali caravan trade. At first colonization seems to have coincided with an expansion of Somali long-distance stock trading. The ecological disasters of the 1890s and early 1900s decimated livestock herds among the Maasai and others. The Somalis, who had been hit by rinderpest somewhat earlier, 'seized the opportunity afforded by this catastrophe to bring in livestock from the Northern Frontier District . . . down the Rift Valley and then bartered to the Kikuyu and Maasai who were desperate for stock'.[81]

The Somali also sold a lot of livestock to European settlers. But by the time of the First World War settlers began agitating against the Somali stock trade, ostensibly because they feared the spread of cattle disease. The government then imposed quarantine regulations against Somali livestock. That marked the beginning of the end of Somali long-distance stock trading. In the meantime, the government also introduced a licensing system intended to restrict the movement of trade in north-eastern Kenya itself. In order to travel, 'a permit, with the names of all Somali with a caravan, was needed . . . For this privilege a trader paid a security deposit of Rs 500.'[82]

While old patterns of trade were being altered or even destroyed, new groups of traders were emerging. Of course these traders faced numerous obstacles. They had 'problems obtaining credit, capital, accurate market information, and access to other resources'.[83] The colonial government actually imposed legal restrictions against granting credit to Africans. Under the Credit to Natives Ordinance, passed in 1903, no credit of more than £10 could be given to an African trader unless approved by a district officer.

It is a testimony to their resilience that African traders increased in spite of all these obstacles. The amounts of capital required to enter trade of course varied from business to business. Barriers to entry were lowest in retail trade. Consequently, this was the first commercial sector to be crowded by African small-scale merchants. In the 1910s African-owned shops began to spread in the Reserves and other African areas, particularly in Central and Nyanza Provinces. A few shops were also set up in places like Machakos district.[84] Most of these early African shopkeepers had 'originally been itinerant traders, "hawking" simple consumer goods in exchange for produce, either on their own behalf or as employees of Asian shopkeepers'.[85] More costly to operate were maize mills. Not surprisingly, only relatively wealthy individuals entered such businesses. Most of them happened to be chiefs, headmen or clerks, that is, people with access to a good income. For instance, chiefs Kinyanjui and Kioi applied for government permission to open up two maize mills and two sugar presses as early as 1910. Poor transportation between the main areas of peasant commodity production and the market centres and towns led to the growth of African traders who owned pack-horses and carts, and from the 1920s motor lorries.[86] These transporters not only carried produce, but some took sand for building, or firewood or manure for sale. By the 1920s, to quote Memon, 'African traders were reported to be gradually being able to compete, here and there, with their Indian counterparts. Thus the groundwork was being laid for the emergence of an indigenous trading class whose interests tended to conflict with those of the immigrant Asiatic traders.'[87] This conflict of course intensified in subsequent decades, and entered a decisive phase after independence in the 1960s.

Indian traders followed the railway line inland and established *dukas* at Voi, Kibwezi and Machakos. They also followed the early military expeditions and established their *dukas* at the new military posts, which subsequently became Fort Hall (Murang'a), Nyeri, Embu, Kisii and so on.[88] With them came the use of rupees, which remained Kenya's currency until 1921. During this period colonial authorities encouraged Indian traders because they saw them as invaluable agents who could help stimulate trade and the consumption of imported commodities among Africans, which would then lead to increased production in the rural areas, and general monetization of rural economies, a necessary pre-condition for the integration of those areas into the colonial and wider international mercantile networks.[89]

Indian traders established shops not only in African areas, but also on European estates, which served the squatters and labourers on the farms. Initially many of them operated as both retailers and produce buyers. Produce was either brought to them, or the Indian traders went to buy it directly from the growers themselves or bought it from African agents and traders. Up to the First World War business grew steadily. The outbreak of the war in 1914 upset and restricted trade. But trade recovered the following year. Business in produce was strong in response to military demands, and prices also rose sharply during the war by as much as 100 per cent. Many Indian traders made handsome profits. After the war increasing numbers of Indian traders engaged less and less in produce buying and began to concentrate primarily on retail trade. It was during these years that large Indian wholesalers began making their impact felt in the import–export trade. Credit facilities, usually for 90 to 120 days, were always available. But the decade ended on a sour note for Indian traders. The collapse of commodity prices and the currency crisis in 1920 ruined many of them. A large number of shops were closed and some traders went bankrupt. A modest recovery began in 1922.

Although Indian traders played an essential role in the commercial life of the country, 'they in no way had a "stranglehold" on the economy. Economic power resided in the European expatriate sector. The large and more important firms were European-owned, and their dominance was reinforced by government policy.'[90] British merchant firms began entering Kenya almost immediately after colonial rule was established. They came to dominate the export of primary produce from Kenya and distribution of imported manufactured goods on the local market. Among these companies were the British East African Company (1906), Smith MacKenzie (1909), Magadi Soda Company (1911) and Brooke Bond (1916). There was also Gailey and Roberts, which was originally a local firm established by settlers in the early 1900s to import agricultural machinery, and was later taken over by a branch of international capital.[91]

The competition among these firms was intense, so they ventured into the production of the commodities which they exported. Some of these firms made heavy investments in plantation agriculture, where one crop was farmed, in which the firms had a global interest. For example, the BEAC established or managed sisal and wattle estates, and Brooke Bond invested in tea plantations. Apart from producing and exporting their own commodities these firms also eventually became involved in the primary processing of their commodities, which gave rise to the establishment of manufacturing or processing units. The merchant firms were compelled to set up processing plants as a result of competitive conditions on the world market. Local processing of items like tobacco and cigarettes by the BAT, or tea by Brooke

Bond, was also intended to give these firms control of the local market against competitors. They provided early cases of import substitution industrialization. These processes of course gathered momentum from the 1920s and 1930s as the penetration of British merchant capital became more intensive and extensive.

At this time and in the years to come foreign investment in Kenya was therefore dominated by merchant capital. The firms concerned 'acted as agents of British industrial capital by linking up East African markets for manufactured goods with metropolitan markets for raw materials'.[92] Thus merchant capital functioned to maintain the metropolitan–colonial division of labour. It was Kay who first made an elaborate distinction between merchant and industrial capital and their inter-dependence at a global level, by arguing that merchant capital was the only form of capital present in the colonial world, yet within the world economy as a whole it was an aspect of industrial capital. Thus in the colonies merchant capital 'existed in its two historical forms simultaneously. At one and the same moment it was the only form of capital but not the only form of capital. This apparent paradox is the *specifice differentia* of underdevelopment.'[93]

The contours of social change

All the processes outlined above – settler domination, peasant commodity production, introduction of a coercive labour control system and growth of commerce and trade – entailed dramatic as well as subtle changes in African social structures and relationships. Old divisions based on gender and age acquired new forms as the household became articulated with the new colonial capitalist economy; and the idiom of social status began to change from acquisition of 'traditional' assets to baptism in the crucibles of the new order: the colonial school and the colonial town.

The first thing to note about colonialism is that its first two decades ushered in a demographic disaster for Kenya as well as other colonies in Africa. From perhaps 4m people in 1902, Kenya's population fell to 3m in 1911, and to less than 2.5m in 1921. It was not until the mid-thirties that the population probably reached its 1895 level.[94] Colonization coincided with the introduction of alien epidemic diseases such as smallpox, venereal diseases, influenza and cholera for people, and rinderpest for cattle. Local therapeutic systems were virtually impotent in the face of this intensive onslaught of alien diseases.[95] Also, food shortage and famine followed in the wake of the wars of conquest. First, livestock and lands were seized. Then thousands of men were forcibly uprooted from the rural economy to build the colonial infrastructure and fight in European wars.

Colonialism in fact drastically altered the social and ecological organization of agriculture and this undermined collective responses to food shortages, which set the stage for the growth and recurrence of famine.[96] 'Cash' crops assumed an insidious omnipresence. Taxation was the most effective weapon with which to whip African peasants into 'cash'-crop production. Whether edible or inedible, crops were commercialized; production for household consumption was increasingly relegated to secondary position. Thus commoditization of peasant production either undermined food production or weakened peasants' ability to retain food surpluses for 'rainy days' ahead. So food shortages became more frequent and slipped into famines more readily than before. Ochieng' has chronicled and analysed two of the major famines that took place in Luoland during the period under discussion, the famines of 1906-7 and 1917-19.[97]

Expansion of peasant commodity production led to noticeable changes in rural social structure in terms of social differentiation, sexual division of labour, and lineage hierarchies. We have already noted the growth of rural social differentiation, whereby a class of accumulators was emerging. This class consisted of those who could get sufficient access to land and could mobilize labour. This often depended on access to off-farm income. No wonder the new class of accumulators came from the ranks of the 'traditional' elite, collaborators, merchants and the new salaried elite. Internal differentiation within the peasantry eventually led to pauperization of some peasants who became a rural proletariat or drifted to towns.

Peasantization also led to important modifications in uses of household labour, particularly in the sexual division of labour. Already by the time of the First World War quite large numbers of able-bodied men were at work at any one time, especially from the Central and Nyanza Provinces. Inevitably the burden of rural production increasingly fell on the shoulders of women. In the absence of any substantial changes in agricultural technology or organization, this simply led to the intensification of female labour time.[98] The extent to which women translated this into greater control in the appropriation of surplus products is not clear and awaits more empirical research. It is generally asserted that colonialism led to increased exploitation of women. It needs to be noted, however, that this growing exploitation of women did not simply emerge out of the 'functionality' of female oppression for the capitalist system, but was also made possible by the patriarchal character of Kenya's precolonial societies, which in part determined that labour migration would be a special male domain.[99]

Finally, expansion of peasant commodity production and the associated pressures from the colonial state forced lineage hierarchies to begin to crumble. Unmarried, propertyless young men gradually lost their dependence on elders for access to means of production and women. Now they could create their personal income by selling crops from their own fields, and above all by selling their labour power. They had less and less need of elders in putting together a brideprice, and gradually escaped their control. Conversely, an elder with fields too small to support his household would send his older children away to look for wage employment.

It cannot be overemphasized, however, that by 1920 these processes, in which the previous forms of generational and sexual division of labour were being altered, and the processes of peasant accumulation and pauperization were taking place, were still in their embryonic stages. But they held a mirror to the future. These social transformations emanating from the sphere of rural production were cemented by the social and ideological permutations reverberating from the colonial school and the colonial town.

The educational system is one of the most important ideological state apparatuses through which the state maintains its control, and relations of production are reproduced.[100] For Rodney colonial education had an economic function in the colonial division of labour, was a vehicle for implanting and encouraging capitalist individualism and was an instrument of cultural imperialism. 'Colonial schooling', he charged, 'was education for subordination, exploitation, the creation of mental confusion and the development of underdevelopment.'[101]

Colonial education had the double task of incorporating the colonized people into the Western capitalist system and reproducing the emerging capitalist relations of production in each colony. At the time the colonial economic system was being imposed colonial schools were vehicles for the transmission of what Kinyanjui calls metropolitan cultural capital (system of meanings, abilities, communication skills, tastes, dispositions, etc.), ideology and skills. Colonial schooling, therefore, sought to undermine the previous cultural heritage. Once colonial capitalism had established its dominance, 'the primary task of education [was] to reproduce the cultural capital, ideological outlook and skills among the social groups which [had] accepted the imported cultural capital and [were] politically and economically incorporated in the dominant mode of production'.[102]

The first Western 'formal' school in Kenya was established at the coast in 1846 by two German Lutherans, Krapf and Rebman. However, up to the end of the century the expansion of Western education at the coast was extremely limited. Some writers have attributed this to the dominant position of Islam in the region.[103] The primary concern of missionaries was evangelization, and Muslims vigorously opposed it. It needs to be mentioned, also, that the limited growth of Western education at this time reflected the limited penetration of capitalism.

Missionaries followed the Uganda Railway into the interior, where their efforts were to bear more fruit. They concentrated their activities around areas where settlers had set up farms and where the administrative officials had imposed 'law and order'. The missions gradually established spheres of influence, whereby certain regions came to be identified with particular missions.[104] Each mission tried to spread its influence as rapidly as possible. Setting up schools was seen as one means to this end.

The task of establishing Western schooling was monopolized by missionaries until about 1910. The need to provide schooling for the children of the growing European community forced the state to intervene directly in the field of education. A Department of Education was set up in 1910 and a Director of Education appointed. Before long the government came to appreciate the need to equip some Africans with skills that were needed in the labour market and were not provided by missionaries. In 1913 the first official African government school was opened in Machakos, and a second one was opened among the Maasai six years later. The government tried to open schools mainly in areas where Christian missions had not penetrated. Also, the government undertook to provide grants to mission schools.

By 1920 missionaries still dominated in the provision of education for Africans, but state intervention increasingly became marked. Direct state intervention in European and Asian education was even more pronounced. By 1918 there were at least three government-run European boarding schools and a day school.[105] A majority of Asian children also attended government-run schools.[106] Missionary agencies had established about 37 schools and mission stations.[107]

Missionaries mainly viewed Western education as a vehicle for spreading the gospel in particular and Western civilization in general. Hence their vehement opposition to African cultural practices; and this opposition was nowhere better articulated than in the school. Government interest in African education was motivated by the needs of the labour market, like the need to train African clerks and junior technicians for the gradually expanding administrative bureaucracy. The few settlers who favoured education for Africans (the majority preferred the uneducated 'noble savage' to the products of the mission schools) emphasized the importance of technical training as a means of preparing Africans for work on the European estates.

Official educational policy, therefore, sought to harmonize these seemingly divergent interests. In 1905 a commission was appointed to look into the question of education. Among other things, it recommended separate racial education, and provision of government grants only to mission schools offering technical education. These proposals were elaborated on by subsequent commissions appointed in 1906 and 1918.[108] The 1918 commission laid three broad objectives that were to guide the organization, structure and ideology of schooling in colonial Kenya. First, it supported the establishment of a separate and superior educational system for European children. Second, it endorsed the need to inculcate Christian and Western moral values among Africans to replace their supposedly 'primitive' cultural heritage. Third, it underlined the need to encourage technical training so as to meet the increasing demands of the labour market.[109]

The organization of three racial school systems was a reflection of, and was intended to reproduce, the racial division of labour in Kenya, with the Europeans controlling the means of production, Asians providing capital and labour in the commercial sector and administrative bureaucracy, and Africans forming the semi-migrant and resident labour on settler farms and in urban centres. Colonial education aimed at turning Africans into acquiescent hewers of wood and drawers of water for the colonial economy. Hence, the cultural onslaught and overemphasis on technical education to which they were subjected in colonial schools. In contrast, European and Asian education was spared this cultural imperialism. 'Asian religious traditions were respected in their educational system, [and] the European schools received hardly any religious indoctrination.'[110]

Africans, of course, resisted the inferior educational system thrust upon them. Strikes by pupils against manual labour were not uncommon.[111] There were also the insistent demands for a literary education rather than technical training, and expressed preference for secular education as opposed to that provided by the missions. All this fuelled the growth of the independent schools movement. The first African independent schools in Kenya 'were probably those organized by John Owalo and the Nomiya Luo Mission which he founded as an Independent African Church in Nyanza Province in 1910'.[112] The independent schools movement gathered momentum from the late 1920s and became an articulate platform of cultural nationalism. The school therefore was an arena of intense social struggle.

Since the penetration and expansion of colonial capitalism was uneven spatially and socially, education also developed unevenly in spatial and social terms. Generally speaking, it was in those regions and among those households that were closely integrated into the new colonial economy that education expanded fastest.

In the first two decades of colonial rule missionary settlements were to be found mostly in districts of the Central and Nyanza Provinces. Thus the dominant ethnic groups in these regions, the Kikuyu, Luo and Luyia, were among the earliest Africans to embrace Western education. Their relatively widespread incorporation into the labour market must have opened their eyes 'to the need for education to fight injustices that prevailed in society, and as a means of earning a better wage (and status) than the jobs in the public service provided'.[113] In contrast, in the coastal region the participation of the people in the labour market was limited and missionary activities were minimized by Islam. Consequently, the task of spreading Western education at the coast fell on the shoulders of the colonial state, which had neither the funds nor the inclination to embark on any large-scale educational enterprise.[114]

The poor development of education among pastoral communities of the Rift Valley, Eastern Province and North-Eastern Province mirrored the peripheral position of these areas in the colonial economy. For the Maasai the position was a little more complicated. The Maasai were among the first Kenyans to go to mission schools. However, unlike the other groups which lost land to European settlers, the Maasai were not induced to sell their labour power to the settlers, or to participate in the colonial economy by selling their livestock. Their experiences with the colonial authorities left them suspicious, if not contemptuous, of any measures undertaken by the colonial state, ostensibly for their welfare. 'In turn, the colonialists built a myth around the Maasai which viewed them as a conservative group resistant to all forms of social change.'[115]

The responses of various groups and regions to Western education was therefore conditioned by the penetration and development of capitalism and its articulation with previous modes of production. On the whole, by 1920 resistance to the introduction of Western education was largely over, especially in the Central and Nyanza Provinces where Western education was now being enthusiastically embraced. The lines of battle were now drawn around the quality, organization and ideology of this gradually expanding educational system.

If the school was the direct agency of cultural imperialism, the colonial town was its social nemesis. Towns had of course existed along Kenya's coast for centuries. Although towns as such did not exist in the interior, except for caravan towns, various types of central places did develop.[116] Colonial urbanization, however, introduced profound changes in spatial organization of towns. Colonial towns in Kenya, as elsewhere in the colonial world, developed as service and administrative centres, and were not centres of production either agricultural, as in some precolonial towns,[117] or industrial as in the metropolitan countries.[118] So economically colonial towns were only entrepôts, parasitic enclaves subsisting on rural production.

As centres of commerce and administration it is not surprising that colonial towns in Kenya were established at key points along the railway. According to Soja, 'the even spacing of these centres reflects the weak influence of local economic factors in initial urban growth, for nearly all were within 100 to 125 mile jumps from one another. Starting from Mombasa there is Voi, Kibwezi-Makindu, Nairobi, Nakuru, Kisumu ... Eldoret and Nyeri'.[119] Generally, each colonial town contained an administrative *boma* where the offices and residential quarters of the government officers were located. Then there was the bazaar which contained all types of stores and shops, mostly owned by Asians. In all colonial towns there was strict residential segregation. The colonial officials and the resident European population lived in the best areas of the towns, which were provided with the available social services and amenities, while Africans lived in slum conditions in the periphery of the towns.

This colonial urban spatial pattern was most evident in Nairobi. Nairobi was founded in 1899 when the railway reached the present site of the city. The railway authorities decided to set up their headquarters here. In the same year the provincial headquarters moved from Machakos to Nairobi. Soon Nairobi attracted Indian traders who established shops. Nairobi began providing commercial services to the European farmers settled in the Central Highlands. In 1908 it became the official capital when the capital was moved from Mombasa. Nairobi had begun its rise to urban primacy in Kenya.[120]

So Nairobi initially grew up as a centre to provide such services as administration, a transportation system, commercial facilities and trade for the running of the settler agricultural economy, and was not itself a source of economic stimulus. Settlement in Nairobi began in the central area. By 1900 the town consisted of railway buildings and two separate bazaars, one European and the other Indian. In 1901 a plague broke out in the Indian bazaar. It was then moved to the present Biashara Street. Residential areas were eventually established outside the central area: each racial group lived in its own area. Europeans lived in the western part of the city in areas like Westlands, Muthaiga and Ngong. Here a house per acre of land was quite common. Asians lived in Parklands under more crowded conditions. Africans lived in slum villages.

These slums grew on the perimeters of Nairobi. Africans in the town were regarded as merely temporary residents, so they had little choice but to build and live in these slums. Among the earliest of these villages were Pangani, Marikini, Karioko, Kileleshwa and Mombasa village. Conditions in these places were appalling. There was hardly any clean water or sanitation. No wonder plagues broke out frequently – for example, in 1901, 1902, 1904, 1911, 1912 and 1913 – which left many people dead. After each major plague epidemic a sanitary commission was appointed. The one appointed in 1913 under Professor Simpson recommended further racial segregation of residential areas, ostensibly to protect Europeans from the spread of diseases from African slums.

In the meantime, the municipality was searching for ways to solve the 'native urban problem' for once and for all. First, in 1917 a decision was made to destroy all the *ad hoc* African villages and to move their inhabitants to just one special location named Pumwani. The decision was implemented in 1923. Second, the administration used an elaborate system of stringent pass laws, the first of which was issued in 1918, to control the flow of Africans into Nairobi. There were various types of passes but they all stipulated the period of time a person could stay in the town depending on whether he was employed, a casual worker, unemployed or looking for work. In order to enforce the pass laws a vagrancy ordinance was passed which empowered the police to arrest suspected vagrants without warrant. Finally, the administration resorted to forcible evictions of 'undesirable natives', sending them back to their reserves.[121]

For Africans life in early Nairobi was nasty, miserable and lonely. The migrant to Nairobi was haunted by the spectre of disease, malnutrition and arrest. Shortage of housing and low wages meant that married men could not bring their families to live with them. Not surprisingly, prostitution flourished. It was sustained by the acute demographic imbalance of the sexes, the lack of wage opportunities for women, and the monopoly of small-scale trading by Asian petty traders. White has argued persuasively that prostitution was officially tolerated, indeed encouraged, because it served as a 'wage depressant, a disincentive for labourers to bring their families to town', and facilitated the daily reproduction of labour power, that is, the maintenance of the worker.[122]

Attempts were also made to impose the colonial urban pattern on Mombasa. Unlike Nairobi, which was a creation of colonialism, Mombasa was a very old city, with at least 750 years of recorded history. It boasted of peoples from diverse cultures and religions – from the Indian subcontinent and Arabia, Africans from the interior and indigenous peoples themselves. In the nineteenth century Mombasa was more of a cosmopolitan trading and distribution centre and less of an area of intensive agricultural production than its coastal neighbours.[123] The railway helped Mombasa eclipse the other old coastal towns, including Zanzibar. It also helped Mombasa stretch its commercial orbit as far as Uganda.

While aspects of Mombasa as a 'native town' were grudgingly recognized, the colonial state sought to remake Mombasa in the image of a typical colonial town. Colonial laws concerning residential segregation, passes, vagrancy, casual labour and repatriation were extended to Mombasa. As early as 1915 the government began to regard the town and island of Mombasa as a 'non-native' area. Many difficulties were encountered in trying to implement these measures. The reliance on casual labour by the port industry militated against employer enthusiasm for stringent controls of labour mobility. Also, it proved difficult to overhaul the town's long traditions of inter-racial and inter-ethnic mingling. And being on the periphery of settlerdom the settler community in Mombasa remained relatively small and politically less powerful.

But even here some features of colonial urbanization reared their ugly heads.[124] Africans were regarded as temporary migrants, so neither the government nor the private employers made any efforts to provide them with housing. African workers were therefore forced to live in conditions of filth and squalor with all the dangers to their health that this entailed. Many upcountry workers, unaccustomed to coastal weather, perished before the scourge of malaria. By 1910 Mombasa had in fact achieved the dubious distinction of having the highest rate of malaria in Kenya. Periodic epidemics of plague crowned it all. As in Nairobi, the cheap migrant labour system meant that men lived away from their wives. This bred prostitution and its attendant evils. By 1913-14, in fact, most of the colony's venereal diseases were reported from Mombasa and Nairobi.

It would be wrong, of course, to assume that African urban dwellers were passive lumps of human clay. They responded to these conditions and made attempts to ameliorate some of the worst aspects. Wherever possible they built their own houses, tried to improve their dwellings, formed welfare associations, and developed and provided their own forms of recreation. All these organizations provided useful links between rural and urban life, and represented creative efforts to reshape the oppressive colonial system to meet African needs. Also, they were later used for mobilizing people into action for diverse purposes, including nationalist politics.

The colonial towns, therefore, provided a milieu for complex and fluid social and political change. In these towns the horizontal pull of ethnic identity was strengthened, while at the same time the vertical thrust of supra-ethnic affinity was engendered. In other words, in the waxen pot of colonial urbanization ethnic particularism and African nationalism developed simultaneously. Behind the slums and poverty lurked growing African political consciousness, which promised eventually to overturn colonial society. The colonial town was a stage where Africa and Europe met and clashed most openly.

Conclusion

In 1920 Kenya changed from Protectorate to Colony status. Like the earlier change from Foreign Office to Colonial Office control, this meant little in practical terms, but represented the burial of a myth that the term 'Protectorate' entailed. All the institutions of colonialism were now in place and the articulation of capitalist and indigenous modes of production was well underway, with all its contradictions and complexities. In this chapter I have traced the salient features of the political, economic and social changes that took place between 1905 and 1920. Many of these changes, it was emphasized, were still in their embryonic stages, but they were the well from which future developments sprang.

Notes

1 George Bennett, 'Settlers and politics in Kenya, up to 1945', in V. Harlow and E.M. Chilver, eds., *History of East Africa*, vol.II (Oxford, 1965), 274.
2 R.D. Wolff, *The Economics of Colonialism: Britain and Kenya, 1870-1930* (New Haven, 1974), 55.
3 In our understanding, the category of peasantry is inclusive of pastoralists. See J.S. Saul and R. Woods, 'African peasantries', in T. Shanin, ed., *Peasants and Peasant Societies* (Harmondsworth, 1979).
4 Claude Ake, *A Political Economy of Africa* (Harlow, 1981); Samir Amin, *Accumulation on a World Scale* (New York, 1974); and John Eaton, *Political Economy* (New York, 1981).
5 Karl Marx, *Capital*, vol.I (Harmondsworth, 1978), 875-6.
6 *Ibid.*
7 Amin, *Accumulation*, 22.
8 Marx, *Capital*, 876.
9 Festus Iyayi, 'The primitive accumulation of capital in a neo-colony: Nigeria', *Review of African Political Economy* 35 (1986), 29-30.
10 Jairus Banaji, 'Backward capitalism, primitive accumulation and modes of production', *Journal of Contemporary Asia* 3(4) (1973), 396.
11 B.J. Berman and J.M. Lonsdale, 'The development of the labour control system in Kenya, 1919-1929', *Canadian Journal of African Studies* 14(1) (1980), 60.
12 See the debates on articulation of modes of production in *Canadian Journal of African Studies* 19(1) (1985).
13 John Lonsdale, 'The State and social processes in Africa', paper presented to the Annual Meeting of the African Studies Association, Bloomington, 1981, p.36.

14 See Crawford Young, *The Rise and Decline of the Zairean State* (Madison, 1985), 8-46.
15 See Ralph Milliband, *The State in Capitalist Society* (London, 1969).
16 See Nicos Poulantzas, *Political Power and Social Classes* (London, 1978).
17 See Walter Rodney, *How Europe Underdeveloped Africa* (London, 1978).
18 Crawford Young, 'The colonial state and its connection to current political crises in Africa', paper presented to the Conference on African Independence and Consequences of the Transfer of Power, 1956-1980, University of Zimbabwe, Harare, 1985.
19 J.M. Lonsdale and B.J. Berman, 'Coping with the contradictions: the development of the colonial state in Kenya', *Journal of African History* 20 (1979), 90.
20 E. Huxley, *Settlers in Kenya* (Wesport, 1975), 7.
21 D.A. Low, 'British East Africa: the establishment of British rule, 1895-1912', in Harlow and Chilver, *History of East Africa.*
22 Wolff, *Economics of Colonialism,* 55.
23 Bennett, 'Settlers and politics', 276, 278.
24 C.G. Wrigley, 'Kenya: the patterns of economic life 1902-1945', in Harlow and Chilver, *History of East Africa.*
25 R.M.A. van Zwanenberg, 'The economic response of Kenya Africans to European settlement: 1903-1939', in B.A. Ogot, ed., *Politics and Nationalism in Colonial Kenya* (Nairobi, 1972), 206-7.
26 Wolff, *Economics of Colonialism,* 86.
27 *Ibid.,* 57.
28 *Ibid.,* 59-60.
29 E.A. Brett, *Colonialism and Underdevelopment in East Africa* (London, 1973), 200-1.
30 Wolff, *Economics of Colonialism,* 87.
31 *Ibid.,* 88.
32 *Ibid.,* 79.
33 R.M.A. van Zwanenberg with Anne King, *An Economic History of Kenya and Uganda* (London, 1975), 296.
34 Wolff, *Economics of Colonialism,* 60.
35 See Wolff, *Economics of Colonialism;* Brett, *Underdevelopment;* and E.S. Atieno-Odhiambo, *The Paradox of Collaboration and Other Essays* (Nairobi, 1974).
36 M. Cowen, 'Wattle production in the Central Province, capital and household commodity production, 1903-1964' Mimeo, Institute of Development Studies, University of Nairobi, 1975; Gavin Kitching, *Class and Economic Change in Kenya: the making of an African petite bourgeoisie 1905-1970* (New Haven, 1980); and Nicola Swainson, *The Development of Corporate Capitalism in Kenya, 1918-1977* (London, 1980).
37 We have to be careful not to divide precolonial societies into watertight compartments of 'nomadic pastoralists' and 'sedentary agriculturalists'. Most East African societies contained elements of both animal husbandry and crop cultivation. See B.A. Ogot, *Economic Adaptation and Change Among the Jii-Speaking Peoples of Eastern Africa* (forthcoming).
38 Isaac Sindiga, 'Population and development in Maasailand, Kenya', Ph.D. Dissertation, Syracuse University, 1986, p.186.
39 H. Hedlund, 'Contradictions in the peripheralisation of a pastoral society: the Maasai', *Review of African Political Economy* 15 and 16.
40 P.T. Dalleo, 'Trade and pastoralism: economic factors in the history of Somali of north-eastern Kenya, 1892-1948', Ph.D. Dissertation, Syracuse University, 1975.
41 *Ibid.,* 275.
42 John Middleton, 'Kenya: changes in African life, 1912-1945', in Harlow and Chilver, *History of East Africa,* 344.
43 *Ibid.,* 341-5.
44 Kitching, *Class and Economic Change,* 31.

45 Middleton, 'Changes in African life', 343.
46 M. Ng'ang'a, 'Differentiation of the peasantry in Central Province of Kenya: 1880-1970s', IDS Working Paper No. 84, 1977.
47 P. Anyang' Nyong', 'The development of a middle peasantry in Nyanza', IDS Working Paper No. 380, 1981.
48 Kitching, *Class and Economic Change*, 25.
49 Settlers had abandoned cotton growing by 1910 essentially for the same reason: that cotton fetched low prices.
50 Kitching, *Class and Economic Change*, 29.
51 *Ibid.*, 26.
52 Frederick Cooper, *From Slaves to Squatters: plantation labour and agricultural labour in Zanzibar and Coastal Kenya, 1890-1925* (New Haven, 1980), 196.
53 *Ibid.*, 173.
54 *Ibid.*, 217.
55 Cynthia Brantley, *The Giriama and British Colonialism: a study in resilience and rebellion, 1800-1920* (Berkeley, 1981).
56 Cooper, *Slaves to Squattors*, 231.
57 *Ibid.*, 255.
58 *Ibid.*, 258.
59 Berman and Lonsdale, 'Coping with the contradictions', 497.
60 Norman Leys, *Kenya* (London, 1924).
61 MacGregor W. Ross, *Kenya From Within* (London, 1927).
62 P. Collier and D. Lal, *Labour and Poverty in Kenya 1900-1980* (Oxford, 1986), 33.
63 A. Clayton and D.C. Savage, *Government and Labour in Kenya 1895-1963* (London, 1974), 37.
64 *Ibid.*, 64.
65 van Zwanenberg with King, *Economic History*, 281-7.
66 Wolff, *Economics of Colonialism*, 95.
67 Clayton and Savage, *Government and Labour*, 135.
68 R.M.A. van Zwanenberg, *Colonial Capitalism and Labour in Kenya 1919-1939* (Nairobi, 1975).
69 P.T. Zeleza, 'Dependent capitalism and the making of the Kenyan working class during the colonial period', Ph.D. Dissertation, Dalhousie University, 1982, pp.115-18.
70 S.H. Somjee, 'Kipande, the symbol of imperialism, 1914-1948: a study in colonial material culture', Staff Seminar, Department of Literature, University of Nairobi, 1980, p.20.
71 Frank Furedi, 'The Kikuyu squatters in the Rift Valley: 1918-1929', in B.A. Ogot, ed., *Economic and Social History of East Africa, Hadith 5* (Nairobi, 1975), 181-2.
72 R.M. Wambaa and K. King, 'The political economy of the Rift Valley: a squatter perspective', in Ogot, *Economic and Social History*.
73 Kenya Protectorate, *Native Labour Commission Report*, Government Printer (Nairobi, 1912), 3.
74 Cooper, *Slaves to Squatters*, 249.
75 M. Parker, 'Political and social aspects of the development of municipal government in Kenya', Mimeo, CO DH65550/1.
76 T. Sleigh, 'Report on the trade conditions in British East Africa, Uganda, and Zanzibar', Union of South Africa, Dept. of Mines and Industry (Cape Town, 1919).
77 Robin Cohen, 'Resistance and hidden forms of consciousness amongst African workers', *Review of African Political Economy* 19 (1980), 15.
78 Clayton and Savage, *Government and Labour*, 85.
79 Makhan Singh, *History of Kenya's Trade Union Movement to 1952* (Nairobi, 1969), 7.
80 R.J. Cummings, 'Aspects of human porterage with special reference to the Akamba of Kenya: towards an economic history, 1820-1920'. Ph.D. Dissertation, University of

California, 1975, p.257.
81 Kitching, *Class and Economic Change*, 212.
82 Dalleo, 'Trade and pastoralism', 103.
83 J.I. Zarwan, 'Indian businessmen in Kenya during the twentieth century: a case study', Ph.D. Dissertation, Yale University, 1977, p.263.
84 A.K. Musyoki, 'The spatial structure of internal trade in staple foodstuffs in Machakos District, Kenya', Ph.D. Dissertation, Howard University, 1986, p.75.
85 Kitching, *Class and Economic Change*, 165.
86 Zarwan, 'Indian businessmen', 259; R.M.A. van Zwanenberg, 'The development of peasant commodity production in Kenya, 1920-40,' *Economic History Review* 27(3) (1974), 453.
87 P.A. Memon, 'Colonial marketing and urban development in the reserves', *Journal of East African Research and Development* 6(2) (1976), 209.
88 van Zwanenberg with King, *Economic History*, 160.
89 Memon, 'Colonial marketing', 201-8. See also his larger work, 'Mercantile intermediaries in a colonial spatial system: wholesaling in Kenya, 1830-1940', Ph.D. Dissertation, University of Western Ontario, 1974.
90 Zarwan, 'Indian businessmen', 94.
91 Swainson, *Corporate Capitalism*, 58-95.
92 *Ibid.*, 67.
93 Geoffrey Kay, *Development and Underdevelopment, a Marxist analysis* (London, 1975), 67.
94 R.R. Kuczynski, *Demographic Survey of the British Colonial Empire*, vol.II (London, 1949), 144; and M.P.K. Sorrenson, *Law Reform in the Kikuyu Country: a study in government policy* (Nairobi, 1967), 34-5.
95 See Paul Richards, 'Ecological change and politics of African land use', *The African Studies Review* 26(2) (1985); H. Kjekshus, *Ecology, Control and Economic Development in East African History* (London, 1977); and M. Dawson, 'Social and epidemology change in Kenya', Ph.D. Dissertation, University of Wisconsin, 1983.
96 T. Zeleza, 'The current agrarian crisis in Africa: its history and future', *Journal of Eastern African Research and Development* 16 (1986), 156-63.
97 W.R. Ochieng', 'Colonial famines in Luoland, Kenya: 1905-1945', Staff Seminar, Department of History, Kenyatta University, 1987.
98 See Sharon Stichter, 'Women and Labour Force in Kenya, 1895-1964,' IDS Paper No.258; and her *Migrant Labour in Kenya: capitalism and African response, 1895-1975* (London, 1982); and M.J. Hay, 'Luo women and economic change during the colonial period', in N.J. Hafkin and E.G. Bay, eds., *Women in Africa: studies in social and economic change*, (Stanford, 1976).
99 B. Bozzoli, 'Marxism, feminism and South African studies', *Journal of Southern African Studies* 9(2) (1983).
100 Louis Althusser, 'Ideology and ideological state apparatuses', in R. Cosin, ed., *Education, Structure and Society* (Harmondsworth, 1972).
101 Rodney, *How Europe Underdeveloped Africa*, 264.
102 Kabiru Kinyanjui, 'The political economy of educational inequality: a study of the roots of educational inequality in colonial and post-colonial Kenya', Ed.D. Dissertation, Harvard University, 1979.
103 See R.M. Mambo, 'Challenges of western education in the Coast Province of Kenya, 1890-1963', Ph.D. Dissertation, Columbia University, 1980; and Roland Oliver, *The Missionary Factor in East Africa* (London, 1952).
104 John Anderson, *The Struggle for the School* (London, 1970).
105 N. Njoroge, 'An outline of the historical development of primary education in Kenya, 1884-1970', Ph.D. Dissertation, Ohio University, 1972, p.77.
106 *Ibid.*, 83.

107 Kinyanjui, 'Political economy', 184.
108 K.P. Lohrentz, 'The politics of educational development in Central and Southern Nyanza, Kenya, 1904-1939', Ph.D. Dissertation, Syracuse University, 1977, pp.71-99.
109 Kinyanjui, 'Political economy', 169-75.
110 Ibid., 175.
111 Lohrentz, 'Educational development', 126-7.
112 Njoroge, 'Primary education', 102.
113 Kinyanjui, 'Political economy', 188.
114 Mambo, 'Challenges of Western education', 96-144.
115 Kinyanjui, 'Political economy', 189.
116 R.A. Obudho, 'Historical perspective of urbanization', in R.A. Obudho, ed., Urbanization and Development Planning in Kenya (Nairobi, 1981), 7-17.
117 J. Gugler and W.G. Flanagan, Urbanization and Social Change in West Africa (Cambridge, 1978).
118 Harold Carter, An Introduction to Urban Historical Geography (London, 1983).
119 E.W. Soja, The Geography of Modernization in Kenya: a spatial analysis of social, economic and political change (New York, 1968).
120 See M.H. Ross, 'Politics and urbanization in two communities in Nairobi', Ph.D. Dissertation, Northwestern University, 1968; and K.G. Macvicar, 'Twilight of an East African slum: Pumwani and the evolution of African settlement in Nairobi', Ph.D. Dissertation, University of California, 1968.
121 R.M.A. van Zwanenberg, 'History and theory of urban poverty in Nairobi: the problem of slum development', Journal of East African Research and Development 2(2) (1972), 29-48.
122 Louise White,'Women's domestic labour in colonial Kenya: prostitution in Nairobi, 1909-1950', Boston University, African Studies Centre, Working Paper No. 30.
123 Frederick Cooper, Plantation Slavery on the East African Coast (New Haven, 1977).
124 Karim Janmohammed, 'A history of Mombasa, c.1895-1939: some aspects of economic and social life in an East African fort town during colonial rule', Ph.D. Dissertation, Northwestern University, 1977, pp.432-43.

3 The years of revolutionary advance, 1920-1929

Robert Maxon

The 1920s were years of revolutionary advance, which were characterized by the continuing contradiction between a mode of production based on European settler agriculture and that of African peasant production, which was typical of Kenya's early colonial history. By the end of the decade, as at the beginning, European settler production, despite the failure of the settlers to capture real political power (through control of the colonial state), enjoyed pride of place insofar as exports were concerned, but this did not lead to the complete stifling of African production. The 1920s would, in fact, witness revolutionary changes in portions of the African inhabited regions of Kenya in the political and economic spheres. While these did not lead to the emergence of a large industrial proletariat, they would produce larger numbers of African migrant workers and a small petty-bourgeoisie, and lead to new forms of African protest. Yet the colonial state was unwilling to adopt a posture which would unleash the social forces that might have further transformed African societies. As a result, the unequal development which had begun to emerge among and within the African regions of Kenya continued and was even magnified.

Towards settler paramountcy

The 1920s opened with the economic and political interests of Kenya's small European settler population seemingly ascendant. Although certainly not economically dominant before the First World War, settler production had come to make up 61.4 per cent of the colony's agricultural exports in 1919, 59.8 per cent in 1920, and 83.7 per cent in 1921.[1] This was the result of support for such production from the colonial state, and the settler mode's ability to hold sufficient African labour to maintain production.[2] Crucial in the latter instance was the fact that Africans could escape service in the Carrier Corps, where conditions were almost always worse, by work on settler farms and estates.

Perhaps an even more important factor in promoting the paramountcy of settler export production at the start of the 1920s was the disastrous impact the war years had upon the territory known before 1920 as the East African Protectorate. Thousands of able-bodied African men were recruited, mostly by coercion and outright force, for service in the military or Carrier Corps. Those in the latter worked as porters, supplying British forces in the unfriendly terrain and climate of German East Africa. Many did not survive the horrors

71

of the East African campaign, and countless others returned disabled.[3] The negative impact of this loss of manpower on African agricultural production, particularly for the export market in the period 1917-19, was considerable.

The end of the conflict coincided, moreover, with the worst drought and disease epidemic to affect Kenya in the twentieth century. Rains failed over much of the colony in 1918 and 1919; famine resulted in many African areas, and the colonial state was forced to import food to meet the distress.[4] On top of this, Kenya was ravaged by the world-wide influenza epidemic, which took many African lives in 1918-19.[5]

In addition to the negative impact on African production for export, the war years had witnessed important gains made by European settlers. These gains were symptomatic of a loss of initiative and control over Kenyan affairs by the Colonial Office (CO). This loss of control was largely a function of the war, which diverted CO attention from the political and economic problems of East Africa to larger imperial interests. The war resulted in the CO coming under the leadership of politicians like Andrew Bonar Law (1915-16) and Walter Long (1916-18), who had no interest in or knowledge of Kenya (unlike their predecessor Lewis Harcourt). The absence of direction in CO policy towards Kenya is most notable after 1915. Increasingly the CO followed a pattern of reaction to and acceptance of the policy initiatives of the colonial state. During the war years, these were increasingly moving towards the ends desired by Kenya's settlers. The result of this would allow the settlers to enter the 1920s in a position to maximize their economic and political dominance.

The passage of the Crown Lands Ordinance of 1915 was one such major measure which exemplifies the loss of control by the CO, leading to a subsequent significant gain for settlers. Faced with strong and persistent pleading from the colonial state on behalf of terms favourable to white farmers, the CO withdrew its earlier opposition to lengthy leases and accepted, in 1915, a measure which had been deemed unacceptable prior to the war. The ordinanace provided extensive security of tenure (999-year leases), relatively easy terms of lease, and the means for ensuring the continued exclusivity of the White Highlands through the power of the governor's veto over land transactions between members of different races. The latter had an important impact not only on Africans but on Kenya's Asian community. Africans would be much affected by the fact that the ordinance defined all lands occupied by African people as crown lands. They thus became tenants at will of the crown.[6]

In the same year, approval was given to a measure providing for registration of African men so as to secure settlers an improved and more reliable labour supply. Long desired by settlers, implementation of the measure was held up by the war and was begun in late 1919. By 1920, therefore, African males over sixteen were subjected to a pass system that required them to carry an identity document which doubled as a work record. Known by the Swahili word *kipande,* the registration certificate was much hated by Africans, not only as it served to facilitate their working for European settlers, but also because it clearly demonstrated their second-class status in Kenya.[7]

Also during the war, the CO conceded the right of elective representation in the Legislative Council to Europeans, while making no provision for similar rights to be extended to the Asian and African inhabitants of the colony.[8] As with registration, implementation of elective representation for whites was deferred until the end of the war. When finally inaugurated in February 1920, the system provided for eleven European unofficial representatives in the Legislative Council. Asians were allowed two nominated representatives, and Africans received no representation at all.[9] Thus, by the beginning of the 1920s, settlers had the means of exercising greater political influence than ever before to safeguard and strengthen the position of economic dominance that emerged from the war, as well as enjoying the advantages provided by the favourable land and labour measures adopted by the colonial state.

As the 1920s opened, moreover, the colonial state took an even more favourable line towards settler interests under the leadership of Governor Sir Edward Northey. Taking up his appointment as Kenya's post-war governor in January 1919, Northey showed extreme favouritism for the settler mode of production right from the start. This patronage, to the almost complete exclusion of the African mode of production, was most clearly seen in the actions Northey took to assist settlers in dealing with the shortage of labour they experienced in 1919. Showing a strong predilection to aid the latter and a disdain of sentiment potentially hostile to his policy in Britain, Northey moved to make sure the state helped provide African workers for settler estates through the issuance of a circular to administrative officers on 23 October 1919. He stressed that they, together with chiefs and headmen, must 'exercise every possible lawful influence to induce able-bodied male natives to go into the labour field'.[10] The colonial state was to directly favour settlers through provision of labour by what amounted to coercion by African and British administrative officials. This policy was then implemented without reference to or approval from the CO.

Northey's favouritism for settler production may also be seen in his ardent support for the Soldier Settler Scheme. The idea of a settlement for veterans in Kenya had been accepted before Northey arrived, but he lost no time in putting into effect a scheme for making land available as rapidly as possible.[11] Dragging a somewhat reluctant CO with him, Northey carried through a settlement project which brought a well-to-do class of ex-officers (most possessed a public school education and had a source of income such as a military pension or investment income) into Kenya as settlers while enhancing the prospects of land sale for the larger pre-war settlers and land agents.[12]

Before very long, this post-war influx of European settlers produced problems for the colonial state and a negative impact on Kenya's African population. An important reason for Northey's labour circular of 1919 was to provide adequate labour supplies for the new settlers. Besides increased pressure on

African men to work in the settler sector rather than on their own lands, the Soldier Settlement Scheme resulted in a loss of land available for African production. Farms were made available from land already set aside for Europeans on the Trans Nzoia and Laikipia plateaus and in the Nyeri area; in addition, land was removed from the Nandi and Kipsigis reserves. The Nandi were the biggest losers, as 100 square miles were taken for the scheme.[13] Because the exchange rate between sterling and the rupee currency used in East Africa hurt the settlers who were bringing capital from Britain, and the start of the scheme coincided with the recession of 1920-2, the veterans had difficulty, and the colonial state, therefore, further subsidized the newcomers. In September 1920, the purchase price of all farms was reduced by 33⅓ per cent.[14]

The colonial state also favoured the settler sector in the early 1920s by raising African taxation to subsidize the settler, while at the same time making no similar imposition on the Europeans. African taxation had been increased during the war, but the end of the conflict found the colonial authorities faced with a severe financial crisis. Revenue fell far short of expenditure, thanks to both a fall in the former and increases in the latter; some of this consisted of war costs which Kenya was forced to bear. After exploring several alternatives, the colonial state decided to raise the rate of hut and poll tax. This was instituted in 1920-1.[15] Raising railway rates or customs duties were rejected as measures to provide additional revenue. Largely at the insistence of the CO, an income tax, directed toward the settlers, was introduced at the same time that African taxes were being raised. An income tax bill actually became law in mid-1920, but settlers opposed the measure from the first. As a result of their representation in the Legislative Council, the settlers were finally successful in obtaining the repeal of the income tax bill in 1922, and the state gained little revenue from this source.[16]

The African sector was thus forced to bear the brunt of the colony's financial problems at the start of the 1920s. As Overton has shown, the colonial state moved to appropriate African resources rather than to adopt measures that would have affected the settler sector of the economy. Taxation, which hit hard on African agriculturalists (rather than pastoralists), was resorted to at a time when Africans could little afford it.[17] This was typical of a pattern that would continue through the 1920s.

So, too, would the trend of expenditure which marked the beginning of the 1920s. Revenue was channelled by the colonial state into two main areas. The largest was for expenditure on administration, the police and public works to provide and maintain the colonial state and its control. A sizable amount was spent, moreover, in subsidizing settler economic development. According to Overton: 'In the spatial sense, this amounted to a heavy net flow of capital from the reserves to alienated lands and urban areas.'[18]

The decision to initiate construction of the Uasin Gishu railway extension represented a similar initiative. Settlers on the Uasin Gishu plateau had pressed for the construction of a railway before the First World War. CO officials had only been willing to consider the scheme if the railway could be constructed to Mumias, so as to tap the productive capacity of North Nyanza.[19] After the war, settlers successfully pressed for the scheme to be undertaken, but the Eldoret to Mumias portion was dropped from consideration. Whereas African production had once been considered vital to the success of the line, it was decided in 1920 to build the railway only to serve European farms, to the corresponding disadvantage of producers in North Nyanza, and this was confirmed when final approval was given for construction in 1921.[20] The colonial state further subsidized the Uasin Gishu railway by undertaking an imperial loan for its construction and by the recruitment, often by coercive means, of thousands of African workers.

The colonial state also sought to assist and defend settler producers in dealing with the currency difficulties which beset Kenya in 1920 and 1921. These difficulties had their origin in the exchange rate for sterling and the Indian rupee currency used in East Africa. Prior to the war the Indian rupee had been valued at 1s 4d, or 15 rupees to the pound. With the war and the suspension of the gold standard, the value of the silver-based rupee began to rise dramatically in 1919. By mid-September, the exchange rate had risen to 2s per rupee, and by late December it had risen to 2s 4d.[21]

The rising value of the rupee in relation to sterling had an impact on producers for export and on consumers of imported goods. As noted earlier, settler production held the greater share of Kenya's agricultural exports at this time, and European farmers were quick to complain and press the state for relief. Many were in debt, and they found their income from exports to Britain falling in value during 1919 and early 1920, while their debt payments and other expenses had to be met in rupees. Likewise, the new settler bringing capital from Britain saw its value reduced in relation to rupees. Consumers of goods of British origin, on the other hand, benefited from the appreciated value of the rupee. The impact on African consumers was probably not overwhelming, however, since the largest item of imports going to such consumers, cotton textiles, originated in India. Cost of such imports would thus not have been affected since the rupee was the standard for both India and East Africa.[22]

Settlers obviously felt the impact of the exchange rate more as producers than as consumers, and they began political agitation, calling for government action. Here again, Governor Northey was sympathetic. He pressed the CO for stabilization of the exchange rate and the adoption of sterling rather than the rupee as the standard for Kenya currency.[23] The CO finally agreed to stabilization. By the East Africa and Uganda Currency Order in Council (No. 2), which came into effect on 1 April 1920, the florin became the new unit of exchange. Its value was fixed at 2s (or 1 rupee).

This stabilization, however, offered little satisfaction to most settler producers. The new exchange rate represented a 50 per cent increase on sterling debts, loans and overdrafts. Railways and sea freight rates were raised to keep in step with the new exchange rate. To further complicate matters, the Indian rupee began to fall in value in the second half of 1920.[24] This led to calls for a drop in exchange rate.

Although the florin became the standard coin, settlers pressed for a coinage system based on the shilling so that Kenya's currency could conform to Britain's. The colonial state and the CO eventually came to agree to the introduction of the shilling as the standard coin. CO officials also accepted the recommendation of a currency committee set up by the Kenya Legislative Council on which settlers were prominently represented. It called for the minting of new shilling coins with the existing 1, 5, and 10 cent pieces becoming 1, 5, and 10 cents of the shilling.[25]

This would have the effect of halving the value of these coins, which were held in greatest quantities by Africans, thus perpetrating what W.M. Ross called the 'shilling swindle'.[26] The measure attracted support from settlers as a means of cutting the cost of wages by paying in cents. CO officials went along with the proposal even though they recognized it would involve 'cheating the native of his twopence'. They felt it would not inflict great harm on Africans, while the minting of new cents would cause great delay in making the currency switch.[27]

The handling of the currency changes in 1920 and 1921 provides a particularly good example of the CO loss of control that characterized much of the war years as well as the period 1919-22. The stabilization of 1920 was accepted by London officials with little enthusiasm or confidence that it offered a solution to the problem. They decided to support the European producers as this was strongly backed by the colonial state.[28] Similarly the CO, though they recognized the switch to a shilling would work a swindle on Africans, considered, in 1921, 'that in deference to the strong body of local opinion it should be adopted', even though 'the prospects of obtaining a reduction in cost of production by its means are very small'.[29]

One other change in policy in the early 1920s which was welcomed by the settlers should be mentioned. This was the July 1920 annexation to the crown of the territory of the East Africa Protectorate under the name Kenya Colony. The coastal strip officially recognized as belonging to the Sultan of Zanzibar was not annexed; it formed Kenya Protectorate.[30] Thus the East Africa Protectorate would thereafter be known as the Colony and Protectorate of Kenya. The major reasons for pressing ahead with the annexation were that it would make it possible to obtain better terms for loans under the recently revised Colonial Stock Act; and that naturalization for residents desiring British citizenship would be far easier legally if Kenya were a colony. The new status would be welcomed by settlers, on the other hand, as a 'marked step toward the grant of Responsible Government',[31] and it would be taken by post-war Africans as a clear sign of favour to the settlers.[32] It was just one of many measures undertaken by the colonial state and supported by the imperial authorities which seemed to benefit the settler at the expense of the African population and its welfare.

Settler paramountcy checked

While the colonial state thus favoured the settlers in the early 1920s, the settler mode of production failed to gain complete pride of place. In contrast to Zimbabwe and South Africa, Kenya did not experience the establishment of a self-governing settler state. The years 1922 and 1923 would witness the re-establishment of CO control over the affairs of Kenya, and this would place a brake on the momentum pushing the colony toward white supremacy. The CO was forced to intervene as a result of several interrelated factors. Protests from liberal humanitarians and capitalists in Britain played a part in this; so too did rising levels of African protest and the pressure of imperial interests highlighted by Asian demands for equality with the settlers. The most fundamental force undermining the settler mode of production was, however, economic. Its weaknesses were clearly demonstrated during 1920-2.

Pressure from humanitarian interests in Britain was particularly influential in bringing about the intervention of the CO in Kenyan affairs so as to alter policies which were perceived as pro-settler. The humanitarian impulse was exemplified by the actions of church and missionary bodies, the Anti-Slavery and Aborigines Protection Society, members of parliament such as J.C. Wedgwood and W. Ormsby-Gore, and, most notably, J.H. Oldham, secretary of the International Missionary Council. In general the concern of these organizations and individuals was that the local colonial state was not ruling Kenya in a manner which brought much credit to Britain. They did not form a unified pressure group, but they were activated by the notion that Britain held its African territories in trust for their populations and that colonial rule should reflect that fact. Oldham, in particular, made the point on many occasions in the 1920s that Britain had a 'duty' to develop its imperial holdings for the good of the empire and its people.[33]

The currency question was one in which such humanitarian pressure brought a change in policy through CO intervention. By early 1921, the CO had begun to feel heat on the issue.[34] The CO at first held firm in its decision to support the Kenya authorities in reducing the value of 10, 5, and 1 cent pieces when the change would be made from florin to shilling. An Order in Council making such a provision was prepared in August.[35] Faced with continuing humanitarian pressure and protests from the government of Uganda, which would utilize the same currency, the CO was, however, forced to give way. The exchange of cents mandated by the August Order in Council was never carried out, and in November another Order in Council was issued, laying it down that 10, 5, and 1 cent coins would circulate at their face value, not as 10, 5, and 1 cents of a shilling.[36]

While averting a shilling swindle, the CO intervention did not save Africans from suffering some loss in the currency conversions of 1920-1. Time limits were set for conversion, but not all Africans were able to abide by these. Some were left holding florins or rupees for which they were unable to obtain compensation. Nevertheless, the loss could have been much higher without the London action.

A second significant area where pressure from humanitarian interests in Great Britain forced the CO to intervene to alter Kenyan policies seen as adverse to African interests and the trust that Britain held to adequately protect them was the labour policy adopted by the colonial state subsequent to the issue of Northey's labour circular of October 1919. For most of the succeeding two years, labour policy in Kenya engendered much criticism in Britain. This followed the lead of criticism from missionaries in East Africa which first crystallized in the so-called Bishops Memorandum of November 1919.[37] Here, and in later criticism from the Anti-Slavery and Aborigines Protection Society and missionary and church groups in Britain, the circular was particularly censured because it was seen as establishing a system of forced labour, the equivalent in many critics' minds of slavery.[38]

Such criticism in the form of questions in parliament, press attacks and memoranda led the CO to press for changes in the circular to make it more palatable to British critics. A revised circular was issued by the Kenya government in July 1920 which stated that administrative officials should see that chiefs did not abuse their authority. The circular was followed by a despatch from the Secretary of State, Lord Milner, which was published as a command paper. CO officials felt that all doubts would be removed by the new circular, and Milner's despatch still laid stress on the need for chiefs to encourage men to go out to work on settlers' estates and farms.[39]

The issue of the amending circular did not, as the CO had hoped, quiet the protest. Oldham was particularly active in succeeding months in calling for further alteration of the labour circular and a change of policy towards Kenya. He orchestrated the presentation of a memorandum of protest signed by the Archbishop of Canterbury and representatives of all British political parties in early 1921, which called for the appointment of a Royal Commission to work out a policy for East Africa more in line with what was seen as Britain's responsibility of trusteeship for Africans.[40] Criticism also continued to be heard in parliament.[41]

These various pressures led the CO finally to order a further revision of the Northey circular. Following the advice of the now retired John Ainsworth, who had served as Kenya's first chief native commissioner, and Oldham, Edward Wood (later Viscount Halifax), who had become Under-Secretary of State in 1921, put together a modification of labour policy.[42] Wood gained the approval of Oldham in August,[43] and in September, Secretary of State Winston Churchill addressed a despatch to the Kenya government which laid it down that 'Government officials will in future take no part in recruiting labour for private employment.'[44] The CO intervention meant that the colonial state would not be able to so openly assist the settler sector in securing labour.

Humanitarian protest in Britain was not the only factor, however, which helped to move the CO to put a brake on the lengths the colonial state was prepared to go to assist the settler mode of production. Though certainly less direct and substantial than such pressure, the emergence of African protest in Kenya in the early 1920s was also significant. Such protest among Africans took both political and religious forms. It was activated by the negative impact of the war and, in particular, by the post-war depression. Nevertheless, African protest in the early 1920s was also directed against the strong favouritism shown by the colonial state for the settlers, which had such negative impacts on many Africans in terms of higher taxes, cuts in wages, the registration system and forced labour, loss of land, and the non-existence of political rights like those enjoyed by the settlers.

In addition to recognizing the difficulties which the colonial system placed on Kenya Africans, it is important to note that the first years of the 1920s were ones of severe economic hardship for Africans, brought about by the depression which affected Kenya from 1919 through 1922. Africans involved in the production of crops for sale were hard hit by the collapse of prices, which made production for external and internal markets unprofitable. Trade in most African areas of Kenya collapsed during this period. In South Nyanza, for example, the period 1919-22 was marked by a virtual cessation in trade. By March of 1919, 75 per cent of the Indian shops in the district had closed and there was little improvement until the latter part of 1922.[45] The situation was similar in other parts of the colony. The colony's annual report for 1921 noted that 'trade throughout the Reserves was dull, and articles of native produce were practically unsaleable'.[46]

The collapse in prices and markets also severely affected the European settler sector. Prices for coffee and sisal fell by more than 50 per cent, and flax prices collapsed to unremunerative levels. This led to an attempt by settlers to cut African wages.[47] As with the collapse of trade, cuts in wages and declining opportunities for wage labour caused hardship for Africans; often men suffered from both disabilities as it became difficult to meet the tax exactions of the colonial state which were not relaxed.

The grievances produced by the depression thus combined with others to foster new forms of political activity and protest in the early 1920s. One of the most important manifestations of such protest was the founding of the Young Kikuyu Association in June of 1921. It was formed and led by 'young' men such as Harry Thuku, who emerged after the First World War as part of a small educated elite produced by mission schools in Kenya. They would be part of a new generation who would seek to more effectively speak for Africans than the chiefs appointed and paid by the colonial state. In the case of the Young Kikuyu Association, labour grievances were particularly significant in the group's formation as the organization protested the cut in wages, registration and the *kipande,* forced labour, and high taxation.[48]

Within a month, the organization changed its name to the East African Association (EAA). This reflected Thuku's desire to build a pan-ethnic protest movement which would provide a voice for Africans of varying background. He gained support from Kamba, Luo, Maasai and Ganda educated young men living in Nairobi and vicinity. With some assistance from Asian political leaders, the EAA sought to voice African demands by addressing protests to the colonial state, the Kenya press, and directly to the imperial authorities in London. Although Thuku and the EAA did not attract much support among the Kamba or the Maasai, it is clear that by early 1922 Thuku had gained considerable backing among the Kikuyu; this was especially so in the rural areas of both Kiambu and Murang'a districts. In doing so, the EAA quickly became the rival of the government chiefs. It called, in fact, for the appointment of a Kikuyu paramount chief.

In this sense, the EAA would be typical of much African political activity to emerge in the 1920s. It provided a forum for the small educated elite to articulate the grievances of the Kikuyu rural population for which, in addition to economic grievances already noted, land scarcity and the security of the land held by Kikuyu was a central concern.[49] Rapid modernization through an expansion of Western education and greater opportunities for agricultural improvement were also desired by many rural Kikuyu. The EAA attracted support from such rural modernizers just as it did from urban workers in Nairobi.[50]

As a result, the Association drew opposition from Christian missionaries and the Kikuyu chiefs who had formed the Kikuyu Association, and was regarded with increasing suspicion by the colonial state. The reason for this hostility is not difficult to understand. The EAA's rapid growth presented a potentially revolutionary threat to the colonial order. It was pan-ethnic in name and appeal, and though the bulk of its support came from the Kikuyu, it obtained backing from educated Maasai, Kamba and Ganda. More important, Thuku had every intention of creating protest links in the Kamba rural areas and in western Kenya as well. The colonial authorities were not prepared to allow such an eventuality to occur. Even more were they not prepared to allow the authority and influence of the colonial chiefs to be undermined. The alliance that had been forged between the colonial state and the chiefs was one of the most important and fundamental foundations of imperial rule in Kenya.[51] The actions of Thuku and his colleagues in the EAA presented a direct challenge to the position of Kikuyu chiefs as intermediaries between the masses of Africans and the colonial state. Unlike the chiefs, Thuku was willing to carry his protests to the British government itself.[52]

The colonial state did not delay for long in suppressing the EAA. With pressure from London for action,[53] Governor Northey ordered the arrest of Thuku on 15 March 1922. He was detained at the police lines in Nairobi. That same evening, a crowd began to gather outside the police station, and armed police were set in place to guard the prisoner. The crowd grew larger on the 16th as most Africans in Nairobi did not report for work. As the crowd grew more boisterous in their demands for Thuku's release, the police lost their nerve and began to open fire. According to official reports, twenty-one Africans lost their lives, but most Kenyans have long felt that this figure was an underestimate. In the aftermath of the violent dispersal of the protesters, Thuku was deported to Kismayu by order of the governor, and the EAA was banned.[54]

The harsh suppression of the EAA had the desired effect so far as the colonial state was concerned. No organization with a similar pan-ethnic aim emerged in Kenya during the 1920s to challenge the colonial state's favouritism for the settlers. Thuku was held in detention for the remainder of the decade.[55]

However, the EAA was not the only protest organization to emerge in the extremely negative conditions for Africans that marked the early 1920s. At about the same time that the EAA came into being in Nairobi, the Young Kavirondo Association (YKA) was launched in western Kenya. Many of the same issues that caused concern among Thuku and his colleagues activated the young, CMS mission-educated men who came to make up the leadership of the YKA, but there were also local grievances which caused concern. Forced labour and the *kipande* ranked high on the list of complaints, as did high taxes and low wages. A particularly important issue was the 1920 annexation of Kenya as a Crown Colony. The leaders of the association regarded the alteration with concern as it seemed to reflect a change in the status of Africans, open the way to greater settler control, and put land in western Kenya at risk for European settlement.[56]

The YKA was formally organized at a meeting held at Lundha in Central Nyanza in December 1921. Mission-educated Luo and Luyia came to discuss their grievances and to advance demands for mitigation. Having chosen Jonathan Okwirri as chairman, the YKA passed resolutions setting out a number of concerns. These included both national and local issues which reflected unhappiness with the impact of the colonial state's economic measures, opposition to government policy, concern about the weakening of the chiefs' position and status, and the desire of the mission-educated to play a greater role in local affairs.[57] The YKA called for the establishment of a separate legislature for Nyanza with an elected African president, abolition of the *kipande*, reduction of taxation (and excluding women from hut and poll taxes), abolition of forced labour and the dissolution of specific labour camps in Nyanza Province, the return of Kenya from colony to protectorate status, granting of individual title deeds for land, the construction of a government school in Nyanza and a general improvement in educational facilities, an increase in wages for the employed (including chiefs), and creation of paramount chiefs for Central and South Nyanza (North Nyanza already had a paramount chief in the person of Mumia).[58]

Having organized and drafted their grievances, the Association sought to place them before the colonial authorities in an atmosphere of rising hostile emotions. The YKA obtained a meeting with Nyanza's provincial commissioner in February 1922. Leaders of the Association strongly stood by their demands that their grievances be met, and they called for a meeting with the governor. The provincial commissioner was impressed by the strong feelings of dissatisfaction displayed at the meeting, but little came of it in terms of positive change. Neither was a May 1922 meeting with the chief native commissioner satisfactory to the YKA.[59]

Amid rising tensions growing out of this dissatisfaction, the colonial state was forced to take steps to defuse the YKA appeal. Just as in the case of the EAA, the organization represented a potential threat to continued settler dominance and to the colonial order itself. In the aftermath of the violent suppression of protest in Nairobi, the authorities could risk no such outcome in western Kenya. They sought, first of all, to reduce the threat of the YKA by concessions. Governor Northey came to meet with the YKA at Nyahera near Kisumu in July 1922. He promised consideration for almost all the demands of the organization save the change from colony back to protectorate and the issue of title deeds for land. Most important, Northey announced a reduction in taxation, forced labour was afterwards withdrawn, and the labour camps closed.[60] In addition to conciliation and some concessions, however, the state would soon seek to change the character and purpose of the organization by enlisting the support of the CMS in western Kenya; as will be seen later, it was very successful in subverting the YKA.

Political associations such as the EAA and YKA were, on the other hand, not the only forms which African protest took in the early 1920s. The conditions produced by settler dominance, labour pressure, high taxation and the depression also formed the background for religious and millenial protest. The best example was the cult of Mumbo, or Mumboism, which gained a substantial following in South Nyanza during and after the First World War. Mumboism grew out of resentment at the colonial conquest and control and the new Western influences which came with it, first among the Luo and later the Gusii of western Kenya.

Mumboism initially developed an appeal among the Luo of Central Nyanza in 1913.[61] It rejected European ways and advocated a return to traditional customs and the way of life before colonial rule. It involved a millenial vision of renewal; an important part of this was the departure of the Europeans from Kenya. The cult of Mumbo quickly spread and found support among the Luo of South Nyanza and, toward the end of the First World War, among their Gusii neighbours.

The religious appeal of Mumboism provides only a partial explanation for the considerable adherence and support it received in South Nyanza. Among the Gusii in particular, the political message of the cult proved more attractive than the religious.[62] Those who believed in the message of Mumboism had only to wait; if they remained true to the faith, a great cataclysm would occur, followed by a golden age of abundance. The Europeans would be swept out of Kenya along with the government appointed chiefs and others who supported the colonial regime.[63]

The appeal of Mumboism at the end of the war may be seen as a significant expression of discontent at the conditions of forced labour, *kipande,* increased taxes, currency changes, and depression of trade. Among the Gusii, moreover, the cult soon came to be associated with a famous prophet, Sakawa, who had lived during precolonial times, and this served to strengthen its appeal.[64] The district commissioner of South Nyanza tried to suppress the movement in late 1918 by sending 68 adherents out of the district for forced labour. He was overruled by his superiors, the Mumbo adherents returned to their homes, and, fuelled by unhappy conditions, the movement continued to find support among the Gusii.[65]

This support caused grave disquiet to the South Nyanza administration in late 1920. The British finally decided that severe action would have to be taken to check the idea that Sakawa would soon return, white men would leave, and black men would rule themselves once again. The district commissioner ordered the arrest of those he regarded as ringleaders in December, and early in 1921 they were deported to Lamu at the coast.[66] This served to curb the threat in the eyes of the colonial administration, but Mumboism did not die out; it would increase its numbers of Gusii adherents, for example, at the time of the Great Depression.

As with the cult of Mumbo, the prophet Ndonye wa Kauti forged a millenial movement among the Machakos Kamba in the depression and oppressive conditions of the early 1920s. Ndonye's movement grew out of the economic setbacks experienced by the Kamba in 1921-2. Increases in taxes and currency changes brought hardship to them. The slump in prices for their produce cut into the Kamba cash income as did the declining opportunities for wage labour outside the district.

From this background of economic distress and general dislike of colonial rule, Ndonye wa Kauti offered a solution. The prophet combined traditional beliefs with those of Christianity. As an example of the former, he claimed an ability to foretell the onset of rain and he invited women to dance *kilumi* at his home as an act of respect. An example of the latter was his concept of God, Ngai.[67] Ndonye also appealed to Kamba beliefs. He held out a view of a millennium which would usher in a golden age when the Europeans would be gone, the land renewed, water would be plentiful, and taxation would be no more.[68]

Ndonye began to preach his doctrine in 1922, and he gained a growing following. He insisted that God had told him to build a house and when it was complete: 'He will send books, clothes, rifles, and a telegraph line . . . As soon as all these articles have been sent to me by God, I shall take complete charge of the whole country.'[69] As Ndonye's following spread, the Machakos district commissioner became worried and sought the prophet's arrest. The European official took Ndonye into custody but lacked evidence to hold him, and his release heightened his popularity. The colonial state thus arrested him again in July 1922, and he was exiled to Siyu at the coast in the following year. He never returned to Machakos, and his movement collapsed in his absence.[70]

These and other manifestations of protest in the early 1920s demonstrate African discontent with the colonial situation in general and specifically the direction in which the colonial state was moving to support the settler mode of production at the expense of that of the Africans. The protests were a factor in causing the imperial government to intervene in Kenya affairs. It would be misleading, however, to maintain that African protest was a major reason for this. Such protest in the early 1920s was diffuse, it was concentrated largely among small numbers of Africans, had not developed a solid and consistent mass following, and effective national links pulling together all major ethnic groups had not developed.

Far more significant, on the other hand, in arousing concern in London for Kenyan affairs was the colony's financial position and economic policies. As noted earlier, Kenya, like many other parts of the world, experienced depressed trade conditions from 1920 through 1922. Prices for Kenya's major exports, now largely European settler-produced crops such as coffee and sisal, dropped precipitously and remained at low levels. Settler flax, which Europeans and the colonial state had viewed with great optimism at the end of the First World War, did not survive, with heavy losses to the producer.[71] Most of the participants in the Soldier Settlement Scheme were in financial trouble, which necessitated further subsidization by the state, and a number were forced to abandon their farms.[72] Currency fluctuations and change also worked to produce a negative impact on trade.

The adverse impact on the colony's finances was substantial. This was all the more so because of a leap in government expenditure under Governor Northey to finance increased administration and support for the European settler sector of the economy (including a registration system, and increase in agricultural support services for settlers). Thus for the 1919-20 financial year, Kenya faced a deficit of expenditure over revenue of more than £440,000.[73] Great pressure was, as a result, placed on the colonial state to balance the budget. This was done, as noted earlier, by increasing African taxation in the following year and by retrenchment. As 1921 brought no real relief, further spending cuts had to be made. Still the colony's finances could not be placed safely on the plus side for, as the 1922 financial year approached, a huge deficit of expenditure over revenue of some £600,000 loomed.[74]

In such a situation, the CO, just as much as authorities in Kenya, had to be concerned with balancing the budget. In London there dawned, in the first half of 1922, the realization that a major problem underlying Kenya's financial woes was not just the depression but the lack of economic sense in basing the economic wellbeing of the colony on the settler mode of production. The most forceful expression of this fact was brought home to the CO by Sir Humphrey Leggett. Leggett was chairman of the East African section of the London Chamber of Commerce and managing director of the British East Africa Corporation, which had extensive commercial holdings in Kenya and Uganda. In January 1922 Leggett minced no words in the criticism he sent to the CO of what he saw as an unwise and uneconomic policy being followed by Kenya's government. He sent another powerful indictment to Labour MP Josiah Wedgwood in late March. The latter passed it on to the CO. Leggett described African taxation as 'deadening their industry and setting them back in every way'.[75] He addressed a further letter to the CO in April.[76]

In these communications to the CO, Leggett maintained that reliance on the European settler mode of production was costing Kenya dearly. The solution to Kenya's economic problems, he maintained, was to stimulate African production by spending more on the reserves while reducing the load of African taxation. This would produce an increase in purchasing power, a matter of some moment to Leggett and his London commercial colleagues. Foreshadowing what would be known as the Dual Policy, Leggett called for African production of low value, bulk agricultural products with the settler production focused on high-value, capital intensive products.[77]

Leggett's criticisms forced the CO to examine the economic situation in Kenya more closely and helped to convince officials to move to reassert control. As Ian Spencer has described, they were at first reluctant to believe Leggett's criticisms, but by May of 1922 the CO had become convinced that African taxation had to be reduced, the African mode of production stimulated, and expenditure on services in the reserves significantly increased.[78] By that time, the Kenya government had changed its position with regard to African production. Pressured by London to effect 'very considerable economies in the public expenditure', the colonial state had established an Economic and Finance Committee under the chairmanship of Sir Charles Bowring to recommend cuts in expenditure and ways of expanding revenue.[79] Among other recommendations, the committee, following Bowring's lead, called for the encouragement of production for export in the African Reserves and a reorganization of the Department of Agriculture to carry it out. The Bowring Committee laid great stress on maize production, both by Africans and settlers, as an answer to Kenya's economic ills.[80] As a result, Northey endorsed the idea of government resources being utilized to support African production.[81]

This was a truly remarkable about face for the governor, who for the previous three years had thrown the resources of the colonial state solidly behind the settler mode of production and given no support to stimulating African agricultural production. Economic reality had finally hit home. The depression had clearly illustrated the folly of depending on settler production. As this was grasped by capitalists in Britain, so too it was a reality that had to be accepted by the colonial state and the British government. The postscript to the change of policy was written on 29 June 1922, when Secretary of State

Churchill sent a secret despatch to Kenya recalling Northey as governor.[82]

The decision to elevate African production from the dustbin was made official policy in the garb of African paramountcy in the following year. Imperial authorities used that doctrine to find a way out of the Indian Question (the term 'Asian' is preferred today in reference to people whose nationality would come to be Indian or Pakistani), which bedevilled them after the First World War. Although it seems less significant in the 1980s, the Indian Question was the CO's most difficult problem when dealing with Kenya in the 1920s. The demand of Kenya's Asian population for 'equal rights' with those enjoyed by European settlers occupied the closer attention of three secretaries of state than practically any other East African issue in the period.

The Indian Question revolved around four specific grievances advanced by East African Asians. First, they objected to the reservation of land in Kenya's highlands for whites only. Settlers had been given exclusive right to the highlands through a pledge by the Secretary of State, Lord Elgin, in 1908, and the Crown Lands Ordinance had given the colonial state the means (the governor's veto on land sales between people of different races) to maintain the White Highlands. Asians demanded the right to purchase land there. A second issue was urban segregation: settlers and the Kenya colonial authorities wished to maintain residential and commercial segregation in towns. Here too, Asians demanded the right to buy or lease any residential or commercial property they wished and could afford. A third grievance involved immigration: settlers maintained the need to restrict immigration from India to Kenya while Asians, claiming equality of treatment as citizens of the British Empire, held out for free entry to the colony. Finally, the major demand was elective representation in the Legislative Council. Asians claimed the right to elect representatives on the same basis as was granted to Europeans after the war.

The last two issues were the most controversial and difficult to find a solution for. The colonial state and the CO never seriously considered opening the White Highlands to Asians. They would be allowed an area for settlement between the highlands and the coast. Although both adhered to the principle of segregation in townships, by the middle of 1921 insistence on segregation had been dropped.[83] Immigration controls were vociferously demanded by the settlers, and they were able to gain support from missionary opinion in East Africa. European settlers, moreover, laid greatest stress on maintaining predominance in political rights. They had obtained the right to elect members to the Legislative Council, and they would admit no sharing with the more numerous Asian community. Settlers adamantly opposed even the granting of voting rights to Asians and strenuously objected to the principle of a common roll for all qualified voters. The right to elections on a common roll was just as strenuously demanded by the Asians. Behind the settlers' strong resistance to equal rights for Asians lay their desire to protect their economic paramountcy, mixed with strong feelings of racism directed at Kenya's Asians.

The settlers drew strength from the advances they had made during and after the war and from the unflinching support of Governor Northey. Here, as in issues relating to the settler mode of production, the governor showed himself to be an ardent believer in European paramountcy. He even went so far as to share secret despatches from the CO with settler leaders and to help and advise them on positions to take in negotiations with London.[84]

Although their claims had little support among Nairobi or CO officials, the Asian case received backing from India. Both Indian nationalists and the government of India gave strong sustenance to Asian claims. The British rulers of India backed the East African Asians because they correctly held that denial of rights there would make it more difficult for Britain to govern india.[85] Strong support for Indian claims was also provided by Edwin Montagu, Secretary of State for India from 1917-22. His pro-Indian stance helped lose him his cabinet position in 1922, but Montagu's championing of equal rights for Asians kept the CO from taking a more pro-settler line.

As neither settlers nor Asians, nor their respective backers, were satisfied with various proposals advanced for settlement, the Indian Question came to a boil in 1922-3. Faced with heavy pressure from the Indian government and its supporters in Britain, CO officials moved in mid-1922 to bring about a settlement which would more closely meet the Asian demands than those of the settlers. To ease the path to agreement, Northey, as noted earlier, was removed as governor; he was replaced by the governor of Uganda, Sir Robert Coryndon. Secretary of State Churchill followed this by arranging consultations between his parliamentary Under-Secretary, Edward Wood, and the Earl of Winterton, who held the same position at the India Office.[86]

The two under-secretaries reached agreement on what would be known as the Wood–Winterton proposals, and Churchill accepted them as a basis for a final settlement. The CO sent the Wood–Winterton proposals to Coryndon on 5 September 1922. They called for a common electoral roll and the enfranchisement of about 10 per cent of the Kenya Asian population. The new Legislative Council would thus have four Asian representatives and seven or eight Europeans. There would be one Asian nominated to the Executive Council. The CO refused to endorse urban segregation and to change its policy on the White Highlands. No immigration restrictions were to be imposed.[87]

These proposals failed to yield a solution, as they were rejected by the Kenya settlers. Coryndon, with his strong South African connexions, was certainly the wrong man to bring about a settlement on these terms. He replied to Churchill that the Wood–Winterton scheme was not palatable to Europeans.[88] At this point in the controversy (October 1922), Lloyd George's coalition government fell and a Conservative Party administration took office. The Duke of Devonshire replaced Churchill as Secretary of State. He continued, however, to press for agreement to the Wood–Winterton proposals, but Coryndon, despite urging from London, failed to gain the agreement of the settlers.[89] In February 1923, the crisis came to a head as the governor reported the threat of a settler armed rebellion.[90]

It is difficult to know how grave the threat of armed action, which included plans to kidnap the governor, really was, but the CO took it seriously. CO officials knew that it would be politically impossible to quell such an uprising of whites when the only troops at their disposal were African.[91] To buy time, the CO called Coryndon home for consultations and agreed to receive settler and Asian delegations.

The parties to the dispute thus made their way to London in the spring of 1923. The Asian delegation was buttressed by representatives from India itself, and the settlers were joined by Dr J.W. Arthur, the Church of Scotland missionary. By the time the parties had arrived in the British capital, the CO had formulated the broad-based outline of a settlement. Indian claims would not be as generously treated as in the Wood–Winterton proposals, but the settlers claim to paramountcy, and an open door to an unofficial majority and self-government on the South African model would not be conceded either. The economic weakness of the settler mode of production had shown the impossibility of leaving the safety of imperial interests in Kenya in their hands.

Thus the CO produced a compromise solution to the Indian Question which proclaimed African paramountcy as the principle which would govern policy in Kenya. It was a clever compromise, as neither the settlers nor the Asians could reject it out of hand; both had claimed a strong wish to promote African advancement. Thanks to the intervention of J.H. Oldham, moreover, such a settlement, which emphasized imperial trusteeship for Kenya's African population, would be acceptable to British opinion.[92]

The CO settlement was published on 25 July as a White Paper entitled *Indians in Kenya*. 'Primarily', the document maintained, 'Kenya is an African territory, and His Majesty's Government think it necessary definitely to record their considered opinion that the interests of the African natives must be paramount . . .'[93] As far as the Indian Question was concerned, common roll elections were rejected; Asians were to have five representatives to the Europeans' eleven in Legislative Council. Arabs would have two representatives, and a missionary would be appointed to represent African interests. Reservation of the White Highlands for Europeans would continue, and urban segregation was ruled out. Restrictions on immigration were to be introduced 'in the economic interests of the natives', but details of these were left until later.[94]

The settlers accepted the Devonshire settlement as did missionary opinion in Britain and Kenya, but Asians did not. Most boycotted the new political structure for much of the rest of the 1920s.[95] Yet the real significance of the CO declaration lies neither with these specific decisions nor with acceptance by the various parties. First and foremost, the CO had reasserted the control which it had abandoned during the First World War to the colonial state, in a fundamental manner. An obstacle which proved insurmountable was placed in the path of settler control of Kenya. This was not so much in the statement that an unofficial majority was out of the question for the foreseeable future; nor was it in the pious but empty words supporting African advancement. As will be seen, British policy for the rest of the decade was distinguished by little concern to genuinely promote African interests to the detriment of the settlers. Rather it was the recognition of the reality that the African mode of production could-not be completely ignored and relegated to unimportance if the colonial state was to survive.

The CO reserved for itself the role of final arbiter in Kenyan affairs by stating: 'In the administration of Kenya, His Majesty's Government regard themselves as exercising a trust, the object of which may be defined as the protection and advancement of the native races.'[96] No matter how hard they might press for it, Kenya's small European settler community would never gain final and effective control of the political and economic structure of the colony. In times of crisis over the next forty years, Britain would fall back on the Devonshire declaration to justify its intervention in thwarting settler aspirations and ultimately facilitating the emergence of an African middle class as a more realistic alternative to the settlers.

Economic realities of the 1920s

The doctrine of African paramountcy was the corollary of the Dual Policy of development. But like the former, the Dual Policy was largely a matter of lip service rather than a policy that would be seriously implemented. As described above, Northey had recommended the stimulation of African production shortly before his dismissal. His successor, Coryndon, adopted the policy with enthusiasm, and it became widely known as the Dual Policy, by which African production in the reserves and settler production in the highlands would both be developed in complementary fashion.[97]

In practice, such a policy was never complementary. For the rest of the 1920s, settler production for export was favoured by the colonial state as is illustrated in table 3.1. Though the Economic and Finance Committee of 1922 had called for the increased production and export of bulk commodities from the African sector, such would never be the case. African production never made up more than 26.3 per cent of total agricultural exports. Of this, hides and skins, not the sort of bulk commodity envisioned by the committee, made up an average 50.4 per cent of exports of African origin between 1922 and 1929.[98] Exports of African-grown maize increased after 1923 but, as table 3.2 indicates, it took clear second place to exports of settler maize.

Thus, despite numerous public statements in favour of stimulating African production by Coryndon and his successor Sir Edward Grigg (1925-31), little was done by the colonial state to favour the African mode of production. As the figures in table 3.1 suggest, the 1920s were not a period of expansion of African production for export; stagnation is a better descriptive term.[99]

Favouritism of the colonial state for the settler mode of production was certainly a most powerful factor in producing this result. High-value cash crops, such as coffee and tea, were kept from African growers,[100] while at the same time the state assisted the settlers in very material ways. Railway

Table 3.1. Origin of Kenya's agricultural exports (percentage of value)

Year	Settler	African	Mixed origin/Asian
1922	78.4	19.4	2.2
1923	70.7	26.3	3.0
1924	71.3	24.0	4.7
1925	71.2	24.8	4.0
1926	74.0	21.8	4.2
1927	79.1	17.2	3.7
1928	77.7	17.8	4.5
1929	73.1	22.9	4.0
8-year average	74.4	21.8	3.8

Source: Colony and Protectorate of Kenya, *Department of Agriculture Annual Report 1929* (Nairobi, 1930), 651.

Table 3.2. Value of Kenya's maize exports (£s)

Year	Settler	African	Total
1922	82,235	73,000	146,106
1923	129,545	120,000	249,545
1924	251,144	130,000	381,144
1925	316,964	100,000	416,964
1926	210,596	70,000	280,596
1927	430,893	75,000	505,893
1928	256,078	50,000	306,078
1929	260,892	45,000	305,892

Source: Great Britain, *Colony and Protectorate of Kenya: Reports for 1925-1929* (London, 1926-30).

rating policies and taxation worked in favour of the settlers in the 1920s. As E.A. Brett has argued, both were used to subsidize the settler sector by transferring resources from the African sector.[101] Tariff policies were arranged to have the same effect,[102] while providing protection for settler production of such commodities as wheat flour, bacon, butter and sugar.[103] Settlers continued to escape the impact of direct taxation, notably the imposition of an income tax. The settler sector was favoured in marketing as well; settler cooperative organizations such as the Kenya Farmers Association (KFA) and the Kenya Cooperative Creameries (KCC) were allowed dominant roles in both internal and external markets.

The colonial state also favoured the settler sector in the provision of transportation and in obtaining external finance. An extensive programme of branch railway lines was undertaken in the 1920s. In addition to the Uasin Gishu railway, lines were constructed from Nakuru to Solai, from Eldoret to Kitale, and from Gilgil to Thomson's Falls. The line from Nairobi to Thika was extended to Nyeri. In all, 397 of the 544 miles of rails constructed in the 1920s passed through European areas and were meant to assist settler farmers.[104]

Finance for these branch lines was largely obtained from imperial loans. A loan of £5m was raised in 1921, and a further £5m in 1927. In the following year, a loan of £3.5m was floated.[105] The bulk of the money from these went to underwrite railway and port development beneficial to settlers.

With this assistance settler agriculture prospered and expanded in the second half of the 1920s. In 1927 and 1928, for example, settler agricultural exports exceeded a value of £2m.[106] Coffee and sisal continued to lead the way, and maize became the third major export of the settler sector in the 1920s. As Sharon Stichter has shown, this success, coupled with increased railway building, created a demand for labour which in turn served to retard African production for export.[107] The prosperity enjoyed by settler agriculture also served to quiet business and humanitarian critics in Britain, and there was thus less pressure in the second half of the 1920s for policies favourable to African agriculture.

A powerful reason for the dominance of the settler sector was the political influence the settlers were able to exercise on the colonial state. While it is usual to see the Devonshire declaration as a defeat for the settlers' ultimate goal of self-government,[108] the statement in favour of African paramountcy actually did little to weaken settler influence in the economic sphere. Settlers continued to have a strong voice in the Legislative Council and were heavily represented on all government appointed committees and boards which had anything to do with agriculture. In most economic issues during the 1920s, settler political influence ensured their protection from measures they deemed inimical. Thus they avoided the imposition of income tax and kept Africans from growing coffee. They were even able to turn the East Africa Commission of 1924 to take a most positive view of the settler mode of production. Although appointed by a Labour government and chaired by W. Ormsby-Gore, formerly a critic of settler agriculture, the commission's report maintained that settler endeavours had 'added greatly' to productivity in Kenya.[109] The commission did much to influence British opinion in favour of the settler mode of production.[110]

Yet the settlers' political influence and economic muscle should not be overemphasized. That these had limitations was exposed in the drive to achieve 'closer union', an East African federation, in the second half of the 1920s. Kenya settlers, led by Lord Delamere, came to back the union of Uganda and Tanganyika, and perhaps also Northern Rhodesia and Nyasaland, with Kenya as a means of increasing their economic and political (the achievement of an unofficial or settler majority in the Legislative Council) influence. L.S. Amery, Secretary of State for the Colonies from late 1924 to mid-1929, was a strong advocate, as was the governor he hand-picked, Sir Edward Grigg; Delamere organized conferences of East and Central African settlers to drum up support.[111] Despite this support, closer union never became a reality. The Hilton Young Commission, which visited East Africa in 1928, did not produce the recommendations desired by Amery and Grigg when its report was published in 1929. Suspicious of the outcome of settler dominance for the African majority and recognizing the fears of such dominance in Uganda and Tanganyika, the committee subordinated closer union to African paramountcy.[112] Amery's despatch of his permanent Under-Secretary, Sir Samuel Wilson, to East Africa to try and save a scheme for closer union proved to be of no avail.[113]

This example of settler inability to become, in a far more comprehensive way than before, the final arbiters of affairs in Kenya would soon be followed by another period of fundamental economic weakness of the settler mode of production. The weakness would be exposed during the Great Depression of the early 1930s. Requiring huge levels of support from the colonial state and subsidization from the African sector, the settler mode of production would still all but collapse.

In discussing the settler sector in the later 1920s, it is necessary also to discuss the beginnings of corporate capitalism in Kenya. Settlers were, after all, responsible for some of the earliest corporate initiatives in the colony. Corporate entities had been successful in gaining land concessions from the earliest days of white settlement. Settler companies had been formed before the 1920s, but they were characterized by instability and interlocking ownership.[114] Company formation expanded and these were marked by a greater degree of stability in the 1920s.

Companies formed and/or registered in the 1920s were owned by Kenya Europeans, Asians or foreign firms. Records indicate no African involvement in the formation of such capitalist enterprises.[115] European private firms predominated in the area of agriculture and property/real estate dealing. Few were involved in manufacturing as the settlers, by the mid-1920s, processed their crops for sale through such state-sponsored bodies as the KFA and the KCC. Most of the larger European public companies, on the other hand, were involved in processing commodities for export.[116] So too were such British firms as Mitchell Cotts, which entered the Kenyan economic scene in the 1920s. Banks operating in Kenya, as before the 1920s, were branches of British-owned financial establishments, such as the National Bank of India and the Standard Bank of South Africa. This source of capital was entirely foreign dominated; while Asian private companies, were almost entirely confined to wholesale and retail trade (especially export/import) in the decade.[117]

It is significant that these examples of capitalism in Kenya did not develop as truly national entities in the decade. Not only were banks foreign owned and Africans not involved in corporate capitalism; settler and Asian firms were generally weak and easily controlled and manipulated by foreign capital.

It is important to note in touching these early examples of corporate capitalism that the colonial system placed powerful limits on its emergence in Kenya and thus on the emergence of a national bourgeoisie. The metropolitan power considered East Africa largely as a market for British industrial goods and a source of raw materials needed for British industry.

The imperial government would not allow manufacturing concerns in Kenya which presented a threat to British industrial interests at home or abroad. Thus, for example, the CO repeatedly frustrated attempts by Asian capitalists to start textile mills in Kenya, which had become by the mid-1920s a large consumer of imported textiles and an exporter, though on a small scale, of cotton.[118] In this way, moreover, Britain placed a substantial brake on the development of capitalist manufacturing enterprises in Kenya. One result of this was that manufacturing made up but a small portion of the gross domestic product in the 1920s.

The attention given here to the considerable influence of the settler mode of production should not blind us to the importance of economic trends in the African sector during the 1920s. These had far greater revolutionary potential for the future than the activities of the settler sector. Here the student is faced with considerable difficulty in reconstructing what was happening in the various African inhabited districts of Kenya because of the dearth of reliable statistics as to production, prices, employment figures, and so on. Gavin Kitching, who has made the most thoroughgoing survey of the African sector during this period, noted this problem time and again.[119] Nevertheless, it can be maintained that, despite the small contribution of African produced commodities in Kenya's exports for the decade, African production was not crushed or stultified. All indications are that in most African districts production increased during the decade.[120] It was production for internal markets: that is to say, production of crops such as maize and beans fuelled exchange within and between African districts, and such production also met the demand of urban centres (such as Nairobi) and settler farms and large estates (such as those near Kericho). This orientation of African produce to internal markets had been accomplished, according to Overton, during the First World War.[121]

The bulk of this expansion of production, however, came from relatively few African districts. On the whole, these were the same areas which had begun to produce for external and internal markets before 1920. Kenya's African economy was characterized at the start of the decade by differential development.[122] Some districts were more immersed in production of commodities, had more men involved in wage employment, and had more men taking part in trade and other business ventures. Thus, they gained more wealth and were more 'developed' than the African districts not so bound up in those activities. Such differentiation continued throughout the 1920s. The Dual Policy played a major role in this. The colonial state spent relatively few resources in promoting African agricultural development during the decade, and thus those districts which attained a head start in development continued to lead the way. When the state did expend resources in African areas, it was almost invariably in those regions which were already most productive. This can be illustrated by the distribution of extension services provided to African areas at the end of the decade. Seven European agricultural officers were assigned to African areas in 1929; four in Kikuyuland, two in Nyanza Province, and one at the coast. Of the 68 African agricultural instructors employed by the Department of Agriculture, 49 were stationed in Kikuyuland and Nyanza, 17 at the coast, and two in Ukamba.[123] With the colonial state doing little to alter the situation and market forces proving inadequate on the whole, the pattern of differential development, which began to emerge before and during the First World War, endured, with tremendous and far-reaching implications for Kenya's future, with little change.[124]

The African areas most involved in production for market or commercial agriculture were the Kikuyu districts of Kiambu, Murang'a and Nyeri and the North and Central Nyanza districts inhabited by the Luo and Luyia. Kitching shows that in the three Kikuyu districts there was a considerable increase in land under crops in the 1920s.[125] The large production for sale seems to have come from Kiambu throughout the decade. Prices were buoyant for all food crops after 1923, and in the mid-1920s expansion of cultivation occurred in Murang'a. With the arrival of the railway in Nyeri district in 1926, there was a notable increase in cultivation and production there in the final years of the 1920s.[126] Much of this took the form of maize and other food crops such as beans, potatoes and wheat, but a noticeable start was made in wattle-bark production among the Kikuyu.[127]

Nyanza Province, specifically North and Central Nyanza, and to some extent South Nyanza, made up the other major area of African production. After 1923 there was a rapid increase in planting and production in these districts. Maize, beans and traditional millets made up the crops produced for the internal market, while simsim and groundnuts were grown for the export market.[128] North Nyanza was the most agriculturally developed district in the province, and by the end of the decade maize production began to expand in the north, in what is today Bungoma district. Kitching notes that 'despite administrative indifference, a sustained expansion of food crop surplus production and export continued until 1930 in all three districts...'[129] Here, as in the Kikuyu inhabited districts, the beginnings of technological change, such as the introduction of ploughs (in preference to hoes) played a part in this process.

Apart from the Nyanza and Kikuyu districts, two other areas commenced the process of commercialization in agriculture in the 1920s. These were Machakos district, where the Kamba expanded production to meet demand from Nairobi and settler estates; and Kericho, where the Kipsigis began commercial cultivation of maize. Here the stimulus was the inauguration of tea estates in the Kericho region from the mid-1920s.[130]

These African areas not only experienced an expansion of cultivation and agricultural production during the 1920s; the decade also witnessed an expansion of African involvement in trade and business there. This took three major forms: market exchange, shop and restaurant keeping, and maize milling. Increasing numbers of Africans were involved in market exchange as the administration of African districts set aside areas as exchange markets and identified particular days as market days. Most individuals involved produced goods they sought to sell, and such exchange often involved barter rather than cash exchange in the 1920s. Some Africans became itinerant traders, buying and selling produce. African shops and restaurants, often under some form of collective ownership, opened all over Kenya in the 1920s, but they were most numerous in Nyanza and Kikuyuland.[131] Mills for grinding maize for sale and consumption within the African reserves also multiplied in the 1920s. Increasingly these were built on streams to take advantage of water as a source of power. Indeed, such mills became a major source of new entrepreneurship among Africans in the decade.

Encouragement of water mills was one of the few ways in which the colonial state assisted such entrepreneurship during that period. European administrators acted during the 1920s to keep this trade in the hands of Africans (and out of that of Asians). The senior commissioner of Nyanza wrote in 1928, for example, that 'non-natives should not in these days as a rule be given mill concessions in the reserves as Natives are quite capable of running these themselves'.[132]

Another way in which the state could provide some assistance to African farmers and businessmen was through the Local Native Councils (LNC) introduced in 1924. Apart from their political role, the LNCs represented, in Kitching's words, the 'first attempt to provide an administrative agency through which a certain amount of African development could be secured, without the resources for such development having to be derived from central government revenue. . .'[133] Beginning in the 1920s, the LNCs came to provide a variety of assistance to traders and farmers seeking to improve their commercial position. Funds were provided, for example, to assist in the inauguration of water mills and ghee factories.[134] In addition to being a source of capital for African business, they also became a source of wage and salary employment in the African areas.

In undertaking this brief survey of African capitalism in the 1920s, the increasing role of Africans as wage earners must also be noted. Most students of the period have seen the decade as one in which a significant increase in the numbers of Africans employed for wages took place. Although the bulk of this took the form of migrant labour, African participation certainly expanded during the 1920s.[135] The major labour-producing districts in the decade were the same ones which supplied the bulk of African commodities for the internal and export markets. According to Kitching, some 30 per cent of adult males in Central and North Nyanza and the three Kikuyu districts were in the labour market in 1925 (up from 25 per cent in 1918), and 40 per cent by 1930.[136]

A variety of factors combined to produce the increasing involvement of Africans in wage employment on settler farms and estates, in Nairobi and Mombasa, and for the colonial state. According to Stichter: 'In the early part of the decade government persuasion and compulsion were prominent features of the labour market; in later years the poor income from crop production in comparison to the income from wages became a more important factor'.[137]

The migrant labourers of the 1920s were almost all single men. These included the first generation of mission educated men going to white-collar employment as clerks, teachers and preachers and a group of unskilled men, lacking Western education, who sought ordinary manual labouring jobs. The educated were likely to be longer-term workers and also to use their wages to improve their economic position in the reserve through purchase of seeds, ploughs, additional land, and so on. The uneducated were more often short-term migrants, whose aim was principally money to buy bridewealth livestock. Some of them undoubtedly did eventually become long-term migrants working in more skilled jobs.[138]

It is significant that most African workers never severed a connexion with their home in the reserves, to which they returned and from which they could proceed again to seek work. Thus the 1920s witnessed no emergence of a large proletariat in Kenya, if by that term one means individuals entirely dependent on wages obtained from capitalists. Most African migrant workers did not meet that definition during the decade. Nevertheless, the increasing numbers of Africans employed in the 1920s would be a factor of immense importance for the future.

Moreover, the great upsurge in squatting in the 1920s held revolutionary potential for the years ahead. Squatters or resident labourers had been a part of the Kenya scene since the earliest days of white settlement. They were one group of Africans who moved more permanently away from the reserves than the normal migrant workers. There was a great outrush of squatters from the Kikuyu districts to settler lands in the Rift Valley, North Nyeri and Thika between 1918 and 1928.[139] Those who left did so normally because of inability to obtain enough land to cultivate or on which to graze their stock. They were able to obtain land for grazing and/or cultivation on settler farms in exchange for offering their labour. By the end of the decade there were some 100,000 squatters on settler land in Kenya.[140] The land shortage in Kikuyu districts that provoked the movement would present crucial difficulties for the colonial state in the future, and the squatters themselves would prove a most volatile element in African protest in the decades ahead.

More significant, perhaps, than either the upsurge in squatting or the expansion in numbers of men involved in migrant labour, was the emergence in the most productive African districts[141] of an African petty-bourgeoisie.[142] In this category may be placed individuals whose income, normally from more than a single source, raised them above their neighbours in that they were able to afford better housing, increased spending on consumer goods, and more education for their children, among other things.

Those whom we may term the petty-bourgeoisie in the 1920s do not fit into any single mould. Most had early access to Western education through mission schools. They thus had opportunities to obtain the better paying jobs which were available to Africans at the time. The position of chief, teacher, catechist or clerk particularly stand out in this regard.[143] They might work in their home district or away from home, but eventually their wages, which were relatively large and stable by the standards of the time for migrant workers, would enable them to save and invest in agriculture or business. In fact it was not unusual for an individual to become involved in both agricultural production for the market and some form of trade.[144] The petty-bourgeoisie were as often as not farmers who had access to off farm income and were thus involved in straddling.[145]

This is not to suggest, however, that the process sketched out above was all-inclusive or applied in every case. There were obviously numerous routes and various forms of straddling involved in becoming a member of the petty-bourgeoisie. A man could just as well get a start as a stock trader as he could as a teacher or chief. What is important is that economic and social differentiation had begun within African districts by the end of the 1920s, just as differentiation had developed between districts during the same time frame. Though still small in numbers by the end of the decade, individuals falling into this category would be exceedingly influential in the years ahead.

Still the most striking thing about those we have categorized as the petty-bourgeoisie was the predominance of chiefs. They were almost always the initial representatives of this class in the rural areas. This should not be surprising, since chiefs had regular employment and, by the 1920s, a reliable salary. They also had better access to technological innovations, such as new varieties of seeds and ploughs, than most of the rural population. Indeed it was not unusual in the 1920s, as earlier, for chiefs to be given large quantities of seeds free. With the power of the colonial state behind them, the chiefs could obtain access to land more readily than others, labour if needed, and permission to start businesses or engage in trade. It can confidently be asserted that, by the early 1930s, the great majority of chiefs in Kenya's most productive districts owned at least one grinding mill. Chiefs were thus the main 'straddlers' of the 1920s, and, as a result, in something of a privileged position. This often caused rivalry and hostility from other petty-bourgeois. Indeed, it would be characteristic of the 1920s and later decades that competition over access to control of local resources and the essentials of modernization (such as Western education, new cash crops and agricultural techniques) would erupt between what may be termed the chiefly and non-chiefly petty-bourgeoisie. This competition underlay a great deal, but certainly not all, African protest and political activities in the latter part of the 1920s.

African protest and politics in the 1920s
African protest after 1922 took a number of forms. It primarily involved local activities growing out of local grievances rather than national organizations

and protest. With the arrest of Thuku and the banning of the EAA, no African protest organization arose claiming to represent the entire colony down to the end of the decade. In emphasizing the local nature of protest, however, it must be stressed that the arenas for political articulation varied from mission station to chiefs' baraza, to a district-wide political organization. Such protest encompassed the actions of organized groups as well as the spontaneous actions of individuals. As E.S. Atieno-Odhiambo has argued, moreover, 'One local issue could be presented at two or more levels at the same time, the initiative for action depending on the perception of the articulators as to what level would be most responsive to the given pressure at the given time.'[146]

This diversity of protest, both in terms of those involved and levels of involvement, makes generalization difficult, but some common trends emerge. Most types of protest sought to work within the system. Those involved in the protest accepted the reality of colonial rule and sought to deal effectively with it. They tried to make the impact of colonialism less harsh and to improve their position within the framework of alien rule rather than trying to get rid of it or drive the British away. Still, not all types of protest in the later 1920s shared this acceptance of the need to work within the system. Adherents of the cult of Mumbo, to take one example, continued to disdain colonial rule and to look to the coming millennium when all European influence would be removed from Kenya.

Another characteristic which may be ascribed to protest in the 1920s is that the motive force behind a great deal of such activity was the drive for modernization. This reflected a desire of individuals and groups to improve their ability to cope with the colonial situation by obtaining greater access to Western education, agricultural improvement (new and improved crops and techniques), enhanced opportunities in commerce, greater employment opportunities, and more equitable treatment when employed. Such desires for modernization could be reflected in the activities of political organizations, separatist churches, or ethnic-based protest groups. While the drive for modernization reflected a desire to adapt more fully to Western civilization, those involved never cut themselves off completely, as the example of the Kikuyu Central Association in the 1920s shows, from their traditional culture and values.

Local political activity through political associations was an important form of African protest in the 1920s. Such associations were, more often than not, made up principally of Western-educated men who, more or less, fit the description set out above as petty-bourgeois. They were normally employed as teachers or clerks and were involved in trade and commercial agriculture. These were men, in J. Forbes Munro's words, 'who had responded to the employment and educational opportunities arising under colonial rule'.[147] The petty-bourgeois membership of these political associations at first included chiefs and headmen, but there often developed rivalry between the state-backed chiefs and others of the petty-bourgeoisie. This rivalry developed because the colonial state favoured the chiefs and was unwilling or unable to cater to the interests and needs of the rest of the petty-bourgeoisie. Thus a significant factor in the activity of many political associations came to be competition for access to local resources and control of them. The non-chiefly petty-bourgeoisie were excluded from the local executive structure and saw official programmes 'not only as generally insufficient but also as tending to favour the official communicators who helped implement them'.[148] Such local political activity may be seen, at this level at least, as a struggle between competing groups of the petty-bourgeoisie.

One of the most important of this kind of political association of the 1920s was the Kikuyu Central Association (KCA). It was launched in 1924 under the leadership of Joseph Kang'ethe and James Beauttah. The KCA came into existence first at Kahuhia in Murang'a and spread from there to Kiambu and Nyeri. It sought to carry on the protest tradition of the EAA but, to avoid hostility from the colonial authorities, the KCA emphasized its concern for the interests of the Kikuyu community.[149]

The prime issue for political organization and action so far as the KCA was concerned was land. The Kikuyu had lost land to European settlement, and land shortage in the Kikuyu districts was, as noted earlier, increasingly felt in the 1920s. A related concern was with land tenure and title to land in the Kikuyu reserve. A 1921 High Court decision had laid it down that since all land reserved for African use in Kenya was crown land, all rights in such land, whatever they may have been in precolonial systems of tenure, 'disappeared, and the natives in occupation of Crown Land became tenants at will of the Crown of the land actually occupied'.[150] Uncertainty as to tenure as well as land shortage were issues with an appeal which extended far beyond the ranks of the petty-bourgeoisie.

The early interests and demands of the KCA may be understood from the list of grievances they presented to Governor Grigg when he visited Murang'a at the end of 1925. The Crown Lands Ordinance of 1915 was objected to because of its negative impact on the Kikuyu. The KCA called for the release of Harry Thuku and permission to hold meetings without the interference of the district administration. It asked for the appointment of a Kikuyu paramount chief with judicial powers, 'who should be well educated and to be elected by majority of our peoples'.[151] The KCA also called for local improvement: erection of a high school, a training facility for hospital workers, a school for girls, and permission to grow cotton and coffee.[152] The Association requested the translation of the colony's laws into Kikuyu and protested against the compulsory rebuilding of houses deemed unsanitary, to prevent plague.[153]

The colonial state took little heed of these grievances and demands; European administrators and chiefs viewed the KCA and its members with scant respect. Faced with government opposition, KCA leaders persevered, and they began in 1925 to use an oath to ensure party loyalty and unity.[154] The colonial state was forced to recognize the growing support obtained by the organization among Western-educated Kikuyu in Murang'a. To meet the challenge posed by such political associations as the KCA and partly to provide a means of co-opting African leadership into the system and subsidize local development, it provided for the establishment, after 1924, of LNCs.[155]

It appears that the initial response of the KCA to the establishment of the LNCs was positive. In 1925, Kang'ethe and another KCA leader, John Mbuthia, were selected for the first Murang'a LNC. Before long, however, the KCA leaders came to realize that the possibilities of achieving significant local reform and progress in redressing their grievances through this medium were limited. The DC was the chairman and chiefs made up a majority of African membership. The former had an effective veto power over all measures discussed and decided upon. Administration control was thus considerable, and the powers of the LNCs at first rather limited.

The KCA nevertheless continued its efforts to build support among the Kikuyu by championing their grievances and aspirations. They moved their headquarters to Nairobi in 1927, and this made for more effective contact with educated Kikuyu from Kiambu. This was symbolized in 1928 when Jomo Kenyatta (from Kiambu) took up the position of KCA general secretary.[156] Kenyatta worked to strengthen and broaden the organization, relying particularly on the party newspaper *Mwigwithania,* which he edited. Published monthly, the journal not only spread news about the KCA and its grievances, but also encouraged cultural pride in its Kikuyu readers.

The organization as a result had increased its support in the Kikuyu districts by the end of the decade, as the colonial administration was forced to admit.[157] In early 1928, the KCA presented a memorandum (as did the rival Kikuyu Association) summarizing its concerns and desires to the visiting Hilton Young Commission. It called for African representatives in the Legislative Council, safeguards for African land, the abolition of the *kipande,* and greater government spending for African welfare. The KCA reiterated its call for a paramount chief, and proposed a 'central native council' for the colony.[158] A KCA delegation also presented oral evidence to the commission. At that meeting, the KCA delegation, which included Kenyatta and Kang'ethe, laid great stress on the desire for title deeds for land and their wish for a Kikuyu paramount chief.[159]

In the same year, the KCA decided to send a representative to London to place their grievances before the CO. Kenyatta was chosen, and he left for Britain in February 1929. He met the Under-Secretary of State for the Colonies, presented KCA petitions to the CO, made a number of liberal and radical contacts in Britain, and travelled in Europe; but Kenyatta returned to Kenya in 1930 without having brought about any significant change in British policy toward Kenya.[160]

While its general secretary was away, the KCA had become involved in what may be termed cultural nationalism. The organization came to take a leading role in defending Kikuyu customs and traditions. The main issue involved was clitoridectomy (or female circumcision), which was an important part of the ceremonies by which Kikuyu girls passed to womanhood. Protestant missions, especially the Church of Scotland, wished to see the practice stamped out. Failing to obtain the support of the state to outlaw clitoridectomy, the missions pressed their converts to agree to desist from the practice, eventually using expulsion from the church as a means to enforce the missionary views. The KCA strongly defended the practice and Kikuyu traditions in general.

The issue was still a burning one at the end of 1929. The Protestant missions (CSM, CMS, AIM) lost a large number of church members while the KCA gained support. Most importantly, it gained support and sympathy outside the petty-bourgeoisie. Above all, the KCA continued to voice the most serious concern of the Kikuyu, the land problem. Thus this organization entered the 1930s as the strongest and most influential local political association formed in Kenya in the previous decade. It would continue to play an influential role in Kikuyu affairs.

The YKA (*Piny Owacho*), formed earlier than the KCA, would not, on the other hand, survive the 1930s. This body had taken shape, it will be recalled, in the discontent of the early 1920s. Supported by Luo and Luyia members of the CMS in western Kenya, the organization had gained some redress for members' grievances as a result of their protest in 1922. This very success and the support the Association was gaining from the people of Nyanza caused the colonial administration concern. The YKA was successfully articulating local issues and grievances,[161] but the organization never went forward to develop this appeal into a truly broad-based following. Rather, it would turn towards an appeal to the petty-bourgeoisie of Nyanza and a concern for their interests instead of for political activism of a more broad type.

A most important factor in this turn of events was the YKA decision to accept the leadership of Archdeacon Walter Edwin Owen of the CMS. A leader in the mission effort in Nyanza in the 1920s and 1930s, Owen was regarded as a most sympathetic missionary who had stood up for African interests. The YKA, Okaro-Kojwang' suggests, decided, out of fear of the fate which had befallen Thuku, to fight their battles through a person of the same race and nationality as their rulers.[162] This choice would be pleasing to the latter, as they hoped that Owen would turn the YKA away from activist politics; they would not be disappointed.

Owen was appointed president of the YKA in July 1923. The missionary quickly moved to, in Atieno-Odhiambo's words, 'make this organization respectable by subverting it'.[163] Owen immediately convinced the members to change the name of the organization to the Kavirondo Taxpayers Welfare Association (KTWA). The change in name reflected a change in concern towards welfare and cooperation with the colonial state. Under Owen's direction, the KTWA turned to demands for better education, better hygiene, and fair treatment for taxpayers. The membership was encouraged, among other things, to adopt Western furniture and eating utensils, practise proper sanitation, and plant trees.[164] The organization thus became more and more elitist after 1923. No longer would there be rivalry with chiefs, but cooperation. Owen 'diluted the radicalism with which the original Association was fired; he neutralized it, played down the true aspirations of the leaders, ultimately converted the Association into a kind of welfare club'.[165]

Owen encouraged the leadership of the KTWA to approach the colonial state with deference and by means of written memoranda. It became the basic tool of their struggle; so much so that the leaders came to be referred to as *'Jo-memorandum'*.[166] The KTWA presented a memorandum to the Hilton Young Commission in 1928. Many of their requests were similar to the KCA's: opposition to closer union and to a settler majority in the Legislative Council, and a desire for African members of that body and the Executive Council. They also called for provincial councils and a national consultative council for Africans. It was nevertheless true that their demands were not made as forcefully as those of the KCA.[167] Because memoranda such as these were elitist and formalized, maintains Atieno-Odhiambo, 'they were effete'.[168]

By the end of the 1920s, therefore, the KTWA had ceased to be a political association of impact. It had become a petty-bourgeois welfare society. Owen's leadership had steered the organization in this direction, but the colonial authorities had also played a part. They moved to co-opt leading members of the Association into the colonial structure. Jonathan Okwirri became a chief. He and YKA secretary Benjamin Owuor Gumba and Simon Nyende were appointed to the Central Nyanza LNC before the 1920s were over. KTWA member Eziekiel Apindi was also drawn into government service, and in 1931 he would be selected by the Kenya government as one of three Africans to serve as witnesses before the Joint Select Committee on Closer Union. This pattern would be typical of petty-bourgeois local politicians of the 1920s and later.

Among the Machakos Kamba, the 1920s witnessed a similar protest from an educated elite, which would likewise be co-opted by the colonial regime in the 1930s. Though in Machakos the elite formed no political association such as the KCA or KTWA, they did assume a lead in protest and as critics of the chiefs. On several occasions these mission-educated young men proved more effective communicators of feelings of discontent than the chiefs; a notable example was the protest regarding the 1924 expulsion of Kamba cattle from the Yatta plateau grazing grounds.[169]

Kamba reformers such as James Mutua and James Mwanthi found a forum for their political interests during the remainder of the decade with the inauguration of the Machakos LNC.[170] In the LNC, these young men pushed for modernization (particularly in the expansion of education), were critics of colonial policies, and on many occasions they were strong rivals of chiefs in local affairs. The latter were not, in the 1920s, influential in the LNC. During the 1930s and 1940s, moreover, the educated men who had been critics of the chiefs and the administration joined its ranks. Mwanthi was made a chief in 1939. Mutua became chief of Maputi location in 1942, having virtually held the job, if not the title, for most of the 1930s. The colonial state appears to have been happy to co-opt them as their criticism now died out and they provided greater efficiency than those holding office as chiefs in Machakos during the 1920s.[171]

African protest and a desire for modernization was also exemplified in the decade by the activities of independent churches. These were formed and led by men who had had contact with Christian missionaries and Western influences. Such individuals and their followers sought improvement outside European control. It is usual to see such churches as belonging to two types. Ethiopian churches came into being as breakaways from established churches. They represented a rejection of European control, possible in the religious sphere if not in the political and economic, and were emancipatory in character.[172] The second type, often termed Zionist, was characterized by churches which sprang up independently and sought to incorporate African beliefs and practices into the church to a greater degree than would be allowed by mission churches. Both represented revolutionary departures from traditional beliefs and the mission churches.

Such independent churches had come into existence in Kenya before the First World War. These continued to thrive in the 1920s as well.[173] That decade also saw the emergence of new independent churches. The Dini ya Roho, for example, took root among the southern Luyia, as a breakaway from the Quaker mission, in 1927. It was formed by Jakobo Buluku and Daniel Sande, who felt the Quakers did not provide a fulfilling Christian experience. They found justification for this position in the fact that the European missionaries down-played certain aspects of biblical teachings. Dini ya Roho insisted on an authentic 'baptism by the Holy Spirit', speaking in tongues, and the free confession of sins.[174] Such independent churches provided not only a means of protest but important spiritual as well as social comfort for Africans and a meaningful way to control their destiny in the 1920s.

Many African protests of the 1920s involved building alliances for a specific result or to deal with a specific grievance. Some of the most successful entailed mobilization of diverse groups to protest changes in colonial boundaries or local leadership. Most common were protests directed against changes in the compositions of locations and against 'alien' chiefs placed over locations. The mission-educated and the masses normally joined forces in such protests.

A good example of protest of this type emerged in Nyaribari location of South Nyanza in 1927. Nyaribari was one of eight locations by which British rule over the Gusii had been made effective. In 1927, the colonial state amalgamated Nyaribari into the neighbouring Kitutu location. This proved quite unpopular. Under the leadership of Musa Nyandusi, an early adherent of the Seventh Day Adventist mission in the district, a campaign was mounted against the amalgamation. The people of Nyaribari did not want to be administered by the chief of Kitutu. Nyandusi, who had been appointed assistant chief for Nyaribari, addressed a letter to the colonial authorities, and when this did not lead to a favourable result he led a campaign of non-cooperation with Chief Onsongo of Kitutu.[175] With the support of all groups in Nyaribari, the campaign eventually convinced the colonial authorities to place Nyaribari under its own chief in 1930. Musa Nyandusi was appointed to the position.[176]

Similar examples of protest against 'alien' chiefs took place among the Luyia in the 1920s as well. Such protest was a reaction to what may be termed Wanga sub-imperialism. Mumia, ruler of Wanga, had collaborated with the Europeans from the first, and he and his family had assisted the British in their conquest of the Luyia. As a result of this, Mumia, in the 1920s, occupied the position of paramount chief of the Luyia, and several of his relatives were appointed as chiefs of Luyia locations outside Wanga.[177] Individuals such as Muranga and Mulama were not popular with the people they were set over. They were seen as outsiders who often used their powers to enrich themselves at the expense of the local population. Popular discontent against Wanga chiefs surfaced in more than one Luyia location during the war and built up force in the late 1920s.[178]

A good example is provided by Samia location, where a Wanga chief, Kadima, had been placed in control before the war. Opposition to the appointment surfaced strongly in the years 1915-17, and it came forth again after the war when the heterogeneous Samia location was placed in Central Nyanza.[179] Kadima's rule was opposed by headmen and mission-educated alike. In 1922, a group tried to 'elect' an alternative chief, but the colonial administration would not recognize him. Protests continued to be voiced against Kadima, however; he was seen as an alien and extortionate chief. Finally, the colonial state brought about his removal in 1927.[180]

While this was typical of one form of African protest in the 1920s, the decade was characterized by several forms of protest and political organization. Much of it foreshadowed patterns of dissent and activism in the decades ahead, but that of the 1920s was particularly significant and indeed revolutionary in its impact, as it represented the first attempts of Africans to organize themselves, by uniting the Western-educated and the masses, for effective protest against the place the colonial state had consigned them in the Kenya political economy.

While capitalism extended its penetration into the rural areas with equally revolutionary consequences during the decade, it produced an uneven impact. Production and trade expanded after 1922 and greater numbers of men were involved in migrant labour than ever before. This expanding impact of capitalism produced a small, but significant, petty-bourgeoisie. This would have great impact on the future. At the same time, however, the extension of capitalist relations to the countryside and the favouritism of the colonial state for the settler mode of production would help to force landlessness, squatting, and wage dependency on greater numbers of Africans than ever before. Thus, at the same time that a petty-bourgeoisie was emerging in rural Kenya, the basis for a future proletariat was being laid.

At the same time that this differentiation was taking place, differential development between districts and regions of Kenya was becoming more firmly entrenched in the colony. This unequal development, which did not begin during the decade, became a part of the economic structure of Kenya during the 1920s. The districts which were more 'developed' then would remain so in terms of agricultural production, communications and Western education until the very end of the colonial period.

This characteristic of the 1920s would have every bit as great an impact on Kenya's future as the blocking of the possibility of settler paramountcy. The economic weakness of the settler mode of production, revealed in the first years of the decade, would ultimately undermine all efforts of the colonial state to subsidize the settler sector. Faced with this contradiction, the metropolitan power intervened to re-emphasize the African mode of production as an important factor in Kenya's capitalist development. In the long run, the colonial state and the imperial government would come to accept the need to promote African capitalism in preference to settler. Though this seemed a long way off in 1929, the events of the preceding decade helped open the way for this most revolutionary occurrence in modern Kenyan history.

Notes

1 Colony and Protectorate of Kenya, *Department of Agriculture Annual Report 1922* (Nairobi, 1924), 8-9.

2 John Overton, 'War and economic development: settlers in Kenya, 1914-18', *Journal of African History* 27 (1986), 88.

3 John Overton, 'Spatial differentiation in the colonial economy of Kenya: Africans, settlers and the state, 1900-1920', Ph.D. Dissertation, Cambridge University, 1983, pp.283-5; A. Clayton and D. C. Savage, *Government and Labour in Kenya, 1895-1963* (London, 1974), 83-8.

4 Clayton and Savage, *Government and Labour,* 87-8.

5 *Ibid.,* 88.

6 P.M.K. Sorrenson, *Origins of European Settlement in Kenya* (Nairobi, 1968), 189.

7 Clayton and Savage, *Government and Labour,* 132-3. Harry Thuku, *Maisha Yangu* (Nairobi, 1971), 19-20.

8 Bonar Law to Belfield, telegram, 27 September 1916, CO 533/169.

9 Marjorie Ruth Dilley, *British Policy in Kenya Colony,* 2nd ed. (London, 1966), 51.

10 'Native labour required for non-native farms and other private undertakings', *East African Standard* (Weekly), 1 November 1919, p.25; R.M. Maxon, *John Ainsworth and the Making of Kenya* (Washington, 1980), 370-2.

11 Northey to Milner, telegram, 14 March 1919, CO 533/207 and Northey to Milner, 31 July 1919, CO 533/212.

12 Michael Gordon Redley, 'The politics of a predicament: the white community in Kenya, 1918-32', Ph.D. Dissertation, Cambridge University, 1976, pp.55-6.

13 Northey to Milner, 11 December 1920, CO 533/238.

14 Northey to Milner, 21 September 1920, CO 533/236.

15 The best discussion of the financial crisis and tax increase is provided by Overton, 'Spatial differentiation', 324-30.

16 Dilley, *British Policy*, 98.

17 Overton, 'Spatial differentiation', 330-1.

18 *Ibid.*, 335.

19 Robert Maxon, 'African production and the support of European settlement in Kenya: the Uasin Gishu–Mumias railway scheme, 1911-14', *The Journal of Imperial and Commonwealth History* 14 (October, 1985), 52-64.

20 Northey to Bottomley, 15 January 1920, CO 533/253; Northey to Churchill, 23 May 1921, CO 533/259.

21 Great Britain, *East Africa Protectorate Report for 1919-20* (London, 1921), 5. The best short summary of this most complicated subject is provided by Clayton and Savage, *Government and Labour*, 139-42.

22 *East Africa Protectorate Report for 1919-20*, 6. Cotton goods made up 73 per cent of total imports. Settler imports made up a higher percentage of those originating in Britain (e.g. machinery and parts, building materials).

23 Northey to Milner, telegram, secret, 11 September 1919, CO 533/213.

24 Clayton and Savage, *Government and Labour*, 140-1.

25 William McGregor Ross, *Kenya from Within*, 2nd ed. (London, 1968), 211. Churchill to Northey, telegram, 19 March 1921, CO 533/237.

26 Ross, *Kenya from Within*, 212.

27 Minute by W.C. Bottomley, 10 May 1921, CO 533/268. Bottomley was one of the most senior officials in the East African department.

28 Minutes by Bottomley, 23 September 1919 and Fiddes, 24 September 1919, on Northey to Milner, telegram, secret, 11 September 1919, CO 533/213. Sir George Fiddes was Permanent Under-Secretary of State for the Colonies. Bottomley revealingly admitted that 'the effect of these proposals may be worse than the condition they were intended to remedy'.

29 EA Currency, memo filed with Northey to Churchill, 11 March 1921, CO 533/257.

30 Northey to Milner, 23 July 1920, CO 533/234. The coastal strip was not annexed because it did not appear that France would accept this without demanding concessions from Britain elsewhere in Africa. Under the terms of an 1862 treaty, France and Britain had agreed to respect the independence and integrity of the Sultanate of Zanzibar. Read to Under-Secretary of State, Foreign Office, 31 January 1920, CO 533/214.

31 Bowring to Long, secret, 12 June 1918, CO 533/196.

32 K.M. Okaro-Kojwang', 'Origins and establishment of the Kavirondo Taxpayers Welfare Association', in B.G. McIntosh, ed., *Ngano* (Nairobi, 1969), 114.

33 George Bennett, 'Paramountcy to partnership: J.H. Oldham and Africa', *Africa* 30 (1960), 356-7. Oldham to Wood, 15 August 1921, CO 533/274.

34 *Great Britain, Parliamentary Debates (Commons)*, vol.142 (8 June 1921), cols. 1851-2.

35 Kenya and Uganda (Currency) Order in Council, 10 August 1921, CO 533/268.

36 Great Britain, *Colony and Protectorate of Kenya Report for 1921* (London, 1922), 11; Clayton and Savage, *Government and Labour*, 142. The change from florin to shilling took place in January 1922.

37 *East African Standard*, 15 November 1919, p.10.

38 Dilley, *British Policy*, 226-8.

39 *Ibid.*, 230. Great Britain, *Despatch to the Governor of the East Africa Protectorate Relating to Native Labour and Papers Connected Therewith*, Cmd. 873 (London, 1920).

40 'Labour in Africa and the principle of trusteeship', Oldham Papers, Box 10, Rhodes House, Oxford University, MSS Afr. 1829. See also: Archbishop of Canterbury to Milner, 5 January 1921, CO 533/271; Oldham, Memorandum on Native Affairs in East Africa, 17 May 1921, CO 533/272. Dilley, *British Policy*, 230-1; Bennett, Paramountcy, 356.

41 Great Britain, *Parliamentary Debates (Commons)*, 142 (14 July 1921), cols. 1565-71 and 1590-91. Dilley, *British Policy*, 231.

42 Maxon, *John Ainsworth*, 410-12.

43 Oldham to Wood, 15 August 1921 and Wood to Oldham, private, 19 August 1921, CO 533/274.

44 Churchill to Bowring, 5 September 1921, CO 533/274. Northey was in Britain at the time the decision was made.

45 *South Kavirondo Annual Reports* 1918-19, 1919-20, 1920-21, 1922, Kenya National Archives (KNA) DC/KSI/1/2.

46 *Colony and Protectorate of Kenya Report for 1921*, 5.

47 Clayton and Savage, *Government and Labour*, 141-3.

48 Thuku, *Maisha Yangu*, 19-20. E.S. Atieno-Odhiambo, 'Politics and nationalism in East Africa, 1919-35', in A. Adu Boahen, ed., *General History of Africa*, vol.VII (Berkeley, 1985), 667. The latter sees the Young Kikuyu Association and its successor the EAA as a 'political association as well as a general workers' union'.

49 Atieno-Odhiambo, 'Politics and nationalism', 667.

50 Thuku, *Maisha Yangu*, 22-3.

51 John Lonsdale and Bruce Berman, 'Coping with the contradictions: the development of the colonial state in Kenya 1895-1914', *Journal of African History* 20 (1979), 497.

52 Thuku, *Maisha Yangu*, 89.

53 CO officials had received their first detailed account of the EAA in early March 1922. Both W.C. Bottomley and H.R. Read urged 'early drastic action' against it. A telegram was sent: 'Are you satisfied that you have all the powers you require for dealing if necessary with combinations having a seditious tendency? Do not understand why a native who expresses these views is retained in government service.' The second sentence referred to Thuku, who was employed at the Treasury. Churchill to Northey, telegram, 8 March 1922, CO 533/275. See also Minutes by Bottomley, 6 March 1922 and Read, 6 March 1922 on Bowring to Churchill, confidential, 25 January 1922, CO 533/275.

54 Northey to Churchill, confidential, 27 March 1922 and Northey to Churchill, confidential, 11 April 1922, CO 533/276.

55 Thuku, *Maisha Yangu*, 35-47.

56 Okaro-Kojwang', 'Origins', 112-16; Atieno-Odhiambo, 'Politics and nationalism', 659.

57 J. M. Lonsdale, 'Political associations in Western Kenya', in Robert Rotberg and Ali Mazrui, eds., *Protest and Power in Black Africa* (New York, 1970), 601.

58 *Ibid.*, 600-2; Okaro-Kojwang', 'Origins', 115-16.

59 Okaro-Kojwang', 'Origins', 116-18; Lonsdale, 'Political associations', 605.

60 Okaro-Kojwang', 'Origins', 118; Lonsdale, 'Political associations', 604.

61 Nyangweso, 'The cult of Mumbo in Central and South Kavirondo', *The Journal of the East Africa and Uganda Natural History Society* (May-August, 1930), 13. Audrey Wipper, *Rural Rebels* (Nairobi, 1977), 42-57.

62 Bethwell A. Ogot and William R. Ochieng', 'Mumboism – an anti-Colonial movement', in Bethwell A. Ogot, ed., *War and Society in Africa* (London, 1972), 172-3.

63 Wipper, *Rebels*, 42-57.

64 William R. Ochieng', 'Black Jeremiah', in William R. Ochieng', ed., *The First Word* (Nairobi, 1975), 77-85.

65 PC to DC, 25 November 1918 and DC to PC, 28 November 1918, KNA DC/KSI/3/2. Minutes of meeting of the Executive Council, 20 February 1919, CO 544/14.

66 DC to PC, 3 December 1920; and PC to Superintendent of Police, Kisumu, 23 March 1921, KNA DC/KSI/3/2.

67 J. Forbes Munro, *Colonial Rule and the Kamba* (Oxford, 1975), 118-19.

68 *Ibid.*, 119.

69 *Ibid.*, 120.

70 *Ibid.*

71 I.D. Talbott, 'The Kenya flax boom', *Kenya Historical Review* 2 (1974), 62-3.

72 The British East Africa Disabled Officers Colony (BEADOC) at Kericho was the most conspicuous failure. *Kericho District Annual Report 1922*, KNA KER/58.

73 Great Britain, *Colony and Protectorate of Kenya Report for 1920-21*, (London, 1922), 3.

74 Northey to Churchill, 15 November 1921, CO 533/265. See also Northey to Churchill, 7 November 1921, CO 533/265.

75 Leggett to Wedgwood, 28 March 1922, enclosure in Wedgwood to Wood, 29 March 1922, CO 533/291. See also Leggett to Masterton-Smith, 26 January 1922, CO 533/291. Sir James Masterton-Smith was then Permanent Under-Secretary of State for the Colonies.

76 Leggett to Bottomley, 27 April 1922, CO 533/291.

77 Ian R.G. Spencer, 'The First World War and the origins of the Dual Policy in Kenya, 1914-1922', *World Development* 9 (1981), 742.

78 *Ibid.*

79 *Ibid.*, 743. Churchill to Northey, confidential, 14 February 1922, CO 533/288.

80 Spencer, 'Dual Policy', 743.

81 Northey to Churchill, 27 May 1922, CO 533/277.

82 It should not be inferred from this, however, that the failure of Northey's pro-settler economic policy was the sole basis for his firing. He was undoubtedly removed also because Churchill had rightly concluded that, given Northey's extreme pro-settler stand in the matter, no settlement of the Indian Question was possible as long as Northey was governor. Northey to Churchill, telegram, 25 July 1922, CO 533/280.

83 Robert G. Gregory, *India and East Africa* (Oxford, 1971), 201. As W.C. Bottomley noted in early 1923, the highlands and segregation were 'not now in the centre of the picture'. Bottomley to Masterton-Smith, 16 February 1923, CO 533/303.

84 Meeting of Members of the Legislative Council, Certain Members of the Executive Council and Delegates of the Convention of Associations with His Excellency, strictly confidential, 7 October 1921, Scott Papers, Section H, File XIV, Rhodes House, Oxford University, MSS Afr. 578.

85 The best source for this is Gregory, *India,* chs.VI and VII.

86 *Ibid.*, 219.

87 *Ibid.* Draft of the proposals dated 14 July 1922 are in CO 533/289. Churchill to Coryndon, telegram, 5 September 1922, CO 533/287.

88 Coryndon to Churchill, telegram confidential, 21 September 1922, CO 533/282. Bottomley, Indians in Kenya, 6 November 1922, CO 533/289. See also Christopher P. Youe, *Robert Thorne Coryndon: proconsular imperialism in southern and eastern Africa, 1897-1925* (Waterloo, 1986), 167.

89 Coryndon to Devonshire, telegram, 11 January 1923, CO 533/292. Gregory, *India,* 224-5.

90 Coryndon to Devonshire, telegram, secret and personal, 3 February 1923; and Coryndon to Devonshire, telegram, secret and personal, 12 February 1923, CO 533/293. Youe, *Coryndon,* 168.

91 Minute by Read, 17 January 1923, on Coryndon to Masterton-Smith, telegram, private and personal, 15 January 1923, CO 533/293.

92 Oldham to Masterton-Smith, private, 15 June 1923, CO 533/303.

93 Great Britain, *Indians in Kenya*, Cmd. 1922 (London, 1923), 10.

94 *Ibid.*, 18; Gregory, *India,* 247.

95 Gregory, *India,* 249-58.

96 *Indians in Kenya*, 10.

97 Dilley, *British Policy*, 184-6.

98 Colony and Protectorate of Kenya, *Department of Agriculture Annual Report 1929* (Nairobi, 1930), 651.

99 Sharon Stichter, *Migrant Labour in Kenya: capitalism and African response, 1895-1975*

(London, 1982), 70.

100 E.A. Brett, *Colonialism and Underdevelopment in East Africa* (London, 1973), 208-9.

101 *Ibid.*, 93, 191.

102 *Ibid.*, 194.

103 *Ibid.*, 203.

104 *Ibid.*, 200.

105 Great Britain, *Colony and Protectorate of Kenya Report for 1928* (London, 1929), 22-3.

106 *Department of Agriculture Annual Report 1929*, 651.

107 Stichter, *Migrant Labour*, 71-5.

108 George Bennett, 'Settlers and politics in Kenya', in V. Harlow and E.M. Chilver, eds., *History of East Africa*, vol.II (London, 1965), 299.

109 Great Britain, *Report of the East Africa Commission*, Cmd. 2387 (London, 1924), 149. The membership of the commission was made up of a member from each political party: Ormsby-Gore, Conservative; A.G. Church, Labour; and F.C. Linfield, Liberal.

110 Brett, *Underdevelopment*, 181.

111 John Barnes and David Nicholson, eds., *The Leo Amery Diaries* (London, 1980), 508-9. R.G. Gregory, *Sidney Webb and East Africa* (Berkeley, 1962), 64-8.

112 Great Britain, *Report of the Commission on Closer Union*, Cmd. 3234 (London, 1929). Sir James Hilton Young was chairman of the commission, but J.H. Oldham was perhaps its most influential member. See also Gregory, *Sidney Webb*, 69-73.

113 Gregory, *Sidney Webb*, 76. Barnes and Nicholson, *Amery Diaries*, 577-81.

114 Nicola Swainson, *The Development of Corporate Capitalism in Kenya, 1918-1977* (Berkeley, 1980), 48-51.

115 *Ibid.*, 51-7.

116 *Ibid.*, 53.

117 *Ibid.*, 54.

118 *Ibid.*, 26-7.

119 For example, G. Kitching, *Class and Economic Change in Kenya* (New Haven, 1980), 38-9, 46.

120 *Ibid.*, 45-6.

121 Overton, 'Spatial differentiation', 279.

122 *Ibid.*

123 *Department of Agriculture Annual Report 1929*, 37.

124 As will be seen, districts such as Machakos and Kericho came to be a part of what Kitching calls 'the process of commercialization', but some regions of considerable agricultural potential, such as those inhabited by the Meru and the Gusii, were only marginally involved in the commercial economy in the 1920s. Kitching, *Economic Change*, 50-1.

125 Kitching, *Economic Change*, 33-7.

126 *Ibid.*, 33-4.

127 *Department of Agriculture Annual Report 1929*, 41 and 48.

128 Kitching, *Economic Change*, 40-1.

129 *Ibid.*, 41.

130 *Ibid.*, 51.

131 *Ibid.*, 163.

132 Handing Over Report of the Senior Commissioner, Nyanza, 10 April 1928, KNA PC/NZA.3/45.

133 Kitching, *Economic Change*, 188.

134 *Ibid.*, 190.

135 *Ibid.*, 248-50; Stichter, *Migrant Labour*, 80; Swainson, *Corporate Capitalism*, 32.

136 Kitching, *Economic Change*, 259. In 1928, some 43 per cent of Kiambu's male population was in wage employment or seeking it.

137 Stichter, *Migrant Labour*, 80.
138 Kitching, *Economic Change*, 270.
139 *Ibid.*, 294.
140 *Ibid.*
141 Kitching includes the three Kikuyu districts, North, Central, and South Nyanza and Machakos as those characterized by petty-bourgeoisie formations by the end of the 1920s. This is reasonable, though I maintain that a petty-bourgeoisie did not emerge among the Gusii in the 1920s. Robert M. Maxon, 'A Kenya petite bourgeoisie enters local politics: the Kisii Union, 1945-1949', *International Journal of African Historical Studies* 19 (1986), 453-4.
142 Many associate the use of the term with Kitching, but as he has noted, 'the terminology is less important than the recognition of the ubiquity of the stratum and its relative privilege'. Kitching, *Economic Change*, 310.
143 *Ibid.*, 309.
144 *Ibid.*, 309, 193.
145 *Ibid.*, 277-9. John Iliffe, *The Emergence of African Capitalism* (Minneapolis, 1983), 31.
146 Atieno-Odhiambo, 'Politics and nationalism', 648.
147 Munro, *Kamba*, 125.
148 J.M. Lonsdale, 'Some origins of nationalism in East Africa', *Journal of African History* 9 (1968), 128.
149 John Spencer, 'The Kikuyu Central Association and the genesis of the Kenya African Union', *Kenya Historical Review* 2 (1974), 77.
150 Quoted in M.P.K. Sorrenson, 'Land policy in Kenya', in Harlow and Chilver, eds., *History of East Africa*, vol.II, 685.
151 Quoted in Carl G. Rosberg and John Nottingham, *The Myth of Mau Mau* (New York, 1966), 98.
152 The colonial state would not allow Africans to grow coffee until the 1930s. Cotton would be encouraged among Africans in western Kenya and at the coast, if not among the Kikuyu, in the 1920s.
153 Rosberg and Nottingham, *Mau Mau*, 97-8. See also *Kikuyu Province Annual Reports 1926* and *1927*, KNA PC/CP.4/1/2.
154 Spencer, 'Kikuyu Central Association', 70.
155 Colony and Protectorate of Kenya, *Native Affairs Department Annual Report 1924* (Nairobi, 1925), 20.
156 Jeremy Murray-Brown, *Kenyatta* (London, 1972), 106-7.
157 As the PC noted in his 1928 annual report, the KCA included in its ranks 'a vast proportion of the more enlightened and progressive youth, and wields an increasing influence in the counsels of elders'. *Kikuyu Province Annual Report 1928*, KNA PC/CP.4/1/2.
158 Rosberg and Nottingham, *Mau Mau*, 93.
159 *Ibid.*, 94.
160 Murray-Brown, *Kenyatta*, 114-33.
161 Atieno-Odhiambo, 'Politics and nationalism', 660.
162 Okaro-Kojwang', 'Origins', 123.
163 Atieno-Odhiambo, 'Politics and nationalism', 660.
164 Members were often required to chant in ritual fashion the pledge to kill so many rats a week and plant so many trees a year, etc. Okaro-Kojwang', 'Origins', 125.
165 *Ibid.*
166 Oginga Odinga, *Not Yet Uhuru* (London, 1967), 67.
167 Rosberg and Nottingham, 'Mau Mau', 95.
168 Atieno-Odhiambo, 'Politics and nationalism', 660.
169 Munro, *Kamba*, 129.

170 *Ibid.*, 130-1.

171 *Ibid.*, 143.

172 K. Asare Opoku, 'Religion in Africa during the colonial era', in A. Adu Boahen, ed., *General History of Africa,* vol.VII (Berkeley, 1985), 529-31.

173 A good example was the Nomiya Luo Church founded in 1910.

174 Odinga, *Not Yet Uhuru,* 69. North Nyanza Handing Over Report, secret, 16 July 1953, KNA DC/NN.2/10.

175 Nyanza Provincial Diary, 19 June 1927, KNA PC/NZA.3/26/2 and *South Kavirondo Annual Report 1929,* KNA DC/KSI/1/3.

176 *South Kavirondo Annual Report 1930,* KNA DC/KSI/1/3.

177 Gideon S. Were, *A History of the Abaluyia of Western Kenya c.1500-1930* (London, 1967), 177-9.

178 *North Kavirondo Annual Report 1928,* KNA DC/NN.1/9 and *North Kavirondo Annual Report 1929,* KNA DC/NN.1/10.

179 Jacob R. Seitz, 'A history of Samia location in western Kenya, 1890-1930', Ph.D. Dissertation, West Virginia University, 1978, pp.117, 185-6.

180 *Ibid.*, 188.

4 Kenya and the depression, 1929-1939

Tabitha Kanogo

The Great Depression of 1929 was caused by a collapse of the world market system. Although the centre of the catastrophe was in the American capital, New York, where the Wall Street stock market tumbled, this economic collapse affected the capitalist market system over the whole world wherever its tentacles were spread. This included the colonies. Here, in general, the prices of primary commodities in the world market dropped sharply and colonial trade was reduced to a new low. In Kenya, the depression greatly dislocated the primary commodities export trade, which was dominated by settlers although Africans were also making a breakthrough into commercial production at this period.

The decade preceding the onset of the depression was characterized by an increased consolidation of the settler sector. The shortlived war-time (First World War) boom brought with it lucrative prices for settler crops. This encouraged the settlers to increase and diversify their production, a trend that was particularly evident in the production of coffee and cereals. On its part the government came out in full support of the settlers and legislated additional labour laws precipitating greater control of labour. The Soldier Settlement Scheme was implemented, expanding the number of settlers and their landholdings. It also improved and extended railway, road and port facilities for easier transportation of settler produce, and upheld the settlers in other ways.[1] Thus, by 1929 the settlers could be said to have been at the strongest and most productive point of their history in the colony. The collapse in the world trade system set the settler community a decade behind. The plight of settler agriculture both in the pre- and post-depression periods has received ample attention.[2] Suffice it to say that the capital-intensive settler agriculture was more grossly affected by the depression than African peasant agriculture. The latter had undergone modest but solid transformation in the decade prior to the depression. As well as expanding the area under cultivation, African farmers were gradually adopting new crops, new varieties of familiar crops and new techniques of cultivation. Above all, production for the market was on the increase.[3] Although the peasant producers did not escape the ravages of the depression, they proved to be more resilient and bounced back with more vigour for the economic reconstruction.

This chapter examines the trend of economic, social and political developments in the post-depression decade. This was a period of widespread consolidation and diversification of peasant production and incipient African political mobilization. Equally, industrialization at the level of processing of primary products emerged, although it had realized very little progress on the eve of the Second World War. The above economic activities of necessity induced social change within the African sector of the colonial society. The nature of this change will be examined. It will be argued that the decade between 1929 and 1939 was crucial in that it provided the forum for the emergence of an African petty-bourgeoisie which was primarily concerned with greater participation in the colonial economy. This in itself created social differentiation among the Africans. The period also witnessed the emergence of modest attempts at 'radical' politics by an African proto-elite from the mission schools. While some of the mission graduates were co-opted into the establishment through their participation in the Local Native Councils established in 1924, the more radical proto-elites articulated the people's grievances through a variety of political-cum-welfare associations, including the Kikuyu Central Association (KCA), the Kavirondo Tax-payers and Welfare Association (KTWA), the North Kavirondo Central Association (NKCA), the Young Nyika Association (YNA), the Taita Hills Association (THA) and the Ukamba Members Association (UMA), among others.[4]

The period under study also witnessed an expansion in wage employment, urbanization and the subsequent emergent labour and political consciousness. Worsening working conditions both in the urban and rural areas resulted in strikes and incipient labour organization.[5] All these changes make this period a very critical one for Africans. It encompasses the first complete decade when African economic entrepreneurship and political expression became a reality.

Africans in the pre-depression period

Despite the 1923 dictum on the paramountcy of African interests and the adoption of the Dual Policy as the basis for the social and economic development of the colony, the colonial state remained largely partisan in its attention to the country's economy. This government partiality was heightened by pressure from the settlers as the latter sought to evolve a privileged and protected nook for themselves. To a large extent the African sector continued to be subordinate to, and structured to service, the settler sector during the 1920s. During this pioneer period, the protectorate authorities bent over backwards to provide favourable conditions for settler agriculture. Hence vital resources and services, including ample fertile land, transportation infrastructure (railways and roads), agricultural and veterinary extension services, freight and marketing subsidies, capital and loan facilities and other concessions were concentrated in the settler sector. Political and financial pressure was applied on Africans to drive them to the labour market on settler farms and elsewhere. To retain this labour, regulations including the 1906 and 1910 Masters and Servants Ordinance, the 1918, 1924, 1937 Resident Native Labourers Ordinances, the *kipande* and other forms of labour legislation were enacted. It was even considered necessary to disrupt African economies by creating limited reserves which would serve as 'a recruiting ground for labour, a place from which the able-bodied go out to work, returning occasionally to rest and beget the next generation of labourers'.[6] To articulate their interests, settlers utilized various forums including the Legislative Council (Legco), the Executive Council and their membership in key decision-making bodies on matters relating to labour, transport, market and finance.[7] They also benefited from informal liaisons with all cadres of colonial administrators who were sympathetic to settler problems. During the First World War, the settlers who were co-opted into various civil positions strengthened their position further. However, their agricultural production was still at a rudimentary experimental stage, so that the first real breakthrough that the settlers made was as a result of war-time demands and the post-war boom. Up to this point, Africans in the reserves together with squatter-peasants in the White Highlands were responsible for the bulk of the export products in the colony.

Despite the half-hearted government concern for peasant production, the latter was propelled by complex internal dynamics which ensured increased production before 1930. Thus, while in Nyanza Province the introduction of cotton as a cash crop was met with a lot of resistance,[8] the production of other commodities, including sesame seed, groundnuts, beans, maize, rice and millet continued to expand. So also did livestock and livestock products. Of the crops, groundnuts, cassava, some varieties of sorghum, beans, white maize and fruits were newly introduced in the area. To enhance production further, the plough began to replace the iron hoe and traditional wooden cultivation implements.

It is evident that the Nyanza peasants readily responded to market changes so that they benefited from the post-1920-1 depression price rise which took place in 1928-9.[9] Basically the export items constituted food crop surpluses except for hides, skins and cotton. The last was slowly picking up in the late 1920s. Of the three districts, North Nyanza was the most productive but also the most densely populated. This was followed by Central and South Nyanza. Although the bulk of these 'exports' were sold within the country, some of the surplus, including maize, sesame and cotton, were sold outside the colony.

Despite this expansion, 'levels of output per capita and per acre in the Nyanza Province were far lower than even the minimal levels reached in Kikuyuland' by 1931. Here, agricultural diversification and production for market was much ahead and already making its mark by the end of the First World War. The 1920s witnessed an expansion of land under cultivation, although the three districts displayed varying capacities, with Kiambu leading the way followed by Fort Hall (Murang'a) and Nyeri. Kiambu's head start can be explained by its close proximity to the Nairobi cash nexus, which obviously stimulated a market economy much earlier than in Nyeri and Murang'a. On the other hand, the presence of settler farms on the edge of Nyeri district provided a market for some of its produce.

For the three Kikuyu districts, potatoes, beans, millets and bananas constituted the more common crops that yielded a marketable surplus. From the late 1920s, wattle became a major export crop, whose rapid adoption and success will be discussed later. This economic buoyancy in the pre-1930 period was not limited to the Nyanza and Central Provinces. Stimulus for additional production among the Kipsigis and neighbouring peoples was occasioned by the establishment of the Kericho Tea Estates. These 'rapidly expanded the market for maize and maize flour' among plantation workers. Hence the Kipsigis adopted maize as a new staple for themselves but also expanded the area under its cultivation in response to the increasing demands from the plantations.

Like their Kiambu counterparts, Kamba peasants within easy reach of Nairobi engaged in market gardening and provided Nairobi with such staples as maize, beans and bananas in the 1920s. Other Kamba producers responded to the needs of settler workers in the nearby plantations and traded in foodstuff either directly with the labourers or through Asian middlemen. As in Central and Nyanza Provinces, the adoption of English iron hoes and ploughs was concomitant with the expansion of acreage under cultivation in Kericho.

At the coast old staples like coconuts and fruit became widely marketed, while cashew-nuts, cotton and sesame were introduced and produced for the market. Those African areas which had access to good communication networks had a greater incentive for production. This was clearly evident in the case of southern Kiambu and Murang'a. The opening of the Thika–Nyeri line was an additional incentive to greater production and trade.

Kenya's economy under the depression
Predictably, the 1929 depression greatly dislocated the colonial economy. As prices of settler crops in the world market dropped sharply and colonial trade fell drastically, so did the settlers fall from their wildly inflated monopoly of commercial production for export. By and large, settler production had never really learnt to stand on its own feet; it called for constant government subsidies and received attention out of proportion to its productivity.

In Kenya, the fall in the prices for export commodities resulted in a parallel fall in government revenue, especially its foreign exchange reserves. As this fall in prices continued unabated until 1935, government revenue suffered irreparable loss. This is clearly illustrated by the fact that by 1934 the value of the country's export earnings was equivalent to the same in the period 1922 to 1923.[10] In this respect, then, the government revenue had reverted to what it was a decade earlier, despite a marked expansion in production, capital and infrastructural investment in agriculture.

This drop in government revenue is better illustrated by percentage falls in the prices of various commodities. Maize, which was the most widely grown crop by peasant farmers and the settlers was hit hardest. By 1931 the maize price had dropped to 50 per cent of its 1929 value — a drop from about Shs 11.10 to Shs 5.06 (and to Shs 3.30 in 1933).[11] Coffee fell by 40 per cent of its pre-depression price, while other major commodities including wheat and sisal fell by 50 per cent. The situation was further aggravated by the invasion of locusts and the onset of drought in 1931.[12]

In general, there was a reduction in the acreage under commercial cultivation after the depression. While the majority of the settlers survived the depression, some of them became bankrupt. Others found temporary relief in the Kakamega 'gold rush', where prospecting promised quick returns.

The effects of the depression were adversely felt among African producers. Wrigley observes that the price of African exports, including sesame, beans, hides, skins and ghee, fell more drastically than those of European cash crops. However, the African maize crop, which largely commanded the internal market, was less severely affected by the depression. On a comparative level, the African producers who had expanded their production in the pre-1929 period without a massive expenditure of capital, as was the case with settlers, withstood the vagaries of the depression better than the settlers did, except for some other problems.

Thus, despite the gaping fall in the price of commodities and the ensuing reduction in household incomes, the colonial government did not adjust the tax obligations of the Africans. When we take into consideration the fact that up to about 40,000 people lost their jobs between 1929 and 1932, we can begin to appreciate the impact of the depression on Africans. Wages were reduced from an average of 14 shillings to 8 shillings a month. By 1930, Africans were responsible for 37½ per cent of the colony's total revenue.[13] This they remitted in direct taxation. Considering the fact that additional revenue was indirectly collected from Africans through customs and excise duties, Local Native Council levies and other indirect taxation, it is evident that Africans contributed much more than was acknowledged. Swainson has estimated that together hut, poll tax and customs duties were responsible for 60 to 80 per cent of the colony's revenue.[14] Paradoxically, the bulk of this income was pumped into the settler sector, this at the expense of the majority African contributors. It was the same settler sector that received priority attention during the depression.

Post-depression reconstruction

The economic setback unleashed by the depression appeared precisely at a time when the imperial government was trying to boost colonial production to the advantage of British industry. Thus in 1929 Britain had introduced the Colonial Development Act. Brett observes that the Act 'grew out of concern with British unemployment rather than with the problem of colonial development'.[15] The Act allowed for the provision of a sum of £1m per year, which would be used to fund infrastructure necessary for colonial production.

It was anticipated that the funds would be used to service interest on capital loans but would not provide money for recurrent expenditure on any of the projects undertaken. The colonies would have to raise money for capital expenditure from financial houses in London.

Like other colonial legislation, this Act offered limited benefits. It operated on the false premise that the economies of the colonies and the metropolitan were complementary. Its basic concern was to keep British industry in operation by supplying adequate raw materials and sustaining colonial consumption of British finished products. An additional bonus would be the avoidance of political disturbances in Britain. The government was especially wary of any socialist protest that might emanate from dissatisfied or redundant labour.

Had the depression not occurred when it did, funds made available by the Colonial Development Act might have stimulated production, albeit in a small way given its limited resources. However, the depression period was no time for initiating new projects. As it was, an appreciable number of existing projects collapsed. In any case, Tanganyika, which was worse hit by the depression, benefited most from the available resources. To a large extent, too, the Act was overtaken by events. The fall in commodity prices which accompanied the onset of the depression was not conducive to an increase in production. For the six-year period between 1929 and 1935 Kenya received £181,000, too little for any meaningful reconstruction of the adversely affected economy.[16]

Although the colonial state could not be said to have realized substantial revenue from settlers, it had continued to give diverse support to them. Right from the beginning the state was committed to nurture settler agriculture at great costs. Hence, although 'the shock of the slump . . . made it necessary [for the goverment] not only to examine the very foundations of the country's economy but also to investigate its effects upon the social development of the people',[17] the government's immediate reaction was to establish ways and means of increasing its own revenue and rehabilitating the settlers.

For a start, the government adopted various austerity measures. Salaries of civil servants were reduced and leave arrangements restructured. Attempts to introduce an income tax for non-Africans was vehemently opposed by settlers. At a time when settlers were calling for greater government support, the tax measure was seen to be in bad taste. This settler resistance to taxation had a long history. At an earlier stage, settlers had opposed taxation on the basis that it was only relevant where there was elective representation. Subsequently, settlers argued that they were making adequate contributions to state revenue through agricultural production. They therefore did not think it fit that they should be taxed separately.

In 1930, the government passed the Agricultural Advances Ordinance, which made provision for finances to the settlers at the initial planting and harvesting period. On a more permanent basis the government established a Land Bank in 1931. Using their land as collateral, settlers could borrow money from the Land Bank, and in this way sustain production without the danger of being declared bankrupt or having their property seized by less tolerant financial lenders. In any case, as the value of land had depreciated tremendously with the depression, other commercial money-lenders were unwilling to lend money against settler land. On the other hand the government-backed Land Bank lent money at lower interest rates, thus helping the settlers further.[18] This, however, does not preclude the fact that the depression forced some of the settler farmers to give up farming due to extreme financial difficulties.

Various other measures were undertaken to keep the settlers solvent. In 1931 the Railways Corporation, which was the major haulier of settler produce to the coast, reduced freight charges for wheat, maize and barley and reimbursed the farmers up to four-fifths of storage charges for these crops. Previously, in 1930, the government had refunded the equivalent of four-fifths of fees charged for grading wheat and maize.[19] Apart from favourable rates for products within the colony, settlers also benefited from preferential tariffs, which allowed their products to enter Britain at lower rates. This protected them from competition from products coming from outside British colonies. The Ottawa Agreement of 1932 was one such tariff.[20]

There is no evidence of direct government attempts to compensate Africans for losses suffered during the depression. However, the Africans were fortunate in that agriculture picked up relatively fast once the traumatic effects of the depression had subsided. In subsequent attempts by the government to revive the economy of the colony, efforts were made to include the welfare of African agriculture in the reconstruction. However, as we have seen, the energies of the government in the decade after the depression were largely taken up with setting the settler enterprise on its feet. But this should not be taken to mean that African agriculture stagnated. By responding to the market forces, Africans expanded their production tremendously. This African initiative was rapidly propelled by government participation in the expansion of peasant agriculture in the inter-war period.

Paradoxically, the depression appears to have been the break the Africans were awaiting to gain official recognition of their productive dynamic. In the decade before the depression, the Africans had demonstrated their prowess in chosen fields of agricultural production. In particular, they had demonstrated that they could produce cereals, especially maize, more efficiently than the settler farmers. Comparatively, the depression did not dampen African production to the same level as the settlers'. With the onset of the depression the colonial government found it expedient to revive and encourage greater peasant production. This would be a cheaper way of production both for the local and export markets. More significantly, it would not entail expensive capital, labour and other overheads characteristic of the settler sector. On the whole, the bulk of African surplus production was in the category of food crops. Surpluses were mainly exported outside their districts of production with the settler farms offering ready markets for maize, beans and potatoes. Some of the maize, sesame, groundnuts and all the cotton were exported outside the country.

African production in the post-depression period

The period between the mid 1920s and 1939 could be said to have been characterized by the consolidation of the commercialization of life in the villages. This means that there was an increasing demand for cash for various services and commodities. Thus, as Africans continued to play an increasingly greater role in the exchange economy, their tastes for alien products, including footwear, clothing, various household utensils, furniture, hoes, ploughs and so on, increased.[21] To meet these new needs, commodity production along with proletarianization were stepped up. To a large extent, then, the increased government participation in the expansion of peasant production in the post-depression period was based on entrepreneurial production already set in motion by the peasants. Government intervention in African agriculture included the supply of better seeds, the maintenance of demonstration plots and limited veterinary extension services. The government was most active in the provision of better strains of seeds and drought resistant seeds (table 4.1).[22] It also encouraged the adoption of better methods of farming including inter-cropping and mixed farming.

Table 4.1. Seeds supplied from departmental votes (lbs)[23]

	Kikuyu	Nyanza	Kerio	Ukamba	Coast	NFD	Total
Maize	52,000	46,000	28,000	4,600	24,000	5,800	161,050
Wheat	26,000	2,000	60	1,200	231	565	26,656
Matama		1,800	9,180			80	11.040
Mwele		1,440					1,440
Buckwheat						14	14
Rice-sena	60						60
Beans		9,000		4,000		200	13,200
Peas	1,000	480					1,480
Chiroko		1,080	540				1,620
Mbaazi		1,080					1,080
Cowpeas				600		7	607
Lucerne		25	60				85
Groundnuts	420	7,200				175	7,795
Simsim	361				3,646	65	4,072
Potatoes	3,400						3,400
Tobacco			2			2	4
Vegetable seed	20	4	9	28			61

At the same time, coordinated attempts were made to provide expert advice in the agricultural and veterinary fields through the use of extension officers. For example, in 1930 the Department of Agriculture dispatched the following personnel to the major agricultural production areas: 11 officers, 4 of whom were sent to Kikuyu, 4 to Nyanza, 2 to the coast and 1 to the head office.

Together with these, 80 instructors and 54 labourers were also employed by the department in various parts of the country. Of the 80 department instructors, 5 were hides and skins demonstrators in Maasailand and Kisii. In general the 80 instructors were distributed as follows:[24]

Nyanza Province (29)		Coast Province (23)	
North and Central		Kilifi	17
Nyanza	22	Malindi	4
South Nyanza	7	Mombasa	1
		Kwale	1
Kikuyu Province (33)		Maasai Province (2)	
South Kikuyu	9	Narok 2	
Fort Hall	5		
Embu	9		
South Nyeri	4		
Meru	6		

In 1930, the Local Native Councils contributed 8 instructors and 30 labourers, who were added to the department employees. Of the 8 Local Native Council instructors, 4 were plough instructors in Nyanza.[25]

Subsequent reports by the Department of Agriculture portray similar official participation in an endeavour to uplift the peasant option. Even in years when there was a drop in the value of African produce, the reports reflected an increase in the quality of native produce, a testament to the beneficial results of the demonstration plots and better seeds distributed by the government and its agents. However, this was not always true for all the crops, cotton being the most obvious 'white elephant'. Generally, in major agricultural parts of the country, the period 1930-8 portrayed a steady increase in agricultural production. The adoption of new crops like maize, tobacco and groundnuts was accelerated in the 1930s. While state intervention in African production had fluctuated and even faltered in the 1920s, in the 1930s there was a more concerted effort to uplift African production. Hence among the Africans the inter-war period witnessed a gradual and sometimes a dramatic leap in commercial production. While prior to 1918 most African products were marketed and consumed internally, these increasingly found their way into the export market. An increasing number of Indian and African traders provided an extensive market network that harnessed agricultural products including potatoes, beans, groundnuts, sugar-cane, sesame, cotton, maize, tobacco, wattle and a decreasing amount of millet. Skins and hides, which earlier constituted the bulk of African exports, continued to be exported in large amounts. But first, let us return to the question of agricultural production.

Kitching estimates that on average Central Province was producing a surplus equivalent to slightly less than one-third of its total agricultural products by 1931.[26] Between the two, maize and beans occupied 72 per cent of the land under cultivation in Central Province, with maize accounting for about two-thirds of this acreage. Although widely cultivated, these two crops, which were both staple and cash crops, only accounted for 30 per cent of the total export value from the province. Among the other exports, bananas ranked quite high, contributing £242,125 by 1932. This was equivalent to 34 per cent of the export value.

Wattle, whose income revenue soon outstripped the other products, was being grown in modest amounts at this period. In less than a decade the value of wattle had grown by about 600 per cent. The wattle was largely grown in southern Kiambu and the western parts of Murang'a. On the export market, the tree was important for its bark from which an extract, tannin, was used in the treatment of leather. Locally, the wood from the tree was used for building, as firewood, or burnt into charcoal fuel. By 1931 wattle production was 'only 11 per cent of the value of maize, 24 per cent of beans, and a mere six per cent of the value of bananas'.[27] Intensive government campaigns executed through the Local Native Councils, chiefs and headmen resulted in a tremendous expansion of wattle production. While in 1929 only 900 tons of dry wattle bark were produced, by 1938 this had risen to 11,649 tons. There was a gradual fall in the marketing of green bark, which by 1938 stood at 2,500 tons from 3,780 tons in 1934.[28] Wattle was also grown in smaller quantities in Kisii, Machakos and parts of Nyanza. This growing importance of wattle in the colony is illustrated by the increase in acreage under the crop in the period between 1925 and 1936 (table 4.2).

Table 4.2 Acreage of wattle planted in Kenya[29]

Year	European	African
1925	8,830	6,000
1930	11,250	20,859
1933	14,613	60,000
1936	16,681	100,000

Wattle was thus the major overseas export from Central Province, while maize established itself, for a period, as the major commercial crop.

Apart from wattle the government also encouraged the cultivation of other cash crops, including cotton and tobacco, in Central Province. By 1938 tobacco growing was on the increase there, while cotton, which was restricted to a few areas by 1935, had increased to 1380 acres by 1937. However, cotton never succeeded in Central Province, initially due to a fluctuation in price but largely because it was not a suitable crop for the area.

Although the cotton crop had been introduced in Nyanza Province earlier, the 1930s saw a more systematic and intensified campaign to increase its production. Here too, the energies of the local administration were harnessed in educating people about the growing of cotton, and enforcing its cultivation. In a more commercialized milieu, opposition against growing cotton was less evident in the 1930s. Here too cotton production showed positive development; increasing from 410 tons in 1931 to over 10,000 tons in

1938.[30] Cotton ginneries were established in areas where cotton production was introduced; including Kendu and Homa Bay in South Nyanza, Ndere in Central Nyanza and in Kibos.[31] This made the processing and marketing of cotton much more manageable. Cotton was also introduced in Kitui, the Coast Province, Embu and Meru. Although cotton fetched higher prices per pound (avoirdupois) and was more profitable per unit cultivated, it did not reflect the anticipated expansion. Both Central and Nyanza Provinces were too high and damp for the cultivation of cotton.[32]

Apart from the concerted official campaign to increase cotton production, the cultivation of other crops, especially staples, continued to increase, albeit modestly. North Nyanza continued to provide the Trans-Nzoia settler farms with maize for *posho* — maize-meal given as rations to the labourers.

Between 1934 and 1937 most crops, including maize, beans, groundnuts, sesame and millet, underwent only gradual expansion with 1938 proving a year of low yields except for wattle and groundnuts in South Kavirondo.[33] In Machakos, market gardening, which was evident in the 1920s, continued to expand in the 1930s. Major crops included onions, fruit and potatoes. Maize, the major African cash crop was a drawback in Machakos as its perpetual production in monocultural patterns resulted in low yields.

While Machakos, which was a marginal area, struggled to expand its production, areas like Nandi which had adequate rainfall had hitherto remained reluctant to adopt cultivation. By the close of our period, however, the Nandi were slowly adopting the cultivation of maize, the surplus of which, a meagre amount, was being sold. However, the Nandi reserve seemed to excel in the exportation of labour. This was estimated at about 90 per cent of the male population by November 1931, averaging at about 70 per cent on the eve of the Second World War.[34] During the Second World War, with good war-time prices, the production of maize improved tremendously compared to the situation in the mid-1930s.

While the maize crop was widely grown in most African reserves, it was particularly important to squatter labourers in the White Highlands. The production of a surplus in this crop was paramount in all squatter households. A conservative estimate for 1931 indicated that squatters utilized 1,061,833 acres of land in the White Highlands. This was equivalent to one-sixth of all the alienated land, or 40 per cent of the land under cultivation or grazing in the White Highlands. It would not be too presumptuous to assert that the bulk of the land under squatter cultivation was planted with maize.[35]

While settlers provided an easily accessible market for maize, their prices were lower. Squatters preferred to sell their produce outside the White Highlands. Asian middle-men, although they undercut squatter profit margins, shouldered the burden of transporting bulky amounts of the maize and potato crops from the White Highlands to the various destinations. With the greater advantage of possessing more and better serviced lorries, the Asians controlled a greater share of this transport and wholesale trade, scouring the reserves,

White Highlands and townships for food crops among other trade items. As indicated below, the government's attempts to eliminate this Indian presence and control of the cereals trade was ineffective and shortlived. The administration was wary about the squatter preoccupation with the production of surplus maize. The district commissioner for Nakuru–Ravine–Naivasha observed that: 'Among the Natives, the Kikuyu, the majority are getting such excellent prices for maize that their whole energies are bent on the production of this crop, leading to difficulties with the squatters, whose land hunger is more voracious than ever and a positive menace in the Elburgon area'.[36]

This, however, was not the whole story about the politics surrounding the maize crop in the colony. We have already noted that before the depression a large percentage of settlers were dependent on the maize crop as their major export. The ease with which Africans in the reserves and in the White Highlands grew maize posed a major threat to settlers. However, the bulk of African-grown maize was rarely exported beyond the Kenya ports on the basis that it was of lower quality – this notwithstanding the fact that a majority of settlers demanded a fixed amount of maize from their squatter labour at the end of each harvest season. With the drastic depreciation in the price of maize during the depression, the government, in seeking to protect the settler farmers and raise revenue, reversed its maize policy.

In 1935, the Native Produce Act was introduced. Essentially, this sought to control the marketing of African produce, especially maize. The maize would be graded on the same basis as settler grown maize. It was projected that this grading would guarantee a higher price. Because maize thus graded could only be sold to licensed traders, the Act, had it succeeded, might have eliminated the bulk of small traders, Asians and Africans, who comprised a wide network engaged in trade in African agricultural products.

More important was the rationale behind the Act. Since settler maize could not be sold profitably at the prevailing world prices, the African-grown maize produced at lower costs was expected to bridge the deficit in the export market. Thus, the Kenya Farmers Association, the settler marketing body, would command a lion's share of the African maize market (offering fixed prices). It would then dispose of the maize in the export or internal markets at a price. In this way, the settler crop would be subsidized by the African-grown maize. Suffice it to say that this maize market strategy never had any chance of success; the government was not committed to spending the kind of money necessary for such a project, neither did the Kenya Farmers Association have either the organizational or storage capacity to cope with such a feat.[37]

The case of maize is only one example of the colonial government's last minute attempt to encourage African production in the wake of economic crisis. Although the colonial government had started, in the mid-1920s' to look into possible ways of alleviating African agriculture, it took the depression for the government to give the matter serious consideration. The depression, however, called for retrenchment, not expenditure on new projects.

The cash crop that generated the most heat among Africans was coffee. Up to 1934, Africans were not allowed to grow coffee. Two major reasons were given for this restriction. In areas where African reserves were adjacent to settler farms, it was feared that poorly kept African coffee would infect settler coffee. It was also argued that if Africans in such areas were allowed to grow coffee, they might become self-sufficient, with the result that they would not avail themselves for wage labour on settler plantations. In 1934, Africans resident in areas away from settler farms were for the first time allowed to grow coffee, notably in the Kisii, Embu and Meru areas. Even then, growing coffee was made a difficult undertaking. For those allowed to grow coffee (Arabica) it was a lucrative crop, but one which was denied the majority of Africans for some time to come.

Squatter and settler economies

The settlers, too, undertook measures to put their enterprise on a firmer basis. Part of the reason why the settler farmers were hit hardest was due to their extreme dependence on the maize crop as their major export.[38] The extensive depreciation of the world maize market convinced settlers of the need to diversify their production. While some adopted new crops, such as pyrethrum and tea, others diversified into the stock industry, keeping dairy and beef cattle, and sheep.

Among the squatters, this settler diversification was not without its problems.[39] These were particularly rife in the stock industry. Kikuyu and Kalenjin squatters especially, who provided resident labour on settler farms, brought with them, and continued to accumulate stock in the White Highlands. Kikuyu squatters built their herds largely through local purchase, coupled with occasional far flung livestock trade networks. In Nakuru district, squatters purchased their livestock from Tugen and Somali livestock traders while in the Naivasha area Kikuyu squatters trekked to the Maasai Reserve to their south to purchase livestock. Crop surpluses were quickly converted into stock so that by the mid-1920s some of these squatters owned hundreds of stock, mostly small stock, including goats and sheep. Here, in the White Highlands, as in Central Province, wealth was accumulated in stock and could be converted into ready cash at short notice. The livestock also served various ritual – social functions, including payment of dowry and circumcision fees.

For the settlers who imported expensive and exotic breeds of livestock, squatter stock was seen as a looming danger; it might infest settler stock with any of the many diseases considered endemic to African stock. Squatter stock were said to be infested with redwater, blackwater and East Coast fevers, rinderpest and pleuro-pneumonia.[40] The settlers also feared that the presence of squatter cattle on the farms would encourage stock thefts from settler herds.[41] Settlers could not sit back and watch their stock destroyed. Depending on whether the area was largely a mixed farming or dairy farming area, settlers advocated for the reduction or elimination of squatter stock

124

respectively. For the squatters, the campaign for the reduction of their stock, which came to be known as *kifagio* (the sweeping away – of stock), was seen as an act of great economic betrayal. For them livestock represented the greater part of their income. A reduction or elimination of their stock would result in dire impoverishment. The settlers further argued that the presence of squatter stock enhanced stock theft and encouraged 'kaffir farming'.

With the help of government personnel from the Ministry of Labour, settlers proceeded to reduce, and in some cases to eliminate, squatter livestock. By and large, the various settler associations took independent actions in their endeavours to deal with the problem. Depending on the ecological zone and the dominant agricultural activity, settlers decided whether to eliminate squatter stock or not. For example, in the drier zones where dairy and beef stock-keeping were predominant, settlers advocated for complete eradication. In areas of mixed farming which were labour-intensive, the need to ensure a regular supply of seasonal labour led the settlers to adopt an accommodating policy. They rejected the complete eradication of squatter stock, opting for a reduction instead.

There was a third category of settlers that was greatly resented by the more well-to-do settlers. These were the poorer farmers who occupied dry marginal lands that produced very little. These settlers entered into symbiotic relationships with their squatter labourers, from whom they got manure, milk, livestock and other produce. They might not be able to afford to pay their labour in cash and therefore resorted to extending unrestricted land rights to their squatters. In reality, these settlers were engaging in 'kaffir farming' and were very dependent upon their squatters. For them, 'it was absolutely necessary that the squatters be allowed to keep their livestock'. This was much to the annoyance of other settlers who saw this squatter independent 'production' as a violation of the sanctity of the White Highlands.

Local options regarding squatter stock were adopted even within the same districts if the settlers were not in agreement. In areas like Naivasha, where stock-keeping was the mainstay of settler enterprise, there was concensus about the elimination of squatter stock. In other areas individual settlers undertook to eliminate their employees' livestock much to the bewilderment of the squatters. Gachago Kagere captures the fate of the squatters thus: '*Kifagio* found me in Ol'Joro Orok. Here some people had up to 300 goats. After a short time some were only allowed to keep 30, 15 or 5 goats. This was not according to the climate, but according to the wishes of the European.'[42] At the height of the destocking campaign no compensation was paid for seized stock. Attempts to repatriate the stock to Central Province proved futile, since the area was itself overstocked.[43] In order to enforce destocking, some district councils resolved to renew squatter contracts only on condition that the squatters met the livestock elimination or reduction conditions. It was not unusual for squatters to be replaced with casual labourers who did not keep livestock.[44]

Squatter appeals to the effect that they had been promised unlimited access to land and had been allowed to graze freely in the first two decades of settler presence in the country went unheeded. It is true that, in some cases, settlers on their recruitment trips in Central Province (in the period prior to 1914) had promised prospective labourers an initial amount of livestock to start them off on the path to livestock accumulation. More importantly, the undercapitalized settlers were unable to pay their squatter labour full wages; the deficit was paid in kind – in the form of access to land on which the squatters grazed and cultivated. Hence squatter stock could be perceived as income in lieu of wages. Within this context, we can begin to appreciate the squatters' feeling of betrayal. The depression also affected the wages of squatters and other agricultural labourers. Before the onset of the depression, squatters earned an average of 8 shillings while casual labourers received 12 to 16 shillings per month. In 1932 the wage of casual labourers fell to 8 shillings per month while, by 1930, squatter wages ranged between 6 and 10 shillings per month. In 1935 this was reduced to 5 shillings and food rations removed.[45]

Settler diversification into the stock industry during the depression was not the only way in which squatters were affected. The adoption of the pyrethrum crop has also been associated with squatter stock elimination, and the introduction of child labour in areas growing it.[46] The effects of the depression on squatter labour were quite extensive. Between 1929 and 1933, labour employed on settler farms fell from 125,885 to 106,875. Shortage of labour, which had been a constant problem among settlers, abated for the first time in the colony's history. This, however, was not restricted to the settler farms. In general, labour supply exceeded demand during the depression period. A large number of squatters from Naivasha, Gilgil, Thomson's Falls and Laikipia were made redundant and forced back to Central Province.[47]

Kenya's agricultural economy was as quick to show signs of recovery from the depression as it had succumbed to the assault. On a world scale, improvement in trade was evident by 1933. Although the overall total of export earnings in Kenya continued to show a fall up to 1935, this was largely due to the slump in prices. Otherwise there was a progressive expansion of production both in the settler and African areas. The extent of the slump in prices is illustrated by the fact that between 1922 and 1938 there was 'no increase in the value of commodities from African areas', although there was a marked increase in production.[48]

It is clearly documented that during the inter-war period there was an expansion of commodity production in the African reserves.[49] Under government encouragement, Africans increased the area under cultivation, responded to demonstrations of better methods of production and in general benefited from the increased commercialization of their agricultural activities. As we shall see later, this expanded African production created massive problems in the African reserves, including land litigations, the disinheritance/dispossession of the landless, soil erosion and overstocking. In another respect, response to increased commercialization of life resulted in drastic proletarianization, urbanization and the attendant labour problems.

It is not possible within the limited space available to analyse the social differentiation evident in African societies as a result of increased participation in commercial production and wage labour. However, it is correct to say that during the 1920s and 1930s many households increasingly participated in the market economy. They expanded agricultural production of marketable surpluses and went out in larger numbers and for longer durations in pursuit of waged employment. Land and wage labour attained a new significance as both provided access to various services and consumer products. In the labour market, coercion was no longer necessary as economic needs dictated that the people go out in search of jobs. Even where direct government intervention in agriculture was minimal or lacking, people seized opportunities to produce a surplus to generate the necessary income.

Obviously, families nearer centres of the cash nexus had greater incentives to produce for the market. Likewise, households with larger pieces of land and adequate rainfall produced more marketable surplus. So that with time, social differentiation became evident in the rural areas as certain homesteads accumulated more than others.

An obvious offshoot of increased cultivation was land litigation, which became a frequent occurrence, especially in Central Province where the commercial value of land had become evident by the 1920s. Tenants (*ahoi*) who had usufructal rights only were evicted by their landlords as the latter expanded their cultivation. Here, landlessness and shortage of land were genuine problems even before the outbreak of the First World War. The cry for the return of the 'stolen' lands played a pivotal role in a political struggle that culminated in the Mau Mau revolt.[50]

The colonial government was aware of this sensitive issue and hoped to provide a final solution in the 1930s. Earlier, constant African protest and petitions about the insecurity of their tenure of land had resulted in the creation of Native Reserves in 1926, which were deemed to safeguard African ownership of land. However, the discovery of gold in Kakamega in 1932 resulted in further violation of African reserves as further land was alienated for the exploitation of the precious metal.

Up to the middle of the 1920s, the White Highlands had offered an escape valve for surplus and discontented population in the reserves. For the Kikuyu, the opening up of the White Highlands provided a new frontier where the landless and big herders could increase their fortunes. By the 1930s, however, the Settled Areas had lost their attraction as settlers imposed stringent labour control measures and sought to reduce and/or eliminate squatter stock. Attempts by some of these squatters to regain their pieces of land in Central Province proved futile as these had been appropriated by their kinsmen.

Thus, while acknowledging the overall security of African lands (Kakamega goldfields notwithstanding), it was increasingly clear that the lands in the reserves were not adequate. In 1931, the Joint Select Committee recommended that this matter be looked into. In 1933, the Morris Carter Commission was set up for this purpose.

The Kenya Land Commission

The deliberations of the Land Commission under Sir William Morris Carter took place at a very opportune time. The dislocation created by the depression was still rife: as a result of extensive retrenchment, hundreds of redundant ex-squatters trekked to the Central Province, joined by those who were trying to escape *kifagio*. The Central Province did not have room for these ex-squatters and their livestock. The Central Province people were themselves engaged in their own battle trying to wrest more land from the state. Retrenchment in urban areas resulted in similar movements back to the reserves.

The terms of reference of the Land Commission included the estimation of African land requirements, and recommendation, if necessary, for the extension of African reserves. The commission was also expected to establish the extent of settler holdings and indicate where these had encroached on Africans' lands.[51] The whole exercise generated a lot of heat as individuals, clans and other bodies, came forward to place their claims. Petitions were submitted to the commission in large numbers. The details of this exercise are beyond the scope of this paper;[52] suffice it to say that Africans were disappointed with the outcome of the commission's deliberations. The addition of a mere 2,600 square miles to African reserves, some of which land was uninhabitable, did not satisfy them.

Apart from actual shortage of land, there was the additional problem of land depletion.[53] As a result of over-cultivation and over-grazing, African lands, especially in Central Province, Machakos and Kitui, were quickly succumbing to soil erosion. By 1938, government attempts to correct this situation through the recommendation of proper farming methods, including intercropping, terracing and use of manure, had had little effect.

In this regard, destocking was particularly resisted and resulted in nasty encounters between the state and Africans. The government adopted a pragmatic approach on this issue, thus missing the socio-economic significance of livestock. This was clearly illustrated in the case of the Kamba. In 1936, the government sanctioned the multinational Liebigs group to establish a meat-processing plant at Athi River on the outskirts of Nairobi, with the promise that it would ensure a constant supply of livestock. Quite obviously the government saw this as a great opportunity to enforce destocking, a step towards the restoration of badly eroded lands. Africans, especially in the eroded area of Ukambani, would be forced to sell their stock to the plant.

The plant was completed in 1938, when the Machakos Local Native Council was advanced a loan of £23,000 from the Colonial Development fund to hire additional staff 'to destock the reserve by compulsory sales'.[54]

Government determination to effect destocking resulted in the seizure of thousands of Kamba cattle, most of which were sold at below market prices. Opposition was met with police reinforcements and petitions to the governor and the Colonial Secretary did not alter the situation. Significantly, the destocking campaign among the Kamba generated massive political mobilization in the reserves and in urban areas including Nairobi and Mombasa. The crisis precipitated the formation of the Ukamba Members Association (UMA), which liaised closely with the Kikuyu Central Association (KCA). An interesting, albeit not novel development was the support UMA got from Isher Dass, the Asian member of the Legislative Council who became UMA's link with the administration.

The Kamba protest culminated in an oath of unity against the administration. Finally on 28 July 1938 about 2,000 Kamba men, women and children marched to Nairobi to present their problem to the governor. Through sheer persistence, the Kamba wrested a major success from the governor, who rescinded forced sales of cattle. Henceforth, sales would be voluntary.

Political organizations and labour mobilization

The success won by UMA could not be claimed by other political organizations operative in the country. The inter-war period witnessed the emergence of many political and welfare organizations which aimed to redress their communities' grievances within the colonial structure.

Initiated by an African proto-elite, these associations embraced the earliest beginnings of inter-regional politics, and by 1939 had the semblance of national perspectives.[55] Thus, during the Kamba protest, UMA worked very closely with KCA, with the former utilizing the latter's newspaper, *Muiguithania,* to advance its protest on the destocking conflict. In general these associations addressed themselves to a long list of common grievances and adopted similar strategies in the articulation of their protests. The issues of forced labour, low wages, long working hours, poor housing conditions, taxation, alienation of African lands, the *kipande* pass system, lack of political representation for Africans in the Legislative Council, industrial education, the restrictions on growing coffee, and racial discrimination, especially with regard to social amenities, constituted the major African grievances.

To a large extent these organizations adopted peaceful methods of resistance, including the sending of petitions, memoranda and delegations to the governor and the Secretary of State for the Colonies in Whitehall. Sit-ins were also employed and in extreme cases delegations were sent to London to present the Africans' case to the British government. Basically, these associations operated within tribal limits, although by the 1930s there was increasing evidence of trans-tribal liaisons and cooperation. The earliest of the associations, the Young Kavirondo Association, which was established in 1921, protested against excessive taxation, the operation of labour camps in Nyanza, the change of the protectorate to colony status and the security of Luo lands. The

129

Association was radical in its demands, which it referred to as the irreducible minimum. The agitation characterizing the demands was only calmed by the arrival of the governor, General Sir Edward Northey, who in his address to the Young Kavirondo Association conceded to some of the demands, reducing the tax from sixteen to twelve shillings, abolished the labour camps and assured the Luo of plans to safeguard their lands. The radicalism of the YKA did not go unnoticed by the authorities. However, it took the wily manoeuvres of Archdeacon Owen to transform YKA from a political organization to a welfare association, the Kavirondo Taxpayers and Welfare Association. Henceforth the Association concerned itself in welfare matters and adopted more peaceful methods of seeking redress. This mellowed approach was not lost on the firebrands, who referred derogatorily to the members of the new Association as *Jo-memorandum* – the people of memoranda.

Apart from YKA, there were other associations in Nyanza reflecting a different historical experience. The Kisumu Native Chamber of Commerce (KNCC), as its name implies, was largely concerned with commercial matters, especially the competition that Asian traders posed to Africans. The absence of government loans and credit facilities to Africans for the latter's improvement of their trading activities further aggravated them. The KNCC members were also concerned about the slow economic development of Nyanza. They attributed this to the government's refusal to allow Africans to grow coffee, and the slow development of cotton.

Faced with a formidable colonial state that seemed to lack a clear native policy, it was left to the Africans to try and unravel colonial policy. Differences of opinion and infighting were not unusual as different groups adopted divergent approaches in articulating their society's grievances. For example, the KNCC derided the KTWA preoccupation with the demand for a land register, since the shortage of land was not a major issue in Nyanza.

In northern Nyanza there emerged the North Kavirondo Central Association, operative among the Luo's northern neighbours, the Luyia. Here, the major bone of contention was the security of native lands, an issue which had been rekindled by the discovery of gold in Kakamega and the subsequent alienation of land. To alienate the land it had been necessary to amend the Native Lands Trust Ordinance of 1930, which had been promulgated to appease Africans and assure them of the security of their lands. The amendment of the ordinance had shaken the confidence of the people further with the provision that alienated land could be compensated for in cash, instead of the return of the land. Like the KCA, which was preoccupied with the issue of land, the NKCA adopted a radical stance in its approach. This, however, did not preclude its chief participation in the rather mundane task of demanding the installation of a paramount chief in Buluyia. Government reticence on this issue resulted in the proclamation of Chief Joseph Mulama as the paramount chief in 1935 by the NKCA. To the colonial administration, this was an act of great defiance which resulted in the suspension of Mulama from his position of chief.

In many other ways NKCA attempted to challenge the colonial state and to widen its style of activities. For example, in 1938 the NKCA joined the UMA, the KTWA and KCA in protesting against compulsory destocking. The protest took the form of a memorandum to the Secretary of State for the Colonies. We have noted that the destocking campaign was deemed necessary for the restoration of badly eroded soils. The colonial government also enforced various other soil conservation measures, including terracing and intercropping. Like other associations, the NKCA expressed its opposition to these measures, misconstruing them as the first steps towards further alienation of land.

The Kikuyu Central Association, which came into being in 1924 and was operative till it was proscribed in 1940, had an active political career that disenchanted the colonial government. Overtly concerned with the issue of land, the KCA was opposed to the 1915 Crown Lands Ordinance and made repeated calls for the return of the alienated land. By the late 1920s the strategic importance of a Western education was common knowledge and KCA advocated higher institutions of learning. It also besought the colonial state for more hospital training facilities, permission to grow coffee, the establishment of African representation in the Legislative Council and the abolition of the *kipande*. In common with other associations, the KCA was opposed to forced labour, especially the employment of young girls away from home. By the 1930s KCA had branches in Central Province, Nairobi and Nakuru. Its activities were well known amongst the squatters in the White Highlands. Here, in the 1940s, KCA assisted in the mobilization of squatters in their anti-settler protests at the height of stringent labour regulations.

However, it is in Central Province that KCA had the greatest impact. Apart from its constant challenge of the colonial government with regard to the lost lands, KCA was caught in a major controversy with the church in 1929.[56] The issue revolved around the Church of Scotland Mission's condemnation of female circumcision, cliteridectomy. In an attempt to enforce the measure, the church excommunicated those of its adherents who engaged in this rite, and also kept them out of the mission controlled schools.

KCA's reaction was to mobilize a major campaign against the church. This resulted in the establishment of two independent churches and two school sponsoring groups. The Kenya Independent Schools Association, closely linked with the African Independent Pentecostal Church, was largely operational in Nyeri, Fort Hall, northern Kiambu and eastern Rift Valley, and concentrated on nurturing schools. The Karinga Schools Association was linked to the African Orthodox Church and flourished in southern Kiambu. Unlike KISA, Karinga was a more politicized group and drew no distinction between educational and political matters. It did not achieve as much success in educational matters as KISA did. However, it did score well in alerting its adherents to the issue of cultural nationalism and the need for self-reliance.

This spirit of self-help was easily adopted by squatters in the White Highlands in their endeavour to provide an educational infrastructure for their children.

In African reserves, missionaries were for a long time responsible for the provision of formal education for Africans. In the White Highlands, up to 1939 neither the missionaries nor the government invested money for squatter children. This is borne out by an observation in 1937 by the Director of Education: 'Up to the present, practically nothing has been done for the education of natives in the White Highlands. There are a few isolated schools run by the church side of societies, but government neither gives nor provides schools.'[57] The churches mentioned only provided limited and occasional supervisory help. The Karinga movement was a major inspiration to the squatters as they pooled their resources to provide education for their children.

Other than problems with education the squatter community faced massive dislocation during the period 1929-39. We have already alluded to the *kifagio* assault. In the years that followed the depression, settlers sought to tighten their hold on labourers by reducing acreage under squatter cultivation, eliminating squatter stock and increasing the hours squatters worked. All these measures were contained in the provisions of the 1937 Resident Native Labourers Ordinance. Technically, the ordinance shifted the government's responsibility over the squatters to the settlers' district councils. As well as increasing the number of hours required from each squatter from 180 to 240, and up to a possible maximum of 270 days per year, the Act allowed the settlers to reduce the number of squatters on their farms.

The subsequent dislocation in the squatter community is beyond the scope of this chapter; suffice it to say that in anticipation of the draconian effects of this ordinance, squatter labourers refused to renew their contracts, squatted illegally and engaged in acts of sabotage by maiming settler stock, setting settler crops on fire and going on strike. Some of the labourers moved to urban areas while others drifted to the reserves. The 1937-8 settler crop was affected as squatters refused to help with the harvesting. This squatter disruption sparked off stringent labour regulations that were to result in the Olenguruone crisis. Elsewhere, between 1934 and 1937 in the Thika sisal estates and among coffee pickers, labour was disrupted in an attempt to get better wages and working conditions.[58] Throughout the squatter–settler wrangle KCA maintained a steady contact with the White Highlands, a contact which was intensely revitalized during the Olenguruone and Mau Mau crises.

At the coast political resistance sparked off by land alienation, forced labour and the imposition of tax coincided with the outbreak of the First World War. Under Mekatilili wa Menza the Giriama in 1914 rebelled in an attempt to resist their eviction from the region to the north of Sabaki River. Despite support from other Mijikenda clusters, including the Rabai, Kambe and Kauma, the Giriama eventually succumbed to the colonial state.

Elsewhere along the coast the alienation of land, which sparked off a series of crises and precipitated political organization, predated the arrival of the Europeans in the area. The alienation of land to the Mazrui Arabs in the first decade of this century displaced a large number of the Mijikenda people,

132

who were pushed to the less habitable inland Nyika region. Some of the Mijikenda were forced to become squatters on coastal plantations while others drifted to Mombasa in search of jobs.[59] The outbreak of the depression in 1929 was preceded by a period of drought in the Nyika area starting in 1925 and lasting up to 1930. This drought resulted in poor harvests. The government's pressure for the collection of taxes despite the poor harvests drove the Mijikenda to desperation. Attempts to resist voluntary employment resulted in forced labour, while some of the Mijikenda settled as illegal squatters on crown land. Those that took up paid employment resented the harsh working conditions on the plantations, and attempts to desert were readily countered by the colonial government. It is within this context of increased impoverishment and proletarianization of the Mijikenda that the Young Nyika Association (YNA) emerged in 1931.[60] It was concerned to champion the grievances of the Mijikenda.

The YNA's memorandum to the Joint Select Committee on Closer Union raised the issues of alienation of land to Arabs and European settlers at the coast, taxation, the *kipande* and forced labour – not very different from those presented by other associations. Indeed, evidence abounds on contacts between these associations at different stages of their formation. The YNA was in contact with KCA, which championed the land grievances of the Mijikenda.[61] Paradoxically, the Carter Land Commission overlooked the alienation of Mijikenda lands during its deliberations. This, coupled with increased government assault on tax defaulters and illegal squatters increased Mijikenda despondency and pushed an increasing number of them to coastal urban towns.[62]

Because the colonial government had hoped to harness the political energy of the Africans through the Local Native Councils, the above associations were seen as errant bodies deserving the strongest condemnation. Although it was not unusual for members of LNCs to join these associations, by and large the colonial government did not condone them, as they were seen to operate as parallel bodies that by-passed the LNCs. Hence, to the colonial government such persons as Harry Thuku, and Samuel Muindi, one of the founder members of UMA, were dangerous leaders whose mobilizing powers needed to be clipped if peace was to prevail. Both were arrested and deported. They were seen to provide an alternative power structure opposed to the state, chiefs, headmen and the LNCs. To the colonial government they were agitators better removed from the masses. Likewise, up to the close of our period, the colonial government did not give adequate attention to the grievances these associations and leaders articulated.

Squatter protest

The increasing deterioration of squatter welfare in the White Highlands was epitomized in the enactment of the 1937 Resident Native Labourers Ordinance. This provided for an increase of squatter labour hours from 180 to 240–270 days per year; it also provided for further reduction of squatter livestock and the acreage of land under squatter cultivation; the settlers were also given the right to reduce the number of employees on farms. Although the application of the Ordinance was postponed while the government sought land for settling those squatters who would be declared redundant, the plight of a majority of squatters was already in jeopardy. While squatters intensified and refined their strategies of resistance in the late 1930s and early 1940s, they had been protesting all along.

In order to evade the *kifagio* ordeal, squatters resorted to a whole range of activities.[63] A squatter might hide his stock at the riverside to escape the labour personnel who enforced the destocking campaign. He might even collude with a colleague to hide the stock in a neighbouring farm, especially if that farm had already been inspected for excessive stock. In some cases, however, the options were not this easy.

Since some settler areas were more tolerant of squatter stock than others, it was quite common for squatters to relocate, moving from one area to another. In some cases, squatters moved to the urban areas in search of wage labour. Many also tried the least favourable of the options, moving back to their areas of origin. Those squatters who hoped to reclaim land from their *mbari* found that even land that had belonged to them had been appropriated by their kinsmen who had remained in the reserves. Most reserves, especially in Central Province, had long attained the optimum carrying capacity. Quite obviously there was a shortage of land and neither the squatters nor their livestock were welcome.

Not all squatter resistance was as peaceful as those strategies discussed above. In desperation, squatters engaged in strikes, maimed settler stock and set settler crops on fire. In very deliberate go-slows, labour was withdrawn, with adverse effects on the settler enterprise. For example, following a period of extensive rumours concerning the impending 1937 Resident Natives Labourer's Ordinance, squatters refused to renew their labour contracts.[64] Neither would they leave settler farms. They obstinately and anxiously awaited the ordinance, fearing that they might renew their contracts only to be confronted with a plight worse than they anticipated. Settlers were anxious that the squatters should help in the harvesting of the 1937 crop.[65]

By the late 1930s, both the colonial state and the settlers were wary of the perpetuation of the peasant option in the White Highlands by the squatters therein. To a large extent, independent squatter production was seen to negate the nature of the squatter contract and the sanctity of the White Highlands. Thus, the colonial equation, whereby the settler owned the land in the White Highlands and engaged in commercial production while the squatters supplied the necessary labour, was not being rigidly observed. The squatters were said to have had:

> the desire for a life wherein for a minimum of work and scanty wage they obtain almost unlimited areas of grazing and haphazard cultivation . . . Unless closely

watched they will bring in the stock of their friends and relatives, cut down forests, cultivate areas along the streams, and proceed to eat the heart out of the land without putting anything back into it.[66]

This observation was an accurate summary of official colonial and settler disenchantment with the squatter community. For this reason the settlers, with the backing of the colonial government, appeared bent on an all-out campaign to remould the squatters to acceptable models. The 1937 Resident Native Labourers Ordinance went a long way to giving the settler district councils the autonomy that they needed to deal with squatters.

Urban unrest

Discontent was not restricted to the rural areas. In the urban areas working conditions for labourers continued to deteriorate. As recruitment in the public and private sectors expanded, so did urbanization. However, this was not matched by an adequate provision of housing, or recreational and other social amenities. Housing was inadequate and squalid. This was made more distasteful by racial segregation in residential areas. In Nairobi, Africans were restricted to the low-lying eastern side of the city, which was prone to flooding and therefore a perfect breeding place for mosquitoes. Wages remained low, and as rural–urban migration increased so did the unemployed population expand. Our period witnessed the incipient development of labour consciousness as men began to organize themselves to lobby for better wages and working conditions. The racial basis of the social and economic policies adopted by the government only helped to fuel despondency among African workers.

Industrialization

At this juncture, it is important to point out that the industrial base of Kenya by the 1930s was extremely thin. Basically, the colony was geared to produce raw materials for British industry. It was also anticipated that it would provide a ready market for manufacturered products from British industries. For this reason there was a tendency for imperial governments to overlook industrial development in colonies.[67] Kenya was no exception. Here, too, colonial manufacturing was seen as a threat to British products.[68] Since the Kenyan economy was expected to complement that of Britain, the local administration was not in a hurry to stimulate industrialization.

Right from the outset of the colonial state, the marketing and processing of primary products was entrusted to various agencies, which amongst themselves set the pace for primary industrialization. For example, the Empire Marketing Board concentrated on the 'marketing of empire food and raw materials'[69] and allocated no funds for manufacturing plants. Throughout the 1920s British manufactured exports dominated the East African market and any attempts at import substitution were seen as competition and therefore harmful to British industry. Pressure was brought to bear on 'infant industries' in British colonies in an attempt to reduce competition with those of the mother country.

For this reason, the Imperial Preference System, established between Britain and her colonies, was subject to manipulation depending on the interests of the metropolitan. For example, under the Ottawa Agreement of 1932, colonial producers were guaranteed 'free access to British and Commonwealth markets'. However, should the commonwealth producer seek to export to Britain similar items to those produced there, then Britain would circumvent the agreement in such a manner as to frustrate any competition. The litmus test to this metropolitan control over local industrialization was more evident in Tanganyika. Here, twine produced locally and exported to Britain proved much cheaper than that produced in Britain, creating an uproar from British manufacturers. It was argued that 'the home market is the only secure market the manufacturers enjoy and it is only in that market that they can make any profit at all [hence] the Secretary of State cannot but admit that the complaint of the manufacturers is a reasonable one...[70]

Paradoxically, the Tanganyikan manufacturers' export comprised 500 tons only out of a total of 10,000 tons sold per year. The message was clear, colonial producers should desist from exporting to the metropolitan stuff similar to that produced therein. The ruthlessness of the metropolitan knew no measure, so that when Tanganyika continued to export twine to Britain, a prohibitive tariff was introduced in 1934 aimed at forcing Tanganyika to raise its price. In 1938 the Twine Company in Tanganyika went out of business.[71]

While Kenya did not face such blatant rebuffs, her plight was not any better. The East African Bag and Cordage Company in Kenya produced twine for local consumption and therefore did not pose any threat to British manufacturers. Even then the metropolitan authorities were indifferent to subsequent expansion of industries in the country. Attempts to set up textile plants in Kenya in the 1930s were vehemently opposed by British textile manufacturers.[72] Thus local capital was barred from setting up industries, while the Colonial Development Advisory Committee only allocated meagre funds for industrial projects: in other words, out of £8m allocated for colonial development by 1919, only £23,000 or 0.3 per cent of the total allocation was used for industrial development.[73] There were, however, a few exceptions when the colonial state together with the metropolitan state supported the establishment of manufacturing plants. The first was the East African Meat Company, for which the government advanced money for the construction of the plant and guaranteed a regular and adequate supply of cattle. This was established in 1935 and was a subsidiary of Liebigs of UK, a meat-processing concern. In many ways the project was in line with government policy. In the first place, it would alleviate the settler pressure for a profitable disposal of their high-grade cattle. Secondly, and more importantly, the establishment of the plant would be a big step towards the accomplishment of the government's destocking campaign; excess stock would find a ready market at the plant. We have referred elsewhere to the political repercussion of this strategy, which forced the government to retract its policy of forced destocking. In as much as the settlers, and their chief marketing body, the Kenya Farmers Association, advocated for an expansion of the industrial base of the country, the establishment of the meat factory was a step in the right direction.

Industrialization in Kenya did not only compete with British manufacturers. It was also pitted against international capital. In Kenya the test case in this direction was in the manufacture of wattle extract. We have indicated elsewhere how the production of wattle expanded tremendously in the 1930s, especially in Central Province. Conflict raged between a local concern, Premchand Raichand, and an international company, Forestal Land and Timber Company, over the extraction of tannin. Supported by the Colonial Office, Forestal, which was established in 1932, was able to override the Asian firm and 'control the conditions of wattle production in Kenya'.[74] Subsequent cooperation between the two groups was on terms favourable to the international company.

By and large 'very little direct assistance was given to the processing and manufacturing industries in the East African Colonies before the Colonial Development Act [of] 1940'.[75] This averaged £5m per year over a period of ten years. The war period encouraged diversification in the manufacturing field, thus enhancing primary industrialization. The significant factors regarding incipient industrialization and import substitution industrialization was that foreign capital was very prominent.[76]

From an early period, import–export groups based in the metropolitan established subsidiaries in Kenya, largely to 'satisfy settler consumer' goods and to cater for the increasing demand for manufactured goods amongst the Africans. These included the firms of Gailey and Roberts, which imported machinery and building materials (largely for settlers); and the United Africa Company, which imported light consumer goods and purchased and exported Kenyan coffee, hides, skins, cotton, oil-seeds, beeswax and sisal among others. Others, such as Baumann and Co., Leslie and Anderson, and Mitchell Cotts & Co. imported a variety of manufactured goods while at the same time exporting primary commodities.

More immediate to our interest were those industries which processed primary products that were marketed widely all over East Africa and beyond. The East African Breweries, which produced beer, was established in 1922; the African Highlands Produce Company, a subsidiary of James Finlay of the United Kingdom, was established in 1924 and concentrated on the manufacturing of tea, a substantial amount of which was exported outside East Africa. Another major tea manufacturing company was the Kenya Tea Company, a subsidiary of Brooke Bond, also established in 1924.

The East African Portland Cement, also a subsidiary of a foreign company – the Associated Portland Cement, was established in 1933. It played the significant role of processing cement and clinker-grinding both of which were vital for the expanding construction industry.

It is evident therefore that in the 1930s there existed a variety of manufacturing concerns, the majority of which were owned by subsidiaries of foreign companies. To a large extent, the establishment of these industries reflected the orchestration of competition in metropolitan capitals. This is best illustrated by the soda ash industry in Kenya. The production of soda ash in Kenya is said to have been closely tied to 'global conglomerates that dominated the chemical industry within the British Empire'. Established in 1911, the Magadi Soda Company was increasingly drawn into the metropolitan hold. Thus in 1926 four British companies, Brunner Mond and Co., the United Alkali Co., Nobel Industries Ltd and the British Dyestuff Corporation amalgamated to form the Imperial Chemical Industries Ltd (ICI) in an attempt to ward off American and German competition in the chemical industry. The Magadi Soda Company was placed under the ICI [77] and the soda ash was exported to the Far East, Britain and Europe.

We have noted that the settler community stood to benefit from the establishment of the meat-processing factory. Unga Ltd, which was partly owned by that formidable settler leader, Lord Delamere, controlled the bulk of the grain milling in Kenya, while another settler body, the Kenya Farmers Association (KFA) marketed the produce. To a large extent, settler capital was too weak to produce any large-scale industrialization.

By the late 1930s therefore, there existed mining, and food, beverage and chemical manufacturing concerns in Kenya. However, the majority of these were owned by local subsidiaries of foreign (mostly British) companies. Maize and coffee milling, a variety of shipping, export and import companies sprung up in the 1920s and were well established by the late 1930s. Significantly, manufacturing remained primary and limited. To some extent this limited development in industry was due to the opposition mounted by British merchant capital against any attempts of industrialization by rival groups.

The argument that the Kenyan situation of the 1920s did not provide a suitable base for industrialization was not a plausible explanation for the strong metropolitan opposition to colonial industrialization. By the 1920s the local population was responding quite positively to a wide variety of manufactured goods and would have provided a ready market. That the area was not as technologically developed as the West would not have precluded incipient industrialization. The basic drawback was the metropolitan's fear of competition from cheap colonial manufactured goods which would undercut metropolitan trade. However, the Colonial Development Act of 1940, together with the increasing decline of British competitiveness on the world markets, pointed to the need for colonial industrialization.[78]

Hence it is evident that industries accounted for a minimal but albeit increasing number of employees. In urban areas the principal employers were the East African Railways and Harbours, the Public Works Department, other government departments, Asian traders and other domestic employers.

The majority of urban workers travelled great distances away from their homes to seek employment. Their distant urban settlements, characterized by overcrowding, a high cost of living, unfamiliar diets and regimes all produced great insecurity. The contraction of job opportunities during the depression resulted in increased unemployment. Although the economy picked up in the mid-1930s, the effects of the depression lasted till the end of the decade. Hence the mid-1930s were characterized by labour unrests as wages fluctuated.[79] Thus in 1934 the Kenya and Uganda Railways and Harbours workers in Mombasa went on strike against a proposed reduction of wages from 2 shillings to 1.50 shillings per day. Likewise in the agrarian sector labour unrest was widespread. In 1934 coffee pickers in Central Province organized boycotts in an attempt to drive wages up. In 1936 and 1937 there were successful strikes on larger plantations, including sugar estates in Miwani, sisal estates in Thika and Mwatate. On the whole, the strikes were better organized and more effective on large plantations which employed long-term labour than on those dependent upon casual labourers. However, the strike which proved to be the Achilles heel of the labour movement took place in Mombasa.

Here, the strike began among the employees of the Public Works Department on 19 July 1939 and soon spread to the workers of the municipality, the Electric Light and Power Company, the Posts and Telegraphs Department and the oil companies. It also spread to those employed by dairy and vegetable growing firms and to the dockworkers. Amongst the major complaints were poor living and working conditions, overcrowding and a low standard of health. The government's immediate reaction was to apply force to disperse the striking workers, pending the appointment of a commission of enquiry. The principal labour officer intimated that the strike was a result of the activities of the Kikuyu Central Association and the East African Labour Trade Union established in 1935. While the trade union was in its infancy, it is true to say that the labour conditions had deteriorated sufficiently to precipitate action. However, from this time onwards labour organization was increasingly consolidated. By the 1940s there existed obvious liaisons between labour movements and political parties.

Social differentiation

We have noted that in the decade after the onset of the depression great changes took place among African societies both in the rural and urban areas. Increased production for the market, increased urbanization and greater attainment of formal education continued to expand. These undertakings were in turn reflected in the society as they enabled the participants to accumulate wealth and invest it in visible forms, alienating them from the majority of villagers. Such indices of social differentiation as the building of permanent houses, setting up of shops, restaurants and maize mills were increasingly visible in the 1930s. The petty-bourgeoisie was already in the making.[80]

The exact combination of the factors that went towards the creation of the petty-bourgeoisie is more complex than portrayed here. In more instances than not, the colonial chief and the mission boy who became a clerk or teacher (or any other profession) had a greater chance of evolving into a petty-bourgeois than the villager who did not think much of colonial beckoning towards greater production and better husbandry. Thus the Musa Nyandusis, Koinanges, Osundwas, Harry Thukus, Jomo Kenyattas and Aworis of the 1920s, who had had some mission education and/or had been colonial chiefs were amongst the most 'progressive' farmers of their day. They had embraced the new ways together with the benefits thereof.

The political orientation of this first crop of mission boys, however, is a different matter altogether. From the same basket, especially from the mission stations, there emerged both the earliest radicals and the earliest retainers of the colonial system. The salient point is that both the collaborators and the political radicals sought to appropriate more of the attributes of the new social order, including formal education, commodity production and political participation among others.

Conclusion

Although our period opened with a crisis over which the colonial state had little or no control, it ended with disturbances which to a large extent were the direct outcome of colonial policies. The espousal of a racially based economy had created massive social and political tensions. Amidst attempts to keep the settler economy afloat after the vagaries of the depression, the colonial state also faced the reality of the need to improve the African sector. There was, therefore, a concerted government effort to graft African agriculture onto the mainstream of the country's economic production.

We have seen how the Africans seized this opportunity. There was an expansion of commodity production; but, there was, too, an expansion of the African population and its expectations from the colonial government. In the settler sector the expansion of settler production seemed to hinge on the contraction of squatter production and the increased proletarianization of the latter. Conflict was bound to arise, and it did.

We have also noted how labour consciousness had began to develop among the urban workers by 1939. Other forms of political organizations which questioned tenets basic to the colonial state did not receive favourable response by the government. All political parties were banned in 1940 with the approach of the Italian invasion. The decade 1929-38 had witnessed diverse and potentially explosive changes. These were evident in the next decade.

Notes

1 For the partisan colonial policy in favour of the settler community, see E.A. Brett, *Colonialism and Underdevelopment in East Africa: the politics of economic change, 1919-1939* (London, 1973); N. Leys, *A Last Chance in Kenya* (London, 1931); W.M. Rost, *Kenya From Within: a short political history* (London, 1968).

2   For a comprehensive analysis of settler vulnerability see, for example, M.G. Redley, 'The politics of a predicament: the white community in Kenya 1918-32', Ph.D. Dissertation, Cambridge University, 1976; Paul Mosley, *The Settler Economies: studies in the economic history of Kenya and Southern Rhodesia 1900-1963* (Cambridge, 1983).

3   G. Kitching, *Class and Economic Change in Kenya: the making of an African petite bourgeoisie 1905-1970* (New Haven and London, 1980), 25-39.

4   See C.G. Rosberg and J. Nottingham, *The Myth of Mau Mau: nationalism in Kenya* (Nairobi, 1966), 35-185 for an account of the nature and activities of the associations.

5   M. Singh, *History of Kenya's Trade Union Movement to 1952* (Nairobi, 1969). This gives a brief history of the trade union movement. However, for the evolution of waged labour in Kenya, see A.H. Clayton and D. Savage, *Government and Labour in Kenya, 1895-1963* (London, 1974); S. Stitcher, *Migrant Labour in Kenya* (London, 1982).

6   C.C. Wrigley, 'Kenya: the patterns of economic life, 1902-1945', in V. Harlow and E. Chilver, eds., *History of East Africa*, vol.II (Oxford, 1967), 246.

7   E.S. Atieno-Odhiambo, 'History of the Kenya Executive Council from 1907-1937', Ph.D. Dissertation, University of Nairobi, 1973, for settler deliberations and use of the above to enhance their welfare; and Redley, 'Politics', on the same issue of settler 'politicking'.

8   H. Fearn, *An African Economy: a study of the economic development of the Nyanza Province of Kenya 1903-1953* (Nairobi, 1961), 68-74.

9   Kitching, *Class and Economic Change*, 40-1. The following exposition of economic expansion in Kenya in our period is largely based on Kitching's work, which affords the most comprehensive reconstruction of African economic activities in the colonial period.

10   R.L. Tignor, *The Colonial Transformation of Kenya: the Kamba, Kikuyu and Maasai from 1900 to 1939* (Princeton, 1976), 186.

11   Kitching, *Class and Economic Change*, 57.

12   Tignor, *Colonial Transformation*, 186.

13   K. Ingham, *A History of East Africa* (London), 337.

14   N. Swainson, *The Development of Corporate Capitalism in Kenya, 1918-1977* (London, 1980), 23.

15   Brett, *Underdevelopment*, 133; Swainson, *Corporate Capitalism*, 22-43.

16   Swainson, *Corporate Capitalism*, 23.

17   Ingham, *East Africa*, 338.

18   Swainson, *Corporate Capitalism*, 38. The government was only able to finance the settlers at great cost. See S.H. Frankel, *Capital Investment in Africa: its course and effects* (Oxford, 1938), 182, where it is estimated that by 1932 loan charges from London financiers constituted 33.6 per cent of the state revenue; J. Lonsdale, 'The Second World War in the transformation of Kenya', in D. Killingray and R. Rathbone, eds., *Africa and the Second World War* (Oxford, 1986), 7.

19   Tignor, *Colonial Transformation*, 187.

20   Swainson, *Corporate Capitalism*, 43.

21   See Brett, *Underdevelopment*, 267.

22   Department of Agriculture annual reports in the late 1920s and throughout the 1930s abound with figures and statements regarding the colonial state's attempts to alleviate African agriculture.

23   KNA, *Department of Agriculture Annual Report 1929*, 45.

24   KNA, *Department of Agriculture Annual Report 1929, 1930*, 29.

25   *Ibid.*

26   Kitching, *Class and Economic Change*, 38.

27   *Ibid.*, 63.

28   *Ibid.*, 64. For a more detailed study of wattle in Kenya see M.P. Cowen, 'Capital and household production: the case of wattle in Kenya's Central Province, 1903-1964', Ph.D. Dissertation, Cambridge University, 1979.

29 Tignor, *Colonial Transformation*, 296.

30 Kitching, *Class and Economic Change*, 74.

31 Fearn, *African Economy*, 194.

32 Kitching, *Class and Economic Change*, 77.

33 *Ibid.*, 81.

34 *Ibid.*, 100. Kitching reckons that these figures would have been relatively exaggerated due to the underestimation of population. Allowing for a 20 per cent exaggeration, Kitching rightly maintains that the figure was indicative of a large out-migration.

35 R.M.A. van Zwanenberg, *Colonial Capitalism and Labour in Kenya 1919-1939* (Nairobi, 1975), 216. Van Zwanenberg observes that 'it was counterargued that in reality the squatters probably occupied as much as 1,850,000 acres, which was just over one-third of the owned alienated land or just under 70 per cent of the land in use'.

36 KNA, *Nakuru–Ravine–Naivasha District Annual Report 1937*, 3-4.

37 Kitching, *Class and Economic Change*, 61.

38 The acreage under settler maize had expanded tremendously from a humble 32,167 acres in 1920 to 200,000 acres in 1929. See D. Anderson and D. Throup, 'The agrarian economy of Central Province, Kenya, 1918-1939', in J. Brown., ed., *The Interwar Depression in Africa and Asia* (forthcoming).

39 For an account of Kikuyu squatter production in the White Highlands and the subsequent conflict with settlers see T. Kanogo, *Squatters and Roots of Mau Mau 1905-1963* (Nairobi, forthcoming), chs.1 and 2.

40 Van Zwanenberg, *Capitalism and Labour*, 236-40; Tignor, *Colonial Transformation*, 310-23.

41 Van Zwanenberg, *Capitalism and Labour*, 241-52.

42 Interview, Gachago Kagere, 28 October 1976, Nakuru.

43 KNA PC/RVP 6A/25/3, PC Central Province to PC RVP, 25 May 1935. See also KNA PC/RVP 6A/25/3, PC RVP to PC Central Province, 30 March 1935.

44 KNA PC RVP 6A/25/7, PC RVP to Colonial Secretary, 21 December 1936.

45 KNA, Native Affairs Department, 1935, 190.

46 Interview, Kiberethi Kanyanja, 13 October 1976, Elburgon; Mrs Wanyoko Kamau, 13 September 1976, Londiani.

47 KNA PC RVP/6A/25/7, Acting Provincial Commissioner RVP to Colonial Secretary, 21 December 1936.

48 Swainson, *Corporate Capitalism*, 23.

49 Kitching, *Class and Economic Change*, 62-107. See also Anderson and Throup, 'Agrarian economy', for changes in peasant production in Central Kenya.

50 For a standard account of Mau Mau and the centrality of land in the struggle, see Rosberg and Nottingham, *Mau Mau*; see also D. Maughan-Brown, *Land, Freedom and Fiction* (London, 1985).

51 Ingham, *East Africa*, 357.

52 R.M. Breen, 'The politics of land: the Kenya Land Commission (1932-33) and its effects on land policy in Kenya', Ph.D. Dissertation, Michigan State University, 1976, 113-38 for reactions to the report and p.174 on Kikuyu right holders; see also *The Kenya Land Commission, Evidence and Memorandum*, 3 vols., Col.91, 1933 and *Report of the Kenya Land Commission*, Cmd. 4556, 1934.

53 See D. Anderson, 'Drought, dustbowl, depression and demography', in *African Affairs* 83(332), July 1984, 321-44.

54 Rosberg and Nottingham, *Mau Mau*, 168.

55 For an account of the origins and articulation of the various associations see *Mau Mau*, 71-188.

56 *Ibid.*, 105-35. The conflict came to be depicted as cultural nationalism.

57 KNA PC RVP/6A/12/11, Director of Education to Provincial Commissioner, Rift Valley in Nakuru on 'Kikuyu Private Schools', 19 October 1937.

58 Tignor, *Colonial Transformation*, 198.

59 See E.M. Aseka, 'Political activities among the Mijikenda of Kilifi and Mombasa Districts: 1920-1963', M.A. Dissertation, University of Nairobi, 1984, ch.1.

60 *Ibid.*, 32.

61 See, for example, KNA, *Kilifi District Annual Report*, 1932, pp.4-5.

62 See K.K. Janmohamed, 'A history of Mombasa, *c.* 1895-1939: some aspects of economic and social life in an East African port town during colonial rule', Ph.D. Dissertation, Northwestern University, 1977. For the question of labour and its attendant problems in Mombasa, see also C. Brautley, 'The Giriama Rising, 1914. Focus for political development in the Kenya hinterland, 1870-1963', Ph.D. Dissertation, University of California, Los Angeles, 1973.

63 T. Kanogo, 'Squatter-peasants. Strategies of survival and resistance', paper presented to the Review of African Political Economy Conference, Liverpool, 26-28 September, 1986.

64 KNA, *Native Affairs Department Annual Report 1937*, 207.

65 *Ibid.*

66 KNA, *Native Affairs Department, Annual Report, 1937*, 187.

67 See Brett, *Underdevelopment*, ch.9 on 'colonial non-industrialization'.

68 Second Report of the Select Committee on Estimates, House of Commons, Cmd.114 of 1928, p.134 quoted in Brett, *Underdevelopment*, 268.

69 *Second Report of the Select Committee on Estimates*, House of Commons, Cmd. 114 g (1928), 134, quoted in Brett, *Underdevelopment*, 268.

70 N. Swainson, 'Company formation in Kenya before 1945, with particular reference to the role of foreign capital', University of Nairobi, IDS Working Paper No.267, p.7.

71 Swainson, *Corporate Capitalism*, 27.

72 *Ibid.*

73 *Ibid.*, 27.

74 Swainson, 'Company formation', 9.

75 See, for example, Swainson, *Corporate Capitalism*, 31.

76 See Swainson, 'Company formation'; A.P. Nyongo, 'The possibilities and historical limitations of import substitution in Kenya', Working Paper No.3, Centre for Asian and African Studies, El Colegio de Mexico.

77 Swainson, *Corporate Capitalism*, 76.

78 *Ibid.*, 31.

79 For example, unskilled African labourers received 33 per cent less in wages than they did in 1935. For the first time, the depression created a situation in Kenya whereby labour supply exceeded demand. See Tignor, *Colonial Transformation*, 189.

80 For this see Kitching, *Class and Economic Change*.

5 Kenya and the Second World War, 1939-1950

Tiyambe Zeleza

The decade between 1939 and 1950 was a very critical one in Kenya's history, having several features at a transitional stage in the development of its political economy. Many aspects lingered on from the earlier phase of primitive colonial accumulation,[1] and new patterns of accumulation began to take shape that later matured into the decolonization drama and eventually independence.

It has long been argued by many Latin American theorists of under-development and dependence that throughout their colonial and postcolonial history Latin American countries experienced relatively faster capitalist development when their ties to the developed capitalist metropoles were at their weakest.[2] Apparently in this century this occurred during the First World War, the Great Depression and the Second World War.

In the case of Kenya it has been shown that war-time circumstances specifically created conditions favourable to capitalist expansion. In the literature we are told how settler agricultural production expanded rapidly and the process of import-substitution industrialization began to gather momentum.[3] On the other hand, we are reminded of peasant impoverish-ment, working-class destitution and African petty-bourgeois alienation.[4]

These approaches and the disparate historical pictures they create are one-dimensional. Certainly while the dependence perspective helps us to understand the external dynamics of accumulation during the war, it ignores the no less important internal forces that were at work and the resultant transformations in social class relations. And to identify accumulation solely with the settlers buttresses that salient half-truth in Kenyan historiography: that settlers accumulated and Africans only struggled. This approach often degenerates into a static dichotomization of colonial society along racial lines, thereby freezing the history of colonialism into a virtually never-changing conflict between the 'colonized' and the 'colonizers' so beloved in nationalist historiography and folklore.[5] Of course the simple fact is that some Africans accumulated and struggled, while others struggled because they did not accumulate. This is to suggest that accumulation was a complex process; while it was not blind to race in a settler-dominated society like Kenya's, it was not exclusive to the settlers either.

In this chapter we will critically examine how the war affected Kenya's political economy, and the contributions Kenya made to the war effort both in personnel and materials. At the same time it will be demonstrated why the war ignited the fires of post-war mass nationalism. It has to be underlined that war-time developments presaged the post-war and particularly post-independence growth of 'national' capital, but simultaneously some of these developments provided the basis for Kenya's further integration into the post-war international division of labour that was characterized by, among other things, the hegemony of American capital and the growing mediation of foreign investment by multilateral institutions and multinational corporations. Between 1939 and 1950 settler accumulation was rapid, but so was the accumulation of some petty-bourgeois Africans. At a general level, this reinforced the extension of capitalist relations of production in the country. But settler and African accumulation increasingly came into conflict. This conflict fused into the unfolding decolonization struggle. After the war the settlers sought to consolidate their war-time economic and political advances; petty-bourgeois Africans grew impatient with colonial-racial structures restricting their chances for faster accumulation; the expanding and increasingly stabilized working class began to flex its labour muscles; and 'poor' peasants resorted to violent confrontation as their exploitation and marginalization deepened. The colonial state was of course not a disinterested umpire in all of this. In fact it was at the centre of the struggles between these crystallizing heterogeneous social forces and classes. So changes in state structures and policies during and after the war reflected the shifting balance of power between the various contending social forces. Needless to say, new state policies actively shaped the trajectory of accumulation and struggle after 1950.

The Second World War years in Kenya

There can be little doubt that the reorganization of Kenya's economy between 1939 and 1945 was, to a large extent, conditioned by the war-time reorganization of the British economy itself. As in peace-time, so during the war, the colonial economies were expected to play a complementary role to the British economy. With the outbreak of the war, Harold Macmillan has written:

> the immediate task of the Colonial Office and the Colonial Governments could be summed up in a single sentence – the mobilization of all the potential resources of the Colonial Empire, both of men and materials, for the purposes of war... We therefore needed to increase colonial production for war purposes on an immense scale.[6]

The Kenyan government of course needed no persuasion. At the beginning of the war the governor, Sir Robert Brooke-Popham, addressed the nation and reminded his listeners of the

> tremendous sacrifices [that] have been made by the people of Great Britain to ensure that the armed forces of the nation are strong enough to overcome the attack of our enemies and to defend the empire and with it this country...
> All the more reason then for all of us in Kenya to help Great Britain by every means in our power, especially by ensuring that we are ready to face any eventuality, that we continue to be self-sufficient in all essential foodstuffs and in so far as we are able, we produce what Great Britain wants most.[7]

145

Among the settlers this call fell on the ears of the converted. The war provoked an outburst of British patriotic fervour among the settlers. But behind the settlers' patriotism lay hard-nosed economic self-interest. The settlers quickly called for increased state support for themselves. They reminded the government how the supposed lack of planning and support for them during the First World War had brought Kenya's agriculture 'to a standstill'.[8]

Conditions during the war conspired to increase settler political power, which was translated into economic power. It is not a little ironical that the war, which prompted the British government to call for intensified production in the colonies and to control the marketing of colonial produce more tightly than ever before, actually led to the decline of Colonial Office control over the colonies. As early as 1940 Governor Moore admitted: 'there has never been a time in Kenya when unofficial opinion has so much influenced policy or been so intimately involved in the counsel of Government'.[9] The Colonial Office could not have agreed more. As Dawe noted, the main object of settlers since 1931 had been 'to secure effective control over the executive government of Kenya. They have made big advances in that direction'.[10] Not all imperial authorities were prepared to watch this usurpation of power by the settlers impotently. In 1942 Macmillan, then Under-Secretary at the Colonial Office, challenged that Kenya was a 'White Man's Country'. He devised a scheme for the Kenya government to buy up the freehold lands of the larger farmers and turn their owners into managers or tenants, and for the purchase of the smaller farms, with a view to reselling them to Africans so that the worsening problem of land shortage for Africans could be arrested before it was too late. He was convinced that failure to take such drastic action would make civil war inevitable.[11] Macmillan's proposal was imaginative but withered in the glare of settler intransigence. His dire prediction of course came only too true a decade later.

It is hard to escape the conclusion that during the war the hand of the settlers vis-à-vis the Kenyan government and that of the Kenyan government vis-à-vis the Colonial Office were undoubtedly strengthened. The British government was naturally more concerned with the execution and fortunes of the war than with the political pretensions of settlers in Kenya. At any rate, the Colonial Office itself was streamlined during the war and operated under severe pressures, so that its powers, not to say its effectiveness, to oversee the colonial empire were considerably reduced.[12] In this regard communication difficulties during the war should not be underestimated. As for metropolitan anti-settler critics, their voices were nothing but whimpers amidst bomb explosions in and out of war-weary London.

The colonial state cooperated with the settlers more than ever before. It may be that government officials did not relish the prospect of a drawn-out confrontation with the settlers under the circumstances of a protracted war. It is also possible that the perennial feuds between officials and settlers were subsumed under a heightened sense of racial solidarity and intense patriotism.

It is certainly the case that 'the extension of government functions, the block placed on further recruitment to the colonial administration, the failure to replace officers who either enlisted or died, all caused the government to seek closer settler cooperation'.[13] In short, the interests of the state to expand and reorganize the war-time economy and administration dovetailed neatly with the interests of the settlers to penetrate the administration. In March 1942 Governor Moore established the Civil Defence and Supply Council, composed of two official and six unofficial (settler) members. Flint calls the council an 'informal cabinet government', and believes it represented 'a kind of clandestine *coup d'état* in which settlers set up, and took over, *de facto* machinery which amounted to a system of virtual self-government'.[14] A settler also headed the Settlement and Production Board formed in September 1939 to coordinate economic activity in the colony.

The restructured colonial state had to respond to British war-time needs and settler demands. In addition, there was the ever-present reality of restive Africans.

At the outbreak of the war the colonial state acquired broad powers of coercion over labour, among a host of other things. Accordingly new regulations were passed, such as the 1940 Defence (Native Personnel) Regulations, which gave the governor power to order provincial commissioners to produce quotas of workers for military and essential services. All such regulations emanated from the Emergency Power (Defence) Acts passed by the British government when the war broke out, which suspended all constitutional guarantees, and were made applicable to the colonies through Orders-in-Council.[15] In Kenya the colonial state used its new and reinforced coercive powers not only to mobilize and recruit labour for the army and services designated as essential, but also to ensure that private farmers and employers received sufficient labour.

Many of the Africans who joined the King's African Rifles in Kenya were conscripted. They were either captured by chiefs on DCs' orders and sent to join the army, or they were ordered to get into lorries while at labour recruitment centres with the promise that they were being taken to places of work, only to find themselves landing at military training depots. Still others were forcibly removed from school and sent to the army, and some unlucky ones found themselves being disposed of by their employers by being told 'to get into the military lorry which was standing there waiting for them'.[16]

Those who joined voluntarily did so either because the army was just 'another one of the European jobs' available, or they fell prey to false rumours that military service would exempt them from paying taxes. Rumour had it, too, that those who waited to be conscripted into the army and did not join voluntarily were always sent to the front lines where fighting was fiercest. Propaganda was indeed extensively used to persuade men to join the army. The Italians and the Germans were painted as devils incarnate, who, Lord forbid, if they conquered Kenya, would have all the men castrated. The propagandists pointed out that the Italians had already threatened the existence of the King of Ethiopia, who until 1935 was the only independent African king. Fear of losing their masculinity and an awakened sense of African patriotism may have moved some, but the most effective and compelling propaganda was simply the promise of a better and fuller life after the war; funds for trade and business, land for settlement, permanent and high-wage employment, and other such tantalizing opportunities were dangled before them like wands that the magic of war would bring.

Apart from requiring men for the army itself, the military authorities, in conjunction with the government, recruited labour for works of urgent operational necessity, such as the construction and extension of airfields, roads, harbours and military training camps. About 20,000 Africans were recruited into the East African Military Labour Service and a further 16,000 into the African Auxiliary Pioneer Corps. Initially recruitment was restricted to the so-called 'martial tribes', but as such sources dried up other nationalities and regions became hunting grounds as well. By 1941 recruitment was virtually extended to the whole of Kenya. All in all, there were about 98,000 Kenyans who served in the armed forces in one capacity or another, at home or in military campaigns as far away as Burma. The maximum total 'serving at any one time appears to have been some 75,000'.[17]

It was agricultural production, however, which was regarded as Kenya's main contribution to the war effort. Consequently, even larger numbers of Africans were conscripted for the settler farmers and other private employers. Such crops as sisal, sugar, pyrethrum, rubber and flax were designated as essential, which meant that it was permissible to use conscript labour for their production. Essential services also included government and local government work.[18] Settlers agitated for conscript labour because of growing labour shortages due to large-scale military conscription and urban employment.[19] There were attempts to strengthen the *kipande* system. Village headmen were empowered to return deserters to their erstwhile places of employment.[20] Further, screws were tightened on the squatter system. In March 1944 the statutory number of days which squatters were allowed to work in a year were increased from 180 to 240 throughout Kenya.[21] New restrictions were placed on forest squatters.[22] Finally, moves were made to control the influx of Africans into the towns in order to offset the imbalance between urban labour over-supply and rural labour shortages for settler farmers.[23]

Settlers relied heavily on conscript labour during the war. The figures show that the numbers of 'free' agricultural wage labourers fell. For example, there were 206,610 monthly paid agricultural labourers in 1941, of whom 159,638 were men, and in 1945 the number was 139,713, of whom 99,424 were men. Part of the shortfall was made up by increases in what was called resident (read squatter) labour. The number of recorded resident labourers rose from 23,325 in 1941 (excludes women and children) to 58,598 (includes women and children) in 1945. This was not enough to make up the shortfall, especially

148

in view of the expansion in settler agriculture. Conscript labourers made up for a greater part of settler labour supply needs.[24]

Some of the glaring technical, commercial and marketing shortcomings which had made settler agriculture so inefficient and unproductive before 1940 were overcome. Backward agricultural techniques and lack of machinery gave way to mechanization. The government used the Anglo-American Lend-Lease Agreement 'to increase her purchases of farm machinery, and mechanization of European farming began in a serious fashion from 1941'.[25] War booty from Ethiopia and Italian Somaliland formed part of the machinery pool; consequently new lands were opened up. Moreover, the use of artificial fertilizers, which had been restricted before 1939 by their high cost, became commonplace, largely as a result of government subsidies, which cut fertilizer prices to farmers.[26] Storage facilities were expanded and improved, again with state assistance. Also, government offered direct credits to farmers so that commercial and merchant banks ceased to be important in the financing of settler agriculture. For its part, the Land Bank lowered its interest rates and offered other attractive terms.[27] District committees and marketing associations also provided finance to settler farmers.[28] Marketing became stabilized as a result of the system of bulk buying and bulk selling of colonial produce introduced by the British government at the beginning of the war. Unlike African peasants in Kenya, or in countries like Ghana and Uganda, who were paid below bulk purchase prices on the proposition that the difference 'was to constitute a kind of collective post-war credit',[29] settler farmers in Kenya received full bulk purchase prices for their produce.

Settler farmers moved into mixed farming on an unprecedented scale. There was great demand for meat by the military authorities. Also, war-time shortage of shipping space made it unprofitable to export bulky commodities like maize, and so more maize was grown to feed the more lucrative livestock. In December 1941 the Agricultural Production and Settlement Board announced a guaranteed price for settler-produced maize. The price was set at Shs.9 per 200 lb bag. African-grown maize of the same quality was set at Shs. 4/90.[30] A number of specious arguments were advanced to justify such a policy of blatant discrimination. It was contended that production costs were lower for African farmers than for settler farmers. Some even went so far as to argue that any vigorous encouragement of African agriculture could only lead to over-production, with the consequent loss of soil fertility in the reserves.[31] By the end of the war prices for settler maize stood at Shs.13, Shs.3 higher than for African maize, the differential having narrowed thanks to a flurry of Colonial Office criticisms, and, more importantly perhaps, as a result of protestations from African producers themselves and the severe food-shortage crisis of 1942-3. Price differentials were also extended to livestock, where settler first-grade beef sold for Shs.34 per 100 lb, while African beef of the same quality sold for Shs.26. In fact, all European cattle, irrespective of quality, were always bought as first-grade beef. So settlers would buy African cattle, use it for a while as work oxen, and sell it as settler cattle. No wonder Africans were reluctant to sell their cattle. The state then resorted to forcible destocking in some areas.[32]

Settler agriculture had never had it so good. Elspeth Huxley, that idiosyncratic muse of the settler conscience gloated: 'this revamping of the [agricultural] industry gave the farmer for the first time in Kenya's history a genuine measure of security'.[33] If economic security was the epitome of settler life during the war, many Africans were condemned to a Sisyphean ordeal of poverty.

The greatest agrarian crisis of the war was perhaps the food shortage of 1942-3. At the time there was a wide divergence of views as to what the causes of the shortage were. In evidence submitted to the Food Shortage Commission of Enquiry, 1943, the settlers predictably blamed it on the lack of 'encouragement to European farmers to produce maize';[34] or the 'lack of machinery and spare parts . . . which reduced the production of European farms';[35] or the failure of the short and long rains of 1942.[36] The commission concluded, correctly: 'neither each of the above reasons, nor the cumulative effect of them all, account for the serious shortage of maize'.[37] But the commission itself did not come up with a convincing explanation either.

The reasons given by Africans who submitted evidence to the commission were closer to the truth. They emphasized that the reserves had been drained of manpower as a result of military conscription and urban migration, so that cultivation of foodstuffs was left to old men and the womenfolk.[38] They stressed, too, that the low prices paid for African-grown maize discouraged many of them from growing marketable surpluses.[39] Finally, in their view the food shortage was the outcome of increased cash-crop production at the expense of food cultivation.[40]

The food shortage was a grim but eloquent testimony to the harsh conditions generated by the war, and an outcome of the cumulative effects of discriminatory agricultural policies. Not surprisingly, the shortage affected the various segments of Kenyan society differently. While hundreds of Africans were dying, especially in the Central and Nyanza provinces, 'the non-natives of Kenya [were] no more than inconvenienced'.[41] The colonial government responded by suspending conscription temporarily.[42] A Reserve Foodstuffs Committee was also set up and empowered with purchasing and distributing food supplies to the reserves. But this was too little, too late. However, the crisis was a sombre inspiration from which future reconstruction of agriculture, in terms of giving official support to peasant farming, sprang.

Notwithstanding the famine and the advances made by settler agriculture during the war, it does not mean that African peasants constituted an undifferentiated mass. During this period the accumulative interests and opportunities for the various sectors of the peasantry diverged further. Although the colonial state continued to impose numerous restrictions on peasant production as a whole, there was still a general extension of commodity relations in the reserves during the war years as a result of expanded commodity production.[43] This expansion was of course uneven spatially and socially. For example, in Nyanza Province, marketed output declined in Central Nyanza, while it rose in North Nyanza. This was partly because an unusually high proportion of the adult male population from Central Nyanza was reported to be working all or part of the year outside the district.[44]

There is evidence to show that during the war more modern and intensive methods of cultivation were adopted by peasants, which led to increased productivity. In the Nandi district, for example, the use of ploughs became widespread. The quantity of maize formally marketed rose from 94.6 tons in 1940 to 2,678.5 tons in 1945.[45] In Nyeri district, the evidence of increased productivity is even more direct. According to some estimates crop yields for maize rose from 600 lb per acre in 1931 to 2,400 lb per acre in 1944; millet from 700 to 933 lb per acre; potatoes from 1.5 to 2.66 tons per acre; beans from 500 to 800 lb per acre; wattle bark from 6.6 to 15.2 cwt per acre; and bananas from 400 to 426 bunches per acre.[46]

It cannot be overemphasized that it was the 'rich' peasants who were more likely to purchase the necessary inputs for increased agricultural output than the 'poor' peasants. This is to suggest that expanded commodity production accentuated the tendencies towards privatization of land tenure and land concentration, and deepened rural class differentiation, all of which typified the spread of capitalist relations of production.

It is more than apparent that even government officials were aware that this process was taking place in the reserves despite all their efforts to stop or turn the clock backwards. According to Sorrenson, in April 1945, Governor Mitchell lamented 'the growth of individual tenure among the Kikuyu, a process that had been hastened by the increase in cash cropping during the war'.[47] Annual district reports, especially from the Central Province where colonial capitalism had advanced furthest, frequently noted the growing incidence of landlessness. It was estimated in 1945, for instance, that Nyeri district was 'so overpopulated that almost half of the people – c.70,000 – would have to be moved if the remainder were to make adequate living'.[48] Apart from natural population increase and the influx of squatters evicted from settler farms, landlessness was a product of growing peasant land concentration. At this time the state did not know what to do with the African accumulators. It was wont to dismiss and caricature them. As one memorandum put it:

> Many of these 'landowners' belong to the more educated section of the people and tend to be antagonistic to tribal influence but as yet have evolved no civic responsibility. . . At the present time they include one or two progressive farmers but the majority are landminers, whose depredations are increased by the use of hired labour. Unless it is the government policy to encourage the evolution of the big landowner and employer of labour, it will be necessary for such men to realise they must re-orient themselves on clan lines sufficiently to ensure their conformation to sound land usage.[49]

This passage aptly captures the reluctance of the colonial state to come to terms with the fact that an African capitalist landowning class had emerged. The official recognition of this class would come in the turbulent post-war years.

Another major bequest of the war which was to change the shape of Kenya's post-war political economy was the expansion of import-substitution industrialization. During the war there was a convergence of two major factors which made this possible. First, there was an intensification of internal pressures for industrialization, and second, external constraints against it slackened. The war made it difficult for the settlers as well as ordinary workers to get consumer goods that they had been used to having previously. Shipping space was limited, so that only essential supplies were sent to East Africa from Europe. Also with the war British consumer industries either switched to the production of war materials or they could simply not produce enough to supply a far-flung empire, especially when it is borne in mind that Germany and Japan had provided significant amounts of manufactured exports to British colonies. By 1939, for example, 72 per cent of all cotton textiles imported into Kenya came from Japan, while Britain's share of this market was a mere 12 per cent.[50]

The only alternative to importing such goods was to begin manufacturing some of them locally, as many bodies, such as the Nairobi Chamber of Commerce, urged.[51] The colonial state responded and began to encourage industrialization. A series of surcharges in the basic tariff were introduced in order to protest local industrial projects. In addition, bodies were set up specifically to foster industrial development. In 1940, for example, the Kenyan government sponsored the formation of the East African Industrial Management Board to manufacture essential items whose supplies had been cut off because of the war. Two years later this was followed by the formation of the Kenya Industrial Management Board (IMB), which was charged with supplying the armed forces with manufactured items. Under the IMB's umbrella there grew up engineering works, woodworking, brick, ceramic and tile manufacturing enterprises. The board was later taken over by the Industrial Development Council in the 1950s, a forerunner of the post-colonial Industrial and Commercial Development Corporation (ICDC).

Thus the colonial state's traditional interventionist role in the economy was extended; support for settler agriculture was being accompanied by support for industrialization. This was a significant development, one which heralded the post-war decline of settler economic and political predominance within Kenya's political economy.

The imperial state relaxed its former undisguised hostility to colonial industrialization partly because 'the prime object of Colonial Office measures towards the colonies during the war was to preserve the gold and foreign exchange reserves of the UK. Colonial governments were instructed to restrict the import of consumer goods and instigate a system of import licences.'[52] Indicative of the new dispensation was the Colonial Welfare and Development Act of 1940. It made available to the colonial governments £50m for a period of ten years for a fairly wide number of projects, including manufacturing. This was in contrast to the CW & D Act of 1929 which offered paltry sums and virtually nothing for manufacturing. British companies were encouraged to set up businesses behind colonial tariff walls now before the war was over. British ministers were acutely aware of American interests in 'the development of colonies after the war'.[53] In other words, they suspected the intentions of American capital to spread its tentacles to the colonial world.

During the war, therefore, grounds were set for import-substitution industrialization in Kenya. Old manufacturing concerns were expanded and new ones established, including blanket, clothing and shoe factories as well as beer and pharmaceutical plants. These enterprises were established by large-scale estate producers, local subsidiaries of international firms, mostly British, and the big Asian merchants. By 1946 there were 280 companies incorporated in Kenya, valued at £46m, among which manufacturing firms were gradually becoming sizeable in numbers and in the share of total value.[54]

The growth of manufacturing industries led to the expansion of the urban labour force. The basis was laid for accelerated labour stabilization after the war. During the war itself the manufacturing companies were too new and fragile to alter in any fundamental way the dominant labour relations system, with its coerciveness tinged by crude paternalism and its low wage ethos. However, during the war there was a trend towards labour stabilization in the towns. This had little to do with rising wages and improving living conditions in the towns themselves. Rather, rural conditions for the wage seekers were deteriorating.[55]

War-time conditions in the town were indeed difficult. In the course of the war employers reduced the quantity and quality of *posho* offered to their workers. It became more difficult to support a family. In fact it became government policy to evict the unemployed, women and children from towns. In 1943, for instance, about 10,000 people, of whom 6,000 were women and children, were evicted from Nairobi alone.[56] A coupons system was introduced in March, whereby employed Africans drew coupons to buy one day's ration at any of the registered shops scattered throughout the town. In 1945 the Phillips Report concluded that 'there is reason to believe that the African's normal diet today is inferior in nutritive value to that which was customary a generation or two ago'.[57] To add insult to injury the shortage of goods provided ammunition for the advocates, including the governor, of a low-wage economy.[58] One commission of enquiry after another harped on the theme that cash wages should remain static and any increase should be paid in kind to avoid fuelling inflationary pressures.[59] Characteristically, European workers were exempt because, it was said, they did not have 'the simpler tastes of Arabs and Africans [which] facilitate the grant of relief in kind'.[60]

It is difficult to make an accurate assessment of the rise in the cost of living between 1939 and 1945 because of the paucity of reliable data. One tribunal at the end of 1942 estimated that the prices of basic goods had risen by over 40 per cent since 1939. The figure was probably much higher, for the tribunal based its calculations on controlled prices.[61] An indication of the rise in the cost of living can be gauged from the fact that between 1942 and 1944 the landed value of imported cloth increased by approximately 100 per cent.[62] Wages failed to keep up with the spiralling cost of living. In 1942 the basic wage was the same as in 1939, and by 1945 it had not risen much.[63] Wages were still based on the needs of a single man and ignored his family responsibilities. But criticisms against this policy began to be voiced in official circles for the first time, although nothing was done about it until the mid-1950s.[64]

The problems of housing were as acute as ever. In fact the war was used as an excuse to postpone taking any action on the housing question.[65] Inevitably this led to overcrowding and overcharging.[66] Overcrowding of course encouraged the spread of disease.

But Kenyan workers did not take all this sitting down. The war years witnessed labour unrest of unprecedented proportions. On the one hand, there was the re-emergence of desertions as a major form of labour protest, and, on the other, workers resorted to strikes on a scale hitherto unknown in Kenya. Indeed, the seeds of trade unionism sown in the 1920s and 1930s firmly began to take root.

Desertions were provoked by the conditions of extreme coercive labour recruitment and control that the whole system of labour conscription represented; so they were widespread among conscripted workers both in military and civilian employment. At one time as many as 15,000 were listed as having 'overstayed' their leave, that is, deserted.[67] The Director of Intelligence and Security reported almost daily about desertions and labour unrest.[68] The war was the last time that desertions would constitute a major form of labour protest. This is because the war marked the last time, save for the detention camps under the emergency in the 1950s, that the coercive labour control system would be implemented on such a large scale.

Strikes were also widespread during the war among all groups of workers, from conscript labourers, soldiers and squatters to the urban workers and those in the public services. The strikes were the result of a complex set of factors, some emanating from the socio-economic hardships generally prevailing in the country and others from specific conditions at work places. For example, scores of strikes erupted in Nairobi, Mombasa and other towns after food rations were reduced in 1942 and 1943. Others agitated against shortages of consumer goods and housing. And of course there was the perennial problem of low wages. For example, in October 1942 African railway workers, the torchbearers of labour militancy in Kenya, went on strike in Mombasa and Nairobi demanding higher wages. Through arrests and police repression the strike was broken. But the government agreed to appoint a tribunal, which recommended modest wage increases.[69]

Some of these strikes were organized by unions or staff associations.

Sometimes during a strike a temporary organization would be set up, and delegates appointed to talk with management or to make representations to a tribunal.[70] It was difficult to organize trade unions during the war, what with frequent arrests and police harassment, all underpinned by repressive trade union legislation.[71] Nevertheless, unions were formed. By the end of 1943 ten unions had been registered. They were mostly organized on racial lines even within the same industry. For example, in the railway Asian and African workers had separate unions.[72] The unions were also crippled by poor finances. Organizational efficiency was another talent in short supply: the veteran trade unionist Makhan Singh spent most of the war in Indian jails. But considerable advances had been made since the 1930s. Kenyan workers were clearly getting more conscious of themselves as a distinct class and of the need to fight for their elemental rights as workers.

The war also proved a fertile ground for the growth of nationalist political organizations. There was certainly no shortage of popular grievances. And people were not blind to the growing power of the settlers either. In the early years of the war the *Dini ya Musambwa* was formed in the Western Province. The movement combined religious and political protest with proto-trade unionism.[73] At the coast the various Mijikenda groups began to flex their political consciousness, and in 1945 merged into the Mijikenda Union.[74] Even the Indian Congress displayed uncharacteristic militancy by calling for the repeal of discriminatory legislation and, more importantly, by trying to forge links with the burgeoning African nationalist movement in resisting settler efforts to consolidate the colonial *status quo*.[75]

The most significant political organization to emerge during the war was the Kenya African Union (KAU). KAU was a successor to the KCA. According to Spencer, KAU was specifically formed as a support group for Eliud Mathu, the first African to be nominated to the Legislative Council.[76] Mathu was nominated in October, 1944. His nomination came in the wake of long-standing agitation by Africans to be represented by one of their own instead of by Europeans, and creeping Colonial Office and colonial government concern about African representation in Legco in the face of growing settler power. Mathu fitted the bill: he was educated at Oxford University, was a successful teacher and a known moderate.[77]

KAU's first president was Harry Thuku, once a fiery nationalist but now mellowed into a conservative businessman. In January 1945 Thuku was ousted and succeeded by the more energetic James Gichuru, a high-school teacher. KAU was formed only a year before the war ended, so there was not much that the movement did during the war itself: its potential lay in the post-war years. In the remaining months of the war KAU tried to promote cooperation with the Indian community and addressed itself to the proposals for a central assembly for the three East African territories. Already KAU had a foretaste of what was to come. The colonial government was wary of it; settler antagonism was palpable; the problem of insufficient funds was chronic;

leadership squabbles were not far from the surface; it was not easy to organize a viable network of party branches; and the ghosts of 'tribalism' were never too far off. Many saw KAU as an elitist and Kikuyu party. But when tested by the raging fires of decolonization after the war KAU would prove itself as Kenya's first truly national African political movement.

The war then had a complex and contradictory legacy. It strengthened settler power and consolidated colonial capitalism, but it also created material conditions from whose womb were born social forces that would soon overturn colonialism on its face.

Post-war Kenya

The year 1945 did not simply mark the end of the Second World War, it also signalled the beginning of a new era for both the imperial metropolitan powers and the colonial world. Even a casual reading of post-war colonial history shows that after 1945 imperial–colonial relations entered a stormy period that was probably unprecedented, and which in most places culminated in formal decolonization within the next two decades.

In the aftermath of the war a fundamentally new hierarchy emerged among the metropolitan capitalist countries, one marked by the hegemony of the USA in the political, economic and military spheres. The war of course had not been fought on American soil, so the USA emerged from it unscathed, a giant ready to impose its will on a tired world. The colonial world could no longer remain the exclusive preserve of the war-ravaged powers of Europe. Britain emerged from the war owing £6,000m and was perhaps the biggest debtor nation in the world.[78] Her dollar deficits were acute and rising;[79] her food situation, especially of oils and fats, was desperate.[80] As British capital became incapable of competing with American capital on a global scale, the British economy was reorganized. Laissez-faire capitalism gave way to a higher level of state intervention, a process which was replicated in the colonies, where of course state intervention was already highly pronounced.

Also, after the war foreign investment in the colonies ceased to be a monopoly of the colonial powers. At first tentatively, then more speedily, foreign investment came to be mediated through multilateral institutions and multinational corporations. New international agencies, such as the World Bank, the IMF, the EEC Investment Bank and EEC Development Fund were established, initially to facilitate the reconstruction of war-torn Western capitalist countries before they reached out to the colonial and dependent world as agencies of the new multilateral imperialism.[81] Multinational corporations also came of age, a reflection of the intensifying concentration and centralization of capital on a world scale. While many concentrated on plantation agriculture and extractive industries, some ventured into secondary manufacturing. So the trend towards import-substitution industrialization was strengthened in some colonies. The import of all this is that the colonies became more fully integrated into the world capitalist system.

Thus colonialism was on the retreat at two levels. First, while the colonial powers with their shattered economies now needed the colonies more than ever, their ability to hold on to them was greatly weakened precisely because of the emerging international division of labour. Internationally the colonial powers were on the defensive politically and ideologically. In a world only recently rid of fascism, the defence of colonialism lost its eloquence. From both sides of the international ideological divide, and for very different reasons, and from the recently formed United Nations and newly independent ex-colonies like India, there came unprecedented and almost universal condemnation of 'old style' colonialism. Second, the colonial world itself was on fire. Social and political struggles were intensifying. Nationalist parties were shedding their elitist timidity, goaded by mass unrest, which spasmodically erupted into demonstrations and riots, boycotts and strikes, petitions and violent protests. The old colonial framework could no longer contain the political crisis in the colonies. It was, therefore, in response to these mutually reinforcing pressures, underlined by the imperatives of British economic reconstruction, that a new post-war colonial policy was unveiled. Its central plank was the Colonial Development and Welfare programme.

A number of institutional mechanisms were created to implement it. First, there was the CD & W Act of 1945 which, together with the amending acts of 1949 and 1950, provided for a total of £140m to be available over the years 1946-56.[82] The colonies were invited to submit ten-year development plans, which were to take into account money provided under the act, money raised from both internal resources and the money markets. By June 1948, 17 plans, including Kenya's, had been received. Kenya's plan earmarked a total expenditure of £17,586,000, of which £3.5m was to be provided from CD & W funds.[83] For the entire post-war period that the CD & W was in operation, Africa received 45 per cent of the funds, with Nigeria ranking as the recipient of the largest grant (£40m), followed by Kenya (£23m). Secondly, two corporations were formed. They were intended to fulfil British economic needs in the short-term, since the CD & W Act concentrated on construction of infrastructure and public services, investments of long-term benefit to capital, but few immediate benefits. The Colonial Development Corporation was formed in 1947 with a capital loan of £100m from the Treasury, and the right to borrow an additional £15m from private sources; later its borrowing powers were increased by £30m.[84] The corporation concentrated on commercial projects, from mining and manufacturing to fisheries and plantations. In order to facilitate its functions the colonial governments were encouraged to form public corporations which established close working relations with the CDC.[85] The second corporation was the Overseas Food Corporation, also established in 1947, with an authorised capital of £50m, including the £25m originally advanced to the United Africa Company, some of whose operations the OFC took over. The brief of the OFC was to organize large-scale plantations and food-growing projects in the colonies. But it got its fingers badly burnt with its largest project, the East African Groundnut Scheme, which was originally started by the United Africa Company. The scheme's eventual failure spelled the end of the OFC itself, and it was dissolved in 1954.[86]

But this investment or 'aid' was only British in name. During and after the war Britain bought colonial produce below bulk purchase prices that she herself had set, and kept the balance in British banks and the Treasury. Of course some of this produce was resold on the world market, particularly to the dollar area, at higher prices, which helped to lessen Britain's severe dollar deficits. Also, Britain refused to return the sterling balances to finance colonial development, because 'while, from a colonial development point of view, the use of balances to finance development expenditure was likely to accelerate growth, the expedient would be likely to involve increased unrequited exports from the United Kingdom, thus aggravating the balance of payments position, and so should be avoided', so minuted one official.[87] And the African colonial sterling balances were not chicken feed. They rose from £573m in 1944[88] to £805.5m in 1947,[89] to over £1,000m by 1951[90] and £1,446m by 1955, or 'more than half the total gold and dollar reserves of Britain and the Commonwealth which then stood at £2,120m'.[91] The conclusion is inescapable. Colonial Development and Welfare represented a 'recycling' of the fruits of colonial exploitation to generate more exploitation.

So after the war the colonies were expected to help in the reconstruction of Britain. The Kenyan government was aware of what was required of it by the imperial authorities. In 1947 the colony's annual report stated quite candidly:

> The dollar crisis and its repercussions on the colony's economy were closely
> examined with a view to falling into line with the needs of the United Kingdom
> in, among other things, reducing expenditure of hard currencies and the
> expansion of production activities.[92]

This was a call to increased agricultural production and accelerated import-substitution industrialization.

The expansion of settler and corporate agriculture gathered added momentum after 1945, which was in part a response to favourable marketing conditions in a post-war world hungry for food and raw materials. Between 1945 and 1960 about £46m was invested in settler and corporate farming, mainly for the construction of roads, dams, buildings, fencing, machinery and vehicles.[93] Existing estates and plantations were able to expand and, in addition, after the war there was an influx of new settlers, mostly British ex-servicemen, for whom large tracts of land had to be found. In 1946 the Agricultural Settlement Board was established and charged with running European settlement schemes. The board bought all the remaining crown land and any uncultivated land that the existing settlers cared to sell, and distributed it to the new arrivals. The number of settler farmers more than

158

doubled from 1,700 in 1948-9 to 3,600 by 1960. Increased European settlement simply meant that many African squatters lost the use of land they had previously occupied for cultivation and grazing purposes. It was in fact the premise of the Settlement Schemes Committee that 'any talk of close [European] settlement is farcical unless the [squatter] system is abolished and abolished very quickly'.[94]

So conditions for squatters worsened. The Labour Department noted in 1952:

> District Councils in the areas of European settlement are limiting the maximum size of plots which might be alloted to the labourer and his family with the intention of limiting 'kaffir' farming and like abuses. . . Resident labour is no longer attractive to Africans.[95]

The Uasin Gishu District Council was one of the first councils to resolve that 'no new Resident Labourer with stock shall be engaged by any occupier. . . no existing contract for resident labourers with stock shall be renewed except from year to year'.[96] Elaborate plans were drawn for the eventual removal of squatter stock.[97] Other district councils adopted similar destocking measures, as did the Forestry Department.[98] Stock reduction went hand in hand with measures to reduce land given to squatters for cultivation and grazing purposes. In 1946, for instance, the Naivasha district council restricted squatter cultivation to two acres and increased the required number of days for a squatter to work from 240 to 270 a year. In Nakuru squatters were allowed a mere 1.5 acres by 1953, down from 2.5 acres in 1946.[99] These measures were not only harsh in themselves, but they were often enforced with calculated cruelty. Sometimes squatters were evicted before they had harvested their crops. Forced seizure of squatter stock became common. Aged squatters were removed from land on which they had lived all their lives and were supposed to return 'home' to the reserves they had never seen. This ruthlessness of course found justification. 'Council believes', the Uasin Gishu district council stated after issuing one of its tough squatter regulations, 'that the African by and large, is still savage and a child and that he understands and responds to firmness, that he fully understands the reasons for council's proposed order, and far from losing confidence if the order is implemented and enforced, will gain respect and liking for the European.'[100] Coming on the eve of Mau Mau these were sentiments of truly monumental self-deception, complacency and utter contempt for Africans.

Squatter marginalization should not, however, be misinterpreted to mean that African agriculture as a whole was being marginalized. Nothing could be further from the truth. Despite continued official biases in favour of settler and corporate agriculture, after the war the colonial state, for the first time, embarked on a planned and long-term assistance programme for African agriculture. In 1946 the Worthington Plan was drawn up, providing £11m to be spent over a period of ten years on agriculture, over half of which was allocated to the African Land Development Programme and earmarked for

African agriculture, mainly for the prevention of soil erosion.[101] The adoption of a policy favourable to African agriculture was determined by three main factors.

First, the government wanted to prevent the recurrence of the disastrous war-time food shortages and the problem of rural poverty from worsening. It was recognized that unless African agriculture was capitalized sufficiently production in the reserves would fall. Second, it became imperative to encourage African agriculture, because increased African production could only help to maximize overall production, enabling the country to feed itself and to produce exports to satisfy British needs. Finally, the colonial state could no longer ignore the growing numbers of increasingly vociferous African capitalist farmers who had risen in spite of great odds. Mathu was speaking for this class when he stated:

> The Private Title or Individual Title Deed is now a necessity in many parts of Central Province. The security it would give the right holders would encourage better farming methods... People are now growing permanent crops; they are establishing permanent buildings and other improvements, like fencing and dips. Individualism in the areas under consideration has come to stay. The Native Lands Trust Ordinance, 1938, will have to be amended to fit with the times.[102]

For a few years after the war the government persisted in its ambiguous attitude towards this class. There were those officials, including Governor Mitchell, who were nostalgically wedded to the virtues of the mythical African 'communal' land tenure system and were antagonistic to the emergence of 'economic individualism' among Africans which, in their opinion, was to blame for most of the problems in the reserves. They proposed that titles should remain with the kinship group which, 'it was thought, would assist in comprehensive planning and agricultural improvements'.[103] This was the basis of the policy of 'planned communal farming' which the government encouraged in some districts up to 1952.

However, from 1948 the reality of capitalist agriculture in African areas came to be accepted. It was recognized that buying and selling of land in many African areas had already gone too far to be reversed; among the Kikuyu *ahoi* tenurial arrangements had irretrievably broken down. In Kiambu district, for example, an estimated 40 per cent of the population had no land. Officials now had nothing but praise for the African land accumulators. In 1950 the annual report from the Central Province enthused:

> A small but growing body of landowners provided an example to their fellows of the benefits and profits to be derived from good farming practice. Paddocking was increased to such an extent that it has now become the local equivalent of the enclosure in England... this will lead to a land owning class... The corollary will be the growth of a large landless class (which already exists in embryo) either staying as agricultural labourers in the Reserve or finding employment in the towns in the Settled Areas.[104]

This landless class 'in embryo' comprised already almost 50 per cent of the population in the Kikuyu Reserve by the turn of the 1950s. The expansion of capitalist agriculture in African areas combined with the expansion of settler and corporate farming violently limited the viability of the squatter system and the choices open to squatters. For the returning squatters there was no respite in the reserves, thanks to land accumulation and concentration there by some Africans. The explosion that was to be Mau Mau, with its intertwined intra-African class struggle and anti-colonial offensive, was brought so much closer. The processes of accumulation and pauperization were subsequently enshrined, in the midst of the Mau Mau emergency, in the Swynnerton Plan which permanently transformed the face of Kenyan agriculture and left an indelible mark on its class structure.

As squatters were being marginalized, there was another movement taking place at the same time almost imperceptibly, but whose eventual effect was to erode the economic hegemony of the settler farmers themselves. That was industrialization. In 1949, the *East African Standard* screamed excitedly:

> Kenya is on the eve – as, indeed, is all of East Africa – of large-scale industrial development. With that development will come a new stability in the colony's economic conditions and an answer to at least some of the very difficult problems which the agricultural character of the country has hitherto created... There is, of course, no lack of capital. In 1948 in Kenya alone £23,000,000 was invested in private and public companies and probably nine-tenths of this money went into industry... Over the last three years at least £54,000,000 has been invested in new companies in Kenya.[105]

Items produced by the new industries included pharmaceuticals, leather and shoes, beer and light drinks, fertilizers, cement, boats and yachts, building materials, furniture and household requisites, gas, metal cans, canned goods, packaged biscuits, plastics and paper containers, textiles, sisal twine, paint, soaps and perfumery, and electrical machinery. Between 1948 and 1952 the output of private industry increased by about 70 per cent.[106] The East Africa Royal Commission estimated that by 1953 'the contribution of manufacturing activity to the monetary economy was in the region of 12% of the total'.[107]

Kenya was ahead of her neighbours Uganda and Tanganyika, where import-substitution industrialization had hardly begun.[108] Kenya's headstart made her an attractive venue for multinational companies looking for investment in East Africa. So Kenya began emerging as an industrial manufacturing and distribution centre. At this time of course Kenya's industrialization was restricted to the early stages of import-substitution. Some of the new industries were established by existing companies, others were set up as branch plants of multinational corporations looking for greener pastures in the 'peripheries'. British capital was still predominant. Of local investment in industry, particularly remarkable was the movement of Asian capital into manufacturing. The expansion of Asian capital after the war was facilitated by the easing of state restrictions against Asian enterprise and the availability of finance capital to Asian entrepreneurs after the Banks of India and Baroda were opened in Kenya in 1945. Some Asian firms even managed to absorb settler-owned enterprises.[109] This was just one manifestation of the cracks appearing in the clay armour of settler economic hegemony.

In fact, though there was an increase in absolute terms, there was a relative decline in the amount of capital formation attributed to settler agriculture and a corresponding rise of capital formation directed into industry and other non-settler farming sectors.[110] Swainson has shown that the colonial state went out of its way to protect locally established industries from external competition. Although a comprehensive tariff system for local industry was not introduced until 1958, war-time measures of imposing surcharges on imported manufactured items were continued after the war, to the obvious satisfaction of firms established in the country. It is in fact evident that it was the imposition of high colonial tariff walls which attracted those fractions of British capital which had become uncompetitive on a world scale to invest in colonies like Kenya. Not only were such firms assured of the exclusion of competitors from the colonial markets, this also allowed them to charge high local prices, which enabled them to enhance their profits on their local operations and recoup losses elsewhere. In addition to the erection of a protective tariff structure, post-war industrial strategy in Kenya was based on Industrial Licensing Ordinances. Under these ordinances a licensee was required to engage in any one of a handful of scheduled industries. The aim was to discourage the proliferation of small firms which would undermine the profitability of the big firms. Thus the licensing system encouraged 'the movement of capital into large, oligopolistic units and a highly concentrated industrial structure emerged'.[111] Industry also became spatially concentrated in Nairobi and Mombasa. This 'differed somewhat from pre-war practice where much industry (which processed agricultural products) was located in rural areas'.[112] This dual concentration of industry had a crucial impact on the development of post-war labour relations, for it was to give a decisive edge to large firms in the formation of the industrial relations system. Thus, as in other areas, the settler farming sector's grip on the labour control system was loosening.

The agricultural and industrial changes outlined above greatly affected the manner in which the Kenyan working class grew after the war. It is evident that, apart from the obvious increases in the overall number of workers, there were significant changes in the composition and distribution of the labour force. It is indicative of the extent to which capitalism had now developed that this expansion owed less and less to overt state coercion. Conscription for essential undertakings was terminated in 1946.[113]

A factor of some importance in the growth of the labour force in the first few years after the war was the return of tens of thousands of ex-askaris. The long-dreamt rewards of the return from war were painfully disappointing to many. Some used their gratuities to make ill-advised or abortive forays into trade and business, while a fortunate few made it and joined the ranks of the growing African petty-bourgeois class of successful traders, farmers, teachers and civil servants. Many were absorbed into the labour force. Lucky were those who received training in the training centres run by the Labour Department. By 1949 when demobilization was completed only 4 per cent had been so lucky. The rest became rural peasants or joined the ranks of underpaid and disenchanted workers prone to militancy.[114]

Table 5.1. Sectoral distribution of employment (including casual and part-time workers and apprentices), 1948 and 1952, in thousands

Sector	1948		1952	
	No.	%	No.	%
Agriculture and Forestry	193.9	46.1	205.8	43.3
Private Industry and Commerce	124.5	29.6	154.3	32.4
Public Services	102.1	24.3	115.7	24.3
Total	420.5	100.0	475.8	100.0

Source: Labour Department annual reports for 1948 and 1952.

Industrial employment began to account for a sizeable share of total wage labour, as table 5.1 shows. It encouraged urbanization as thousands flocked from the rural areas to work in the towns. For example, employment of adult male Africans in the nine main towns increased from 97,718 in 1948 to 135,385 in 1954.[115] In spite of attempts by the state to curb the influx, rural-urban migration intensified. As more people flocked to towns so did the numbers of those who became long-term residents increase. The rising trend towards urban labour stabilization was observed for Nairobi and Mombasa.[116] As urban labour showed signs of becoming stabilized, rural labour displayed marked tendencies towards greater proletarianization. This was reflected in the steady decrease in the reported number of resident labourers, from 24.4 per cent of the total African agricultural labour force in 1946 to 20.6 per cent in 1952, while the shares of both monthly and casual labour rose.[117] Another development, though less noticeable, was the entry of African women into wage employment in steadily increasing numbers, from about 35,000 in 1946 to just over 40,000 by 1952, of whom 3,453 were in non-agricultural employment. There was also a fairly rapid advance of Asian and European employment, from about 35,000 in 1948 to around 41,000 six years later. This can partly be explained by the importation of skilled manpower for manufacturing industries. Employers were encouraged to submit applications for entry permits for immigrant workers. In 1947 alone 10,000 new immigrants entered the colony, half from India and the other half from Britain.

Despite the growth of the working class and the fact that many workers were staying at their jobs for longer periods than before, the weight of the evidence seems to point to the conclusion that during the period under review improvements in working and living conditions were minimal. Arguments and rationalizations for a system of low wages still guided wage policy.[118] As could be expected, the wage structure reflected the racial divisions within the society. Overall, European workers earned about 24 times as much as African workers and Asian workers ten times as much. In 1947 the East African Salaries Commission argued forcefully that the time had not yet come for introducing a common salary scale for all races,[119] a recommendation fully endorsed by the government. To be sure, in 1946, for the first time, the government introduced minimum wages, although those for agricultural workers were excluded. Minimum wage rates were based on inadequately calculated cost of living indexes, and the needs of a single worker and not those of his family. It was one thing to enact minimum wage orders and quite another to implement them. In 1952 the Department of Labour was alarmed when a survey it had conducted revealed that no more than 10 or 11 per cent of the workers in Nairobi earned the barest statutory minimum.[120] In the Nairobi of that time the 'average' African worker spent 90.3 per cent of his income on his food alone.[121] This should go some way to dispel the myth that urban workers were better off than rural peasants. Rural wages were of course also low, and as in the case of resident labour, even fell sharply.[122] On the whole, in 1947 'average' wages for unskilled Africans were Shs.10-16 per month, the same as in 1941, and for skilled workers Shs.80, also the same as in 1941. By 1952 the unskilled 'average' had risen to Shs.18-40 and the skilled 'average' to Shs.120.[123] In real terms, that is, taking into account the rise in the cost of living, there had been no real improvement since the late 1930s. The Northcott Report wondered 'whether wage rates were not seriously below the level of 1939'.[124] The Booker and Deverill Report was more categorical. 'All the evidence,' it stated, 'is therefore, that some of the urban Africans are living at lower standards than they were before the war.'[125] And standards before the war were nothing to boast about.

The provision of adequate housing and social services remained as elusive as ever. The government and railways tried to provide accommodation for their own employees, but they only scratched the surface of the housing problem. Of the 80,000 Africans estimated to be in Nairobi in 1949, for instance, about 25,000 of them reportedly 'had no fixed abode'.[126] Shortage of housing was only one side of the problem; the existing houses themselves were in a deplorable state. Commenting on government housing in one of the African locations in Nairobi, an observer noted that 'the shortage of latrines, standard pipes and other amenities and the absence of storm drainage . . . are the same today [as in 1941] except that another four years of damage and filth has been added'.[127] The Wilson Report found PWD housing in Mombasa 'perfectly disgraceful . . . latrines are either non-existent, too shallow or without a proper house over them to protect them from the rain . . . they [the PWD] are setting an extremely good and criminal example of how they [workers] should not be housed'.[128] Railway housing was not much better.

It was provided in 'barrack-like structures built in rows of 20 . . . many were living three in a room, even five in a room'.[129] The conditions in the expanding teeming slums were of course worse. Slum development was thinly endorsed by the Vasey Report on African housing, when it declared categorically that employers could not be expected to build houses for their workers and the solution lay 'in the building by the African of houses for himself or for the accommodation of other Africans'.[130]

Such living conditions conspired to lead, in the words of the labour commissioner, 'to a great deterioration in the actual physical state of the African worker today',[131] a conclusion borne out by investigations and reports by the Labour and Medical Departments and other observers. Many workers suffered from what one team called 'malignant malnutrition'. For its part overcrowding made workers susceptible to respiratory infections, like pneumonia and tuberculosis, which became 'the commonest cause of death and absence from work'.[132]

It was such conditions which gave rise to growing militancy by African workers after the war. Between 1946 and 1952, 12 new trade unions were registered, covering a wide range of industries and occupations, excluding the agricultural sector. In 1952 there were 27,589 reported paid-up union members. The largest union was the Transport and Allied Workers Union with 9,823 paid-up members. It was formed in 1946.[133] All the unions concerned themselves with bread-and-butter issues and demanded higher wages, shorter working hours, social security and pension schemes, improved accommodation and better working and living conditions generally. The way these demands were articulated of course varied depending on the industry and strength of the union.

The African Workers Federation and the East African Trades Union Congress, in succession to each other, sought to act as central trade union organizations. AWF enjoyed a brief if spectacular history. It emerged during the 1947 Mombasa general strike and quickly spread its tentacles to Nairobi, where a branch was formed in July. Plans were afoot to establish branches in Kisumu, Nakuru and other towns when its president, Chege Kibachia, was arrested the following month. The organization began to crumble after that. The EATUC was founded on May Day, 1949, by five registered trade unions at a mass rally attended by trade union leaders and nationalist politicians, including Kenyatta. The EATUC had in Fred Kubai, its president, and Makhan Singh, its general secretary, able and militant leadership, which made the congress a potentially formidable organization. The EATUC like the AWF also failed to survive the arrest of its main leaders in 1950.

Trade unions swam in the waters of persistent labour unrest. The number of strikes and workers involved were high in the post-war years. There were 80 recorded strikes in 1947, 87 in 1948 and 84 in 1952. Out of the 87 strikes in 1948, 32 were major strikes, that is, they involved more than fifty workers and lasted for more than a day. In 1947 and 1950 the country was rocked by general strikes in Mombasa and Nairobi, respectively.

The Mombasa general strike was the culmination of scores of strikes that had plagued the town since the 1930s. It lasted 11 days from 13–24 January and involved more than 15,000 workers, from skilled and semi-skilled to unskilled and casual labour, whose demands concerning pay, employment and living conditions were as comprehensive as they were unwelcome to the government and other employers in the coastal town.[134] The government used all its power through show of force and arrests, employment of scabs, and despatches of amiable peacemakers like the Rev. L. J. Beecher and Mathu to break the strike. The strike ended when the government agreed to appoint a tribunal to look into the workers' grievances.

The Nairobi general strike followed on the heels of a wave of strikes that shook the city and its surrounding areas in 1949 and 1950, including the boycott of the Nairobi civic celebrations in March, 1950. The EATUC urged Africans to boycott these Nairobi Charter Day celebrations because workers had nothing to celebrate when they lived in 'dirty and unhealthy slums... when plans are being secretly hatched to add to Nairobi more land of Africans'.[135] Boycotting the celebrations touched a raw nerve among the ultra-royalist settlers, who called for swift and stern action to be taken against the labour leaders. Kubai and Singh were subsequently arrested on 15 May. The Nairobi general strike broke out the next day. It lasted eight days and involved about 100,000 workers. It spread to many surrounding areas. The strike was called off when the government agreed to raise the minimum wage by Shs.6. Both the Mombasa and Nairobi general strikes displayed a measure of working-class power that impressed the workers themselves and frightened the government.

Workers and trade unions played an active role in the growing nationalist movement. This movement had many currents, which did not always cross, in fact some run in parallel antagonism to each other, but they all flowed, with varying intensity, into the sea of anti-colonialism. In addition to trade unions, there were politico-religious movements like the Dini ya Musambwa, whose followers were massacred in February 1948 and April 1950. Disenchanted ex-servicemen had their associations, such as the Nyeri District Ex-Servicemen's African Friendly Association and the Kikuyu and Murang'a District Ex-Soldiers Associations, which articulated the grievances of returned African soldiers. Then there were the ethnic welfare associations such as the Luo Union, the Abaluyia Association, the Nandi-Kipsigis Union, and the Mijikenda Union, all of which served as vehicles of ethnic solidarity and diffuse nationalist sentiments. More expressly political was the age-old KCA. Although it had been banned in 1940, by 1946 the KCA was as alive as ever. Throughout 1945 and 1946 its leaders petitioned the government to have the ban lifted. The government refused. In spite of this the KCA kept its branches functioning. It continued organizing in various parts of the Central Province and the Rift Valley, especially among the embittered squatters.[136] In 1946 the KCA paid for the return passage of its long-absent general secretary from Britain. That man was Jomo Kenyatta, destined to become the first President of independent Kenya.

Up to that time KAU had been muddling along. Its attempts to gain recognition from the colonial government had not been very successful. Its geographical spread was still limited largely to the Central Province, although it established fledgling branches in the Coast, Rift Valley and Western Provinces. It had practically no success in Nyanza, especially in central Nyanza district, the Luo heartland and the home of the Kavirondo Taxpayers and Welfare Association. KAU's leadership was undecisive; even Mathu grew distant from the party. Its attempts to mobilize the educated African elite in government employment, and forge links with the various ethnic associations and those beloved 'masses' of nationalist leaders, had still not borne much fruit. Certainly KAU did not endear itself to squatters when it urged them to sign the very restrictive new labour contracts being forced on them by the settler farmers and the government.

Kenyatta became president of KAU in June 1947, and immediately revived its sagging fortunes. Such was the new enthusiasm that the meeting which elected him collected some Shs.4,565, KAU's largest single contribution in one day. Wherever he went Kenyatta pulled very large crowds. But it became increasingly clear that Kenyatta was no firebrand. His message usually cautioned moderation. This was anathema to young militants such as the '40 Group', composed of ex-soldiers living in Nairobi but originally from Nyeri and Murang'a. The 'masses' were also now too politically roused to appreciate Kenyatta's and KAU's counsels of moderation. So Kenyatta's authority began to weaken, and KAU membership fell. Also, African Legislative Council members, whose numbers had increased, distanced themselves from KAU. Charges that it was a Kikuyu party were heard frequently once again.

Kenyatta had taken many KCA members into KAU, but the KCA apparently did not entirely lose its identity. In fact, it seems that as KAU's national influence ebbed during 1948 and 1949, the KCA revived its underground activities. The underground movement used oathing as an instrument of enhancing members' allegiance to the movement's goals and a means of cementing their solidarity. According to Spencer, centres and forms of oathing changed from 1944 to 1950-1. The final pre-emergency phase and form of oathing 'began in late 1948 and early 1949, with the spread into Nairobi of a new oath reflecting new aims of militancy and violence. By 1951 the initiative had shifted from the conservative Kiambu elders to the Nairobi militants'.[137]

The Nairobi militants were trade unionists led by men like Kubai, president of the EATUC, J.M. Mungai, president of TAWU, and Bildad Kaggia, leader of the Clerks and Commercial Workers' Union. The first two took the oath in 1948, and Kaggia a year or so later. They helped to spread the oath first to chosen trade union leaders, Nairobi taxi drivers and some carefully selected 'criminals' and prostitutes who were to collect any information that might help the movement. Later, mass oathing was introduced and Nairobi taxi drivers helped organize the transportation.[138] In June 1951 the militants took control of KAU's Nairobi branch, with Kubai as branch chairman. KAU was reinvigorated and it entered its most militant and active period. The party extended its influence further afield in the country as branches opened or were revived at the coast, in the Rift Valley and even in Nyanza where Achieng' Aneko opened a KAU branch at Kisumu, although he did not at first call it that.

From this time KAU articulated the traditional demands for African political representation, land reform, improved economic opportunities and abolition of the registration system with greater assertiveness than ever before. And there was more: KAU demanded independence. KAU's first call for independence was made at a joint KAU and East African Indian National Congress chaired by Mathu in April 1950. The moderates, including Kenyatta, were pushed along. When Kubai and his colleagues took over the KAU Nairobi branch they called for independence in three years. The government had no intention of remotely meeting the radical nationalists' demands. In education the much-awaited Beecher Report published in 1949 failed to satisfy demands for the expansion of African education. In 1950 Glancy's Report appeared to cave in to settler opposition for a new registration system to be introduced for all races as promised in 1947 to replace the *kipande* which was only for Africans. And in 1951 Governor Mitchell reneged on his proposal made in October 1950 to increase the number of African and Asian seats in the Legislative Council, again because of settler opposition.

Such intransigence emboldened the resolve of militants to intensify the struggle and made the position of moderates within KAU quite difficult. Leaders like Kenyatta walked a tightrope; any false move and they would fall into the hands of either the government or the radicals and attract the retribution of one or the other. This came home to Kenyatta when the government pressed him to condemn political violence and he did so on a few occasions, only to be warned by the radicals in KAU against going too far. Violence was indeed escalating. Disgruntled peasants and squatters in rural areas were sabotaging crops and farm machinery, maiming and killing settler cattle, refusing to follow government agricultural conservation measures, and village headmen were also being killed. On 7 October 1952, Senior Chief Waruhiu was murdered. About two weeks later, the new governor, Sir Evelyn Baring, declared a state of emergency and 187 KAU leaders, including Kenyatta, Kubai, Kaggia, Mungai and Oneko were arrested.

Conclusion

The colonial crisis had burst into the open. By 1952 the various currents in the Kenyan nationalist movement had converged into an irresistible torrent. Unable to deal with the crisis by itself, the colonial state called upon the imperial state, which reasserted its control, and thereby began the gradual erosion of power for the dominant power bloc in the colonial state, namely, the settlers. The various contradictions in agriculture and industry, the labour control system and politics which had brought the crisis to a head of course did not go away. Under the emergency they took new forms. As new social, economic and political processes were generated, the institutional and class basis of the colonial state was further transformed. The only thing that was certain on that night of 20 October 1952 was that Kenya was entering uncharted and stormy waters.

Notes

1 On the concept of primitive colonial accumulation see R.M.A. van Zwanenberg, *Colonial Capitalism and Labour in Kenya 1919-1939* (Nairobi, 1975); Philip McMichael, 'The concept of primitive accumulation: Lenin's contribution', *Journal of Contemporary Asia* 7(4), 1977; and Jairus Banaji, 'Backward capitalism, primitive accumulation and modes of production', *Journal of Contemporary Asia* 3(4), 1973.

2 See, for instance, A.G. Frank, *Capitalism and Underdevelopment in Latin America*, Monthly Review Press, 1967.

3 See Ian Spencer, 'Settler dominance, agricultural production and the Second World War', *Journal of African History* 21(4), 1980; R.M.A. van Zwanenberg with Anne King, *An Economic History of Kenya and Uganda* (London, 1975); and N. Swainson, *The Development of Corporate Capitalism in Kenya, 1918-1977* (London, 1980).

4 See C.G. Rosberg and J. Nottingham, *The Myth of Mau Mau* (Nairobi, 1966); M. Singh, *History of Kenya's Trade Union Movement to 1952* (Nairobi, 1969); and B. Kaggia, *Roots of Freedom* (Nairobi, 1975).

5 See T. Zeleza, 'African history: the rise and decline of academic tourism', *Ufahamu* 13(1), 1983; and A.J. Temu and B. Swai, *Historians and Africanist History: a critique* (London, 1981).

6 Harold Macmillan, *The Blast of War 1939-1945* (London, 1967).

7 *East African Standard*, 8 September 1939.

8 *East African Standard*, 1 September 1939.

9 Governor Moore to Dawe, 6 June 1940. CO 533/517 38077.

10 Sir A. Dawe's Memorandum on a federal solution for East Africa, 27 July 1942. CO 967/57.

11 Macmillan's memo, counterproposal to Dawe, 15 August 1942. CO 957/57.

12 Macmillan, *Blast of War*, ch. 7.

13 Spencer, 'Settler dominance', 503.

14 J. Flint, 'Last chance for the White Man's Country: constitutional plans for Kenya and East Africa, 1938-1943', paper presented to History Seminar, Dalhousie University, February 1983, 14-15.

15 Circular telegram, Secretary of State, 15 September 1939, CO 533/503.

16 See O.J.E. Shiroya, 'The impact of World War II on Kenya: the role of ex-servicemen in Kenyan nationalism', Ph.D. Dissertation, Michigan State University, 1968.

17 See A. Clayton and D.C. Savage, *Government and Labour in Kenya 1895-1963* (London, 1974), 232.

18 See, for instance, the 'returns of conscript labour', Governor Moore to Secretary of State, 20 April, 24 July, 4 December 1944, CO 533 38091/12.

19 For details see P.T. Zeleza, 'Dependent capitalism and the making of the Kenyan working class during the colonial period', Ph.D. Dissertation, Dalhousie University, 1982, 190-2.

20 G.M. Rennie (Chief Secretary) to Seel, 5 March 1943, CO 533 38091/2.

21 Governor Moore to Secretary of State, 12 June 1944, CO 533 38091/12.

22 Some of the relevant correspondence can be found in Kenya National Archives (KNA) Labour 9/10.
23 See *Sunday Post*, 15 June 1941; and correspondence in KNA Labour 2/64.
24 *Labour Department Annual Report*, 1950.
25 See van Zwanenberg with King, *Economic History*, 44.
26 Spencer, 'Settler dominance', 504.
27 See E. Huxley, *No Easy Way: a history of the Kenya Farmers' Association and Unga Ltd.* (Nairobi, 1957), 140-1.
28 R.M.A. van Zwanenberg, 'Neocolonialism and the origin of the national bourgeoisie in Kenya between 1940 and 1973', *Journal of Eastern African Research and Development* 4(2), 1974, 164.
29 Macmillan, *Blast of War*, 174-5; Also see van Zwanenberg with King, *Economic History*, 215.
30 See *Food Shortage Commission of Enquiry Report* (Nairobi, 1944).
31 Spencer, 'Settler dominance', 505. Also see *East African Standard*, 8, 11, 14, 22 and 25 August 1942, on the maize control controversy.
32 See *Food Shortage Commission of Enquiry Evidence*, KNA Agr. 3.
33 Huxley, *No Easy Way*, 140.
34 *Food Shortage Commission of Enquiry Report*, 23.
35 *Ibid.*, 29.
36 *Ibid.*, 27.
37 *Ibid.*, 29.
38 *Ibid.*
39 *Ibid.*, 23.
40 *Ibid.*, 29.
41 *Ibid.*, 4-6.
42 See relevant correspondence between Governor Moore and Secretary of State; and CO minutes between 1943 and 1944 in CO 533 38091/12.
43 Van Zwanenberg, 'Neocolonialism'; Swainson, *Corporate Capitalism*, Chapter 5.
44 G. Kitching, *Class and Economic Change in Kenya: the making of an African petite bourgeoisie, 1905-1970* (New Haven, 1980), 130-5.
45 *Ibid.*, 146-8.
46 *Ibid.*, 149-50.
47 M.P.K. Sorrenson, *Land Reform in Kikuyu Country* (London, 1967), 56.
48 See *Kiambu District Annual Report*, 1945.
49 Tomkinson to Chief Secretary, 14 May 1945, KNO LO LND 30/2/2.
50 See *East African Standard*, 28 April 1939.
51 *East African Standard*, 26 August 1942.
52 Swainson, *Corporate Capitalism*, 104.
53 Macmillan, *Blast of War*, 179. For more details on American attitudes towards the British Empire at this time see W.R. Louis, *Imperialism at Bay: the role of the US in the decolonization of the British Empire* (London, 1977).
54 Swainson, *Corporate Capitalism*, 125.
55 P.T. Zeleza, 'Dependent capitalism', 198-206.
56 *Food Shortage Commission of Enquiry Report*, 61.
57 *Report of Committee of Inquiry Into Labour Unrest at Mombasa*, Nairobi, 1945 (also known as Phillips Report).
58 Governor Moore to Secretary of State, 19 September 1943, CO 533 38091/12.
59 President, Nairobi Chamber of Commerce to Chairman, Trade Disputes Tribunal, 30 October 1942, KNA Labour 2/14. Also see Phillips Report, 67-8.
60 The statement was made by the General Manager of the KUR & H and quoted by the Phillips Report.

61 V.S. Cooke, Member of Trade Disputes Tribunal, 8 November 1942, KNA Labour 2/14.
62 The Phillips Report recommended amendment of the customs tariff.
63 See P.T. Zeleza, 'Dependent capitalism', 216-20.
64 Phillips Report, 66; *East African Standard,* 7 March 1945.
65 See relevant correspondence between Governor Moore and Secretary of State in 1941, in CO 533 526 38091/6; and correspondence on labour in towns, in KNA Labour 2/64.
66 See Committee Appointed to Examine African Housing for Government Employees in Nairobi, 30 May 1942, No. B/HO/2/9/1/1/28. KNA Labour 3/3.
67 Shiroya, 'Ex-Servicemen', 36.
68 Director of Intelligence and Security to Chief Secretary, 13 December 1942, KNA Labour 9/59.
69 P.T. Zeleza, 'Dependent capitalism', 226-36.
70 Singh, *Trade Union Movement,* 114.
71 P.T. Zeleza, 'Dependent capitalism', 237-41.
72 See Clement Lubembe, *The Inside Labour Movement in Kenya* (Nairobi, 1968), 61.
73 G.S. Were, 'Politics, religion and nationalism in Western Kenya', in B.A. Ogot, ed., *Politics and Nationalism in Colonial Kenya* (Nairobi, 1972).
74 R.M. Mambo, 'Colonial rule and political activity among the Mijikenda of Kenya's coast to 1960', History Staff Seminar, Kenyatta University College, November, 1980.
75 D.A. Seidenberg, *Uhuru and the Kenya Indians* (London, 1983).
76 J. Spencer, *The Kenya African Union* (London, 1985), 116.
77 J.R. Rockler, *Mathu of Kenya* (Stanford, 1976).
78 D.J. Morgan, *The Official History of Colonial Development* (New Jersey, 1980), vol.V, 89.
79 *Ibid.,* vol.II, 4-17.
80 *Ibid.,* 177; vol.IV, ch.4.
81 D.W. Nabudere, *The Political Economy of Imperialism* (London, 1977), parts 4 and 5.
82 Morgan, *Official History,* vol.I, ch.5.
83 G. Padmore, *Africa: Britain's Third Empire* (New York, 1949), 168.
84 Morgan, *Official History,* vol.IV, 118-20.
85 *Ibid.,* chapter 5; and vol.I, ch.6.
86 *Ibid.,* vol.II, chapter 5; and vol.IV, ch.4.
87 *Ibid.,* vol.II, 60.
88 *Ibid.,* vol.I, 201.
89 *Ibid.,* vol.II, 59.
90 *Ibid.,* vol.V, 311.
91 Walter Rodney, *How Europe Underdeveloped Africa* (London, 1972), 188.
92 *Kenya Colony Annual Report,* Government Printer, Nairobi, 1947, p.4.
93 Van Zwanenberg with King, *Economic History,* 45-7; L.W. Cone and J.F. Lipscomb, eds., *The History of Kenya Agriculture* (Nairobi, 1972).
94 *Report of the Settlement Schemes Committee,* Government Printer, Nairobi, 1944, 9.
95 *Labour Department Annual Report,* 1952, 11.
96 Uasin Gishu District Council Minutes, 24 June 1942, KNA Labour 9/9.
97 See KNA Labour 9/9, Labour 9/304 and Labour 9/309.
98 Divisional Forest Office to Conservator of Forests, 19 July 1947, KNA Labour 9/10.
99 See *Annual Reports, 1942-52,* for Trans-Nzoia, Uasin Gishu, Nakuru, Naivasha and Kiambu.
100 Uasin Gishu District Council Minutes, 1 May 1947, KNA Labour 9/9.
101 P.T. Zeleza, 'Dependent capitalism', 269-70.
102 *Report of Committee on Agricultural Credit for Africans,* Government Printer, Nairobi, 1950, 24-5.
103 M.P.K. Sorrenson, *Land Reform,* 60.
104 *Central Province Annual Report,* Government Printer, Nairobi, 1950, 11.

105 *East African Standard,* 7 June 1949; also see *Kenya Colony Annual Reports, 1947,* 42-3; and *1949,* 33, 43-4.

106 A. Amsden, *International Firms and Labour in Kenya, 1945-70* (London, 1971), 50.

107 Van Zwanenberg with King, *Economic History,* 133.

108 See papers in M. Fransman, ed., *Industry and Accumulation in Africa* (London, 1982) .

109 Swainson, *Corporate Capitalism,* 124-30.

110 *Ibid.,* 110-11.

111 *Ibid.,* 123.

112 Amsden, *International Firms and Labour,* 51.

113 See Sessional Paper 7 of 1945.

114 Shiroya, 'Ex-servicemen,' 115-19; *Labour Department Annual Report 1948,* 19.

115 *Reported Employment and Wages in Kenya, 1948-60,* East African High Commission, East Africa Statistical Department, Kenya Unit, August 1961.

116 See van Zwanenberg with King, *Economic History,* ch.13; *Labour Department Annual Report 1952,* 21.

117 P.T. Zeleza, 'Dependent capitalism', 288-9.

118 *Ibid.,* 303-17.

119 *East African Salaries Commission,* 1947, paragraphs 73-97.

120 *Labour Department Annual Report 1952,* 8.

121 *Pattern of Income, Expenditure and Consumption of African Labourers in Nairobi,* Oct-Nov. 1950, East African Statistical Department, February, 1951.

122 *East African Royal Commission 1953-1955 Report,* Cmd. 9475 of 1955, p.33.

123 Kitching, *Class and Economic Change,* 274.

124 *African Labour Efficiency Survey,* Colonial Research 3, edited by C.H. Northcott, 1949, 66.

125 *Report on the Economic and Social Background of Mombasa Labour Disputes,* by H.S. Booker and N.M. Devril, 1947, unpublished.

126 Minutes, Labour Commissioners' Conference, Dar-es-Salaam, June 1949, KNA Labour 10/92. For details see P.T. Zeleza, 'Dependent capitalism', 317-25.

127 Acting Labour Commissioner to Chief Secretary, 10 July 1947, KNA Labour 3/3.

128 P.E.D. Wilson, 'Labour conditions generally in the PWD with special reference to housing', 16 November 1947, KNA Labour 3/3.

129 *African Labour Efficiency Survey,* 76.

130 *Report on African Housing in Townships and Trading Centres,* by E.A. Vasey, 1950, 4.

131 See Statement on Labour Policy by the Labour Commissioner, Hyde Clark, KNA Labour 9/2.

132 *African Labour Efficiency Survey,* 83-116.

133 P.T. Zeleza, 'Dependent capitalism', 327-49.

134 See correspondence in CO 533/544 38091/6 part 1; CO 533 545 1947; KNA Labour 3/12-17; reports and returns monthly intelligence in KNA Labour 2/67; and press reports of the *East African Standard* and *Mombasa Times,* 14-25 January 1947.

135 Statement issued by Central Council of the EATUC; see Singh, *Trade Union Movement,* 253-4.

136 Spencer, 'Settler dominance', 173-8.

137 *Ibid.,* 210.

138 *Ibid.,* 208.

6 Nationalism and decolonization, 1947-1963

Wunyabari Maloba

I

The period of decolonization in Africa, stretching from 1956 to 1964, was about the most optimistic period on the continent in recent times. It was a period that held high hopes for the masses and the elite alike in Africa. Having been kept under foreign rule for so long, with consequent loss of pride and initiative, it was generally believed that political independence would be the magic cure of all of Africa's problems. In retrospect, cynics and objective observers alike might be tempted to dismiss such excesses of hope as naive and unrealistic. This would be unfair. At the time when these hopes were entertained, the masses genuinely expected a radical change in their lifestyles and an increase of available opportunities to advance, to develop, to move forward in security and stability. Army coups, hunger and drought, economic mismanagement and foreign debts, political repression and detention without trial had yet to show their ugly heads under local management and direction. Political repression was familiar to many Africans as the usual weapon employed with ruthless efficiency by colonialists in their bid to stifle the growth of nationalism. It must have been the hope of many on the continent, that independence would relegate such a practice to the ugly past and that in the future independence would indeed mean freedom. As can be seen, these were hopes, wishes; they did not in most cases constitute a programme of action or elaborate ideological pronouncements. This was true in spite of the many promises made by African political parties prior to independence. How had this freedom been won or attained?

This chapter addresses itself to this crucial question of decolonization with particular emphasis on its evolution in Kenya. It would be both unrealistic and unfair to discuss the decolonization of Kenya without paying any attention to the international dimension of the dissolution of European empires after the Second World War. It should be remarked that decolonization, like colonialism, is an emotive topic. Decolonization is dissolution of empire, and it cannot be conceivably thought that this was the result of magnanimity on the part of the imperialists. It has been alleged that in the case of Britain, the British people knew very little about the empire, that they were ignorant of the details of the empire and by implication were not sorry to have it dissolved. This can hardly be true. Even if the common man in Britain did not know the names of all the British colonies, there can be little doubt that the value of these colonies to Britain was a well-established fact in British informed and ruling circles – the circles that controlled the economic and political destinies of both the colonial subjects and the common man in Britain. No plebiscite had been taken in Britain before colonization and certainly none was taken to dissolve the empire. Appropriate explanations were found and fed to the public. The empire made Britain 'Great Britain', a title whose employment had both economic and political implications on international balance of power and prestige. After listening to all the arguments about the religious factor, the civilizing mission and the spread of law and order in the colonies, it is necessary to remember that 'colonialism should be looked at for exactly what it is; a money making business. . .'.[1] Colonialism was serious business, it was certainly not a peripheral part of British society; especially its economics, politics and international relations. Why then did Britain undertake to decolonize most of its empire after the Second World War? The portrayal by imperialist historians of decolonization as a 'pre-emptive policy developed in London or Paris during the Second World War for a variety of reasons, but not in response to the mounting nationalist tide in Africa itself'[2] is generally not true.

The African nationalist looks at decolonization as the regaining of independence lost during the scramble for Africa. It is therefore inevitable that an analysis from the nationalist should place more emphasis on the African local initiative, which in one gigantic upheaval threw out the hated colonialists. In this regard more emphasis is placed on instances of resistance towards colonialism, and however dispersed these may be in historical time, they are all seen to be organically linked as contributions towards the ultimate decolonization. In some respects this is true. Colonialism was never a popular rule and it would be tempting to look at any sabotage, work stoppage or defiance as being diverse expressions of nationalism. This stretches the argument a bit far. For the purposes of this chapter, we shall limit our discussion to the forces in both the colonies and the metropolitan country that converged to give way to political freedom after the Second World War.

II

After the Second World War, Britain was an exhausted country. It had suffered immense material loss during the war. Indeed its war effort had to be greatly aided by the USA. This aid continued after the war in the now famous Marshall Plan, a gigantic economic aid plan for the reconstruction of war-torn Europe and its dislodged economies. British dependence on American aid during and after the war inevitably entailed some concessions being made to the American anti-colonial sentiments, especially under Roosevelt. The American view was that they were not pouring their economic and material resources into the war to save empires for Europeans. The salvaging of empires intact had economic and political implications which USA found objectionable. In particular there was the question of economic spheres of influence, whereby colonies were assured markets for British or French goods. So long as empires persisted, American companies could not hope to penetrate the colonies effectively for investment and other extractive activities. Ochieng' puts the point rather strongly when he says, 'America, which emerged from the Second World War as the richest nation on earth, and with a glut of capital, was looking for investment possibility all over the world and this was being frustrated by European colonies.'[3] American pressure on Europeans to decolonize need not have arisen solely because of a 'glut of capital'. American industry was certainly the most vibrant after the war and the US government felt that having emerged as the strongest power after the war it needed to capitalize on that strength. It certainly was not going to pretend to Europeans that they were equals. The American ascendancy effectively meant the subordination of Europeans and their peculiar interests. What the United States needed was the opening up of markets overseas and the winning of as much of the world as possible for *Pax Americana,* basically an informal economic empire that arose out of the ashes of the Second World War. This American pressure was not ignored in Britain. Roger Louis and Ronald Robinson state that 'as the danger from Washington reached its peak in 1943-1944, the Colonial Office succeeded in persuading the British Treasury to contribute on a large scale to African welfare for the first time'.[4] This in effect meant more capital being channelled into the colonies for welfare services than ever before – largely in response to American pressure but also because of an increasingly vocal group of 'British liberals, humanitarians, and socialists. . .'[5] The American pressure therefore pushed the British almost unwillingly into increasing their capital expenditure on the welfare of the colonized masses. Colonialism was being given a face lift. The results were not adequate. Although American pressure on European colonial empires weakened as the cold war became a major preoccupation of Washington in international relations after 1945, it did not mark the end of it. The Europeans could not afford to ignore this pressure. This alone could not of course lead to decolonization, but it was crucial in that it questioned the existence of colonialism at the highest and most critical level of international relations. The USSR, for reasons obviously different from those of the USA, consistently criticized the whole concept of colonialism. Lenin and others that followed him looked on colonialism as plunder,[6] and after 1945 the USSR was in a much stronger position to have its opinions on this issue listened to with concern in the corridors of power in Europe. Indeed the rise of any nationalist party in the colonies was suspected of having ideological ties to Moscow even when none were possible. It can be argued that the fear of the spread of communism became an American obsession after 1945 and with it the fear that protracted colonial struggles might lead to its spread in former colonies. The international political climate after 1945 did not favour the existence of colonialism.

Besides, it must be noted that the exhaustion of Britain economically and politically after the war seriously limited the possibilities of endless military intervention in the colonies. There was the war in Malaya, and Kenya, and the Suez Canal crisis, but for how long could Britain afford to militarily intervene overseas? Military intervention was an expensive alternative.

It would be inaccurate to attribute decolonization wholly to the strength and efficacy of the two factors already mentioned; namely British economic decline after 1945, and Soviet (but more fundamentally for Britain, American) anti-colonial sentiments and pressure. These were important factors: they ensured that the imperial powers realized the limitations of their power and influence in the new international balance of power. They alerted the imperial powers to the perils of possible stubbornness to hold on to colonies in an age when there was immense international pressure to decolonize. Active colonialism, we might add, had 'gone out of fashion'; it was now risky and expensive. This does not mean that imperial exploitation of colonies was not profitable at this time. The value of colonies to post-war Britain was even more crucial than before. What had made colonialism expensive was the emergence of restive and increasingly politically conscious populations in the colonies. Although most troubles in each colony could be contained (as happened in Malaya and Kenya), there was the danger that such troubles might become a marked and permanent feature of post-war colonialism, necessitating perpetual British military intervention. This prospect, together with the possibility that such continuous warfare might cost the British the 'friendship' of their colonial subjects and thereby interfere with the flow of commerce, caused a radical change in outlook in British imperial policy. The point to be stressed here is that there would have been no decolonization at the time it occurred without sustained nationalist resistance to colonialism in the colonies. Although, to be sure, this resistance was not uniform in intensity, those occasions when Britain faced sustained resistance were serious, expensive and complicated. The international political climate after the Second World War prepared favourable ground in which to sow the seeds of nationalism. Nationalist agitation accelerated the rate of decolonization. Without it there might still have been decolonization, although occurring at a much slower rate; and it is probable that it would have taken a long time. In the international political climate that prevailed after the war, decolonization proved to be a shrewd move by Britain to divest itself of formal control over its colonies while retaining immense influence through cultural and economic links and especially through the Commonwealth. Decolonization can therefore be explained as being largely the outcome of the convergence of international forces and local nationalist politics on a given colony. In this fatal convergence of forces for the empire, local initiative played a crucial role which must not be underestimated. It is important at this stage to illustrate this point with examples from Malaya and Ghana.

III

In 1941, Japan invaded Malaya and defeated the British in one of the most humiliating military blows to British prestige as an imperial power. Japan continued to rule Malaya alongside other countries in South-East Asia until 1945, when the USA dropped atomic bombs over Hiroshima and Nagasaki, forcing Japan to suddenly but expectedly surrender. Before the defeat of Japan, the local populations in South-East Asia waged varying 'wars' of resistance against Japanese occupation. In themselves alone, such wars were never a military threat to Japan's hegemony over the area. They however ensured that Japan's rule was not a peaceful episode. Normally it was Japan's style of government, consistently ruthless, which turned the local populations against it. In Malaya after the British defeat, the most sustained opposition to Japanese rule was provided by the Malaya Communist Party. It was the most organized group and had a military wing, the Malayan People's Anti-Japanese Army (MPAJA). MPAJA was supported in its war-time activities of resistance by the British. Naturally at the end of the war in 1945, the Malayan Communist Party (MCP) hoped that the British would include the party in its post-war reconstruction of the colony's administration. It has been alleged that in 1945 the MCP could have seized power in Malaya if it wanted to, for it was the most organized party in the colony and it also had its own army — the MPAJA. That the MCP did not undertake to seize power is perhaps a reflection of its trust in constitutional politics which it hoped Britain would enact after the war. These hopes were soon disappointed. 'MCP was rapidly disillusioned regarding British post-war intentions. No immediate plans were made for the introduction of representative politics nor for basic economic and social reform. Indeed the British envisaged a very gradual advance towards independence.'[7] MCP soon realized that the major thrust of British post-war policy in Malaya was aimed at excluding it from the centre of activities in the trade unions. But it is here that the MCP immediately confronted British intransigence and hostility. Trade union activity was closely controlled and in the end the Pan-Malayan Federation of Trade Unions was destroyed. Backed by the colonial government's policies and decrees, employers in Malaya from 1946 to 1948 sought to 'enforce strict discipline and terms of employment on workers'.[8] It is significant that 'after 1947 comparatively few wage increases were granted and virtually none as the result of union negotiation or strike pressure'.[9] In such repressive circumstances, which also left 'the overwhelming majority of the Chinese and Indian population as aliens',[10] as a result of the withdrawal of the 'liberal citizenship proposals of Malayan Union', the MCP felt driven into considering an armed uprising. Let it be emphasized that the leadership of the MCP was most reluctant to enter into an armed uprising, as can be seen by their refusal to take advantage of their organizational and military superiority in 1945. The British colonial government's hostility meant that the MCP could boast of very few victories and it paid heavily for this in the decline of membership to the party. Even for those of its members who remained faithful, the MCP found that their enthusiasm was low. On 18 June 1948, a state of emergency was declared in Malaya. The MCP had hoped to create a 'Communist People's Republic of Malaya'. The rebels aimed at breaking down the existing machinery of government as well as creating economic chaos. An immediate objective was to create limited areas of Communist control from which further conquests could be made until the whole country had been gained. The attacks on Europeans were part of the policy of bringing the tin and rubber industry to a standstill, and at the same time driving out British personnel altogether.[11]

The communist fighting forces did not manage to control 'a liberated area', but they caused a lot of problems for the British administrations in both London and the colony. It was an expensive exercise involving a lot of troops, drawn not only from Britain but also from other Commonwealth countries. This was resistance to colonialism and capitalism by a local communist party. It was a development which the British colonialists could not tolerate at all. Even if in principle Britain had come to accept the reality of self-determination or independence for the colonies, it was not prepared to allow, and never allowed, its former colonies to be taken over by communist nationalists. The strategy was always to steer nationalism away from communism. In Malaya's case we see this point again very well developed. After the war, the British government prepared a new constitutional framework for Malaya, which came to be popularly known as the Malayan Union. The major focus of the Malayan Union was to create a more centralized administration over the colony, while in the process tightening British overlordship over the sultans of the various Malayan states. The state administrations were in this constitution completely subordinated to the central administration. It is not surprising that as soon as the details of the constitution were known there was considerable protest from the people in Malaya. Leading these protests were not the communists or radical nationalists, but rather they were the traditional rulers – the sultans – and other conservative elements in Malayan society. The new constitution aroused the anger of the conservative segment of Malayan society. This was the most powerful segment, and the resultant nationalism was essentially conservative nationalism. Faced with communist rebellion after 1948, the British felt that it was in the immediate and future interests of the empire to cooperate with this traditional conservative nationalism. A new party was formed in 1946 to lead the Malayan people in their opposition against the Malayan Union. The party was called the United Malay Nationalist Organization (UMNO). As a result of these protests, a new constitution was drawn up in 1948. It is significant that this new constitution was the result of direct participation by UMNO and the sultans, presided over by Malcolm MacDonald, the commissioner-general for South-East Asia. Britain had gone out of its way to seek the cooperation of the conservative nationalists, who were to it naturally more preferable than communist nationalists. From 1946 until Malaya's independence on 30 August 1957, Malayan nationalism was led largely by the sultans, their relatives or other conservatives. When a Malayan delegation went to London in 1956 to negotiate for independence, 'they met with little opposition to their demands. The British Government had no intention of delaying independence in Malaya with the risk of provoking the breakdown of all the cooperation which had been achieved to end the Emergency.'[12]

Ghana did not have a Communist Party nor was there any armed rebellion as was the case in Malaya. However, as in Malaya, the evolution of its nationalism and subsequent independence can only be sensibly explained if due attention is paid to its internal history. In Ghana's case the crucial years, at least insofar as this chapter is concerned, are from 1946 to 1952. In 1946, Ghana got a new constitution replacing the one formulated in 1925. The memorable aspect of the 1946 constitution was that the elected African members of the Legislative Council were in the majority over the ex-officio members. 'The elected members were . . . in a decisive majority over the ex-officio and nominated members together: eighteen against twelve, a stage of political advance which no other colonial territory had hitherto reached.'[13] This constitution came to be known as the Burns Constitution, named after Sir Alan Burns, who as governor had been instrumental in devising it. It was considered at the time as a very 'imaginative constitution'. The constitution however did not confer self-government to Ghana. Although in the majority in the Legislative Council, the African members

> had no responsibility for making Government policy, only for criticising the policy which the officials had laid before them. The elected members had of course the power of the purse, and in the last resort they could, in theory, refuse to vote the estimates. In fact, however, their powers of this nature were limited by the powers which the Burns constitution reserved for the Governor . . .'[14]

In spite of this 'imaginative constitution', criticisms of colonial policies and colonial administration continued to come from Africans. In fact these criticisms became more sustained and virulent after 1947. This state of affairs had more to do with economics than with politics, although in a colonial context the separation between these two can sometimes be artificial.

At this time in Ghana, cocoa, which was and is still the country's chief export crop, was 'smitten by a new disease called, from its most conspicuous symptom, swollen shoot'.[15] It spread rapidly and it was feared that it might damage the cocoa crop altogether. It is the remedy for these tragic events that aroused the anger of rural peasant farmers and even large African farmers against the colonial state. The colonial administration's prescription to the farmers was that they had to cut down all diseased trees. This was drastic and naturally aroused resentment and suspicion from the rural population. The rural masses looked at the directive as a deliberate effort by the colonial administration to destroy them and their economic welfare. While this agricultural problem had not yet been resolved, there also arose the problem of food prices in the towns. Food and other commodities cost a lot of money in towns in the post-Second World War period. There was inflation and it hurt the urban workers severely. What, however, made the colonial state a target of African anger and revolt was that it was identified as being linked to both of these unpleasant and intolerable issues – the destruction of cocoa crops and exorbitant prices for goods and commodities in the cities.

> The government knowing that the problem of scarcity and high prices was world-wide, felt that there was little or nothing which it could do in the Gold Coast to solve it. When the supplies improved, prices would fall; and the public must wait for that to happen. It considered the problem of scarcity and high prices to be a purely commercial problem, concerning the shopkeeper and his customers only. It did not see how dangerous its own position was. Many people assumed that, as a foreign government, it must of necessity be in league with foreign merchants.[16]

Added to this there was also the problem of the frustration felt by the local citizens who had recently served as soldiers in the Second World War, fighting for Britain. Now most of them were being demobilized and they felt frustrated over their benefits, especially over 'pensions and resettlement and other grievances peculiar to them'. As a result of all these grievances,

> In February 1948, the Gold Coast erupted in terrifying violence. Riots, which first flared up in Accra, quickly spread to all other major towns. Mobs made vicious attacks on European stores and offices, as well as shops and homes of Indian and Syrian traders. This outburst of arson, violence and looting, with sombre racial overtones, took the British administration almost completely by surprise.[17]

The surprise must have been connected to the 1946 constitution, which although 'imaginative', was now found to be no solution to the colony's economic and political problems. Indeed in the commission of enquiry's analysis of causes and the recommended remedies, a deliberate effort was made to link economic to political problems, in itself a rare admission on the part of British colonial officials at this time. The commission of enquiry found that the rioters had genuine grievances, among which were 'discontent among ex-servicemen; political frustration among educated men who regarded the Burns Constitution as inadequate; the concentration of economic power in European and Syrian hands; high prices; unequal distribution of scarce consumer goods over the country; the cutting out of diseased cocoa; and the housing shortage'.[18] These are essentially economic problems, other than the frustration felt by the educated elite over the Burns Constitution, which is indeed political. However, in its recommendations, the commission of enquiry urged among other things that further constitutional reforms were crucial. It did not curb the growth of constitutional nationalism, it merely wanted it controlled, and if this was done, the hope was that this would avert the occurrence of further riots like those of 1948. As a result of these riots, which clearly demonstrated a loss of trust by Africans in the colonial state, there was an accelerated advance in nationalism and demands for self-government became common. The British government, in response to these local political pressures and acting against the background of 1948, appointed another committee to advise it on further constitutional changes. The result was the Coussey Report of 1949, written by 'an all African committee under the chairmanship of Mr Justice J.H. Coussey'.[19] Unlike the Burns Constitution, the Coussey Report recommended a much more forthright inclusion of Africans in the administration of Ghana. The Africans were to be involved more in the formulation and execution of policies, these policies thereby being seen as responsive to African demands. This new emphasis on African participation was aimed at making the colonial administration less remote and more in touch with Africans, a move which would make the government 'responsive to less forceful expressions of public feelings than a trade boycott'.[20] Of course it is known that even the Coussey Report did not satisfy the African demand for self-government. It was to Nkrumah's credit that he understood this underlying hunger for freedom. He exploited it, like any other politician would, and demanded in 1950, 'self-government now'. In the general strike called in January 1950, Kwame Nkrumah tried to put more pressure on the colonial administration to grant more constitutional reforms. After the inevitable imprisonment, Kwame Nkrumah emerged in 1952 as the country's most dominant political personality and his party, the CPP, which had 'insisted on self-government now' as the country's largest and best organized party. Indeed the story of Ghana after 1950 becomes all too familiar. It culminated in Ghana's self-government and Nkrumah being named prime minister in March, 1952. Independence was to follow in 1957.

The illustrations from Ghana and Malaya demonstrate that even when decolonization had been accepted as inevitable, this acceptance alone would not lead to decolonization in the colonies; there had to be local demands for independence. Almost invariably the story started as demands for reforms within the framework of the colonial state and later there were agitations for more fundamental constitutional reforms aimed at transferring political power to the local nationalists.

IV

After the government's triumph over local resistance against colonialism in Kenya, there continued to exist within the colony feelings and sentiments of resistance and hatred against the newly imposed colonial state and the economic and social order that it defended fervently. Colonialism was rule by coercion, and even when it found local collaborators and administrators, it still remained an alien coercive political and economic system with no local mandate. It was essentially a political system maintained into being by the maxim gun. In Kenya, there was the added complication that it was a settler colony. The fact that Kenya was, in terms of settler population, the smallest settler colony in Africa,[21] did not make much difference in terms of the legislation enacted and colonial policies adopted to enforce settler colonialism. Chief among the needs of the settlers, other than land, was labour. It is not my intention to offer an analysis of settler colonialism and labour policies in colonial Kenya, since such an analysis has been done in the previous chapters and is found in recent studies.[22] What needs to be emphasized here is that African protest movements in Kenya were in large measure reactions to the punitive economic and political policies of the colonial state. Avowedly racist, the colonial state in Kenya from the initial stages discounted African contributions to the economic development of the colony.[23] Africans were to provide labour needed to develop settler farms and government labour needs. In later years, Africans were to be faulted by both the government and the settlers for their laziness and primitivity and little attention was paid to the fact that the symbols of progress in the colony and later the country were invariably the results of African labour given under duress for very minimal wages, and certainly no gratitude.

The protest movements in Kenya arose first in those areas that had undergone profound social and economic transformation under colonialism. This transformation involved more direct involvement in the colonial cash economy, and exposure to Christianity and literacy. Involvement in the cash economy was basically through the supply of labour. Mission education produced in central Kenya and in Nyanza groups of literate Africans. Because these areas were integrated in the colonial economy as suppliers of labour, markets, and profitable 'hunting grounds' for missionaries, they produced the initial protest movements against colonialism. What should be emphasized here is that the initial protest movements were not national in focus or in constituency. These were local movements, addressing themselves to local issues. They arose out of local outrage and frustration over specific grievances; in most cases these grievances were economic. This was in many respects expected. As the colonial state tightened its grip on Kenya after 1914, tribes were generally administered separately from each other. Kenya was then a very rural society with very limited means of inter-tribal communication. 'British administration stabilized boundaries, recognizing each tribe as a separate entity through a system of tribal reserves. These units became the focal point of administration. Government policies in, for example, law, primary and intermediate education and local government had the effect of strengthening tribal loyalties. . .'[24] The administrative isolation of tribes meant in effect that there were limited chances of the members of various tribes developing a national awareness. National awareness, or nationalism even in a rudimentary form, was slow in developing in Kenya. In this context the protest movements that arose from 1920 to 1940 were basically tribally based with specific grievances to be redressed. It would be premature to talk of supra-ethnic nationalism.

The grievances that gave rise to the East African Association were economic. Reacting to economic pressures brought into being by the depression, European employers in Kenya sought to drastically cut the wages of African workers. This cut in wages, it was argued then, was a sound economic move to assure themselves of profit even in the depths of depression. The African response was predictably hostile. Low wages had been one of their perennial complaints.

When, therefore, European employers proposed to cut African wages by a third, the Africans in Nairobi under Harry Thuku formed the East African Association. It is alleged to have had as members many Africans from outside Kenya, most notably from Uganda and Nyasaland. There can be little doubt, however, that its membership was overwhelmingly Kikuyu. The EAA did not just concern itself with wages, but widened its list of grievances to include dissatisfaction over forced labour, and the *kipande* system. Later, when Harry Thuku formed the Young Kikuyu Association partially in response to the formation of the Kikuyu Association by chiefs and moderates under missionary influence, he again used the new organization to voice African (Kikuyu) dissatisfaction over low wages, forced labour, land alienation, and the *kipande* system. It should be noted that these were basically the same grievances that the more conservative Kikuyu Association had on its agenda. The difference between YKA and KA was one of style, leadership and pace. The Young Kikuyu Association under Thuku appeared to want a speedy resolution to the grievances and even went as far as sending a telegram to the Colonial Office in London. Grievances over labour recruitment and wages also inspired the formation of the Young Kavirondo Association. This organization also expressed great disapproval of the *kipande* system. The causes of the formation of all these bodies may have been similar, but they were crucial because they were local. The local people related themselves to these grievances; they were not imaginary. The next task would have been to forge a trans-tribal organization to form a national platform for articulation of these problems. This did not happen. Indeed after 1922, local problems continued to occupy the local elders and elite. The protest movements were until 1944 basically fragmentary, small, moderate and weak. We did not have anything close to mass nationalism. Even at the height of cultural nationalism in Kikuyuland from 1928 to 1930, the emphasis was on preserving Kikuyu cultural traditions within Christianity. Those who broke away mainly from the Church of Scotland Mission (CSM) over the question of female circumcision were trying to hold on to what they considered crucial cultural attributes of the tribe. They tried within an almost impossible situation to maintain an honourable position in colonialism. They were not rejecting Christianity nor even colonialism for that matter; what they were expressing was a deeply held desire to have their customs respected by the new evangelizing culture. They were asking a fundamental question: how can one be an African and a Christian at the same time? Like all other movements before it, cultural nationalism in Kikuyuland, which gave birth to independent churches and school systems, arose out of specific local grievances. It did not develop into a countrywide protest movement.

The Kikuyu Central Association, formed in 1924, has continued to be a source of great historical interest. This is in large part because of its alleged militancy and the supposedly uncompromising positions that it took with regard to colonial policies in Kikuyuland at this time. Its aim had of course been to give a united voice of Kikuyu opposition. This united voice did not emerge at all, but continued to be an elusive goal, as subsequent politicians were later to find. However by the 1920s and 1930s KCA and its members continued to be seen as the uncompromising voice of resistance to colonial policies. When in the 1930s other protest movements arose among the Kamba, Taita and Luyia, they all looked to KCA for inspiration. The Kikuyu Central Association's chief grievance was of course land alienation. To this main source of contention were added the subsidiary, although equally significantly resented, policies governing labour procurement, taxation and racial discrimination.

The Ukamba Members Association arose in 1938 as an organization formed to protest an impending government destocking decree. By this decree cattle from Ukambani were to supply the meat factory at Athi River, which opened in 1938. Later the government reconsidered its decision over the forced sale of cattle, but only after about 2,000 Kamba had marched and camped in Nairobi with a protest petition for the governor. In this instance, a misguided government policy was halted as a result of communal protest. The Taita Hills Association, formed in 1939, arose largely to protest lack of land for expansion of the population. The alienation of large areas below the Taita Hills for a 'European sisal plantation' seemed to foreclose the possibility of the Taita expanding into the valleys below the hills. It is as if their 'next frontier' had been robbed from them. It is also noticeable that the Kikuyu Central Association gave a lot of strategic help to the Taita Hills Association. As in the Ukamba Members Association, the cooperation between the Taita Hills Association and the Kikuyu Central Association was largely in the realm of ideas and organizational strategies. At no point did these organizations hope to join to form one national organization. The major focus of protest was local grievances over the implementation of colonial policies in specific areas. KCA, THA and UMA were proscribed in May 1940, even after they had jointly pledged their loyalty to His Majesty's government. The North Kavirondo Central Association voluntarily dissolved itself 'at a meeting with the DC at Kakamega . . . voluntarily for the course of the war. In fact the DC continued to use their [leaders] to help with the recruiting campaign and other wartime measures.'[25] All the protest movements mentioned illustrate the results of local people's efforts at organizing themselves to resist specific colonial policies. It could of course be argued that although many of their grievances were economic in character, they were actually expressions of nationalism. This would be correct; but it would be correct only in so far as it relates to ethnic nationalism and not territorial nationalism. The members and leaders of these organizations sought for local answers to their grievances. Their objections to colonialism were specific and local. It can be argued that in a colonial context any grievance, even if local, has a national bearing. Although this may be so on a general level, it would not be able to explain why these several and disparate organizations arose and how they strove to maintain the enthusiasm and loyalty of their members. Political organization had become a marked feature amongst Africans by 1938. This was especially true in Nyanza and central Kenya. But this was small-scale organization, which tended in its emphasis to foster rather than counter the growth of ethnic or tribal nationalism. Colonial administrative policies and economic development did much to mold this phenomenon of ethnic nationalism. It is against this background that we must analyse the growth of African nationalism and subsequent decolonization of Kenya in 1963.

V

In 1945, the Kenyan political scene was characterized by tension and inter-racial suspicion. At the heart of the matter was the intransigence of the settlers, supported by the colonial state. Even the policies of 'multi-racialism' of Sir Philip Mitchell were in effect a continuation of previous colonial policies. The major difference was that some investment of capital was to be made in African subsistence economies and thereby hopefully to uplift the living standards and culture of the Africans, who could only then aspire to 'civilized standards' and 'citizenship'. This entailed the cooperation of the settlers and Mitchell sought to win their support for his colonial schemes. These schemes and plans for development were, to be sure, long-term. Their fruition was to be in the distant future and at no time in the near or middle future was it ever envisaged that Africans would have political power. Change in African society was to be through the agency of the state initiated from above. After 1945 'there was. . . a more purposeful emphasis on constitutional advance, but it was constitutional advance at a pace to be carefully regulated from above: gradually widening representation on the local legislature; the building up of responsibility through local government; a cautious extension of approved trade unionism'.[26] It was to be a significant feature of Kenyan history, that African nationalism and development did not follow this imperial design. Local events altered its face. Specifically the intransigence of the colonial state and the consequent frustration of African nationalism brought the two forces into a memorable collision course from 1948. By 1952, there was an explosion.

The formation of KAU (Kenya African Union) in 1944 should rightly be seen as the first serious attempt to organize a party with territorial ambitions – the first formal attempt at territorial nationalism. Although it was started in modest circumstances and with the immediate aim of giving African support to Eliud Mathu, newly nominated to the Legislative Council, it also had as one of its aims the unity of Kenyan Africans and advocacy of their social and economic progress. It was a moderate party, highly conscious of the power of the colonial state and the hostility of the settlers. Its leadership was composed of educated Africans who no doubt strove to advance constitutional legal nationalism. Centred in Nairobi and with a membership and leadership that was largely Kikuyu, it can be argued that KAU, although national in outlook, tended to be supremely concerned with the problems that were closest to the Kikuyu, especially land. Its tactics were to advance its positions through written appeals and representations to the colonial authorities in both London and Nairobi, and to organize the Africans into a credible mass political movement. Its greatest task was to raise the national political consciousness of the Kenyan people. As subsequent experience amply demonstrated, this was not an easy task. KAU was competing not only against ethnic nationalism but also functioning against the background of inter-tribal suspicion and even apathy. It is therefore true that up to 1947 when Kenyatta assumed its leadership, KAU had scored very few if any political victories. What altered this situation of apathy and fruitless appeals was the return of Kenyatta to Kenyan politics and the significantly worsening economic position of the Africans in Kenya after 1948. It was the latter however which accomplished the radical politicalization of the African masses, especially in Nairobi and central Kenya.

By 1946, landlessness had become a crucial factor in Kikuyuland. This in itself created enormous rural strain, worsened by the fact that there was no more room for expansion. The colonial government perpetually denied that Africans had a genuine land grievance. As late as 1951, when tension over land had significantly increased, the provincial commissioner for Central Province categorically refused to acknowledge the existence of land grievances against the colonial state by the Kikuyu. He noted that 'The land problem among the Kikuyu and the northern Kamba has grown more difficult by the measure of another year of population increase among two fertile tribes. The numbers of landless men are greatest among the Kikuyu of Kiambu and Fort Hall'. His advice to the Kikuyu was that

> the African must learn like all other races of the world that he can no longer expect by right of birth to have the world provide him with a farm, whatever the circumstances of his father; the surface of this planet cannot expand, whatever the universe may be doing; and the addition of adjacent lands would only be a palliative for a few years to this problem. Nonetheless, it is hard not to sympathise with the Kikuyu who loses the means of rearing cattle and goats, with all that those things meant to the social and magico-religious functions that made up the web of his tribal life.[27]

All that the administration could do was to sympathize, but it was not going to make any more land available to Africans. The colonial government considered that all land problems had been adequately solved by the recommendations of the Carter Land Commission. The landless Kikuyu, mainly young men, poured into the urban areas, especially Nairobi, with the hope of finding employment. Young, unskilled and not well-educated, many of these young people came to constitute the vast pool of unemployed Africans in Nairobi at this time. Conditions were not any better for those Africans who were lucky to secure urban employment. 'In towns, although the cost of living rose by 40 per cent between 1949 and January 1952, the minimum wages rose from 7 shillings, 62 cents per week in 1949 to 14 shillings, 13 cents per week in 1952, plus a house and medical attention.'[28] These appalling working and living conditions were later on to lead to militant trade unionism. As of 1951 wage rates in Kenya 'were intended to provide a reasonable living wage for an adult male African living under urban conditions as a single person and without reference to family responsibilities'.[29]

It is these conditions of economic desperation in both urban and rural areas of Kikuyuland which in 1950 onwards led to doubts being expressed about the efficacy of cautious constitutional nationalism as championed by KAU. These doubts, which led to militant nationalism, were reinforced by the ill-advised publication of the *Kenya Plan* by the Electors' Union, a European semi-political party. In this plan of 1949, Europeans restated their determination to continue to dominate Kenya. It was an authoritative restatement of racial dominance which did a lot to inflame African anger and arouse an equally uncompromising position from Africans determined to gain power. It is in these uncompromising years from 1950 to 1952 that politics and strategies of defiance were embraced and adopted by African nationalists.

> Between 1945 and 1953, KAU engaged in a long and futile struggle to achieve change by reform. In addition to the commanding issue of land and to its demand that the report of the Kenya Land Commission be revised, KAU's policies were directed toward achieving equality with Europeans. Its influence on government policy, however, was negligible.[30]

And so in these circumstances of desperation, young men of militant tendencies sought to capture the leadership role in KAU and hopefully to reformulate its strategies. Many of these militant young men[31] came into nationalist politics via trade unionism. Their militancy can in large part be explained by economic desperation and the consequent restiveness of their constituency – the urban population, employed and unemployed. Their capture of office of the Nairobi branch of KAU and subsequently of the KAU executive committee the same year goes a long way to illustrate the desperate nature of the situation. But it was not only the fight over the direction and effectiveness of constitutional nationalism that was involved. From 1950, the Kikuyu actively employed oathing as an effective way of forging tribal unity behind their leaders in their struggle (constitutional initially) against the colonial government. As oathing spread, it brought into nationalist politics many people who would have otherwise remained indifferent to the struggle. But oathing also brought with it a lot of problems. Its spread from Kiambu in earnest from 1950 to other parts of Kikuyuland and Nairobi was not uniform in style or intensity or even results. The militancy of the Nairobi branch of KAU, and its subsequent regrouping as the Central Committee, directed the oathing in Nairobi and exported it to the districts of Nyeri and Fort Hall. This thrust to the northern districts was independent of the Kiambu oathing activities, which continued on the whole to be controlled by 'parliament', based at Banana Hill and under the influence of old KCA members and ex-senior chief Koinange. 'Parliament' did not abandon the politics of petitions and appeals.

There is no evidence that 'parliament', which continued to be very influential in the KAU, ever supported armed rebellion. What can be said is that the oathing based at Banana Hill and in the Nairobi slums under the Central Committee brought a new style and emphasis in the development of nationalism in Kenya. Oathing accelerated the pace of politicization among the Kikuyu, initially peacefully but increasingly by coercion, by 1952. But this was a strategy which complicated nationalist politics immensely. KAU under Kenyatta had by 1952 two faces: there was the national open face which sought to unite all Africans in Kenya in the nationalist struggle. There was the other face, which was open only to the Kikuyu, which was closed, controlled and militant. This militant side of KAU was under the influence of 'parliament' and the Central Committee and had to a large extent alienated itself from the general body by 1952. Although continuing to struggle for the same goals as the KAU, the militant conspiratorial politics of the Kikuyu excluded other tribes. The spread of the oath, which was responsible for Kikuyu militancy by 1952, was not always properly controlled. This meant that neither the 'parliament' nor the Central Committee was able to exercise control over the activities of their various adherents. Lack of adequate control in effect meant that militant nationalism was to a large extent unsupervised. The picture that emerged in 1952 was of a splintered nationalist movement. Kenyatta's aim had been gradually to extend the influence of KAU from central Kenya to the rest of the country. This ambition was never fulfilled. Economic desperation in central Kenya and Nairobi, both populated mainly by the Kikuyu, was confronted with the racial arrogance of the settlers and the intransigence of the colonial state. This state of affairs made constitutional nationalism no longer tenable and gave way via oaths to militancy in Kikuyuland. As has been remarked, this militancy lacked coordination. 'Parliament' and the Central Committee both continued to exist as separate entities; in the middle was KAU. By 1952, Kenyatta, although still regarded as a towering national figure in African politics, did not exercise control over these militants. He still had faith in constitutional nationalism, whose realization he saw as the product of long-term struggle. As early as 1950 Kenyatta had agreed to denounce Mau Mau.

> In October 1950 the Kenya Citizens' Association was formed. It was sponsored by Peter Mbiyu Koinange; it was non-racial and its aim was to further human relationships. The inaugural meeting was held at the United Kenya Club and was attended by seventeen Europeans, eight Indians, and eleven Africans, of whom Kenyatta was one. The chairman of the Association, Sir Charles Mortimer, asked Kenyatta to denounce Mau Mau at a public meeting; this he did in February 1951.[32]

Kenyatta's denunciation of Mau Mau was to continue up to 1952. In fact it continued during his trial in 1953 and even after his release from detention in 1961 and beyond.

What needs to be understood is that the characteristics of the African nationalism, that had emerged in Kenya in all its forms and variations by 1950, were caution and conservatism. This was conservative nationalism. Neither the militancy of the Central Committee nor the conspiratorial politics of 'parliament' could alter this fact. The cry was for eventual African freedom. The cry for freedom is of course the most basic demand of any nationalism. There was also the opposition to racial discrimination and the demand for a resolution on the question of landlessness in Kikuyuland. These demands do not constitute revolutionary nationalism. The militancy that emerged after 1950 was a strategy to accelerate the achievement of essentially basic and conservative demands from an obdurate colonial state. The stubbornness of the colonial administration precipitated a crisis.

VI

Soon after his arrival in Kenya as governor, Sir Evelyn Baring made a short familiarization tour of Central Province. During the tour he conferred with chiefs, priests, headmen, African administrative officers, settlers, and of course members of the white provincial administration. He felt compelled to agree with the evaluation of these groups that a state of near anarchy existed in the country and that this could only be arrested and reversed through a declaration of a state of emergency. He cabled the Secretary of State for the Colonies on 10 October 1952, asking for permission to declare a state of emergency in the colony.[33] In his reply on 14 October 1952, the Secretary of State for the Colonies stated, 'I approve your proposal to declare state of emergency under Emergency Powers order in Council, 1939, and to take action against Kenyatta and his henchmen. I shall give you my full support in thus maintaining law and order.'[34] In his submission the governor had argued that it was KAU under Kenyatta which had masterminded Mau Mau: 'KAU leaders and particularly Kenyatta, were at the back of the Mau Mau movement and violent crime'. The hope of the governor had been that, with the removal of Kenyatta, tranquillity would be restored in central Kenya. This was not to be. The removal of these political leaders who in any case had no control over Mau Mau as they emphatically stated during their trial at Kapenguria in 1953, went a long way to alarm the rest of the population in central Kenya. Emergency measures, beatings, rape, and indiscriminate shooting from the colonial military forces went a long way in expanding the rebellion. The expansion of the movement was largely the result of the government's draconian emergency measures. It was to be a bitter struggle. The arrival of the British army in Kenya in 1952 effectively meant that the colony was now ruled from London. The pace of events and their direction was now to be determined by London and not by the local colonial state.

Throughout the emergency the colonial administration denied that Mau Mau was the product of economic hardships or of frustrations of nationalist politics. The general colonial wisdom held that Mau Mau was the psychological breakdown of a people and their weak cultures when confronted with strong and bewildering Western European culture.[35] The Mau Mau fighters in the forests were generally seen as ignorant gullible young people who had been led astray by ruthless African demagogues. E.B. Wakefield, M.P., a member of a British parliamentary delegation to Kenya to enquire into the causes and remedies of Mau Mau, felt strongly that economics was not behind the armed rebellion.

> We are often asked to what extent economic grievances, and grievances relating to land are connected with Mau Mau. The answer is, I think, that a misconception of the real history of the Kikuyu tribe and their position in the past has been used for political purposes by a people who are endeavouring to get support to achieve their own political ambitions. The land grievance is certainly connected with Mau Mau but is not, I think, the cause of it anyway.[36]

In spite of these denials and contradictory statements, the British government undertook to prosecute the war against Mau Mau alongside reconstruction in Kikuyuland. Physical brutal war was to be waged alongside economic reforms, which if fulfilled would erode local support for Mau Mau significantly. Chief among these reforms was the Land Consolidation Programme conceived under the Swynnerton Plan.[37] This was an ambitious agricultural reform programme that completely changed the agricultural geography of Kikuyuland. It created a stable African landowning class with access to capital and income to be derived from the growth of cash crops hitherto preserved for white farmers. This was a drastic step with tremendous political implications. The British were not ashamed to admit that the aim of this programme was not only to increase the income of the Africans in the rural areas, but also to create a new class, a rural-based middle class which would offer a moderating influence on African politics. In an influential article published in *The Round Table* (a quarterly review of British Commonwealth affairs) of June 1954, this point was elaborated upon.

> The more responsible elements among the Kikuyu have not yet been able to achieve a recognised and established status. One reason for this is that opportunities open to an African to earn a middle-class standard of living are practically non-existent. Not only does the social vacuum thus created provide an opening for an explanation for such uprisings as Mau Mau, led by misguided and evil men, but makes emergence of a real multi-racial society problematical . . . the creation of an African middle class is essential if the colony is to look forward to social stability in the future . . . If the European community in Kenya wishes to avoid a repetition of Mau Mau in the future, with perhaps greater emphasis on its economic than on its racial aspects, every effort must be made now to create a class of Africans whose interests are identical to their own.[38]

In the context of Kenya of 1954, this middle class was to be carved out of the landholders in central Kenya with access to capital and income. It was also hoped that they would be rural employers of labour. The creation of this class reinforced conservative values in central Kenya. It undermined the basis of Mau Mau agitation and brought to prominence the voices of the

190

loyalists and other property owners. When nationalist politics re-emerged in 1960, the political initiative in central Kenya lay securely in the hands of the conservative elite.

This conservatism was further reinforced by British tactics of rehabilitation in emergency camps of those who had been arrested for alleged involvement in Mau Mau activities. Rehabilitation principally involved the renunciation of Mau Mau and its aims and a commitment to the Christian faith. Indeed there could have been no reconstruction and rehabilitation without the pivotal role played by the Christian churches in Kenya. The chief priest in charge of rehabilitation in detention camps held the title of 'Director of ideology'. The Mau Mau detainees were released back to the 'reserves' after going through a number of stages, and at each stage their loyalty was gauged. Only those who had 'completely renounced an allegiance to Mau Mau will be permitted to return to their Reserves'.[39] In his handing-over report of 26 February 1957, A.N. Savage spelt out to his successor in Githunguri division what he called 'The Golden Rule on the release of detainees'. In this he stated: 'The Golden Rule with regard to the release of detainees is that no release is effected without the agreement of local loyalists. These are Chiefs, or Chief's Headmen, and local loyalists.'[40] In thus determining the rate of entry of former Mau Mau to the 'reserve' out of detention camps, these loyalists demonstrated an 'ideological victory' on their part. This 'ideology' was conservatism hostile to radical pronouncements and posturings. The former Mau Mau activists or sympathizers were being reabsorbed on terms certainly disadvantageous to them into changed rural areas in which they had lost influence, power and sometimes land. It is necessary to emphasize this point to illustrate the conservative environment which dominated Central Province by 1960.

Alongside economic reforms in Central Province, the colonial government allowed limited African political activities throughout the country by 1955. There was permission to form district based organizations in which Africans were to learn the complexities of government before ever aspiring for national politics. Only at a later date, not specified in 1955, were Africans hopefully to participate in national political deliberations. The political reforms proposed by the administration in 1955 were aimed at engaging African political energies at a local level. These reforms naturally pointed to a slow growth of African nationalism, controlled tightly by the administration. It was in this spirit that the Lyttelton Constitution of 1954 was proposed, which was meant to regulate and control African political consciousness and growth. It would be a mistake to think that the British were in a hurry to leave Kenya by 1954. The situation, however, altered dramatically in 1957 with the first direct African elections in which eight Africans were elected to the Legislative Council. It is the activities of these moderate men which altered the pace of constitutional reform in Kenya, much faster than had originally been planned when African politics were allowed again in 1955. These new members profitably utilized parliamentary immunity and criticized several policies of the colonial administration. But perhaps more crucial was their collective refusal to participate in the multi-racial government as ministers according to the Lyttelton Constitution. They demanded equal parliamentary representation with Europeans. This resulted in the Lennox-Boyd Constitution of 1958, which substantially increased African representation in the Legislative Council from eight members to fourteen. However, it preserved many of the provisions of the Lyttelton Constitution, especially those concerning multi-racial government. It was again the refusal to participate in this type of government which increased the political tempo in the colony from 1957 to 1960. The cry now was for freedom, and a recognition of Kenya as an African country. These elected members of Legco acted as individuals; they did not represent a national political party. Their demands were for political independence and the release of Kenyatta. They had been elected to represent districts populated largely by specific ethnic groups. In this way it could be true that they were 'sent to represent their tribal groups as "ambassadors" in the Legco in Nairobi'.[41] These were the new elite in their various ethnic areas, conscious of the social prestige and power that they enjoyed amongst their people. By 1952 militant nationalism was associated only with a section of the Kikuyu, so that, other than Central Province, the other areas had not experienced any militant expressions of nationalism at all. Since the start of the emergency and subsequent reconstruction and rehabilitation in Central Province, militancy had been defeated and in its place had emerged conservative cautious nationalism that rested on the shoulders of loyalists and ex-Mau Mau detainees, who after release from detention were known to be quiet and exemplary citizens. The African members who were elected to the Legco in 1957 were not in any way associated with the militancy of 1952. They demanded independence, the abolition of discrimination, the release of detainees, and an increase in wages; but never the destruction or reformulation of the social and economic system that prevailed in Kenya. Their various constituencies were conservative and cautious. What, however, distinguishes this group of elected African members is their refusal to participate in the multi-racial government. This refusal and persistent demand for independence precipitated further constitutional reforms – reforms which would have otherwise been slow in coming.

VII

Problems associated with personality clashes, petty feuds, exaggerated fears about the future, and rivalry had immeasurable influence on the relationships between African elected members by the time KANU and KADU were formed in 1960. These members were keen to increase their influence on the national stage. When KANU (Kenya African National Union) was formed in 1960, it, like KADU (Kenya African Democratic Union), merely brought together pre-existing district organizations and their leaders. These parties were not the result of a few individual idealists starting a party and extending its influence in the country through an elaboration of its programme. No. These parties in 1960 formed alliances of convenience between pre-existing political organizations. The major thrust of activity was therefore expended not on elaboration and discussion of party policies but rather on campaigns for leadership in the party. It was easy for the distribution of leadership roles in these parties either to offend or to gratify ethnic sensitivities, for after all these members of the Legislative Council had over time come to be seen as ethnic spokesmen. The formation of KANU and KADU in 1960 marked the second attempt at territorial nationalism. But as in the first attempt under KAU, there were still problems associated with ethnic nationalism which the colonial authorities had so carefully fostered in the district organizations formed after 1955. Oginga Odinga tells us that 'the district associations up and down the country were to be converted into branches of KANU'.[42] He correctly states that 'for many [the leaders] the outcome of the elections would determine their political allegiance. . .'[43] And indeed this was true. What needs to be stressed here is that by 1960 the veneer of unity which had characterized the relationship between African members of the Legislative Council from 1957 was now shattered. The nationalist movement was again splintered. This lack of unity was to have tragic consequences for future national politics, for its feasted on rumours, personality clashes and petty rivalry. These are not points of ideological difference. They are however tragic in the sense that they basically utilize people's fears of security. In the absence of ideological discussions, powerful personalities became the points of reference in national politics by 1960.

In its manifesto of 1960/61 KANU spoke of its aims in general terms. It pledged itself 'to undiluted democracy. KANU pledges itself to ensure fundamental freedoms'.[44] Even on the key question of economic policy the manifesto was agonizingly general. It stated: 'KANU wants to ensure that the means of production, distribution, and exchange are under the best obtainable system and administration consistent with all the interests of the country.' At some points it was emotional: 'After long years of domination Kenya wins freedom not to let her children suffer again because of want of accommodation, or the like, but to lead them into a world of plenty, equality, liberty and brotherhood.'[45] As early as 1960, KANU had committed itself to respect for individual property. While acknowledging that resettlement of displaced persons and landless people was going to be its chief problem, the manifesto however noted that it should be 'resettlement not at the cost of the high standard of agriculture already attained, but definitely at the expense of absentee landlordism. . .' This question of land and its utilization received considerable attention at the Lancaster House Conference of 1962.

KADU was of course no clearer than KANU in its aims and policies. Other than the perceived fear of domination by the Luo, and especially by the Kikuyu in post-independent Kenya, KADU did not differ in any substantial manner in its policies from KANU. The only major difference was the proposition by KADU of a regional system of government which was seen as a safeguard against this domination. At the heart of these fears and therefore the major point of contention between these two parties was the question of land; landownership and control in post-colonial Kenya. These differences were perhaps spelt out most clearly in the constitutional conference of 1962. In the minutes of the conference, Dr Kiano said 'that land and property rights should be enshrined in the Bill of Rights. KADU had quoted land tenure as one reason for regionalism, on the assumption that after independence some groups might take advantage of others. But land was so important to the economy of Kenya that it should be under the control of the Central Government. . .'[46] In his contribution, Daniel Arap Moi picked up on this issue of land: 'As regards Dr Kiano's remark that, unless KANU's policy on land was accepted, there would be a breakdown and bloodshed, his people of Kalenjin were prepared to fight and die for their land, which after all in Kenya belonged to the people of the various tribes and not to the Kenya Government'.[47] Questions related to land received considerable attention at this conference. What all this highlighted was the place of ethnic groups in post-colonial Kenya. It goes far to illustrate that even on the eve of independence questions related to a national agenda and territorial nationalism had not been settled. As independence drew near, the leaders of both parties devoted most of their time on assuring the world and resident minority property owners – especially settlers – that they would respect private ownership of property in post-colonial Kenya. In his address to the Royal Institute of International Affairs in London on 27 September 1960, Mr Gichuru, in speaking on the future of Kenya, stated 'We believe in personal freedom, in security of private property, in the maintenance of law and order and definitely the British judicial system with each independent test. . .'[48] KADU in its manifesto on the question of land went even further. It acknowledged that 'Individual tenure is considered, for the country generally, to be the best form of holding, since it ensures personal care of the land and livestock, but it must be recognised that in some areas this is impractical and will always be so.'[49] It all the same stated that 'Kenya citizenship is not an essential condition for the development of a farm or ranch to the benefit of the Kenya economy. Citizenship rights should be confined to the political arena, such as the right to vote.'[50]

By 1963 both parties in their pronouncements and manifestos showed clearly that the goal of their activities was political independence. There was a regrettable absence of any serious attempt to analyse the colonial economic and social system to see how this could hinder or frustrate the aspirations of the Kenyan people after independence. The singular aim of the political elite by 1963 was to inherit the state. But they failed to realize that the state, as constituted in Kenya in 1963, was oppressive, ruthless and a vehicle through which settlers and Britain exploited the Africans. To inherit the state intact was unfortunately to advance the aims for which it was so uniquely suited and created. This flaw on the part of the nationalist leaders, of being unable to comprehend adequately the complexities of colonialism and especially of the colonial state and its political economy, can in part be attributed to the brevity of time from the formation of the political parties in 1960 to the attainment of independence in 1963. Many of these politicians were making their début in national politics, having only recently started their career in politics in district-based organizations. It was to be some time before they mastered the art of self-confidence in their career. This was to happen alongside their contributions in the Legislative Council against belligerent settler politicians. Their knowledge of the complexities of international politics and economics was therefore limited. Besides, we must never forget that in the three years before independence most of the time was spent on hurriedly compiling party manifestos, party organization and registration of members and preparations for elections. The manifestos themselves clearly reflect the mood of the times in which they were formulated – hurried, general, and filled with excitement, but slim on analysis, reflection and comprehension of the options and strategies needed to solve the problems that lay ahead. It is also worth noting that the ideas expressed in the manifestos came from the leaders. There is no evidence that the general population in the villages or even towns was in any significant way involved directly in the formulation of these documents. The manifestos were compiled by the leadership and subsequently presented to the people at huge mass rallies for token oral approval; for example, the 'KANU Manifesto for Independence, Social Democracy and Stability' was presented to the public at a mass rally of 100,000 people at Thika on 20 November 1960, and predictably approved.

When independence was achieved in 1963, the colonial state and the colonial economic system remained largely intact. It was then and in subsequent times that the political elite sought to Africanize (or Kenyanize) the system. Efforts in this direction meant that the leadership in 1963 officially endorsed capitalism as the country's economic system: 'when national independence was achieved the political aim of taking over the economy became merged almost imperceptibly with individual aspirations to take over the jobs, positions, and life styles which the economy made possible'.[51] The new political elite had political power and used it to gain entry into the world of economic privileges. The companies that had hitherto operated in Kenya could not neglect the new situation. It was in their long-term interests to find accommodation with these new political masters. The government's aim of Kenyanization was essentially the Africanization of the colonial economy built on injustice. This process took several forms. In the first place, the government insisted that jobs previously held by expatriates should be Africanized, starting with key posts in the civil service. These top positions carried with them immense power. The new occupants maximized their newly found opportunities to advance their economic welfare. This was achieved through increased access to loans and credit, buying of land and company shares. Lacking financial power, the ruling elite came to rely increasingly on their political power to squeeze benefits from foreign and local capital.

Apart from the Africanization of jobs, there was also the essential element of buying land previously held by European settlers. The rapid entry of Africans in these areas led the previous owners to shift their capital into manufacturing, or they migrated overseas. Again here the African petty-bourgeoisie relied on the state to provide capital through various loan agencies and the political rationalization for their actions.

After independence many of the companies not previously represented in Kenya arrived to take advantage of the country's economic policy, which of course subscribed to capitalism. After 1965 this manufacturing was basically to meet internal needs, a sort of import-substitution strategy. Naturally they flourished under protected markets. The government passed a number of legislative measures to attract foreign capital. The chief one was the Foreign Investment Act of 1964, which in effect 'constitutes a bill of rights for foreign investors, guaranteeing freedom of repatriation of profits (in proportion to the foreign share of equity), interest and repayment on foreign loan capital, and abjuring expropriation without good cause'.[52] Since it was in manufacturing that most profits could be made from invested capital, the local capitalists quickly shifted their attention from agriculture to manufacturing, working in alliance with foreign capital in various capacities. This alliance, forged as the result of political power, constituted a neo-colonial connexion with all its complexities. In this way, then, an African ruling elite emerged politically powerful and economically allied to international capital. This linkage, achieved through cooperation, competition, and forever moderated by the state, merely expanded the colonial economic system without significantly altering its structure nor its aims.

Conclusion

The emphasis in this chapter has been to look at the decolonization of Kenya within an international context. Only this approach can explain the linkage between local agitation and changing international opinions and forces which, together combined, led to the end of colonialism in Kenya. The start of it is generally acknowledged as the end of the Second World War, and the desperate economic situation which imperial powers found themselves in. Their loss of economic power severely curtailed their supremacy in international relations. Before the war, colonialism had been viewed by the imperial powers as essentially an internal matter and therefore not subject to international scrutiny. This changed after the war. Its value and right of existence was questioned at the highest levels of international relations by the USA and USSR for different ideological reasons. It has been maintained throughout this chapter that this opposition to colonialism, especially from USA, led to some reforms, basically very minimal, being undertaken in British African colonies. These reforms, however, were seen by the imperial powers as a way of consolidating their power, although self-government as an end was to be granted at some distant unspecified future. To argue that the imperial powers of their own volition granted independence as an act of magnanimity would be wrong. Acting against international pressure, the imperial powers were more receptive to calls for reform than had been the case before 1945. What needs to be stressed is that increased demands for fundamental reforms in the colonies and demands for self-government made colonialism harder to manage in the traditional manner. Reluctantly the imperial powers came to concede to self-government and then independence of the colonies as a way of extricating themselves from a complex situation, and also an effective means of safeguarding their enormous economic interests in these colonies. The decision to grant independence even when under militant pressure should be seen as constituting a tactical retreat for imperialism. But this retreat was never viewed as defeat. Defeat was experienced in very rare circumstances. Decolonization was undertaken in such a manner that the economic and social systems which had been established in the colonies over half a century or more were never disturbed or altered. This fact alone ensured the continued reaping of profits by imperial powers from their investments in their former colonies. The economic basis of colonialism was retained but now without the difficult task of maintaining law and order. This task was to be passed on to the new local rulers. For imperialism, this new era, as subsequent events clearly indicated, was now one of exploitation without responsibility. In a speech to the Conservative Party conference in 1956, the British Colonial Secretary, Mr Lennox-Boyd, said that 'any other policy but that of moving towards self-government and satisfaction of nationalist aspirations in the colonies would be "fraught with disaster" '.[53] He went on to mention that 'in this process, the British Empire "is not breaking up, but growing up" '. The economic basis of colonialism was reiterated by the Colonial Secretary at this conference. He said, 'the increased volume of inter-imperial trade resulting from an expanding Commonwealth would assist in solving economic problems'.[54] For this to happen power had to be bestowed in the hands of collaborators, being the nationalists who had promised to safeguard this trade link between the former colony and the imperial powers. Such collaborators were always found and it is they who assumed leadership while espousing conservative economic and social policies.

The rate at which reforms were granted in each colony depended to a large extent on the internal factors. In those instances where there had been a violent expression of nationalism, as in Malaya and Kenya, the initial efforts were to crush the rebellion, then talk to 'responsible' moderate leaders. After the military defeat of the communist uprising in Malaya, Britain granted power to a conservative elite hostile to communism and radical pronouncements. To avoid further violent outbursts in Ghana like those of 1948, Britain accelerated constitutional reform in the colony that led to self-government in 1952 and full independence in 1957.

In Kenya, the frustrations which led to the Mau Mau rebellion were skilfully attended to alongside fighting to crush the armed rebellion. On an elementary level the colour bar had started to be broken down slowly but surely from 1953. We are told that by 1953 'The Nairobi Hotel Keeper's Association announced it has no objection in principle to anybody entering their hotels. Discrimination against African farmers growing their own coffee crops has been removed. . .'[55] Although token gestures, these actions were significant in slowly eroding the basis for militant nationalism. The land consolidation in Kikuyuland created a class of conservative nationalists who, though eager for political independence, were not at all inclined to support or encourage radical policies or politics. Rehabilitation in emergency camps was so successful, according to the aims set out by the British, that the graduates of detention camps were seen as model citizens. In his annual report for 1958, the district commissioner for Kiambu felt strongly that 'there was continued evidence to support the view that returned detainees were less inclined to crime, either of a violent or of a subversive nature, than the "normal" citizen'.[56] There was still, to be sure, a lot of frustration over land. But after 1956, it was generally seen that this grievance would be redressed through petitions and legal channels rather than through a violent uprising. Even Kiama Kia Muingi held to this non-violent agitation. Many of those who were members of this loosely organized informal underground movement sought to 'achieve compensation either from the Loyalists or government for any losses suffered by Mau Mau adherents . . . To take revenge on the Loyalists; to continue to fight for Mau Mau aims but to do it without resort to violence.'[57] By 1960, the stage was set for cautious conservative politics not only in Central Province but in other parts of Kenya which had not in any case been part of the militancy of 1952. This stage had been reached through constitutional reforms which were in themselves made inevitable as a result of the Mau Mau violence. The direct intervention of the British army in the conflict, to rescue the settlers, clearly indicated the weakness of the settler dominated state. Settlers and other minorities could not be relied upon to safeguard vital British economic interests. In terms of political power, it is the settlers who lost in the aftermath of Mau Mau. The perennial fear of successive British governments that these settlers would rebel if upset or 'betrayed', and thereby cause intolerable political problems in London, were now easily overcome by the fact that there was a resident British army that would have easily subdued such settler mischief.

The story of nationalism and decolonization in Kenya is complex and multifaceted. As a result, to argue that the Mau Mau rebellion directly and singly brought independence to Kenya would be a gross simplification of the historical events which have been detailed in this chapter. It is a tempting argument to take, but largely mistaken. It would be wrong for it would fail to deal with the complex nature of the district-based political organizations that were formed after 1955. It would also not comprehend the international dimension of the decolonization process, and would fail to acknowledge the crucial role played by Tom Mboya and the trade union movement in shouldering the task of legal nationalism after 1952 at the height of the emergency. The trade union movement, under Mboya's able and widely acknowledged brilliant leadership, kept the national spirit and indeed national politics alive at a time when Central Province was effectively under military siege. It is this ceaseless agitation on Mboya's part and that of his union that clearly pointed to the need for further urgent reforms to allow for a mild political activity. By 1955, district-based organizations were permitted. In the subsequent election of 1957, the African elected members refused to participate in the multi-racial government. This was a point of major crisis. The gradual timetable envisaged by the British in 1955 was rendered useless and further reforms were inevitable. The point to be emphasized is that the basic aims of KAU, which were seen as intolerable in 1952, were now granted after sustained agitation in 1960. It had taken Mau Mau violence, Mboya's ceaseless agitation and the united demand for *Uhuru* by the elected members in 1957 to reach this far. Each one of the steps and stages grew as a result of the other. The distinguishing feature in all these stages was the basic demand of nationalism – the right of a people to self-determination. At no stage was nationalism in Kenya ever socialist, or left-wing, in ideas or inspiration. In outlining KANU's aims for an independent Kenya at the 1962 Lancaster House Conference, Jomo Kenyatta spelt out what became the party's permanent concerns in subsequent periods. He said: 'KANU had accepted the principle of private ownership in land and free enterprise. . .'[58]

Notes

1 Negley Farson, *Last Chance in Africa* (London 1949), 5.
2 Bethwell A. Ogot and T. Zeleza, 'Kenya: the road to independence and after', unpublished paper, Kenyatta University, 1985, 1.
3 William R. Ochieng', 'The Mau Mau, the petit bourgeoisie and decolonization in Kenya', unpublished paper, Kenyatta University, 1984, 8.
4 W. Roger Louis and Ronald Robinson, 'The United States and the liquidation of British Empire in tropical Africa, 1941-1951', in P. Gifford and W. Roger Louis, eds., *The Transfer of Power in Africa: decolonization 1940-1960* (Harvard, 1962), 38.
5 *Ibid.*, 37.
6 V.I. Lenin, *Imperialism, the highest stage of capitalism* (Moscow, 1947). See also N.I. Bukharin, *Imperialism and World Economy* (New York, 1929).
7 Michael R. Stenson, *Repression and Revolt: the origins of the 1948 Communist insurrection in Malaya and Singapore* (Ohio, 1969), 2.
8 *Ibid.*, 6.
9 *Ibid.*, 6.
10 *Ibid.*, 9.
11 J. Kennedy, *A History of Malaya* (London, 1962), 271-2.
12 N.J. Ryan, *The Making of Modern Malaya* (London, 1963), 200.
13 W.E.F. Ward, *A History of Ghana* (London, 1967), 324.
14 *Ibid.*, 325.
15 *Ibid.*, 327.

16 *Ibid.*, 330.
17 David Rooney, *Sir Charles Arden-Clarke* (London, 1982), 82.
18 Ward, *Ghana*, 333.
19 *Ibid.*, 335.
20 *Ibid.*, 335.
21 Kenneth Good, 'Settler colonialism: economic development and class formation', *Journal of Modern African Studies* 14(4), 1976, 598.
22 See, for example, Anthony Clayton and Donald C. Savage, *Government and Labour in Kenya* (London, 1974). See also R. van Zwanenberg, *Colonial Capitalism and Labour in Kenya 1919-1939* (Nairobi, 1975).
23 M.P.K. Sorrenson, *Origins of European Settlement in Kenya* (Nairobi, 1968).
24 George Bennett and Carl Rosberg, 'The formation of nationalist parties in 1960', in C.J. Gertzel, M. Goldschmidt and Don Rothchild, *Government and Politics in Kenya* (Nairobi, 1969), 103.
25 Carl Rosberg and John Nottingham, *The Myth of Mau Mau: nationalism in Kenya* (New York, 1966), 186.
26 George Bennett and Alison Smith, 'Kenya: from "whiteman's country" to Kenyatta's state, 1946-1963', in D.A. Low and Alison Smith, eds., *History of East Africa*, vol.III (Oxford, 1976), 109.
27 *African Affairs Department Annual Report 1951*, Government Printer, Nairobi, 1952, 32.
28 B.A. Ogot, 'Kenya under the British, 1895-1963', *Zamani* (Nairobi, 1968), 283.
29 *East Africa Royal Commission, 1953-1955 Report*, London, 1955, 157.
30 Rosberg and Nottingham, *Mau Mau*, 220.
31 *Ibid.*, 269.
32 Guy Arnold, *Kenyatta and the Politics of Kenya* (London, 1974), 106.
33 Sir Evelyn Baring to Secretary of State for the Colonies, inward telegram, top secret, 10 October 1952, CO 822/443.
34 Secretary of State for the Colonies, 14 October 1952, CO 822/443.
35 J.C. Carothers, *The Psychology of Mau Mau* (Nairobi, 1954). See also Official government response to Carother's Report, WCOM 1/43-1/52. Reel no.6. Kenya National Archives.
36 E.B. Wakefield, 'The situation in Kenya', unpublished paper presented to the Royal Institute of International Affairs, London, 10 March 1954, 3.
37 R.J.M. Swynnerton, *A Plan to Intensify the Development of African Agriculture in Kenya* (Nairobi, 1954).
38 'Reconstruction in Kenya: the prospect beyond Mau Mau', *The Round Table* 175 (June, 1954), 254-5.
39 *East African Standard*, 11 September 1953, 68.
40 A.N. Savage, *Handing Over Report, Githunguri Division.* 26 February, 1957, DC/KBU 2/1, Kenya National Archives.
41 W.R. Ochieng', 'The gestation period of tribalism in Kenya', in *The First Word* (Nairobi, 1975), 170.
42 Oginga Odinga, *Not Yet Uhuru* (London, 1967), 193.
43 *Ibid.*, 194.
44 *Kanu Manifesto for Independence, Social Democracy and Stability*, KANU, 1960/1961, 12.
45 *Ibid.*, 14.
46 Minutes of Kenya Constitutional Conference Meeting, 1962. KNA, Record of the fourth meeting, 16 February 1962, 26.
47 *Ibid.*, record of the fifth meeting, 19 February 1962, 34.
48 James Gichuru, 'Kenya', unpublished paper presented to the Royal Institute of International Affairs, London, 27 September 1960, 1.
49 *KADU's Plan on Land Tenure and Agricultural and Pastoral Development for Independent Kenya.* KNA MAC/KEN/36/7, 2.

50 *Ibid.*, 4.

51 *Employment, Incomes and Equality: a strategy for increasing productive employment in Kenya,* ILO Report, Geneva, 1972, 87.

52 Richard Sandbrook, *Proletarians and African Capitalism: the Kenya case 1960-1962* (Cambridge, 1975), 6.

53 *East African Standard,* October 13, 1956, 1. Decolonization became a crucial aspect of government priorities under Harold Macmillan after 1960. For an exhaustive analysis of this change of attitudes and priorities within the Conservative government of Harold Macmillan, see Dan Horowitz, 'Conservatives and Africa', *African Affairs* 69 (274), 1970. For Ian MacLeod's views on decolonization see *Spectator,* London, 20 March 1964 and 23 April 1965.

54 *Ibid.*, 1.

55 Colin Legum, 'Progressive policy emerges in Kenya', *East African Standard,* 22 August 1953, 4.

56 *Kiambu District Annual Report, 1958,* KNA DC/KBU/1/46.

57 *Kiambu District Annual Report, 1957,* KNA DC/KBU/1/45. See also *Kiama Kia Muingi: Appreciation by the Kenya Intelligence Committee,* KNA WC/CM/1/1/6. Flag E.

58 Minutes of Kenya Constitutional Conference Meeting, 1962. KNA, Record of the ninth meeting, 21 February 1962, 77.

7 Independent Kenya, 1963-1986

William Ochieng'

The history of independent Kenya has been approached from three main perspectives. One perspective views it as a continuing and expanding continuum, reflecting institutions and ideas that trace their origins to the colonial period. It is argued in this genre that African nationalism was merely concerned with eliminating the colonial barriers to its rise within the structure of monopolistic exchange, 'rather than with changing the structure itself'.[1] This school of thought accuses Kenya of developing without an African ideology, a sin in the eyes of those for whom the absence of Kenyatta's and Moi's writings in radical anthologies 'is equated with the absence of national interest and dignity or sense of nationhood'.[2]

The second perspective, pioneered by Oginga Odinga's book, *Not Yet Uhuru*, and very much loved by radical and Marxist scholars, is the one which regards the history of independent Kenya as a tale of betrayal of pre-independence popular hopes and aspirations of the masses for a socialist transformation of society. Scholars who adopt this approach regard Kenya as an excellent example of a neo-colonial African state. Inherent in this analysis of neo-colonialism is the argument, which is explicitly stated, that there have been no significant economic and structural changes since independence and that the British policy of the late 1950s was designed to contain the nationalist movement within the framework of colonial institutions and the ideas which support such institutions.[3]

The third perspective, which is transparently simplistic, is the one which applauds post-colonial Kenya as the 'success story'. According to this school of thought Kenya's 'general economic and social stability and highly developed system of hotels and other amenities have made it the most popular and successful country in black Africa'.[4]

What, however, are we to make of these contradictory approaches? Does the history of independent Kenya simply depend on every observer's opinion? It is the position of this chapter that the above perspectives are overdrawn and obscure reality. It is increasingly becoming clear that the various and early critics of independent Kenya's development strategy did not give the Kenyan 'system' a chance to unfold, a chance to take off. It is today apparent that the forces of neo-colonialism are not as deeply embedded in Kenya as Colin Leys, Steve Langdon and Oginga Odinga asserted in their various works.[5] Despite the powerful presence and influences of the multinational companies and agencies of the metropole, there has evolved a new nationally based petty- and national bourgeoisie class. This class is not only providing an autonomous ruling elite, in control of the Kenyan state, but is also playing a vital role in 'institutionalizing' commodity relations throughout the country.[6]

The attainment of Kenya's independence on 12 December 1963 marked the culmination of 68 years of anti-colonial struggle waged by the Kenya Africans to free themselves from British domination, oppression and exploitation. But the attainment of independence also marked the beginning of the process of nation-building. By nation-building was understood the elimination of poverty, disease and ignorance and the emergence of a relatively egalitarian and participatory society. In his address to the nation during the Independence Ceremony Kenyatta confronted the challenge of independence in a language which he was to echo and re-echo throughout his presidency:

> Fellow countrymen, many people may think that, now that there is *uhuru*, now that I can see the sun of freedom shining, riches will pour down like manna from heaven. I tell you there will be nothing like heaven. We must all work hard, with our hands, to save ourselves from poverty, ignorance and disease. . .
>
> In the past we used to blame the Europeans for everything that went wrong. When things went wrong we used to say the Europeans are bad, they are sucking our blood. Now the Government is ours . . . You and I must work together to develop our country, to get education for our children, to have doctors, to build roads, to improve or provide all the day-to-day essentials. This should be our work, in the spirit that I am going to ask you to echo, to shout aloud, to shatter the foundations of the past with the strength of our new purpose . . . HARAMBEE!

Thus, the *Harambee* era, the *Harambee* spirit and the new nation came into being. Harambee was a clarion call for dedication, hard work and unity. Hard work, according to Kenyatta, was the only way to achieve prosperity, to keep people from being confused by idle leaders and young radicals. It was the way to political stability which, according to Kenyatta, was essential to attract investments and grants.

Yet, to observers, the call for hard work was not in itself clear, or enough. A blueprint, or guideline, for the development of the country was necessary, for Kenya had emerged from the colonial period with conflicting social, economic and political philosophies which had emanated from the past racial, ethnic and class conflicts and interests. Indeed, to understand the tensions and conflicts which have been at the base of independent Kenya's political and economic debate it is important to understand Kenya's colonial legacy and the multiplicity of values with which Kenyans emerged into independence from the womb of colonialism.

Between 1895 and 1952 the assumption within the settler and imperial circles was that Kenya would 'forever' remain a white man's country, with the white settlers providing political and social leadership. Between 1940 and 1954 the imperial government did not only pour much money into Kenya to boost European agriculture and industry, but a number of settler leaders were also made responsible for groups of government departments. Indeed, between 1945 and 1952 it seemed as if the imperial government was set to hand over power to Kenyan European settlers. However, the emergency generated new social and political processes and destroyed the basis of settler power and aspirations, restructured the class and institutional bases of the colonial state, and altered the balance of class forces, so that both the settlers and the armed freedom fighters – the loud protagonists in the political crisis of 1952 – became marginalized by the time of Kenya's independence. Indeed, by 1957 a new generation of African politicians had come to the centre stage. It was this new generation, and not the colonial governor or his overlords in London, who held the initiative and dictated the pace of events.

But were the African leaders ideologically agreed on the type of society which they wished to create after independence? The answer is that the majority of the African nationalist leaders who took over the running of the state from the British had already accepted, and were committed to, the bourgeois tenets of Western democracy and capitalist production. Remember that the constitution and the future shape of independent Kenya were effectively negotiated at the 1960 Lancaster and 1962 Marlborough House Constitutional Conferences in London. In both conferences it was the new generation of African leaders – the Mboyas, Ngalas, Mois, Kianos and Muliros – who were the most effective, and influential representatives. What is important for our argument is that on the issues of Kenya's future economic structure, and the values underlying it, there were no serious difficulties between the British government and the African leadership. If anything, most African leaders were in full agreement with the economic philosophy of free enterprise and the institution of private property and were visibly eager to maintain that economic system.

Equally the African elites had come to accept and respect the role of private investment in Kenya's economy. In other words, the basic issues at the Lancaster and Marlborough Conferences were not concerned with the nature of Kenya's future economy but with the structure of government which independent Kenya should assume. KADU emphasized the value of regionalism against a strong central government as a means of controlling allocation of revenues and land. They maintained that reallocation of white settler farms ought to be left within the jurisdiction of regional administrations. On the other hand KANU initially downplayed the regionalism issue and concentrated on advocating national unity, a strong central government, East African federation and pan-Africanism. But, as we said earlier, both KADU and KANU were basically agreed on the creation of a democratic, capitalist society. This basic agreement explains why KADU leaders were later very easily absorbed within KANU after independence.

But while the above observations are mostly valid, it should be recorded that the vice-president of KANU at the Lancaster House Conferences – Jaramogi Oginga Odinga – was visibly distressed by the wholesale acceptance of the colonial economic structure. In his book *Not Yet Uhuru*, Odinga records that he only agreed to go along with his KANU colleagues in order not to impede Kenya's *uhuru*. Odinga represented, and would continue to represent, the radical element in Kenya's nationalist movement, which after independence would agitate for wide-ranging nationalization of foreign companies and industries and socialist policies.

Contradictions within Kenya's nationalist movement were simply a reflection of a class-divided capitalist society. In a class-divided society the most important type of conflict is that between the different social classes. Karl Marx has underlined this point: 'All historical struggles, whether they proceed in the political, religious, philosophical, or some other ideological domain, are in fact only the more or less clear expression of struggles of social classes.'[8]

People differ in a great number of ways. They have by nature different interests, different needs, different aspirations and different values. Additionally, differences occur in society because there are many forces which divide the population culturally, politically and economically, and however much people may cooperate, they will still be in technical conflict because their interests and the way they see things will be different. Conflict seems to be an inescapable aspect of community and, hence, of being human.

Conservative and radical politics
Right from the imposition of British colonial rule to the present, Kenyans had never agreed ideologically. There were those who collaborated with the British advent and those who opposed the imposition of colonial rule. There were those who embraced Westernism and Christianity and those who resisted these. And even when the Kenya African Union (KAU) was formed in 1944, to mobilize Kenya Africans towards an African nation and, ultimately, to win *uhuru* for the country, ideological differences continued to manifest themselves within the nationalist party. Within KAU were the conservatives – people like Francis Khamis, Joseph Katithi, Jomo Kenyatta, Eliud Mathu and B.A. Ohanga – who believed in constitutionalism and dialogue with the imperialists. But within KAU were also radicals – people like Stanley Mathenge, Fred Kubai and Bildad Kaggia – who, as early as 1947, were calling for independence 'now' and advocating violence to hasten the departure of the British. Since the terms 'conservative' and 'radical' are analytically ambiguous, some operational definitions of them are in order for the purpose of this chapter. By 'conservatives' is meant those nationalists who espoused a constitutionalist and reformist approach and were after independence concerned with the maintenance of the colonial legacy. By 'radicals' we mean those politicians who stood for fundamental changes in the social, economic and political fields. These people advocated the use of force to achieve independence and after independence called for a total transformation of Kenyan society in the interest of the masses who had been at the forefront of the struggle for independence but who had been 'neglected' after *uhuru*.

Although there were periodic conflicts between the two factions, as is exemplified in the conflict between the freedom fighters and the loyalists during the Mau Mau uprising, articulate cleavage between the conservatives and radicals within the nationalist movement did not begin to clearly manifest itself until 1960. In that year the ultra-conservative nationalists banded together to form the Kenya African Democratic Union (KADU), and hoped that together with small political groupings of settlers and Asians they could lead Kenya into independence and maintain the *status quo*. Most of the radicals banded together to form KANU, but KANU also attracted a large number of conservative politicians. As it later turned out, the bitterest ideological struggles between the conservatives and radicals were to take place within KANU in the period after independence.

As independence approached, politics within KANU began to polarize. One wing consisted of Oginga Odinga, Bildad Kaggia, Achieng' Oneko, J.D. Kali and Pio Gama Pinto and their political associates, together with some ex-Mau Mau detainees. These were the radicals. They preached some form of socialism and advocated cooperation with socialist countries. They stood for rapid Africanization, nationalization of foreign industries and enterprises and free distribution of former settler farms to the landless. The other wing of KANU consisted of conservatives, led by Jomo Kenyatta, Tom Mboya and James Gichuru. This group espoused a reformist approach and advocated close cooperation with Britain, the United States and countries of the European Economic Community. In the economic field the conservatives advocated the retention of the *status quo*, and strongly supported the controversial clause 75(i) of the Independence Constitution which protected property rights of white settlers and other immigrants.

The acceptance of the above clause by the KANU leadership meant that Kenyatta, Mboya and their associates were prepared to betray the party's strongly nationalist and socialist ideology and were ready to cooperate with the white settlers. As John Haberson has put it:

> The beginning of a serious ideological schism within the future ruling party (KANU) occurred when Kenyatta and many of his principal lieutenants were persuaded to accept the two most important European conditions: (i) that Africans must pay for the land they were to receive, and (ii) that resettlement must be accomplished as far as possible before independence.[9]

One of the leaders of the radical wing of KANU, Bildad Kaggia, was later to comment:

> KANU leaders lost the battle against immigrant races when they accepted those sections in the constitution which safeguarded private property and interests. Many people thought that the constitution was going to be amended soon after the achievement of *uhuru*. But government policies after independence strengthened the entrenched clauses instead of weakening them.[10]

The first two years of independence were years of political readjustment.

The opposition members of parliament (both from KADU and the African People's Party (APP)) were lured to join KANU in the government. They immediately strengthened the conservative wing of KANU, but the ideological differences between the radicals and conservatives in KANU continued. The radicals accused the KANU government of betraying the pledges which they had made to the masses before independence.

Land policy, in particular, became a major bone of contention, and no one tried more consciously than Bildad Kaggia to put the government on the road to a land policy that would be good for the expanding Kenyan economy, the interests of the landless, and the confidence of the poor people who had elected the *uhuru* government. On 5 September 1963 Kaggia wrote a letter to the Minister of Agriculture and told him:

> Everyone in this country is very well aware of the landhunger that has existed among Africans as a result of the robbery of their land by the British colonial imperialists. The logical method to solve the problem posed by this robbery would have been to nationalize all big estates owned by the Europeans and make them either state farms, so as to alleviate unemployment, or hand them to cooperatives formed by landless Africans.

Apart from advocating for free land distribution to the landless, Kaggia also called for free education and free medical facilities for the people, but nobody senior in Kenyatta's government listened to him. In fact by championing the interests of the poor Kaggia did not know that he was making many enemies among Kenyatta's close lieutenants. Indeed on 22 May 1964 the Prime Minister, Mzee Jomo Kenyatta, wrote to Kaggia and, among other things, told him: 'I am seriously concerned at your repeated attacks on the policies of the Ministry of Lands and Settlement, and with your interference with land consolidation in Fort Hall [Murang'a].'[11] This was a veiled warning to Kaggia; and a request to him to resign from the government if he did not like its policies. In June 1964 Kaggia resigned his parliamentary secretaryship in the Ministry of Education with the following comment: 'As a representative of the people I found it very difficult to forget the people who elected me on the basis of definite pledges, or to forget the freedom fighters who gave all they had, including their land, for the independence we are enjoying.[12]

Kenyatta and his close associates were not impressed. On many occasions Kenyatta had made it abundantly clear that 'Those Africans who think that when we have achieved our freedom they can walk into a shop and say "this is my property", or go onto a farm and say "this is my farm" are very much mistaken, because this is not our aim.'[13] On 4 May 1965, Tom Mboya told an attentive parliament: 'there is no society or country where social services are completely free. So far as the nation as a whole is concerned, every service must be fully paid for.'[14]

But the disagreement between the radicals and Kenyatta's government continued, and went beyond land, medical and educational issues. As we have observed already, the radicals were also calling for rapid Africanization of the civil service and economy and the publication of a blueprint for economic and social development. More importantly, the radicals were also pressing the government to honour the party pledge on the necessity of an East African Federation.

To placate the radicals Kenyatta instructed Tom Mboya, his Minister of Planning and Economic Development, to formulate the famous Sessional Paper No.10 of 1965, otherwise known as 'African Socialism and its application to planning in Kenya'. The publication of the Sessional Paper in May 1965 sparked off fresh controversies that eventually led to the breakaway of the radicals from KANU. The blueprint clearly had no intention of altering the inherited colonial economic and social structures, and particularly their law and order aspects. Argued Kaggia: 'I do not mind calling our socialism African Socialism, Kenyan Socialism, Kikuyu Socialism, or even Luo Socialism, but I believe that whatever prefixes we use it must be socialism and not capitalism.' The radicals accused the government of advocating 'capitalism under the cover of socialism'. Kenyan academicians also dismissed the document as a 'fraud'. The document, according to Dharam Ghai, 'commits the government against a revolutionary break with the past in its attempt to transform Society'. According to Barak Obama, African Socialism, as contained in the document, remained 'undefined'.

But Mboya disagreed with government critics who were calling for scientific socialism. He called them 'prisoners of foreign propaganda'. He said: 'It was our concern to define a system and to identify policies that will meet our needs, solve our problems and further our ambitions . . . Each country has its history, its own culture, its own inheritance of economic institutions and resources, and its own problems. To impose on a people a rigid system (Marxism) that takes no account of their needs, desires, aspirations and customs is to court disaster and failure.'[15]

In March 1966 the radicals, led by Oginga Odinga, Bildad Kaggia and Achieng' Oneko, broke away from KANU and formed the Kenya People's Union (KPU), which was supported by urban workers, trade unions and students and advocated socialist policies, but in 1969 the KPU was banned following a disturbance in a Kisumu political rally at which Jomo Kenyatta was pelted with stones and at which the police shot and killed 43 people in the demonstrating crowd.

But the radical tradition continued in the ruling party, led by the radical populist member of parliament, Josiah Mwangi Kariuki (J.M.), who championed the people's right to free medical services, education and land. Finally, in 1975, after a series of bomb outrages in Nairobi, J.M. Kariuki was brutally murdered, but Kariuki's murder did not deter factionalism and dissidence within KANU. Between 1975 and 1977 a number of critical members of parliament, including J.M. Seroney, George Anyona, Flomena Chelagat and Martin Shikuku, were detained. After the death of President Jomo Kenyatta on 22 August 1978, and the rise to power of President Daniel Arap Moi, there was a lull in radical activity, but early in 1982 the government unearthed a clandestine movement which called itself 'The December Twelve Movement' and which published a seditious newsletter known as *Pambana*. Although only Wang'ondu wa Kariuki was formally brought before court and jailed for possessing the publication, several university lecturers, including Edward Oyugi, K.K. Wachira, Willy Mutunga and A.M. Mazrui were arrested and detained. On 1 August 1982 there was a bloody attempted coup which was quickly suppressed by President Moi's government. The rebels claimed in their broadcast that they wished to rid Kenya of 'dictatorship, neocolonialism, capitalism and corruption'. For a while, after the suppression of the rebellion, the radicals went underground. Others escaped to Europe, but early in 1986 the adherents of the December Twelve Movement surfaced again, this time calling themselves *Mwakenya,* and with a new underground leaflet called *Mpatanishi*. One of the apprehended adherents of the movement, Gakaara Wanjau, claimed in a press conference in Nairobi that 'the main objective of the movement was to educate the masses on their rights and the shortcomings of the present system so that ultimately the people themselves could rise against the government and bring about a socialist change and instal a Marxist regime'.[16]

Economic and social development since 1963

The achievement of independence in 1963 had implications that extended beyond political change, to include economic and social changes as well. Besides bringing vital political decisions under the control of the indigenous bourgeoisie, independence also enabled some leaders to make important economic decisions which have enhanced economic independence. Right from independence Kenya's leadership opted for a clear strategy of economic growth, based on a determination to keep existing ties with Western countries and gain foreign aid and investment. In addition, the KANU government concentrated on growth, rather than redistribution.

If one looks at the overall picture of Kenya's economic performance since 1963, one is bound to admire much that has been achieved. Rapid economic growth has been achieved in a remarkably sustained way. Except for the slump of 1973-5, when the economy was shaken by a 'quadrupling of petroleum prices', the gross domestic product has grown steadily at 5.4 per cent annually since independence. An important source of this fairly rapid growth was the country's political stability, pragmatic leadership and the economy's ability to sustain rather high rates of investment. What is even more noteworthy is that the country has, on the whole, been able to finance most of its investments out of domestic savings.

Agriculture, in particular, was regarded from 1963 as a crucial springboard of Kenya's economic and social growth. Yet Kenya's agricultural problems were acute at independence. During the colonial period the cash-crop agricultural sector was completely dominated by European settlers. As the land issue had been at the root of most of Kenya's political troubles, it was necessary to find a solution to it in the interest of stability and growth. The KANU government tackled the land issue by a massive resettlement of African farmers on the previously European-owned farms. Between 1961 and the mid-1970s the British government loaned to the Kenyan government a large sum of money to enable the latter to buy the farms of the departing white settlers for the resettlement of Africans. The scheme involved the sub-dividing of large farms into smaller farm units which African farmers could afford. By about 1971 over a million acres of land had been settled by about 50,000 families. A large number of former European farms had also been transferred to Kenyan citizens as intact units, usually with financial assistance from public funds.

In other words, the first thrust of state support to indigenous development involved the rapid transfer of land in the former White Highlands through the settlement schemes. By 1975 several large foreign-owned estates still remained, producing commodities such as tea, sisal and coffee. We learn, however, from Gavin Kitching in his book *Class and Economic Change in Kenya* that in the period 1958 to 1968 the gross farm revenue of African smallholders in Kenya grew from a little under K£8m to over K£34m, an increase of 420 per cent in a decade. The largest single item in this growth was coffee production, 'which was worth a little over K£1 million in 1958 and nearly K£8.5 million nine years later'.

Since independence the majority of Kenyans have believed that greater industrialization is essential for improving the quality of their lives. Kenya has no major minerals so the industrial sector consists mainly of processing. In that framework there have been impressive advances since 1945. The last census of industrial production before independence was taken in 1957, when a survey was made of industrial establishments which employed five or more persons. It was found that manufacturing industry in Kenya principally engaged in the production of consumer goods, or in the processing of agricultural and forestry products for export. There were also many establishments for the repair of machinery and equipment. By mid-1950s manufacturing industry in Kenya was providing nearly 10 per cent of GDP.

Though the origins of Kenya's industrialization can be traced to the colonial period, it was in the period after independence that substantial progress in the field of industrial development was realized. Manufacturing firms of different types and sizes were set up. In particular, the second half of the 1970s saw substantial industrial expansion, and a substantial entry into manufacturing by the indigenous capitalist class. The coffee and tea boom of the mid-1970s generated savings and a large proportion of these were subsequently invested in the industrial and commercial sector of the economy – particularly in food, chemicals, leather, rubber, plastic and metal processing. The 1970s also saw the establishment of three vehicle assembly plants: Leyland at Thika, another plant at Mombasa funded jointly by the Industrial Development Bank, Inchcape Mackenzie and Kenya Motor Holdings, and a General Motors plant in Nairobi.

In the fourth National Development Plan it was estimated that some K£317m would be required for investment in the industrial sector over the period 1979-83. As Kenya had opted at independence for an open capitalist economy foreign investment was encouraged, especially in priority industries, which include basic steel, machinery, heavy chemicals and machine tools. Both the British and Americans have been the major foreign investors in Kenya. In 1986 the British had the largest stake in the country with a total of KSh.24 billion in both joint and direct investments. They were followed by the US firms which had invested about KSh.5.3 billion. Some of these investments require advanced technology and management skills which had to be initially imported. However, in May 1986 President Moi's government made a ruling to the effect that in the future for any foreign enterprise to be registered it needed to go into partnership with indigenous capital, which must command 51 per cent or more of the investment.

The result of Kenya's industrial policies and performance since 1963 is that Kenya is today self-sufficient in the production of many goods which previously had to be imported. Reasonable success has also been realized in introducing some of Kenya's industrial products to the international market. Impressive achievements were made, particularly in the sugar, textile, and pulp and paper industries by the government and by private investors. For example: in 1963 Kenya produced 33,000 tonnes of sugar; in 1982 she produced 400,000 tonnes. In 1960 Kenya produced 3,000 tonnes of paper; this figure had risen to 85,000 tonnes by 1982. By 1982 the Kenya textile industry was able to meet 85 per cent of the local demand for clothes and cloth materials with good quality products.

The rapid expansion of the agricultural and industrial sectors has contributed much to the expansion of marketed production either in response to increased demand for capital and consumer goods and services or through making available surplus goods and services to be used for getting export earnings. The major functions of the Ministry of Commerce since independence included stimulating the growth of domestic marketed production, facilitating Kenyanization of trade, ensuring continuous availability of essential commodities throughout the country, promoting and protecting consumer interests, and promoting exports from Kenya.

In terms of internal trade, the Kenyanization of wholesale and retail business was seriously pursued in the process of implementing the Trade Licensing Act of 1967. By 1982 the majority of licensed businesses were being run by citizen traders whose number was estimated at 110,786. Indeed, by 1982 some 27,248 small-scale indigenous traders had benefited from loans totalling some K£796,000 issued by the District Loan Boards since 1963. In terms of external trade Kenya's major trading partner since *uhuru* has been the

European Economic Community, which has been absorbing one-third of Kenya's exports, which include coffee, tea, pineapples, cashew nuts, hides and skins, pyrethrum extract, fresh and processed horticultural produce, flowers, mushrooms and other products. The African continent takes the second place as a major consumer of Kenyan exports – importing particularly Kenya's industrial products. A few other regions, such as the Far East, the Middle East, India, Japan and Australia, absorbed about 20 per cent of Kenya's total exports in 1981, while the USA and Canada accounted for 5 per cent of the 1981 export. In the same year some 1.3 per cent of Kenya's external trade went to Eastern socialist countries.

Who controls Kenya's economy?

During the first twenty years of Kenya's independence both right-wing and left-wing scholars in Kenya and abroad were engaged in a bitter controversy over the nature and direction of the Kenyan economy. The left-wing was on the offensive. Led by Steve Langdon, Colin Leys and Raphie Kaplinsky, they adopted the underdevelopment, or 'dependency', thesis as expounded by Gunder Frank and Paul Boran for Latin American development, to analyse the performance of the Kenyan economy.

The underdevelopment school argues that the patterns of subordinate development established at the periphery of imperialism before and during the colonial phase are self-perpetuating. Gunder Frank, in particular, identified a historical sequence of mechanisms through which metropolitan capital secured monopolies enabling it to appropriate the surplus generated at the periphery and largely transfer it to the metropole, 'the latest and apparently most invulnerable mechanism being the monopoly of technology possessed by the leading multinational corporations'.[17]

With regard to Kenya, both Kaplinsky and Langdon argued that the indigenous bourgeoisie is still incipient and has not transcended its essentially petty-bourgeois or comprador character. It is largely unproductive and not capable of spearheading a transition to real capitalist development. The principal source of this incapacity is the complete dependence of this indigenous bourgeoisie on foreign capital for which it operates either as an agent, a transmission link or as a junior, subordinate partner.[18] Thus looked at, the Kenyan economy is a neo-colonial economy whose development is both distorted and slowed down by continuous transfers of surpluses to the various metropoles whose monopolies operate in Kenya. With regard to the Kenyan bourgeoisie, the 'dependency' school dismisses it as 'auxiliary', and the Kenyan state power is seen as a direct instrument of foreign bourgeoisie.

What, however, is the right picture? The truth is that although Kenya from 1963 opted for a capitalist development and invited foreign investors, the interests of the indigenous bourgeoisie and foreign capital *have never* been 'harmonious'. Available evidence indicates that over the first two decades of independence there was a steady growth of indigenous capitalist enterprise in Kenya. Originally based on merchant capital, this national bourgeoisie is gradually moving into manufacturing, and far from this bourgeoisie being 'auxiliary' to international capital 'it has used its connection with the Kenyan state successfully to establish itself in direct competition with foreign firms'.[19]

The African capitalist class is not a creation of the post-colonial state. Research findings of Gavin Kitching, Nicola Swainson and Michael Cowen indicate that this class had been forming since the 1920s and that the primary source of accumulation for this bourgeoisie was land and agriculture. Before independence its development was impeded by the limits imposed on it by settler capitalism, but by 1960 the economic and political weight of the indigenous owners of capital was already decisive. We are told, for example, that between 1955 and 1964 their capital accumulation increased from K£5.2m to K£14.0m per annum. From 1963 this indigenous capitalist class was to extend the basis of its accumulation assisted by the power of the state. In her book *The Development of Corporate Capitalism in Kenya,* Nicola Swainson tells us that preferential access to certain areas of the economy, such as trade, was secured through the mechanism of licensing.

The first legislation to this effect was the Trade Licensing Act of 1967, which excluded non-citizens from trading in rural and non-urban areas and specified a list of goods which were to be restricted to citizen traders only. These included most basic wage goods such as maize, rice and sugar, and was to be extended later on in the 1970s to include most commodities like textiles, soap and cement.[20] The Kenya National Trading Corporation, which had been formed in 1965 to handle domestic import–export trade, was also used extensively after 1967 'as an instrument by the emergent bourgeoisie to penetrate the wholesale and retail sectors, which had formerly been the exclusive preserve of non-citizens'.[21] In 1975 the Trade Licensing Act was amended to the effect that all goods manufactured by foreign firms in Kenya must be distributed through the KNTC-appointed citizen agents. Again, as Swainson puts it, 'This move cut out a substantial proportion of the wholesale trading profits to foreign corporations and brought a wider range of commodities under the control of African merchant capital.'[22] It should also be appreciated that another important feature of the transfer of the economy to the Africans has been the large-scale extension of state credit institutions, such as the Agricultural Finance Corporation (AFC) and Industrial and Commercial Development Corporation (ICDC). The ICDC, which has been in operation since 1964, is in charge of the Commercial Loans Revolving Fund through which it helps progressive citizen traders, especially those who acquire businesses from non-citizens through the government's Kenyanization of trade programme. Between 1964 and 1972 more than 2,542 citizen traders received financial assistance worth KSh.70m through this ICDC scheme, and between 1974 and 1975 total loans given out by ICDC to 1,087 citizen traders and industrialists amounted to K£2.7m.

The effects of massive transfer of land and commercial facilities and capital to the African farmers and citizen traders since independence is that 'African capital became first significant, and then predominant'. By 1977 it was estimated that only 5 per cent of the mixed farms within the former White Highlands remained in expatriate hands. By 1974 the Development Plan claimed that most small commercial firms had 'already been transferred to citizen ownership' and that 'larger and more intricate firms still in foreign hands would be Kenyanized by 1978'. And as Colin Leys puts it: 'The transfer to African capital of urban real estate, already well advanced by 1976, received fresh impetus from the sudden rise in liquidity due to exceptional coffee sales of that year'.[23] In addition, passenger road transport was largely in African hands by 1977, 'as were tour companies, laundries and dry cleaning, and a rapidly growing share of the hotel and restaurant sectors'.[24]

In 1986 alone Kenyan businessmen acquired subsidiaries of several multinational companies. In April of that year Kenyans acquired 5 million shares of the Barclays Bank of Kenya, one of the biggest banks in the country. Between May and July 1986 Marshalls Kenya Ltd and Twentieth Century Fox Theatres Ltd were bought by Kenyan citizens. Kenyans also took equity control of the local tyre manufacturing subsidiary of the American conglomerate, Firestone, as well as buying interest in Mobil Oil, which changed its name to Kobil Oil Ltd. On the above evidence the underdevelopment thesis, as applied to Kenya, disappears behind ideological misconception. Kenyans, from independence, have progressively and impressively taken charge of their economic and political affairs.

This is not to say, however, that poverty, landlessness, unemployment and inequalities have been arrested to any large extent in Kenya. Indeed Kenya remains a land of a few very rich people and millions of poor folk. Within the rich few are Kenyan citizens of Asian origin who still dominate retail and wholesale business in Kenya's major urban areas. For example, by mid-1986 Kenyan Asians owned 98 of the 116 shops on the rich Biashara Street, 114 of 139 shops on Moi Avenue and 180 of the 242 shops on River Road, in Nairobi. In the same year Kenyan Asians also owned much of Kenya's large-scale import-substitution manufacturing industries.[25] The control of merchant finance in Kenya's urban areas by Asians had led to intermittent calls by African politicians for 'Africanization' instead of 'Kenyanization' of the country's commercial life. However, commerce in most of rural Kenya is in the hands of indigenous Africans.

The politics of state control

Since the formation of the first African nationalist party (KAU) in 1944 there have existed in Kenya two types of politics. The first type is the ideological politics which we talked about earlier in this chapter. Ideological politics in Kenya is concerned with the type of state which Kenyans should build and it has been expressed in terms of those who prefer a Marxist state versus those who favour capitalist development.

The second type of politics is played within the camp of those who favour capitalism, but its concern is with which ethnic group (tribe) should control state power, and therefore the economic and social life of the state. The politics of state control can thus be called the politics of tribalism.

The term 'tribalism' has been variously viewed by scholars who have attempted to discuss it. According to J.A. La Fontaine, tribalism entails, among other things, a clinging to traditional life, as opposed to rapid change. Tribalism has also been used to designate (and often deplore) nepotism in modern African states, where ties of common ethnic origins may be given precedence over other, more modern, allegiance. A man may be described as 'tribalist' when he is devoted to his particular tribe against the wider, more approved aims of national unity, modernization and justice. Similarly a society or political party may be described as 'tribalist' when it recruits members on the basis of birth into a particular linguistic, cultural or regional group. With regard to this definition GEMA (Gikuyu, Embu and Meru Association), New Akamba Union and Luo Union were tribalist organizations.

There is, of course, a world of difference between the man who, on behalf of his ethnic group, strives to maintain its traditional integrity and culture, and the man who invokes tribal ideology in order to maintain a power position and whose philosophy is ethno-centric. In Kenya, tribalist mentality and ideology developed during the colonial period due to ethnic competitions over colonial jobs and patronage, especially among the emerging educated petty-bourgeoisie. The British also manipulated ethnic differences by tribalizing local governments, schools and political associations in order to divide and rule. A few individuals, like James Beauttah, Makhan Singh, Achieng' Oneko and Jomo Kenyatta, attempted to provide political bridgeheads across ethnic and racial boundaries, but they were quickly spotted by the British, who screened or detained them. By thus keeping ethnic units apart, the spirit of ignorance and suspicion was kept alive throughout the colonial period.

If Kenyans have so far failed to dislodge tribalism from their political life it is because, at the core of nationalist parties, like KAU, KADU and KANU, were strong tribalist tendencies. Indeed each time any of the above parties called for party elections, painstaking efforts were made to ensure that each major ethnic group was given an important party post to assuage tribal feelings. This tradition has continued in Kenya, with balanced tribal representation in KANU and at cabinet.

Towards independence the small tribes in Kenya banded together in KADU in fear of the alliance of the Kikuyu and Luo in KANU. By 1965 it was certain that the Kikuyu–Luo alliance had failed. The Luo accused Kenyatta of tribalism and selfishness. On his part Kenyatta regarded the Luo as the ambitious and bitter rivals of the Kikuyu for political power. In this struggle Kenyatta forged some loose alliance of most Kenyan ethnicities with the Kikuyu and isolated the Luo throughout his rule. It was perhaps only in Luoland where the people danced gleefully when Kenyatta died.

In an interesting paper which he read at the sixth annual conference of the African Studies Association of Australia and the Pacific in August, 1983, entitled 'Organizing the political representation of the Kikuyu bourgeoisie in Kenya', Dr Scott MacWilliam argued that there was a tremendous growth of tribalism in Kenya between 1965 and 1978. This development, according to Dr MacWilliam, was brought about by the ambition of the Kikuyu bourgeoisie to dominate and monopolize Kenya's political and economic life. The path to this dream was cleared in stages: by the expulsion of the radicals from KANU in 1966, the assassination of Tom Mboya and the banning of the KPU in 1969. The killing of Mboya, in particular, brought a big rift between the Luo and the Kikuyu. In the circumstances of the suspected assassin being identified as a Kikuyu, and a spontaneous demonstration of the Luo in Nairobi against President Kenyatta at Mboya's requiem service, the Luo and Kikuyu leadership each organized a tribal response. Colin Leys described the reaction in Central Province in these terms: 'The Kikuyu leadership responded by inaugurating a mass oathing programme among the Kikuyu, Embu and Meru and also part of the neighbouring Kamba. In the course of about twelve weeks virtually every adult Kikuyu took an oath to keep the flag in the house of Mumbi (i.e. keep the government in Kikuyu hands).' In October 1969 Kenyatta was pelted with stones by the Luo when he officially opened the Russian-built hospital in Kisumu. He died nine years later without setting foot in Nyanza again.

Between 1970 and 1978, with stronger leaders like Mboya, Oneko, Odinga and Kaggia out of the way, the key jobs in government, industry, commerce and education were placed in the hands of the Kikuyu. During this period, GEMA Holdings, a supposedly commercial association, was formed to consolidate the Kikuyu, Embu and Meru economic fortunes. It issued shares to members as a means of financing the increasing agricultural, industrial and commercial ambitions of the Kikuyu bourgeoisie – particularly the Kikuyu of Kiambu and Nakuru. GEMA Holdings, incorporated with a minimal capital of one million shillings, had by 1974 raised 20 million shillings from shareholders' subscriptions and by 1976 had extended this to over 50m shillings. By 1979 it was estimated that GEMA had over 64m shillings. These figures should not surprise us since the leaders of the association were among some of the top richest political leaders as well as governors and chairmen of national banks.

What is important about GEMA, however, is not that it was a somewhat successful commercial venture, but its meddling in KANU and national politics. There is evidence that GEMA was deeply involved in the 1974 national elections, particularly in Nairobi and the Rift Valley. More importantly, from 1974 the GEMA leaders, particularly Kihika Kimani, Jackson Havester Angaine, Njoroge Mungai, James Gichuru and Njenga Karume, were at the centre of the 'Change the Constitution Group' of politicians who were opposed to Vice-President Daniel Arap Moi succeeding Kenyatta in the event of Mzee's death, because they wished to keep the government in 'the house of Mumbi'. What eventually deterred the anti-Moi forces was the attorney-general's warning, backed by the government, that it was 'a criminal offence for any person to compass, imagine, devise or intend the death or deposition of the President', for which the mandatory penalty was death.[26]

Jomo Kenyatta was both a strong nationalist and pan-Africanist, but as he grew old and senile some henchmen around him, led by Mbiyu Koinange, made many appointments and decisions that were openly tribalist, and this tended to alienate and disillusion many non-Kikuyu. All these developments dramatically changed when Daniel Arap Moi took over the presidency at the death of Jomo Kenyatta. There was instant relief and a realignment of ethnic politics. Although Mwai Kibaki became the vice-president it soon dawned on the Kikuyu that they no longer occupied the number one position in the government, but they consoled themselves by regarding Moi as a 'passing cloud'.

Since 1979 politics within the Kikuyu society has centred on how to recapture the presidency. For example, in 1981 a Kikuyu by name Andrew Mungai Muthemba was tried and acquitted of treason on charges that he was plotting to overthrow the government and kill the President. He was alleged to have recruited an assassination squad which was training at an abandoned quarry at Ndeiya, Kikuyu. Later in 1983 the member of parliament for Kikuyu and Minister for Constitutional Affairs, Charles Njonjo, was alleged to be plotting to take over the government. A judicial commission of enquiry upheld the allegations, but President Moi later pardoned Njonjo and no action was taken.

For their part the Luo saw no reason to continue with the politics of opposition after Kenyatta's death. The Luyia, who in the past divided their support between the Kikuyu and the Luo, had, by mid-1980s, also emerged as strong contenders for the presidency. To eliminate inter-ethnic rivalries and in a bid to forge unity among Kenyans, in 1980 President Moi outlawed tribal associations like GEMA, the Luo Union, the New Akamba Union and the Abagusii Union, as well as parliamentary ethnic pressure groups. In 1982 Kenya became officially a one-party state, as it was feared that a multi-party system might encourage tribal groupings in several parties.

Notes

1 S. Langdon, 'The political economy of dependence', *Journal of Eastern African Research and Development* 4(2), (1974), 30.
2 H. Bienen, *Kenya: the politics of participation and control* (Princeton, 1974), 4.
3 R.M.A. van Zwanenberg, 'Neocolonialism and the origin of the national bourgeoisie', *Journal of Eastern African Research and Development* 4(2), (1974), 168.
4 G. Arnold, *Modern Kenya* (London, 1981), 1.
5 Colin Leys, *Underdevelopment in Kenya* (London, 1975); Oginga Odinga, *Not Yet Uhuru* (London, 1967); Langdon, 'Political economy'.
6 Van Zwanenberg, 'Neocolonialism', 161.

7 W.R. Ochieng', *A History of Kenya* (London, 1985), 151.
8 K. Marx and F. Engels, *Selected Works*, vol.I, 396-7.
9 J. Haberson, 'Land reform and politics in Kenya', *Journal of Modern African Studies* 9(2), (1971), 244.
10 B. Kaggia, quoted in Paul Ogulla's unpublished manuscript, 'A history of the Kenya People's Union: 1966-1969', 27.
11 O. Odinga, *Not Yet Uhuru* (Nairobi, 1967), 266.
12 *Ibid.*, 266-7.
13 J. Kenyatta, *Suffering Without Bitterness* (Nairobi, 1968), 161.
14 T. Mboya, *The Challenge of Nationhood* (London, 1970), 80.
15 *Ibid.*, 73-105.
16 *The Standard*, 21 May 1986.
17 C. Keys, in M. Fransman, ed., *Industrial Accumulation in Africa* (London, 1982), 170.
18 B. Beckman, 'Debate on Kenyan capitalism', *Review of African Political Economy* 19, 50.
19 N. Swainson, 'The rise of a national bourgeoisie in Kenya', *Review of African Political Economy* 8, 39.
20 *Ibid.*, 41.
21 *Ibid.*
22 W.R. Ochieng', *A History of Kenya* (London, 1985), 157.
23 M. Fransman, *Industrial Accumulation in Africa*, 178-9.
24 *Ibid.*, 179.
25 *Financial Review*, 30 June 1986, 3-7.
26 See J. Karimi and P. Ochieng', *The Kenyatta Succession* (Nairobi, 1980).

8 Foreign policy, 1963-1986

Katete Orwa

Some perspectives on Kenya's foreign policy

Kenya's foreign policy has been subjected to various interpretations. One view portrays Kenya as a country which pursues two types of foreign policy: the one is perceived as radical and applied to international issues, the other is conservative, aimed at creating stable conditions in East Africa where Kenya has vested interests.[1]

A more recent view, and perhaps the best articulated to date, denies that Kenya has a foreign policy independent of those of the metropolitan powers. Thus, Kenya is described as a neo-colonial state[2] which has a 'cooperative link with the world economy and multinational corporations',[3] a country joined in alliance with 'imperialism' to form 'a substantial opposition to progressive regimes' in eastern Africa.[4]

This conception has been expressed best by Timothy M. Shaw, who sees Kenya as a 'sub-imperial power', a 'middle power'. Kenya and the white-ruled South Africa, another sub-imperial power, are presented as being 'of special importance in Africa where they are increasingly able to determine continental affairs in the interests both of themselves and their external associates'.[5] He adds that 'A sub-imperial state is at the centre of the "periphery", a "client" which is able to exert dominance in a region of the Third World.'[6]

In eastern Africa, Kenya is such a power. It is the leading diplomatic and economic centre where most corporate branches are located. This enables Kenya to act to advance foreign and national elite interests, a role which produces 'dependence and regional inequality'.[7] The conclusion reached is that Kenya is a dependent, neo-colonial state whose foreign policy is basically an extension of the policies of the imperialist capitalist states and their multinational corporations.

Samwel M. Makinda has been even more forthright. Denying John Okumu's thesis that secessionist threats to the newly independent state of Kenya shaped the country's foreign policy, he asserts that 'indeed, from the beginning, Kenya's foreign policy was shaped by the need to attract more foreign capital, maintain commercial links with neighbouring states, ensure the security of its borders and consolidate the domestic power base'.[8] Makinda goes further to say that this policy only entrenched dependence on 'foreign investment' which, in turn, called for the perpetuation of Kenya's dependence on the 'East African market'. Dependence on the East African market and foreign investment was to facilitate and maintain Kenya's regional dominance. Probably, though

Makinda does not clarify the point, this regional dominance also depended on a military arrangement with the British and an alliance with Ethiopia.[9]

It is difficult to deny that Kenya is a dependent state whose development, especially economic, reflects development in Western European and North American economies. It is also true that Kenya's economy is dominated by European and American multinational corporations, itself a consequence of colonial history.[10] These may at times influence both domestic and foreign policies. Professor D.W. Nabudere has noted the impact of the multinational corporations on East African regional organization, starting with the 1964 Kampala–Mbale agreement through to the collapse of the East African Community in 1977. Some members of the former East African General Assembly have also confided that they were witnesses to the contribution of European and American aircraft manufacturers to the break-up of the East African Airways. William Attwood, United States Ambassador to Kenya during the 1960s, has given us inside information into the role of the great powers in influencing the policy of a dependent state.[11]

But it is unrealistic to assume that Kenya is led by naive leaders who have no perception of national interests except those of the multinational corporations and of a national elite. In fact, both Shaw's and Makinda's analyses are pregnant with contradictions. Kenya is supposed to be a neo-colonial state; it is at the same time said to be witnessing 'a revival of realpolitik' as a result of 'the elusiveness of development and growth'.[12] *Realpolitik* is strictly a balance of power politics and operates mainly to serve, promote and protect vital national interests. Furthermore, most of the variables Makinda cites in support of his thesis basically confirm realists' proposition of power politics. Therefore his interpretation of Kenya's dependency boils down to a balance of power explanation: Kenya entered into military arrangement with Great Britain and alliance with Ethiopia to 'ensure the security of its borders'.[13]

States are run by people. It is their character which makes up the character of the state. The foreign policy of a country and its vital interests are what those who manage national affairs perceive them to be.

Kenya, like all sovereign states, has its vital national interests, which she pursues both within the international and regional systems. Some of these cannot be realized solely through the extension of the foreign policy of a globally dominant power or by the sole promotion of a combination of external and internal group interests.

Kenya's foreign policy in perspective
The basis of post-independence Kenya's foreign policy is found in three documents, the 1960 Kenya African National Union (KANU) constitution and the 1961 and 1963 KANU Manifestos. In the constitution, four of the stated aims relate to foreign policy. There is a commitment by the nationalists to 'vigilantly safeguard national interest' and work 'with the other nationalist democratic movements in Africa and other continents to eradicate imperialism,

colonialism, racialism and all other forms of national or racial or foreign oppression'. In addition, Kenya would join with other United Nations Organization (UNO) members to promote and consolidate 'international peace and the peaceful settlement of international disputes'. Finally, a KANU government would work with other African leaders to foster 'closer association of African territories and states by promoting unity of action among the people of Africa'.[14]

This document reveals an obvious realism. The aims are couched in moderate tones. Collective action through multilateral organizations in handling international disputes was preferred to a unilateral or violent approach. Even on the issue of African unity, the document does not refer to African federation but to 'unity of action'. The founding fathers already recognized that continental political unity could not be attained and shelved the idea. Are these the people who are said to have pursued radical African policies?

The 1961 and the 1963 KANU Manifestos, the latter signed by Mzee Kenyatta, followed the tone of the constitution, thus suggesting a degree of consistency in the thinking of leaders. A KANU government would 'take the necessary measures to protect the security of the people and to preserve the national integrity of Kenya within the present borders'. To achieve this, the armed forces were 'to be maintained at a level' that would facilitate their carrying out this role. Furthermore, party leaders resolved not to pursue 'aggressive' policies or harbour imperialistic intentions against Kenya's neighbours. At the same time, the country, upon the attainment of statehood, would seek a defence arrangement with other African countries, with special attention to 'an Eastern African defence policy', so that neighbouring countries could work together to maintain regional stability.[15]

By 1963, Kenya leaders had already accepted the necessity of upholding the pre-independence *status quo* in eastern Africa. That year's KANU election manifesto declared that Kenya would 'build on the foundation of the East African Common Services Organization and of the East African Common Market to bring the people of Kenya, Uganda, Tanganyika and Zanzibar into closer political co-operation'. The colonial economic policy which had encouraged foreign private investment in Kenya would remain unchanged, while local private investment and state participation in the economy would receive governmental support.[16] Thus in East Africa no radical changes were expected. Things were to remain the way they had been, although evolutionary changes would be acceptable. No critic has shown that the three KANU documents were drafted with the aid of the imperialists or at the request of multinational corporations.

As far as Africa was concerned, KANU adopted an anti-colonialist policy, committing the country to the support of liberation movements. Leaders agreed to work together with other African states toward the gradual realization of 'continental unity'.[17] Finally, non-alignment would constitute the basis of Kenya's global policy, with Kenya offering friendship to every country that

221

would 'return it'. But the policy of non-alignment would not mean neutrality in world affairs. Far from it: Kenya planned to participate fully in international developments, supporting what the 'country believed is right' and judging each case 'on its merit'. To this end, Kenya would not permit 'the existence of foreign military bases on our soil', and the soon-to-be government committed itself to supporting world efforts for universal disarmament.[18]

The foreign policy of the new state

When Kenya gained her independence she chose to be guided by a number of principles in the conduct of her foreign relations. The division of the world into two antagonistic blocs gave birth to a principle that such division constituted a hindrance 'to the development of world peace and welfare'.[19] Consequently the new state rejected this world system. This logically led to the adoption of the principle of non-alignment in international affairs. It was a principle by which the new state asserted her right to independence and sovereignty. As a corollary the new state postulated the principle of 'positive independence', which expressed the country's determination to be an effective actor in world affairs and her opposition to 'imperialism, neo-colonialism, racialism and all other forms of foreign or national oppression'.[20] Internal and regional conditions produced the principle of a regional *status quo,* from which emerged the policy of 'good neighbourliness'. To this was tied an economic ideology known as African Socialism, which rejected 'Western Capitalism and Eastern Communism'.[21]

From these principles four levels of policy become discernible. At the first level concern centres on global issues which come under the general policy of non-alignment. At the second level focus is on continental affairs, while at the third and final level of policy concentration is on the attainment and maintenance of regional stability. Collectively, activities at all these levels seek specific foreign policy goals. At the top of the objectives list are what K.J. Holsti calls *'core'* interests, which comprise territorial integrity, independence and sovereignty, and national security. Connected to these are the 'middle-range' objectives – economic, cultural and commercial relations, diplomatic representations and political influence.[22]

Although the ruling party, KANU, evolved Kenya's foreign policy principles and identified international goals before independence, implementation had to wait until after independence. How well foreign policy was conducted would depend in turn on the new country's diplomats. Yet in 1963 Kenya did not have professional diplomats and was bound to rely on inexperienced diplomats. This situation no doubt influenced the evolution and the style of foreign policy management.

The period between 1963 and 1966 was therefore characterized by a search for a workable system of foreign policy management. It was, in addition, marked by a fairly vocal parliament which sought to put its imprints not only on foreign policy formulation but also on implementation,[23] contrary to conclusions reached by Ngunjiri and Okumu;[24] a foreign affairs department determined to manage the conduct of the new state's international relations, especially under Joseph Murumbi as minister of state in the office of the President, in charge of foreign affairs; a President who was inactive in foreign affairs, contrary to what Howell thought;[25] and a clique around President Kenyatta led by Njoroge Mungai, who determined that most foreign policy issues had to be vetted by it so as to avoid the pursuit of irresponsible foreign policy. It was because of this fear that Njoroge Mungai enunciated the policy, particularly after the resignation of Murumbi and the departure of the radical left from the government and the ruling party in 1966.

Pragmatism, therefore, meant that Kenya would pursue a conservative course in her foreign policy. The position that the country took following the 24 November 1964 American–Belgian paratroopers intervention in Stanleyville, Congo, and that has been used to justify a policy of radicalism on global and intra-African affairs, seems to have been Murumbi's personal assertion. He was disowned by the government in the same way as he was when he said that Kenya and Tanzania were ready to form a federation without Uganda.[26]

At the continental level, much of Kenya's policy posture expressed principle rather than a radical commitment. Support for decolonization efforts and the struggle against 'racialism' in southern Africa evolved from domestic conditions and was also in conformity with the general commitment of independent African states and the Organization of African Unity (OAU) Charter. At home Kenya had been a victim of white racism. After independence the country adopted the policy of racial accommodation. It was and is fair that Kenya should oppose racialism and call for a multiracial society in southern Africa. In a similar vein support for liberation movements has consisted of collective diplomatic action and financial contributions to the OAU's Liberation Fund. All factors considered, this posture was consistent with the policy of 'wait and see'. It was a pragmatic policy because it did not alienate our trading partners, who also have entrenched economic interests in southern Africa; it kept Kenya within the mainstream of intra-African politics and protected our economic interests in Africa, as Kenya's trade with eastern and southern African countries before 1977 made up over 40 per cent of the country's external trade.[27] Not until the 1980s did the country begin to implement in letter and spirit UN sanctions against racist regimes, although she had earlier implemented fully the OAU's ban on diplomatic contact with white-ruled South Africa and Portuguese Angola, Mozambique and Guinea Bissau, among others. Indeed, until the 1981 OAU Nairobi Summit, Kenya's direct role in inter-African politics had been low-keyed. Our efforts to reconcile the liberation groups in Angola in 1975 arose from the position of Kenyatta as an African elder statesman.

Non-alignment in Kenya's foreign policy

Kenya's adoption of non-alignment as the basis of her international policy simply expressed a sense of conservatism and uncertainty in a bipolar international system. The perceived threat of neo-colonialism, which in the 1960s was thought to constitute a potential danger to formal political independence, called for a posture that could protect the formal political independence, especially when there was no doubt about the inability of the new states to defend their independence and sovereignty with military force.[28] Thus, to Kenya as to other Third World states, non-alignment 'came to denote a policy as well as a strategy designed to avoid entanglement in the cold war which characterized this bi-polar structure' of the new international system.[29]

Non-alignment sought to enable the new state to be an actor in international politics without losing her identity. As a part of a collectivity Kenya hoped to effectively pursue her international interests. The collective strength was to derive from a moral force rather than military power. The moral force was conceptualized as pervasive and salient, encompassing security, defensive strategy and economic realms. Rapid economic development required diversification of both sources of trade and aid. But such diversification also meant increased politico-economic independence and security as it would enable the state to skirt the superpowers' 'camps in which [they provided] the philosophy, way of life and the wherewithal of life in their [respective] camps or spheres'.[30]

That Kenya saw non-alignment as a strategy to protect the nation's independence and sovereignty from extra-African threat is clear. Speaking at Makerere University on 17 August 1964, the late Tom Mboya objected to the policy of isolation or neutrality in international politics. Since Kenya 'belonged to the growing "Third World" which believed in the policy of positive non-alignment', her policy was also one 'of positive non-alignment'. Following from this fact Kenya could not 'be used as tools of any of the rich countries' nor could she be expected to ally herself 'permanently and automatically with either the Western bloc or the Eastern bloc'.[31]

Characteristic of this thinking was the 1965 Sessional Paper No. 10. In this major policy document, 'foreign ideology' was rejected and an apparent indigenous ideology of African Socialism adopted. Other elements of neo-colonialism and imperialism, such as foreign military bases, would not be permitted to be established in Kenya, nor would the country 'belong to any permanent military alliance'. A subordinate relationship with one or more countries would be avoided, as that could not be consistent with the policy of positive independence.[32] Consequently, the closure of the British military bases at Kahawa, Nairobi, now the seat of Kenyatta University, after independence was intended to underscore this policy.[33]

This line of thinking carried on to the economic field. The ideology of African Socialism, as conceived by the ruling elite, rejected both capitalism and communism as systems of economic and social organization.[34] Here an indigenous 'African . . . economic system that is positively African' was preferred. In pursuit of this 'African economic system' Kenya would 'borrow from any country technology and economic methods ... without commitment; seek and accept financial assistance from any source – without strings; participate fully in world trade – without political domination'.[35] This policy was expected to achieve two basic international economic objectives. First, the avoidance of economic imperialism, and second, the facilitation of the diversification of 'both the markets for our exports and sources of imports whether of goods, capital or manpower'.[36] When viewed from the perspective of the movement for New International Economic Order, the policy seeks the achievement of 'the establishment of a new global economic order' and promotion of 'causes of international stability as well as justice'.[37]

Positive Independence or Positive Non-alignment (the two terms have been used by government officials interchangeably) required that Kenya's relations with the major powers be carefully balanced so that the country's ability to act in international affairs was not hampered. It was on this account that the British were forced to close their base at Kahawa, and Kenya pledged that her territory could not be used by either NATO or Warsaw Pact powers in any 'localized conflicts' in which 'any part of Africa or Asia or the Middle East' was involved.[38] Ideological rigidity was equally rejected.[39] These assumptions led to the assertion that:

> We shall continue to join and co-operate with other developing nations in the fight for a new international economic order in which there will be greater justice, trade and control of international institutions that determine world economic priorities.[40]

In more concrete terms, non-alignment was formulated to mean 'a policy of equidistance' between East and West. 'Equidistance' thus underscored the existence of 'a coincidence of interests' between Kenya and the capitalist countries of Western Europe and North America.[41] This conception of non-alignment clearly described Kenya's relations in the world economy. Kenya's apparent advanced economy rested on a continued reliance and dependence on the capitalist world system. For this reason nationalization of private capital (mainly Western European and North American) was rejected on the grounds that it could 'not serve to advance the cause of African socialism';[42] that it 'would discourage additional private investment', which would reduce 'further the rate of growth of the economy'; that it would interfere with the effective utilization of 'foreign aid funds leading to an even greater reduction in development expenditure'. Therefore, nationalization would be limited to instances where private capital threatened national security; or 'when productive resources are being wasted; or when operation of an industry by private concerns has a serious detrimental effect on the public interest'.[43]

The objectives of the policy were to guarantee foreign private capital, to create conditions for additional foreign capital investment, and to attract foreign aid funds from international and Western banking and financial institutions as well as official assistance. Towards the realization of these goals

Kenya passed the 1964 Foreign Investment Protection Act (amended in 1977 and 1984), which guaranteed these investments against nationalization and made it incumbent upon the government to compensate immediately any capital nationalized. It further allowed transfer of profits, management, patent and brand name fees as well as dividends. In addition, the act created tax incentives and allowed for the creation of outright monopolies as exampled by agreements with Delmonte, Firestone and Magadi Soda.[44]

Partners in development: Kenya and the capitalist world

During the debate on the 1964 Foreign Investment Protection Bill, many backbenchers had sensed the contradiction between the policy of non-alignment and the obvious pro-West policy emerging from the cabinet. There were charges that Kenya's economic structure and arrangements could not allow the country to act independently in international affairs. This could only inhibit the realization of the country's non-alignment objectives, a situation that ought to be corrected by a slight tilt to the East. But the government, through Tom Mboya, maintained that Kenya was already non-aligned and 'prepared to establish such economic and political relations with other states as the country's interest demanded.'[45] The country's interests appear to have demanded that economic and political relations be intensified with the Western European states, since their interests coincided with those of Kenya.

Foreign private investment in Kenya increased rapidly following the passage of the 1964 bill. By 1977 the United States of America ranked second to the United Kingdom with more than $320m in capital investment. West Germany, Japan, Italy and France had also made significant inroads.[46] The contribution of foreign aid and investment to GNP also assumed an increasing importance, while a substantial part of saving and investment came to be 'financed increasingly by foreign aid and investment'.[47] (See Table 8.1.).

Table 8.1. The contribution of foreign aid and investment to GNP (K£ million)

	1965-69	1970-74	1975-79	1980-84
Gross investment*	19.7	25.4	23.9	25.6
Foreign saving	3.2	7.5	7.8	9.5
Gross national saving**	16.5	17.9	16.1	16.1
Government saving	(0.2)	2.0	2.4	(0.8)
Private saving	16.7	15.9	13.7	16.9

* Measured as the deficit on current account and exclude transfers.
** Minus debt service and profit remittance.
Source: Republic of Kenya Sessional Paper No. 1 of 1986, 15.

Almost any other economic indicator confirms the reality of the policy of coincidence of interests with the West. Kenya is most indebted to the capitalist world both in terms of funded and unfunded external debt. Tables 8.2 and 8.3 show what the situation looked like in the 1970s, which Makinda, and

Hveem and Willetts have characterized as periods in which Kenya was non-aligned and played an effective role in intra-African affairs.[48]

Table 8.2. Total public debt: funded and unfunded (K£ million)

1971	1972	1973	1974	1975	1976
94.88	105.76	126.50	136.34	167.51	209.89

Source: Republic of Kenya, Economic Survey, 1977, 59.

Table 8.3. Sources of unfunded external debt (K£ thousands)

	1971	1972	1973	1974	1975	1976
UK	46,314	47,209	48,014	47,098	43,826	40,786
USA	5,733	7,272	13,611	13,476	15,902	18,380
W. Germany	4,583	4,889	4,869	6,319	14,223	16,122
USSR	130	113	97	89	69	57
Japan	598	599	690	1,058	2,788	6,710
Israel	566	471	374	275	173	87

Source: Republic of Kenya, Economic Survey, 1977, 60.

Table 8.4. Kenya's external trade exports (K£ million)

Receiving country	1980	1981	1982	1983	1984
EEC					
United Kingdom	58.85	59.81	72.25	96.25	142.27
W. Germany	56.02	58.42	60.83	82.01	98.05
Italy	23.73	20.12	15.20	14.76	21.28
France	6.35	5.88	11.35	11.35	11.18
Netherlands	17.69	21.05	27.76	32.57	52.58
Others	12.47	12.63	15.14	17.90	22.94
Other Western Europe	23.55	18.92	21.53	24.94	33.69
Total	198.66	196.83	218.70	279.88	381.99
Eastern Europe	4.94	6.95	8.11	5.48	6.78
USA	16.93	19.52	35.18	39.10	38.82
Japan	3.83	3.74	3.46	4.63	6.13
China (Peoples Republic)	1.96	0.63	0.31	1.88	3.29

Source: Republic of Kenya, Economic Survey, 1985, 96; Republic of Kenya, Economic Survey, 1977, 76.

Table 8.5. Kenya's import trade (non-African) (K£ thousands)

From	1977	1978	1979	1980	1981	1982	1983
EEC							
UK	95,218	145,933	141,311	162,369	156,850	135,756	121,535
W. Germany	57,851	87,755	68,809	77,659	75,115	75,627	70,319
Italy	22,007	33,490	23,745	37,682	25,229	22,959	15,690
France	26,316	30,831	17,627	32,690	31,149	28,111	38,632

Netherlands	10,901	15,961	14,111	20,879	21,103	23,114	27,718
Others	27,528	40,417	35,916	38,995	37,359	36,159	47,433
Other W. Europe	17,470	13,714	18,131	19,722	27,668	16,929	24,947
E. Europe	4,247	5,340	4,737	6,606	6,210	5,405	4,054
USA	30,482	41,096	34,925	60,964	63,651	53,377	56,541
Japan	65,603	67,912	49,927	88,409	73,456	70,137	85,523
China (People's Rep.)	5,814	5,103	4,804	7,192	8,184	6,608	3,076

Source: Republic of Kenya, Statistical Abstract, 1984, 73.

Although Kenya's foreign policy sought to diversify sources of trade so as to reduce her dependence on one state or group of countries, in practice diversification has been mainly within the capitalist market system, although limited participation in the planned economies has been maintained. This demonstrates the distinction between idealism and realism in international politics. As already indicated above, Kenya's real economic world lies in the capitalist world system and nothing short of revolution could change that fact. Tables 8.4 and 8.5 indicate the direction of Kenya's external trade – trade outside Africa. Both show conclusively that Kenya has taken measures to diversify her trade sources, but that the process has been largely concentrated in the capitalist economies. Socialist countries account for less than 3 per cent of both exports and imports. Yugoslavia is the only one that has capital investment in Kenya, while the People's Republic of China is currently engaged in the construction of a multi-million shilling sports complex in Nairobi.

The same pattern exists with respect to diplomatic and security relations. Kenya has resident diplomatic representation at ambassadorial level with only the People's Republic of China and Union of Soviet Socialist Republics. Yugoslavia has a trade mission. Kenya has yet to recognize North Korea, although it recognizes South Korea and has allowed the latter to be represented in Kenya. Another point worth noting is that Kenya does not post a military attaché to her embassies in Moscow and Peking, while such have been found in London, Bonn, Paris and Washington since 1976. Most of Kenya's ambassadors are concentrated in Western Europe, North America, Japan, Australia and India. With the exception of North Korea, Cuba and Romania, all the major socialist countries of Eastern Europe and the People's Republic of China are represented at ambassadorial level in Kenya. Ambassadorial representation in Moscow and Peking must therefore be attributed to the importance of these countries in the international power structure rather than to the policy of non-alignment.

Although diplomatic and economic relations do suggest that Kenya interacts with the socialist countries, military relations do not conform to the other two levels of relations. For purposes of military training, Kenyan military officers have since independence been sent to the United Kingdom, Israel and the United States, the last having acquired greater importance than Israel after 1976, for advanced training. This training has influenced equally the sources of arms, with NATO countries supplying 80 per cent and the United States 14 per cent of all arms imported by Kenya during the 1970s. Of the NATO countries, the top suppliers are the United Kingdom, Italy, France and West Germany. Outside of NATO and the United States, Israel remains a leading supplier.[49] In addition, Kenya has since 1964 maintained direct military links with the West. After closing the British military base at Kahawa she signed a military pact with Britain, the object of which was and still remains the guaranteeing of Kenya's security from both internal and external threat. At the same time she rejected a Soviet economic and military aid package in 1966. The 1980 military agreement with the United States not only contradicted the principle of not allowing Kenya to be used as a stage-off base in conflicts involving Africa, Asia or the Middle East, but also underscored the contradictions that exist between Kenya's acceptance of non-alignment as a principle and the pursuit of national interests in partnership with Western Europe and North America.[50]

Throughout the 23 years of her independence Kenya has rejected only military and economic aid from the Soviet Union and ordered closed only the embassies of the Peoples' Republic of China, and Czechoslovakia.[51] No official visits have been exchanged at the highest level of government between Kenya and the Soviet Union. Thus relations with the Soviet Union have 'continued on a polite formal basis'.[52] This is what makes President Daniel Arap Moi's visit to China in 1980 of special significance. This visit took place only after Peking normalized relations with the United States and declared the open door policy, that set the stage for military cooperation with the United States and closer economic relations with the capitalist countries of the West, including Japan and the United States. This visit to China was followed by another to Yugoslavia, a member of the non-aligned movement.

One is therefore inclined to observe that Kenya has always had special relations with Western Europe and that this relationship is explained by a feeling that Kenya's economic and social development can best be achieved through a capitalist system of production at home, but which must receive a steady inflow of external capital. Diplomatic and security relations are therefore essential if the economic goals based on the capitalist mode of production are to be achieved. But this development strategy also requires that special relationships and conditions prevail in Africa generally and eastern Africa in particular.

Kenya's objectives in eastern Africa

During the colonial period regional commerce was a major factor in Kenya's economic development. Kenyan nationalists did not anticipate a major restructuring of this economy.[53] After independence they sought to preserve regional economic structures together with all the benefits that had accrued to Kenya before independence. Towards this end Kenya enunciated the policy of good neighbourliness. 'Good neighbourliness simply meant the maintenance of pre-independence status quo'.[54] The new state wished and desired to 'dwell in unity, peace and liberty' and to receive political goodwill from her neighbours, so that 'plenty be found within our borders'.[55] The call for the preservation of the pre-independence regional system was not idealistic. It was necessitated by the apparent precarious position in which Kenya found herself upon the attainment of statehood in 1963.

Kenya's special economic position in East Africa 'risked being challenged by Tanzania and Uganda' following the departure of British colonialists,[56] who had created a dependency relationship among the East African states. Kenya had developed into an East African metropol and Tanzania and Uganda constituted her periphery. In turn, Kenya formed the periphery that linked Tanzania and Uganda with metropolitan Europe and North America. Through such institutions as the East African Common Services Organization, the East African Currency Board and the East African Common Market, with a more or less uniform external tariff and a virtually free-trade system in the region, she completed the linkage. Common services – East African Posts and Telecommunications, East African External Telecommunications, East African Railways and Harbours and East African Airways – were established for the region with headquarters in Nairobi. Thus, Nairobi became the centre of economic and communication activities in post-Second World War British East Africa. Foreign investors responded well, investing their capital in Nairobi, where industries manufactured goods for a protected East African market.[57]

Consequently, Nairobi became the centre for international capitalist penetration of East Africa. The inflow of external capital into Kenya at the expense of her neighbours enabled her to develop ahead of her neighbours. Tanzania and Uganda, therefore, grew to form the peripheries that supplied raw material for use by Kenya-based industries. They also constituted the principal markets for Kenya's manufactured goods. In addition, foreign firms based in Kenya acted as middlemen for major exports from Uganda. As Tanzania and Uganda developed into dependencies of Kenya, the latter also became inextricably tied to external capital.

After independence it was expected that Tanzania and Uganda would seek to redress the imbalance by adopting policies that would lead to regional economic reorganization, especially when it became apparent that political federation was unattainable.[58] Kenya's policy of good neighbourliness arose in part out of the recognition of this fact. A reckless foreign policy could endanger the economy which, by any measure, depended on the East African market, regional and internal stability and the continued inflow of Western foreign private capital. Hence, the *status quo* must not be disturbed, even though incremental changes in the regional system could be agreed upon. It is on the basis of this perception that Kenya's refusal to ratify the 1964

Kampala–Mbale agreement ought to be read. The agreement sought radical changes in the regional economic *status quo*. Similarly, the failure of the East African federation proposal ought to be seen in this light.[59] Even the 1967 Treaty of East African Co-operation, which created the now defunct East African Community, was signed only after significant concessions had been made by all parties involved, even though Kenya knew the treaty would bring problems.[60] Therefore the provisions, when they appeared to conflict with Kenya's development objectives, were violated altogether.[61]

Ideological differences that emerged among the East African states at the beginning of the second half of the 1960s can partly be explained by the failure to redress the economic imbalances. Tables 8.6 and 8.7 underscore the nature of inter-state trade disparity in East Africa. The table demonstrates conclusively that Kenya had a massive favourable balance of trade against both Tanzania and Uganda; that she remained exporter of finished products and consumer of raw materials from Tanzania and Uganda; and that between 1959 and 1966 Tanzania was the worst off of the three East African countries.

Table 8.6. Inter-territorial trade in East Africa, 1959 and 1966.

	Kenya		Uganda		Tanzania	
	Exports	Imports	Exports	Imports	Exports	Imports
	(£ thousands)		(£ thousands)		(£ thousands)	
1959	12,232	5,484	5,224	6,494	2,571	8,049
1966	28,792	11,108	10,430	16,404	4,637	16,347

Table 8.7. Percentage of total inter-territorial trade by commodities

1959						
Food stuffs, beverages and tobacco	60.1	25.6	26.8	33.9	13.0	40.4
Raw materials and mineral fuels	14.9	71.3	51.4	13.1	33.7	15.6
Manufactured goods and chemicals	81.2	12.7	14.7	37.6	4.1	49.7
Total	61.1	27.4	26.1	32.4	12.8	40.2
1966						
Foodstuffs, beverages and tobacco	63.6	29.7	24.0	36.0	12.5	34.3
Raw materials and mineral fuels	68.7	27.7	18.9	39.0	12.4	33.2
Manufactured goods and chemicals	65.7	22.5	25.2	37.6	9.1	39.9
Total	65.6	25.3	23.8	37.4	10.6	37.3

Source: Okumu, 'Kenya's foreign policy', 278.

The publication in 1965 of Kenya's Sessional Paper 10, which purported to be a blueprint on African Socialism, marked a restatement of Kenyan leaders' commitment to capitalism,[62] which had produced the country's dominant economic position. Two years later, Tanzania adopted a socialist economy

231

based on self-reliance as a way out of dependency on Kenya and Western capitalism, and Uganda appeared ready to follow suit when Obote unveiled the Common Man's Charter. Kenya's ruling elite perceived in these developments a threat to vital interests, a political conspiracy against the country that must be carefully monitored. One factor which appears to have mitigated against over-reaction on the part of Kenya was the fact that political and security relations with Ethiopia, Tanzania and Uganda remained relatively warm throughout the first decade of independence. This does not mean that there were no disagreements. Tanzania had misgivings about Kenya's coolness on the issue of East African Federation. But the policy of good neighbourliness, to which Tanzania also subscribed,[63] continued to prevail. Thus, Kenya continued to emphasize peaceful coexistence and peaceful settlement of disputes among the region's states.[64]

While economic conditions influenced the evolution of Kenya's policy posture in East Africa, national security issues acted to condition her approach to Eastern African affairs. In this area Kenya appeared most vulnerable on the eve of independence. Concern arose out of real threats and potential ones. The Republic of Somalia had been demanding north-eastern Kenya from the British as early as 1960. As Kenya approached independence, it intensified its claim to the territory. Kenya responded by offering to Somalia a hand of good neighbourliness while warning that she would never give up even an inch of her territory.

The North-Eastern Province issue was very critical to the survival of the new state. Much of western Kenya had once formed part of Uganda and the Kampala government had raised questions about Uganda's eastern border with Kenya. The frontier with Ethiopia also called for adjustment. The movements of Somali between Kenya and Somalia appeared to be paralleled by those of Maasai between Kenya and Tanzania. Could the Somali irredentism trigger similar interest on the part of Tanzania? A determined deterrence policy toward Somalia, coupled with a policy of good neighbourliness, could pre-empt the spread of irredentist interests.

This situation, indeed, influenced the evolution of the policy of good neighbourliness.[65] What Kenya wanted was respect of the pre-independence equilibrium in the region.[66] Emperor Haile Selassie, who also faced similar territorial claims by Somalia, underscored the point when he declared in 1964 that 'The territorial integrity must necessarily be respected, because disregard for their fundamental principles is contrary to the interest of mankind.[67]

Territorial integrity was considered a very vital national interest by the new Kenya government. It spent '$70,000,000 in unplanned for military expenditure' between 1964 and 1967 in a war of attrition with shifta over the 'North-Eastern Province.[68] The army grew from about 6,500 at independence to 16,000 in 1967 before it declined to the original size. Kenya did this while seeking a peaceful settlement. President Kenneth Kaunda of Zambia, acting on behalf of the OAU, mediated the conflict and in October

1967 President Kenyatta and Prime Minister Mohamed Ibrahim Egal of Somalia signed an agreement in Arusha, Tanzania, committing the two countries to a negotiated settlement of their disputes. Kenya's position regarding territorial issues underscored the importance her leaders put on this matter. Kenya entered a reservation that she would never consider any proposals touching on her territorial integrity.[69] This was a restatement of the stand Kenya had taken in 1965 when she recognized the jurisdiction of the International Court of Justice. Kenya reserved to herself jurisdiction over

> Disputes concerning any question relating to or arising out of belligerent or military occupation or the discharge of any functions pursuant to any recommendation or decision of any organ of the United Nations, in accordance with which the Government of the Republic of Kenya has accepted obligation.[70]

It is important to note that Kenya's first diplomatic moves in eastern Africa sought to protect the territorial integrity of the new state. This concern is what explains Kenya's decision to enter into military alliance with Ethiopia in 1964, and partly accounts for the 1964 Anglo-Kenyan military agreement. Following these military arrangements Kenya proceeded and signed two additional treaties with Ethiopia and Uganda, settling their respective border differences. In each of these treaties Kenya did not concede territory. Kenya's objective was, above all, the maintenance of regional balance and stability, because regional balance or the *status quo* has always been crucial to continued economic growth in Kenya. Eastern Africa provides an indispensable market for manufactured goods and raw material and makes a significant contribution to Kenya's balance of trade position.

Table 8.8. Kenya's external and East African trade (£ thousands)

Type of trade	1975	1976	1977	1978	1979	1980	1981
Imports							
External	352,195	393,773	529,243	658,795	619,251	957,515	931,123
East Africa	10,652	13,224	2,203	2,330	905	1,515	1,283
Total	362,847	406,997	531,446	661,125	620,156	959,030	932,406
Exports							
External	176,532	278,458	440,004	354,513	370,965	444,109	478,310
East Africa	61,450	66,604	61,814	41,822	41,820	71,595	58,918
Total	237,982	345,062	501,819	395,712	395,712	515,704	537,228
Visible balance							
External	−175,663	−115,315	−89,239	−304,282	−248,286	−513,406	−452,813
East Africa	+50,798	+53,380	+59,611	+38,689	+40,917	+70,080	+57,635
Total	−124,865	−61,935	−29,627	−265,413	−207,369	−443,326	−395,178

Source: Republic of Kenya, *Statistical Abstract*, 1984, 52.

The shifting of regional equilibrium

Generally speaking, the eastern African region had been a fairly stable subsystem between 1961 and 1970. In spite of inter-state hostility, the region did not experience any explosive wars save for skirmishes along the north-eastern front. Political goodwill tended to prevail while economic relations continued normally, despite imbalances and misgivings about these among some countries of the region. Furthermore, a balance had been maintained through restrained armament, and military alliances between Tanzania and Uganda (1963), and Kenya and Ethiopia.[71] The East African Authority performed important political functions by providing a forum for direct contacts among the East African presidents and in this sense served as a moderating factor. This condition contrasted a great deal with that of the 1970s. While in the preceding period ideological, economic and even security differences had been confined to diplomatic manoeuvre and verbal confrontation, the 1970s deteriorated into violent conflicts.

The shift began with the overthrow of Prime Minister Egal in 1969. The coup brought to power a military leadership whose Greater Somalia strategy centred on a military solution and which had no legal obligation to honour the terms of the 1966 Ethio-Somali and the 1967 Kenya–Somali agreements. Somalia proceeded to forge an alliance with the Soviet Union, from whom she expected to receive arms already denied her by the United States and other Western arms suppliers. The Soviets, in turn, saw an opportunity to counter the US presence in Ethiopia and the Horn of Africa.[72] To the north-west of Kenya another pro-Russian regime appeared momentarily in the Sudan in 1969. Uganda, under Obote, had provided the scale on which the political pendulum in the former British East Africa balanced. The coming to power of General Idi Amin in 1971 began a process which eventually disturbed the delicate equilibrium.[73] Finally, the overthrow of Haile Selassie in 1974 left a vacuum in the power equation. The new military government declared Ethiopia a socialist state, creating a prospect for Soviet dominance in the Horn of Africa.

Events moved rapidly towards the total collapse of the system. First, by 1974, Kenya risked being surrounded by socialist countries. Uganda, too, relied on the Soviet Union and Libya for military support. Although Sudan had renounced socialism in 1971 and denounced the Soviets, her ties with Kenya were just beginning to take hold. However, the presence of the Soviet Union in Somalia and Uganda was disturbing to a country which was the vanguard of capitalism in the region, particularly when the policy of coexistence that had characterized inter-state relations in East Africa collapsed as a result of hostility between Idi Amin and President Nyerere. Tanzania had also expected Kenya to denounce the military regime in Uganda. When Kenya failed to do so and continued to have normal diplomatic intercourse with Amin, relations with Tanzania deteriorated, setting in motion an unending ideological war that heightened suspicion on the part of both parties.

Kenya's policy toward Uganda may have been influenced by a number of considerations. First, economic self-interest. Under Amin, Uganda's economy increasingly became a hostage of Kenya. Second, realism cautioned against interference in the internal affairs of other countries as long as the equilibrium remained undisturbed. Thus, to Kenya, the military coup and all the accompanying internal atrocities were matters better left to the Ugandans themselves. Finally, ideological consideration may have also played a part. Obote had been more pro-Nyerere and he had leaned toward socialism. Amin ended this trend and acted as a check against the spread of Tanzania-type socialism in the region.

The economic conditions that prevailed in the 1970s also tended to blur the perception of some of the ruling class in Kenya. Idi Amin's economic policies led to the collapse of Uganda's economy and Kenya's exploitation of Uganda heightened. Thus, Uganda became increasingly more important for commercial purposes than the East African Community arrangement. Or so it seemed to the inner circle in the government. A feeling grew that the Community's Common Services in Tanzania lost money and were being subsidized by Kenya.[74] The *Daily Nation* captured the mood in an editorial on 8 August 1976:

> Our posture must be to diversify our exports and imports to other areas and to find alternative routes so that economic blackmail should not succeed . . . especially given irreconcilable ideological difference between us and our neighbours . . .

Finally, in January 1977, Kenya took a bold step by breaking up the East African Airways. Tanzania had earlier pleaded with members of the East African General Assembly to save the airline, and later retaliated by closing all its borders with Kenya, an act which ended the Community system. Tanzania explained her action: 'If Kenya did not want air, railway and sea links with her neighbours, there should be no reason why she should want a road link with the same neighbours.' Kenya was thus mistaken in thinking that Tanzania could not block her access to the southern African market.[75]

The collapse of the Community left a regional vacuum. It had provided a framework for consultation among the East African leaders. After Amin took over power in Uganda the forum never functioned properly again, but it had continued to provide psychological security. In its aftermath, both Kenya and Tanzania sought alternatives. Kenya looked northwards, trying to build political and economic links with the Sudan.[76] As for Tanzania, she sought to create new economic groupings, such as the Southern African Development Coordination Conference (SADCC) and the Kagera Basin Development Council. But attempts at creating new power centres did not yield immediate dividends and they failed to provide mechanisms for balancing regional power at a time when there was occurring an apparent arms race in the region.

Between 1963 and 1969, Kenya's most aggressive enemy, Somalia, had an army of about 4,000 men, which compared well with Kenya's estimated force of 6,500 after the Arusha Agreement, and Ethiopia's 35,000-man army. Kenya's military arrangements with Ethiopia and Great Britain also enabled Kenya to balance out Somalia's power, especially when other neighbours did not represent an immediate security threat.[77] Both Tanzania and Uganda, under Obote, had maintained their forces at 7,000 and 10,000 men respectively and were members with Kenya in the East African Community, a situation which contributed to the policy of peaceful coexistence during the 1960s and the early part of the 1970s.

The arrival of the Soviets in Mogadishu, following the 1969 coup, the existence of military governments in Ethiopia and Uganda and the internal instability that developed in the latter two countries eventually destabilized the region. The Somali army increased from about 4,000 men in 1968 to 53,000 in 1977. Somalia also introduced the largest and most advanced military arsenal. Equipment included 250 T-34, T-54 and T-55 Soviet battle tanks; more than 300 BTR-40 and BTR-152 armoured cars; while the air force possessed 66 combat aircraft consisting of Soviet MiG-15s, 17s, and 21s.[78]

In Ethiopia the coup removed from power Kenya's most trusted ally in the Horn of Africa,[79] and the revolution momentarily dismembered Ethiopia's 35,000-man army. Moreover, American-supplied military equipment was thought to be no match for Soviet-armed Somalia. Ethiopia's air force had a few US F-5A and F-5E fighter aircraft and some battle tanks, but her military weakness was made worse by civil war and secessionist movements which intensified with the revolution.[80]

In East Africa Amin duplicated Somalia. He began to claim much of western Kenya and part of Tanzania's Kagera enclave. His regime also brutalized citizens of Uganda's neighbours, particularly Kenya and Tanzania.[81] Uganda's army increased from 10,000 in 1970 to about 21,000 men in 1976. Amin built one of the largest air forces in East Africa. He acquired 12 Soviet MiG-21s. Other equipment included an unknown number of battle tanks and Sam II ground-to-air missiles, all of Soviet origin. Even if the army was incapable of effectively using the equipment, neighbours felt threatened.[82]

Tanzania foresaw the danger, and quietly increased and modernized her forces. In 1974, these were thought to number about 10,000 men in the army, 1,000 in the air force and a similar number in the navy. When the country mobilized against Uganda in 1978, the army consisted of over 50,000 men. Equipment included Chinese T-59 and T-62 battle tanks, one to two squadrons of MiG-17s and 19s and some ex-Chinese P-6 Swaton Class patrol boats for the navy.[83]

In the emerging power structure Kenya's position appeared weak. Kenya had demobilized her forces after the 1967 Arusha Agreement. Therefore, by the early 1970s, the armed forces stood at about 6,950 men. The army had no battle tanks, while the air force flew 6 BAC-167 aircraft, 5 Bulldog armoured trainers, 10 Beaver light transport planes and two Bell helicopters.[84] As tension increased during the second half of the 1970s Kenya entered the regional arms race. The three branches of military increased steadily from 1976 onwards. Military expenditure rose from less than 1 per cent of GNP in 1973 to 4.6 per cent in 1978, while spending as a percentage of total governmental recurrent expenditure increased from 6.3 per cent in 1967 to over 10 per cent in 1970. Defence allocation in the 1980/81 fiscal year accounted for 25 per cent of the budget. The country also acquired 12 US F-5E and F-5F fighter aircraft, a number of anti-insurgency attack helicopters, and an assortment of battle tanks from Britain, in addition to transport planes, armoured cars and many other weapons from Israel, France and the Federal Republic of Germany. This growing concern with security dictated that military alliance with socialist Ethiopia be maintained, and when Somalia went to war with Ethiopia in 1977, Kenya intervened and asked the United States not to supply Somalia with military material. Kenya acted in self-interest and ignored the ideological difference between herself and Ethiopia.

The 1977/78 Ethio-Somali war and the 1978/79 Tanzania–Uganda war arose out of the collapse of the eastern African system that had operated since 1961. Economic self-interest on the parts of Kenya and Tanzania and an uncompromisingly antagonistic personality clash between Amin and Nyerere led to the collapse of the East African Community and with it went its role as a stabilizing political institution. Political changes in Somalia, Uganda and Ethiopia combined with massive armament postures to disturb the equilibrium that had existed in eastern Africa up to about 1974. A strongly armed Somalia felt more confident in invading Ethiopia, which found herself polarized by internal power struggles and weakened by secessionist wars. Kenya, which had relied on Ethiopia to balance out Somalia's aggression, increasingly felt threatened and responded by maintaining alliance with a vowed Marxist–Leninist state at the same time as she was breaking the East African Community, purportedly because of Tanzania's socialist policies.

In addition, she was forced to enter the regional arms race, thereby obeying the dictates of power in international politics. Regional equilibrium had been disturbed and each member of the system not only had to protect itself but also had to work towards the re-establishment of the lost equilibrium.

The politics of stabilization and the return to equilibrium

When a balance of power is disturbed the tendency is for the situation to return to equilibrium. The balance of power that had contributed to regional stability in the 1960s was grossly disturbed in the 1970s mainly because of developments in Somalia and Ethiopia; partly because of suspicion and ideological differences between Kenya and Tanzania; and partly because of irresponsible leadership in Uganda, all of which culminated in the break-up of the East African Community, the closure of borders between Kenya and Tanzania; and wars between Ethiopia and Somalia and between Tanzania and Uganda. Kenya and Tanzania made attempts to redress the systemic imbalance, Kenya by seeking to foster new relations with Sudan and Ethiopia, while

Tanzania looked south, where she helped form SADCC.

Kenya's northern oriented strategy led to the establishment of permanent ministerial and border consultative committees with Sudan and the invitation of Colonel Mangestu Haile Mariam to pay a state visit to Kenya in 1980. While in Nairobi, Colonel Mangestu and President Moi reaffirmed their countries' continued commitment to the 1964 military treaty. Earlier, President Moi had been on a state visit to Mogadishu, aimed at improving relations in the Horn of Africa. In 1981 President Moi brought together Colonel Mangestu and General Numeiry in a diplomatic effort to have Ethiopia and Sudan settle their difference over support for liberation movements based in their respective countries. These efforts by Kenya and Tanzania were part of various attempts to re-establish the collapsed East African equilibrium. Ethiopia, with the assistance of the Soviet Union and Cuba, also re-emerged as a major factor in the power equation in the Horn of Africa. Ethiopia's new massive military power, together with the enlarged and modernized Kenyan security forces, eventually re-established the military balance in the Horn of Africa that had been lost in the 1970s.[85]

The return of Milton Obote to power in Uganda in 1980, instead of undermining the re-establishment of the lost equilibrium, contributed towards its achievement. Obote's presence on the East African political scene led to improved relations among the three East African states. He successfully brought the East African leaders together in Kampala, setting the stage for future summits aimed at normalization of relations. The process was given momentum by the widening political instability that threatened to engulf all of the eastern Africa states following the conflicts of the late 1970s. Obote's government faced a Museveni-led rebellion along with other minor opposition groups. These groups sought to use neighbouring countries as their operational bases against the Obote regime. In Kenya the now-defunct Kenya Air Force mutinied on 1 August 1982, and the ringleaders fled to Tanzania where they were given political asylum. Two months later a coup plot against Nyerere was uncovered in Dar-es-Salaam and the leaders of the plot fled to Kenya where they received protection. Sudan and Ethiopia had their own perennial secessionist movements with which they had to contend. These developments underscored the problem of regional security – that is, insecurity in one country seemed to influence events in another.

It was with this background that the heads of state of Kenya, Tanzania and Uganda held their first official summit in Tanzania in October 1983. No such meeting had taken place since 1971. The three leaders, Moi, Obote and Nyerere, signed a secret security agreement, the effect of which was the repatriation of dissidents from Kenya to Tanzania and Uganda, and from Tanzania to Kenya to stand trial in each of these countries for treasonable offences. It seems that future summits were conditioned on these extraditions, because the October meeting was followed immediately by the November, 1983 Arusha Summit at which the leaders agreed to settle once and for all the issues concerning the division of the assets and liabilities of the defunct East African Community.[86]

The Arusha agreement marked the end of hostility between Kenya and Tanzania and thence normalization of relations proceeded apace. It also opened the door for solving the perennial problem of how to divide the EAC assets and liabilities, totalling K.sh. 12m. The Joint Ministerial Committee set up by the heads of state was directed to reach agreement by January 1984, demonstrating the determination of the three presidents to have the experiences of the 1970s behind them. On 25 January 1984 the countries reached agreement by which the EAC liabilities were divided proportionately – Kenya 42 per cent, Tanzania 32 per cent and Uganda 26 per cent. Assets were also divided proportionately, with Kenya and Tanzania receiving the lion's share but only Uganda had to be compensated by transfer of hard currency. It appears that the desire for regional stability was more important, because none of the parties achieved what it had originally demanded.[87]

President Moi captured the new spirit of cooperation emerging in East Africa during Kenya's Jubilee independence celebrations on 12 December 1983. 'Our foreign policy continues to be guided by the principles of good neighbourliness, non-alignment and non-interference in the internal affairs of other countries.' Kenya subscribes to these principles because the interests of all the countries in the region require adherence to them. The President added that the East African leaders had agreed on renewed cooperation because they wanted to restore 'peace and tranquillity in East Africa'.[88]

In Kenya experience appeared to have taught that regional 'peace and tranquillity' required a broader regional cooperation that went beyond the traditional East African countries. Even before the normalization of relations with Tanzania, Kenya had signed an agreement with Sudan that outlawed the use of their respective countries by subversive groups intent on destabilizing their respective governments. Furthermore, the nature of Kenya's international trade patterns that developed during the 1970s made almost all the eastern African states indispensable in national economic strategy. While Uganda remains the most important trading partner, Rwanda, Burundi and Sudan have emerged in importance since 1977. Uganda is the gateway to Rwanda, Zaire and Burundi, while the Sudanese market is in Southern Sudan (see tables 8.9 and 8.10). The continuation of this western/north-west commerce hinges on stability in all these countries.[89]

A number of observations emerge from tables 8.9 and 8.10. First, Kenya enjoys an overwhelming advantage in regional trade. Second, Uganda, Burundi and Sudan have become extremely important in economic calculus. Third, the 1977 border closure affected Kenya and Tanzania economically. As can be seen on table 8.9, Kenya exported goods worth K£20.4m to Tanzania in 1975 and K£23m in 1976. She imported K£9m and K£12.4m from Tanzania during these respective years. After 1977 there occurred a sharp fall in trade between the two countries. The border problem, further, affected Kenya's

Table 8.9. Kenya's domestic exports* (Eastern Africa): value by country of destination (K£ thousands)

Country	1975	1976	1977	1978	1979	1980	1981	1982	1983
Uganda	25,703	26,871	45,498	31,498	30,588	55,531	46,795	55,161	62,782
Tanzania	20,365	22,995	7,677	1,837	3,074	3,477	4,535	5,547	4,782
Zaire	1,797	1,975	3,187	2,086	2,306	3,643	5,315	5,095	6,770
Rwanda	4,103	4,857	5,621	7,376	8,087	12,313	20,830	20,963	23,066
Burundi	678	1,107	1,735	3,160	4,267	7,077	12,751	13,035	13,402
Somalia	2,244	2,030	1,756	2,914	2,189	4,298	1,783	3,915	2,581
Sudan	712	1,807	3,504	5,071	6,228	8,103	10,910	13,601	20,204
Zambia	6,712	6,400	6,126	5,165	5,191	4,644	1,884	1,816	1,552

*Excludes transfers and re-exports.
Source: Republic of Kenya, Statistical Abstract, 1984, 59.

Table 8.10. Kenya's imports (Eastern Africa): value by country of origin (K£ thousands)

Country	1975	1976	1977	1978	1979	1980	1981	1982	1983
Uganda	1,466	818	581	1,975	803	1,206	1,010	1,390	855
Tanzania	9,166	12,406	1,622	353	102	309	273	860	1,015
Zaire	461	410	606	466	533	157	720	987	1,214
Rwanda	—	765	1,259	2,333	3,289	2,623	3,690	2,311	3,391
Burundi	32	5	—	—	1,158	115	274	189	331
Somalia	126	103	105	20	71	44	30	33	40
Sudan	—	136	1,161	23	210	8	22	18	17
Zambia	549	824	1,030	1,575	1,243	1,518	1,592	1,372	1,040

Source: Republic of Kenya, Statistical Abstract, 1984, 73.

trade beyond Tanzania. In 1975 Kenya's African trade accounted for about 40 per cent of total exports and by 1984 this figure had dropped to 26 per cent in spite of a significant increase in exports to Rwanda, Burundi and Sudan after 1977.[90] Finally, Kenya enjoys a massive favourable balance of trade with all the eastern African countries which, as shown on table 8.7, helps reduce the volume of her international trade deficit. Therefore, Kenya must put greater value on regional stability in order to promote her economic interests.

Kenya's efforts to assume eastern African leadership following the retirement of President Nyerere must therefore not be seen as idealistic and adventuristic. It is a pragmatic approach to the politics of a region which has become of immense importance to Kenya. By sponsoring the Uganda peace talks in Nairobi, Kenya was largely promoting her own interests. The failure of the Nairobi peace agreement was thus accepted philosophically, with Presidents Moi and Hasan Mwinyi of Tanzania declaring simply that whatever was happening in Uganda, the Nairobi agreement offered the best hope for a lasting peace.[91] Realism dictated that, although Museveni had slapped Kenya on the face by floating the Nairobi agreement, his government should be accepted if the broader objective of creating regional stability conducive to inter-state cooperation was to be realized. Thus, immediately after Museveni took Kampala, President Moi joined Mobutu Sese Seko of Zaire and Juvenal Habyarimana of Rwanda at the eastern Zairian town of Goma, and declared support for the Museveni government. The Goma meeting marked the beginning of a regional-wide summitry system, and was followed by another at Entebbe, Uganda in March 1986, attended by the Presidents of Tanzania and Burundi in addition to the original four heads of state. The July 1986 Nairobi Summit brought also Sadeq El-Mahdi of Sudan, while on 27 November 1986, Burundi hosted 'the fourth regional summit of Heads of States and Governments of East and Central Africa'.[92] It is important to note that at all these summits the dominant issues have been security and economic cooperation, with the heads of states and government repeatedly undertaking not to allow their respective territories to be used by dissidents or refugees for purposes of destabilizing their home governments.[93]

Conclusion

A number of conclusions may be drawn with respect to Kenya's foreign policy. First, Makinda is wrong in suggesting that Kenya's non-alignment and active involvement in inter-African affairs ended when the country granted the United States Rapid Deployment Force the right to use Kenya's military facilities.[94] Kenya's non-alignment has always been ambivalent except at the level of principle and public articulation. This also goes for Howell's conclusion that there may have been a time when Kenya pursued a radical foreign policy on global issues. Second, Kenya's pro-West policy has never changed since 1963. This posture is explained by the acceptance of a capitalist mode of production as the best strategy for national development. Tied to this is the continued dependence on external sources for financing the budgetary deficit and development budget. In this sense then, one has to accept the existence of a coincidence of interests between Kenya and the metropolitan powers. Any policy designed to promote and protect Kenya's economy must out of necessity promote and protect external capital. It is, therefore, at this level that Kenya can be seen to promote international capitalism in eastern Africa. But does the ruling elite do this consciously, aware that it is not promoting Kenya's interests? Inter-state trade is an important national interest that has a lot of bearing on national wealth. It is clear that eastern Africa is important to the country's international commerce, a condition that even a non-pro-West ruling class would hardly wish to see reversed.

Kenya's reliance on the West and North America for security assistance by and large arises from the need to defend national territorial integrity. The defence of territorial integrity is a duty for both radical and conservative leaders alike. A policy designed to ensure national security cannot be said to promote the interests of external powers. If this were so then Kenya would have had to withdraw from her military alliance with Ethiopia after the latter adopted socialism. Does it not look strange that a 'sub-imperial state' intervened on behalf of Ethiopia during the 1977/78 Ethio-Somali war? While it is true that the foreign policy of a country reflects the interests of the class that controls economic and political power,[95] this does not mean that such policies deliberately promote the interests of metropolitan powers. Kenya's foreign policy seeks 'to promote economic and social modernization', an aim which had formed a major ideology of the pre-independence nationalists. Once they assumed political power they applied their foreign policy with a view to achieving these objectives. It is for this reason that 'relations with' other states, African or non-African, 'have been handled with a great deal of caution', avoiding racialism on even such controversial issues as colonialism, racialism, neo-colonialism and non-alignment,[96] lest a radical posture drive out and inhibit the continued inflow of external private investment capital as well as official development aid. Therefore, the 1980 military agreement with the United States of America, although a contravention of the principle of non-alignment, was not a deviation from Kenya's pro-West policy.

Notes

1 John Howell,'An analysis of Kenya's foreign policy', *Journal of Modern African Studies* 6(1), 1988 30; S. Makinda, 'From quiet diplomacy to cold war politics: Kenya's foreign policy', *Third World Quarterly* 5(2), 1983, 300-1; C. Legum, ed., *Africa Contemporary Record 1972/73* (London, 1974), B161.
2 C. Leys, *Underdevelopment in Kenya: the political economy of neocolonialism 1964-1971* (London, 1975).
3 C. Ake, 'Review of Colin Leys' *Underdevelopment in Kenya'*, *Canadian Journal of Political Science* 9(2), 1976, 341.
4 G. Lamb, 'Review of Colin Leys' *Underdevelopment in Kenya'*, *Review of African Political Economy*, May-Oct., 1975, 84-5.
5 T.M. Shaw, 'International stratification in Africa: sub-imperialism in Southern and Eastern Africa', *Journal of Southern African Affairs* 2(2), 1977, 145.
6 *Ibid.*, 146.
7 *Ibid.*, 151-2.
8 Makinda, 'Cold War politics', 302.
9 *Ibid.*
10 D.K. Orwa, 'The impact of foreign policy on the Kenyan economy', paper presented to the 3rd OSSREA Conference, Eldoret, Kenya, 28 July to 1 August 1986, 6-7.
11 W. Attwood, *The Reds and the Blacks: a personal adventure* (New York, 1967); D.W. Nabudere, 'The role of Tanzania in regional integration in East Africa: old and new patterns', in K. Matthew and S. S. Mushi, eds., *Foreign Policy of Tanzania* (Dar-es-Salaam, 1981).
12 Shaw, 'International stratification', 147.
13 Makinda, 'Cold War politics', 302-3.
14 KANU Constitution (1960), 1-2.
15 KANU Manifesto (1961), 3; (1963), 17.
16 KANU Manifesto (1963), 17, 23, 24; (1961), 14-15.
17 KANU Manifesto (1961), 28-9; (1963), 26.
18 KANU Manifesto (1961), 28-30; (1963), 27-8.
19 D.K. Orwa, 'Non-alignment; the East African perspective', in L. Adele Jinadu and I. Mandaza, eds., *African Perspectives on Non-Alignment* (Harare, 1986).

20 KANU Constitution (1960), 1-2; KANU Manifesto (1961), 28-9; (1963), 26; Orwa, 'Non-alignment', 42.

21 Sessional Paper 10 of 1965; Orwa, 'Non-alignment', 42. See KANU Manifesto (1969), 22.

22. K.J. Holsti, *International Politics: a framework for analysis* (1977), 132.

23 D. Rothchild, *The Politics of Integration* (Nairobi, 1968), 126-54; C. Gertzel, *The Politics of Independent Kenya 1963-1968* (Nairobi, 1970), 51-2.

24 N. Ngunjiri, 'The interaction of Kenya parliament back-benchers and the Kenya foreign policy', BA Dissertation, University of Nairobi, 1974; J.J. Okumu, 'Some thoughts on Kenya's foreign policy', *The African Review* 111(2), 1973, 265.

25 Howell, 'Analysis of Kenya's foreign policy', 30.

26 Rothchild, *Politics of Integration.*

27 See *Kenya Economic Survey* (1977), 75; Okumu, 'Some thoughts', 265.

28 D.K. Orwa, 'National security: the African perspective', in Bruce E. Arlinghaus, ed., *African Security Issues* (Boulder, Colorado, 1984), 205.

29 L.A. Jinadu, 'West African perspectives on the Non-Aligned Movement', in L. Adele Jinadu and I. Mandaza, eds., *African Perspectives on Non-Alignment* (Harare, 1986), 3.

30 KANU Manifesto (1961), 28-30; Orwa, 'Non-alignment', 41.

31 T.J. Mboya, *Challenge of Nationhood* (London, 1970), 234; Orwa, 'Non-alignment', 43.

32 Sessional Paper 10 of 1965, 2-3, 8-9; Orwa, 'Non-alignment', 43.

33 Mboya, *Challenge of Nationhood,* 237.

34 Sessional Paper 10 of 1965, 1.

35 Orwa, 'Non-alignment', 43; Sessional Paper 10 of 1965, 8-9.

36 KANU Manifesto (1969), 22; Sessional Paper 10 of 1965, 8-9.

37 KANU Manifesto (1979), 9; (1983), 25.

38 KANU Manifesto (1961), 30; Mboya, *Challenge of Nationhood,* 237; Orwa, 'Non-alignment', 42.

39 KANU Manifesto (1979), 8.

40 KANU Manifesto (1983), 25.

41 Orwa, 'Non-alignment', 45.

42 *East African Standard,* 30 September, 1964.

43 Sessional Paper 10 of 1965, 26-7.

44 ILO, 1972; Orwa, 'Non-alignment'.

45 Gertzel, *Independent Kenya,* 51-2; House of Representatives, *Official Report,* vol.III, part 3: First session, 7 October 1964; vol.IV, 3 March, 1965.

46 I. Gershenberg, *Multinational Enterprises, Transfer of Managerial Know-how, Technology Choice and Employment. Effects: a case study of Kenya* (Geneva, ILO, 1983); D.K. Orwa, 'The multinational corporations and Kenya's development', Seminar Paper, 2-4 December, 1985, Nairobi University.

47 Sessional Paper 1 of 1986, 15.

48 Makinda, 'Cold War politics'; H. Hveem and P. Willetts, 'The practice of non-alignment. On the present and future of an international movement', in Y.A. Tandon and D. Chandarana, eds., *Horizons of African Diplomacy* (Nairobi, 1974).

49 US Arms Control and Disarmament Agency, 1967-76 and 1971-80; *Military Balance,* 1980; R. Luckham and D. Bekele, 'Foreign powers and militarism in the Horn of Africa', *Review of African Political Economy* 31 (1984), 10.

50 Orwa, 'Non-alignment', 45.

51 Okumu, 'Some thoughts'.

52 C. Legum, ed., *Africa Contemporary Record 1978/79* (London, 1981), B280; *Africa Contemporary Record 1980/81* (1983), 225.

53 Sessional Paper 10 of 1965.

54 Orwa, 'National security', 12.

55 National Anthem, Republic of Kenya.

56 Orwa, 'National security', 12.
57 Cf. W. Elkan, 'East Africa Community', in C. Legum, ed., *African Contemporary Record 1968/69* (1969), 14-15.
58 Rothchild, *Politics of Integration.*
59 *Ibid.*, 162-3.
60 T.J. Mboya, 'The East African treaty of co-operation: how far is it a step towards African unity?' Speech at Makerere University, 19 December 1967.
61 Nabudere, 'The role of Tanzania in regional integration'; A. Chemonges, 'Uganda and the disintegration of the East African Community 1971-1977', MA Dissertation, University of Nairobi.
62 Mboya, *Challenge of Nationhood*, 73-105.
63 T.M. Shaw, 'Foreign Policy of Tanzania, 1961-1968', MA thesis, University of East Africa.
64 *Africa Contemporary Record 1972/73*, B161.
65 Okumu, 'Some thoughts', 272.
66 Okumu, 'Kenya's foreign policy', in O. Aluko, ed., *Foreign Policy of African States* (London, 1977), 143.
67 *Africa Contemporary Record 1978/79*, 145.
68 Okumu, 'Some thoughts', 271.
69 *Africa Contemporary Record 1968/69*, 159; Okumu, 'Some thoughts', 271.
70 C. Gertzel, *Government and Politics in Kenya: a nation building text* (Nairobi, 1969), 598.
71 D.K. Orwa, 'Balance of power theory and Kenya's policy in Eastern Africa', paper given at the Historical Association of Kenya Annual Conference, Nairobi, August 1981.
72 O.J.C.B. Ojo, D.K. Orwa and C.M.B. Utete, *African International Relations* (London, 1985), 98, 137-8.
73 Chemonges, *Uganda.*
74 *Ibid.*
75 *Africa Confidential*, 1 April 1977, 5.
76 See *Africa Contemporary Record 1973/74*, B184; R. Hall, 'Islamic zeal plunges Sudan into turmoil', *The Observer*, 20 May 1984, 6.
77 *Weekly Review*, 12 July 1976, 3-5; *Africa Diary*, 7-13 December, 1963, 1487; *Keesing's Archives*, 21-8 March, 1964.
78 *Strategic Survey* (1977), 19.
79 *Africa Contemporary Record 1974/75*, B193-4.
80 *Ibid.*, 19-23.
81 *Weekly Review*, 13 February, 1976, 5.
82 *Military Balance, 1979/80* (London, 1980).
83 *Africa Contemporary Record 1973/74*, B309, B269-70.
84 *Ibid.*, B176; *Weekly Review*, 12 July 1976, 3-5.
85 *Military Balance*, 1983.
86 *Weekly Review*, 16 December, 1983, 13.
87 *Ibid.*, 27 January, 1984, 29.
88 *Ibid.*, 12 December, 1983, 7.
89 *Ibid.*, 23 August, 1985, 13-14.
90 Republic of Kenya, *Economic Survey* (1977), 75, 78; (1985), 94.
91 *Weekly Review*, 31 January 1986, 7.
92 *Daily Nation*, 28 November, 1986, 1, 36.
93 *Weekly Review*, 18 July, 1986, 11; *Daily Nation*, 10 July 1986, 28; 28 November 1986, 1, 36.
94 See Makinda, 'Cold War politics'.
95 I.D. Levin in R.B. Farrell, ed., *Approaches to Comparative and International Politics* (Evanston, 1966), 213.
96 Okumu, 'Some thoughts', 263.

B.A. Ogot: a bibliography

Hudson A. Liyai

Introduction

Our aim is to bring together in one source all the creative and scholarly works of Professor B.A. Ogot and his critics. The bibliography includes Ogot's published and unpublished works. It is divided into six broad sections according to the form of the works rather than the contents of the items entered. The aim is to identify the type of work and its source including, as far as possible, the full bibliographic details.

The first section lists published books and monographs both singly or co-authored, including edited volumes. Similarly, the second section lists Ogot's contributions to books including chapters, introductions and prefaces. The third section includes articles, review articles, and significant letters published in journals. Also included in this section are the numerous editorial contributions published under the *nom de plume* 'Iconoclastes' in the *East Africa Journal,* which Ogot edited for over eight years.

Sections four and five include unpublished materials ranging from conference papers, mimeographs, lectures and manuscripts at various stages of preparation. The final section contains criticism of Ogot's writings. This includes general criticisms published in journals and books, and reviews of Ogot's books. In this section the items are entered alphabetically by either the author's name, the title of the critique, or the title of the work under review.

It is our hope that this bibliography will serve as a guide to the range and depth of intellectual output that Professor Ogot has fostered during his illustrious academic career. It is further hoped that it will be useful to scholars and researchers and stimulate intellectual exchange on the ideas and issues brought forward by Professor Ogot.

Books and monographs

1 Ogot, B.A. with J. Lonsdale. *The African Voice in Kenya*. Nairobi: East African Publishing House, 1978.

2 Ogot, B.A. *The Challenge of Nationhood: a collection of speeches and writings* by Tom J. Mboya. London: Heinemann in association with André Deutsch, 1970.
   B.A. Ogot inspired the idea, researched and selected the material, planned, edited and wrote the linking passages.

3 Editor of *East Africa, Past and Present*. Paris: Présence Africaine, 1964, 217pp., maps.
   Essays from the East African Society of African Culture (EASTASAC) symposium held in 1962.

4 Editor of *Hadith 1: proceedings of the annual conference of the Historical Association of Kenya, Nairobi, August 1967*. Nairobi: East African Publishing House, 1968, 172pp., ill.

5 Editor of *Hadith 2: proceedings of the annual conference of the Historical Association of Kenya, Nairobi, August 1968*. Nairobi: East African Publishing House, 1970, 267pp., maps.

6 Editor of *Hadith 3: proceedings of the annual conference of the Historical Association of Kenya, Nairobi, August 1969*. Nairobi: East African Publishing House, 1971, 210pp.

7 Editor of *Hadith 4: politics and nationalism in colonial Kenya; proceedings of the Historical Association of Kenya, Nairobi, August 1971*. Nairobi: East African Publishing House, 1972, 275pp.

8 Editor of *Hadith 5: economic and social history of East Africa; proceedings of the 1972 conference of the Historical Association of Kenya*. Nairobi: East African Literature Bureau, 1975, 256pp., ill.

9 Editor of *Hadith 6: history and social change in East Africa; proceedings of the 1974 conference of the Historical Association of Kenya*, Nairobi: East African Literature Bureau, 1976, 235pp., ill.

10 Editor of *Hadith 7: ecology and history in East Africa; proceedings of the 1975 conference of the Historical Association of Kenya*. Nairobi: Kenya Literature Bureau, 1979, 242pp.

11 Editor of *Hadith 8: Kenya in the 19th century*. Nairobi: Bookwise and Anyange Press, 1985, 258pp.

12 Editor of *Historical Dictionary of Kenya*. Metuchen, N.J. and London: Scarecrow Press, 1981, 278p. (African Historical Dictionaries, No. 29).

13 Editor of *History of the Southern Luo*, vol. I, *Migration and Settlement 1500-1900*. Nairobi: East African Publishing House, 1967, 250pp. (The Peoples of East Africa).
   A revised version of Ph.D. thesis presented to London University in April 1965.

14 Editor of *Kenya before 1900*. Nairobi: East African Publishing House, 1976, 291pp., ill.

15 *Kenya under the British, 1895 to 1963*. Nairobi. (Reprint, pp.255-89) East African Publishing House and Longmans, 1968.

16 Editor of *Kenya's Trade Unions 1952-1956* by Makhan Singh. Nairobi: Uzima Press, 1980, 330pp.

17 Edited with R.E. Leakey, *Panafrican Congress of Prehistory and Quaternary Studies: proceedings of the 8th Panafrican Prehistory and Quaternary Studies Conference, Nairobi, 5-10 Sept. 1977*. Nairobi: The International Louis Leakey Memorial Institute for African Prehistory, 1980, 400pp., ill. (in English and French).

18 Edited with F.B. Welbourn, *A Place to Feel at Home: a study of two independent churches in Western Kenya*. London: OUP, 1966, 157pp, ill.

19 Ogot, B.A. *Reintroducing Man into the African World*. Nairobi: Bookwise (forthcoming).

20 Editor of *UNESCO General History of Africa*, vol.V: *Africa from 1500 to 1800* (forthcoming).

21 Editor of *War and Society in Africa: ten studies (selected papers from the 5th Annual Social Science Conference of the University of East Africa, Nairobi, 8-12 December 1968)*. London: Frank Cass, 1972, 268pp.

22 Edited with J.A. Kieran, *Zamani: a survey of East African history*, Nairobi: East African

Publishing House, 1968, 407pp., ill.

B.A. Ogot edited the second revised edition, published by East African Publishing House and Longman, Nairobi, 1974, 405pp.

Chapters and contributions in books

1 'African ecology in historical perspective: problems and prospects', in *Hadith 7: ecology and history in East Africa, proceedings of the 1975 Conference of the Historical Association of Kenya*, ed. B.A. Ogot. Nairobi: Kenya Literature Bureau, 1979, pp.1-8.

2 With R.S. Herring and D.W. Cohen, 'The construction of dominance: the strategies of selected Luo groups in Uganda and Kenya', in A.I. Salim, ed., *State Formation in Eastern Africa: Selected papers from a Conference organised by the Department of History, University of Nairobi, held at Nakuru, September 1979*. Nairobi: Heinemann, 1984, pp.126-61.

3 'The Church of Christ in Africa', in F.B. Welbourn and B.A. Ogot, *A Place to Feel at Home: a study of two independent churches in Western Kenya*. London: OUP, 1966, pp.21-71.

4 'Description of the project: the drafting of a general history of Africa', in J.K. Kizerbo, ed., *General History of Africa*, vol.I: *Methodology and African prehistory*. Paris: UNESCO, 1981, pp.xxiii-xxv.

5 'Description of the project' in D.T. Niane, ed., *General History of Africa*, vol.IV: *Africa from the twelfth to the sixteenth century*. Paris: UNESCO, 1984, pp.xxiii-xxv.

6 'The development of African politics in the plural societies of East Africa', in J.C. Anene and G.N. Brown, eds., *Africa in the Nineteenth and Twentieth Centuries*. Ibadan: Ibadan University Press and Nelson, 1966, pp.487-503.

7 'Economic adaptation and change among the Jii-speaking peoples of Eastern Africa', in *Languages and History of the Nilotic Peoples*. University of Cologne, 1982.

8 'The external factor in African history', in *Proceedings of the Colloquium of Second World Black and African Festival of Arts and Culture (FESTAC)*. Lagos, 1977.

9 'Foreword' in B.G. McIntosh, ed., *Ngano: studies in traditional and modern East African history*. Nairobi: EAPH, 1969, p.vii (Nairobi Historical Studies, 1).

10 'Foreword' in B. Onyango-Ogutu and A.A. Roscoe, *Keep my Words*. Nairobi: EAPH, 1974, p.7.

11 'Foreword' in W.H. Whiteley, ed., *Language in Kenya*. Nairobi:. OUP, 1974, pp.ix-x.

12 'From Chief to President: a study in traditional and modern African leadership', in W. Frohlich, ed., *Symposium on Changes of Social Structures in Africa (Afrika im Wandel Seiner Gesellschaftsformen)*. Leiden, 1964, pp.84-95.

13 'The Great Lakes region, in D.T. Niane, ed., *General History of Africa*, vol.IV: *Africa from the twelfth to the sixteenth century*. Paris: UNESCO, 1984, pp.498-524.

14 'Historians and East Africa', in J.D. Fage, *Africa Discovers her Past*. London: OUP, 1970, pp.66-82.

15 'The historical development of African societies, 1500-1800', in B.A. Ogot, ed., *UNESCO General History of Africa*, vol.V: *Africa from 1500 to 1800* (forthcoming).

16 'History, anthropology and social change – the Kenya case', in B.A. Ogot, ed., *Hadith 6: history and social change in East Africa: proceedings of the 1974 Conference of the Historical Association of Kenya*. Nairobi: East African Literature Bureau, 1976, pp.1-13.

17 'History, language and culture', in *Languages and History of the Nilotic Peoples*. University of Cologne, 1982. (Dedicated to Professor Oswin Kohler on the occasion of his 70th birthday.)

18 'The impact of the Nilotes', in Roland Oliver, ed., *The Middle Age of African History*. London: OUP, 1967, pp.47-55.

19 'Introduction' in *Hadith 5: economic and social history of East Africa: proceedings of the 1972 conference of the Historical Association of Kenya*, ed. B.A. Ogot. Nairobi: East African Literature Bureau, 1975, pp.ix-xii.

20 'Introduction' in *Hadith 8: Kenya in the 19th century*. Nairobi: Bookwise and Anyange Press, 1985, pp.v-xiii.

21 'Introduction' in *Kenya's Trade Unions 1952-1956* by Makham Singh, edited by B.A. Ogot, Nairobi: Uzima Press, 1980, pp.i-vii.

22 With T. Zeleza, 'Kenya: the road to independence and after', in Roger Louis and Prosser Gifford, eds., *Decolonization in Africa*. Yale University Press, 1987.

23 'Kenya under the British, 1895-1963', in B.A. Ogot and J.A. Kieran, eds., *Zamani: a survey of East African history*. Nairobi: East African Publishing House, 1968, pp.249-94.

24 'Kinship and statelessness among the Nilotes', in Jan Vansina, R. Mauny and L.V. Thomas, eds., *The Historian in Tropical Africa: studies presented and discussed at the fourth International African seminar at the University of Dakar*, Senegal 1961. London: OUP, 1961, pp.284-304.

25 With J.B. Webster, 'The Lake Region, 1500-1800', in B.A. Ogot, ed., *UNESCO General History of Africa*, vol.V: *Africa from 1500 to 1800* (forthcoming).

26 'A man more sinned against than sinning: the African writer's view of himself', in A. Gurr and P. Zirimu, eds., *Black Aesthetics: papers from a colloquium held at the University of Nairobi, June 1971*. Nairobi: East African Literature Bureau, 1973, pp.20-31.

27 'The movement of peoples in East Africa', in B.A. Ogot, ed., *East Africa, Past and Present*. Paris: Présence Africaine, 1964, pp.36-48.

28 'Mumboism – an anti-colonial movement', in B.A. Ogot, ed., *Warfare and Society in Africa: ten studies*. London: Frank Cass, 1972, pp.149-77.

29 'On the making of a sanctuary: being some thoughts on the history of religion in Padhola', in T.O. Ranger and I.N. Kimambo, eds., *The Historical Study of African Religion with Special Reference to East and Central Africa*. London: Heinemann, 1972, pp.122-35.

30 'Oral traditions and the historian', in M. Posnansky, ed., *Prelude to East African History: a collection of papers given at the first East African vacation school in Pre-European African history and archaeology, Makerere, December 1962*. London: OUP, 1966, pp.140-8.

31 'Population movements between East Africa, the Horn of Africa and the neighbouring countries', in *The African Slave Trade from the Fifteenth to the Nineteenth Century: reports and papers of the meeting of experts organised by UNESCO at Port-au-Prince, Haiti, 31 January to 4 February 1978*. Paris: UNESCO, 1979, pp.175-82 (UNESCO General History of Africa, Studies and Documents, 2).

32 'Preface' in Basil Davidson, *The Growth of African Civilization: East and Central Africa to the late nineteenth century* (written with the assistance of J.E.F. Mhina and the advice of Bethwell A. Ogot). London: Longmans, 1967, pp.vii-viii.

33 'Racial consciousness among the Africans: a colonial heritage', in *Racial and Communal Tensions in East Africa: papers presented at the seminar organised by the East African Institute of Social and Cultural Affairs, Nairobi, 26-30 November 1964*. Nairobi: East African Institute of Social and Cultural Affairs, 1966, pp.104-12. (Contemporary African Monographs Series, No.3).

34 'The remembered past: reflections on the nature and value of traditional evidence, in B.A. Ogot, ed., *Hadith 2: proceedings of the annual conference of the Historical Association of Kenya, Nairobi, August 1968*. Nairobi: EAPH, 1970, pp.1-5.

35 'Reverend Alfayo Odongo Mango 1870-1934', in K. King and A. Salim, eds., *Kenya Historical Biographies*. Nairobi: EAPH, 1971, pp.90-111.

36 'Revolt of the elders: an anatomy of the Loyalist crowd in the Mau Mau uprising 1952-1956', in B.A. Ogot, ed., *Hadith 4: proceedings of the annual conference of the Historical Association of Kenya, Nairobi, August 1971*. Nairobi: EAPH, 1972, pp.134-48.

37 'The role of the pastoralist and the agriculturalist in African history: the case of East Africa', in T.O. Ranger, ed., *Emerging Themes of African History: proceedings of the International Congress of African Historians held at University College Dar es Salaam, October 1965*. Nairobi: EAPH, 1968, pp.125-33 (proceedings edited by P.E. Mveng, also published in French).

38 'Some approaches to African history', in B.A. Ogot, ed., *Hadith 1: proceedings of the annual conference of the Historical Association of Kenya, Nairobi, August 1967*. Nairobi: EAPH, 1968, pp.1-9.

39 With F. Hassan, 'Sudan 1500-1800', in B.A. Ogot, ed., *UNESCO General History of Africa*, vol.V: *Africa from 1500 to 1800* (forthcoming).

40 With James de Vere Allen, 'Summary and conclusions' to theme IX – Historical archaeology in Africa, with emphasis on trade; relations between prehistoric peoples of the interior of Africa and the outside world, in R.E. Leakey and B.A. Ogot, eds., *Proceedings of the 8th Panafrican Congress on Prehistory and Quaternary Studies, Nairobi, 5-10 September 1977*. Nairobi: The International Louis Leakey Memorial Institute for African Prehistory, 1980, pp.381-4.

41 'Towards a history of the relations between African systems', in B.A. Ogot, ed., *Hadith 3: proceedings of the annual conference of the Historical Association of Kenya, Nairobi, August 1969*. Nairobi: EAPH, 1971, pp.1-5.

42 'Why is Africa stagnant?', in *The Challenge of Development*. Nairobi: EAPH, 1968, pp.13-14 (Contemporary African Monographs Series, No.7).

Papers, lectures and reports

1 'African ecology in historical perspective: problems and prospects'. Presidential address to the Historical Association of Kenya, Nairobi, 30 August 1975, 8 p.

2 'As others saw us: being an analysis of grassroots imperialism in 19th Century Kenya'. Paper presented at the Historical Association of Kenya Annual Conference 1978, 9 p.

3 'Aspects of British administration in Kenya'. Paper read at the Institute of Commonwealth Studies, Oxford, November 1962.

4 'British administration in Central Nyanza, Kenya'. Lecture given to the Historical Association, Uganda Branch, 1962.

5 'Chronology in the Nilotic zone of influence'. Paper read at the Conference on African Chronology, Farnham, England, 11-15 July 1966.

6 'A community of their own: a study of the search for a new order by the Maria Legio of Africa Church'. Paper delivered to the Conference on the Religious History of Eastern Africa, Limuru, Kenya, August 1974.

7 With D.W. Cohen and R.S. Herring. 'The construction of dominance: the strategies of selected Luo groups in Uganda and Kenya'. Paper presented at the Conference on 'The process of state formation in Eastern Africa in the eighteenth and nineteenth centuries', organized by the Department of History, University of Nairobi, sponsored by the Goethe Institute and held at Nakuru, 13-16 September 1979, 31 p.

8 'East Africa and the Nile Valley: contacts in classical times'. Staff Seminar Paper No.1, Department of History, University of Nairobi, October 1970, 7 p.

9 'From chief to president: traditional and modern African leadership'. Lecture given at the Seminar on Changes of Social Structures in Africa, organized by the German African Society (Deutsche Afrika-Gessellschaft), Cologne, November 1962.

10 'Historical research in Kenya: 1963-1973'. Paper presented at the Third International Congress of Africanists, Addis Ababa, 9-19 December 1973, 3 p.

11 'History, ideology and contemporary Kenya'. Paper presented at the Historical Association of Kenya Annual Conference, 1981.

12 'Kenya: the way ahead'. Lecture given to Gayaza High School (Uganda), April 1963.

13 'Movements and cultures in the interior'. Lecture delivered at the Royal College, Nairobi, in the series 'East Africa's Past', organized by the Department of Extra-Mural Studies, 10 September 1963.

14 With W.R. Ochieng'. 'Mumboism – an anti-colonial movement?' Paper presented at the University Social Science Council Conference, Nairobi, 8-12 December 1969.

15 'Oral tradition and cultural development'. Keynote address given at the seminar on 'Oral traditions: past growth and future development in East Africa', organized by the Institute of African Studies, University of Nairobi, sponsored by UNESCO, held at Kisumu, 18-21 April 1979, 8 p.

16 'Oral traditions and history'. Lecture given at the Vacation School in pre-European African history and archaeology, organized by the British Institute of History and Archaeology in East Africa, Makerere, December 1962.

17 'The origins of the Western Kingdoms of Uganda'. Lecture given to the Historical Association, Uganda Branch, 1963.

18 'The place of history in nation-building'. Paper presented at the Historical Association of Kenya Annual Conference, on 'Teaching and the place of history in Kenya', held at Kenya Technical Teachers College, Nairobi, 25-28 August 1980, 16 p.

19 Also given as a lecture at Kabarak High School on 8 September 1984, the audience including President Daniel arap Moi of Kenya.

20 'Politics, culture and music in Central Kenya: a study of Mau Mau hymns, 1951-1956'. Paper presented at the Historical Association of Kenya Annual Conference, 1976, 11 p.

21 'Problems of Continental African history'. Paper presented at UNESCO Conference on the revision of African history textbooks on East and Central Africa, Nairobi, 25-30 March 1985, 7 p.

22 *Report of the Select Committee on East African Harbours Corporation.* Arusha: East African Legislative Assembly, 1975, 266 p. Report presented by B.A. Ogot, Chairman of the Select Committee.

23 'Revolt of the elders: an anatomy of the loyalist crowd in the Mau Mau Uprising, 1952-1956'. Paper presented at the Historical Association Annual Conference, August 1971, 15 p.

24 'The role of arts in a developing country'. Public lecture delivered at Kisumu on 15 September 1977, 10 p.

25 'The silences in the old narratives or new trends in cultural history'. Paper presented at the University of Nairobi, Dept of History Conference on 'Social and cultural history of Eastern Africa', sponsored by the Ministry of Culture and Social Services and the Goethe Institute, Naivasha, 12-15 November 1981, 16 p.

26 'Social change among the Luo up to 1920'. Research paper, Makerere University College; won the Arts Research Prize, 1951.

27 'The theoretical basis of socialism'. Address given to a seminar organized by the East African Institute of Social and Cultural Affairs, Nairobi, February 1964.

28 'Traditional religion and precolonial history of Africa'. Paper read to the Conference on African History at Lauterbach, West Germany, 6-7 June 1966.

29 'The transcription of ethnonyms in Kenya in relation to their historical study, a report'. Paper presented to the Historical Association of Kenya, 1978, 30 p.

30 'Whose history? – the dilemmas of research in early African history'. Chairman's address to the Historical Association of Kenya Annual Conference, Nairobi, 23-29 August 1984, 15 p.

Unpublished manuscripts

1 *Africa and the Caribbean* (forthcoming).
2 *An African Prophet: the life and teaching of John Owalo.*
3 With Grace Ogot. *Dholuo – English Dictionary.* Incorporating words, expressions and usages.
4 *Historical Myths and Legends of East Africa.* Recorded legends of the various peoples of

East Africa. Different variations rewritten with notes.
5 *History of the City of Nairobi* (forthcoming).
6 *Luo Historical Texts,* vols. I and II.
7 With Grace Ogot. *Luo Proverbs* (forthcoming).
8 'Migration and settlement among the Southern Luo Peoples, 1500-1900: a case history of oral tradition as a historical source'. Ph.D. Thesis, University of London, 1965.
9 'Padholla historical texts, vols.I and II'. Recordings made in Padhola on the traditional history of the Padhola. The texts have been translated into English and annotated, and are available in the History Department, University of Nairobi.
10 *Sanjasanja,* 2 vols. Luo folktales for primary schools.

Ogot and his critics

1 Amollo-Odhiambo, Peter. 'Cake on a dirty plate'. Letter in *E. Africa Journal* 2(3), 1965, p.3.
2 Austen. 'War and society in Africa: ten studies' (1972). *International Journal of African Historical Studies* 1972, p.707.
3 Barrett, David B. 'A place to feel at home' (1966). *E. Africa Journal* 3(12), 1967, pp.32-4.
4 Clayton, Anthony. 'Hadith 5: economic and social history of East Africa' (1977). *Journal of African History* 18(2), 1977, pp.142-3.
5 Clayton, Anthony. 'Historical dictionary of Kenya' (1981), *Journal of African History* 23(3), 1982, p.431.
6 Cohen, David W. 'History of the Southern Luo, vol.1' (1967). *Journal of African History* 9(3), 1968, pp.480-2.
7 Cohen, David W. with E.S. Atieno-Odhiambo, *Siaya: a historical anthropology of an African landscape.* (Nairobi: Heinemann and James Currey, UK (forthcoming).
8 Denoon, Donald. 'Hadith 3: proceedings of the Annual Conference of the Historical Association of Kenya, 1969' (1971). *E. Africa Journal* 8(12), 1971. pp.26-8.
9 Diagne, Pathe. 'History of the Southern Luo, vol.1'. *Présence Africaine* 69 (1st quarter), 1969, p.219 (in French).
10 'Education in East Africa: refuge for conservatism' (commentary). *E. Africa Journal* 2(4), 1965, pp.34-6.
11 Frontera-Rial, A. 'Kenya before 1900: eight regional studies' (1976). *American Historical Review* 83(5), 1978, pp.1314-15.
12 Gavin, 'War and society in Africa: ten studies' (1972). *Journal of the Historical Society of Nigeria* 1973, p.440.
13 Gray, Richard. 'A place to feel at home; a study of two independent chuches in Western Kenya' (1966). *Journal of African History* 9(1), 1968, pp.178-9.
14 'Hadith 2: proceedings of the Annual Conference of the Historical Association of Kenya, 1968' (1970). *Times Literary Supplement,* 21 May 1971, p.601.
15 'Historical dictionary of Kenya' (1981). *ARBA* 13, 1982, p.185.
16 'Historical dictionary of Kenya' (1981). *Choice* 19, July 1982, pp.1541-2.
17 Kamundia, C.A. 'Zamani: a survey of East African history' (1968). *African Affairs* 69 (275), 1970, pp.193-4.
18 Kimambo, Isaria N. 'Zamani: a survey of East African history' (1968). 'Hadith 1 (1968). *E. Africa Journal* 6(2), 1969, pp.41-2.
19 Kiwanuka, M.S.M. 'History of the Southern Luo: vol.I' (1967). *Uganda Journal* 33(1), 1969, pp.97-9.
20 K'Ombudo, Ojwang. 'An African man needs no introduction'. Letter in *E. Africa Journal* 5(3), 1968, p.3-4. Ogot's rejoinder, *ibid.,* p.4.

21 McCall, 'Zamani: a survey of East African history' (1968). *Journal of Interdisciplinary History* 1(1), 1970/71, pp.137-61.

22 McCracken, John. 'Zamani: a survey of East African history' (1968). *Tanzania Notes and Records* 70, 1969, pp.68-70.

23 Norton, R.F. 'War and society in Africa' (1972). *International Journal of African Historical Studies* 8(4), 1975, pp.702-4.

24 Murray, Francis. 'African heritage lauded'. *E. Africa Journal* 2(6), 1965, p.3.

25 Nyeko, Balam. 'Hadith 5: economic and social history of East Africa' (1975). *Transafrican Journal of History* 5(2), 1976, pp.185-90.

26 Odhiambo, Peter Amolo. K'Ombudo le petit progressif'. Letter in *E. Africa Journal* 5(6), 1968, p.5.

27 Okelo, Jasper A. 'Approach creates doubt'. Letter in *E. Africa Journal* 2(1), 1965, pp.3-4.

28 Okelo, Ondiek. 'Who's right?' Letter in *E. Africa Journal* 1(8), 1964, pp.3-5.

29 Okwach, Oteng' Wuod. 'Ogot and K'Ombudo and the Ombudsman'. Letter in *E. Africa Journal* 5(6), 1968, pp.2-5.

30 Oliver, Roland. 'Zamani: a survey of East African History' (1968). *Journal of African History* 10(3), 1969, pp.497-9.

31 Oludhe-MacGoye, Marjorie. 'Mr Iconoclastes breaks images vaguely conceived' (on inter-racial marriages). *E. Africa Journal* 5(11), 1968, pp.4-5.

32 Osogo, John. 'History of the Southern Luo' (1967). *E. Africa Journal* 4(3), 1967, pp.42-3.

33 Roberts, A.A. 'War and society in Africa: ten studies' (1972). *Bulletin of the University of London (SOAS)* 1974, p.284.

34 Smith, R. 'War and society in Africa: ten studies' (1972). *African Affairs* 72, 1973, p.203.

35 Steinhart, Edward I. 'Zamani: a survey of East African history' (1968). *African Historical Studies* 3(1), 1970, pp.237-9.

36 Stoll, Gerhard. 'Integration and no assimilation'. Letter in *E. Africa Journal* 2(2), 1965, pp.3-4.

37 Thurston, A. 'Historical dictionary of Kenya' (1981). *African Affairs* 81(324), 1982, pp.444-6.

38 Trappes-Lomax, Hugh. 'His intermarriages case was grossly overstated'. *E. Africa Journal* 5(12), 1968, pp.4-6.

39 Twaddle, Michael. 'War and society in Africa: ten studies' (1972). *Journal of African History* 14(2), 1973, p.354.

40 Twaddle, Michael. 'Zamani: a survey of East African history' (new edition, 1974). *Kenya Historical Review* 4(1), 1976, p.153.

41 Ukpabi, S.C. 'War and society in Africa: ten studies' (1972). *Journal of Modern African Studies* 13(1), 1975, pp.167-8.

42 Waller, Richard. 'Kenya before 1900' (1976). *Journal of African History* 20(4), 1979, p.580.

43 'War and society in Africa: ten studies' (1972). *Choice* 10, July 1973, p.832.

44 Wenkere-Kisembo, S. 'The University, the students and the society'. *East Africa Journal* 6(2), 1969, pp.6-8.

45 Wilks, Yorick. 'Histrionics'. *East Africa Journal* 8(7), 1971, p.44.

46 Wrigley, C.C. 'Hadith 5: economic and social history of East Africa' (1975). *Kenya Historical Review* 5(1), 1977, pp.141-4.

47 Yambo, Mauri. 'Hadith 4: politics and nationalism in colonial Kenya' (1972). *Kenya Historical Review* 2(2), 1974, pp.299-303.

48 'Zamani: a survey of East African history' (1968). *Choice* 6, 1969, p.1087.

49 'Zamani: a survey of East African history' (1968). *Times Literary Supplement*, 17 July 1969, p.773.

Articles, review articles, commentaries and letters

1 'Academic and political choices in nation-building'. *E. Africa Journal* 9(5), 1972, p.2.
2 'African brotherhood vs. economic realities'. *E. Africa Journal* 7(10), 1970, pp.2-3.
3 'Answer to Okelo' (letter). *E. Africa Journal* 1(8), 1964, p.6.
4 'Authors, publishers and milch cows'. *E. Africa Journal* 8(1), 1971, p.3.
5 'The battle for educational Uhuru'. *E. Africa Journal* 4(6), 1967, pp.7-8.
6 'British administration in the Central Nyanza district of Kenya 1900-1960'. *Journal of African History* 4(2), 1963, pp.249-73.
7 'A budget of great relief, but . . .' *E. Africa Journal* 5(8), p.9.
8 'The concept of Jok'. *African Studies* 20(2), 1961, pp.123-30.
9 'Corruption in public life'. *E. Africa Journal* 4(7), 1967, pp.5-8.
10 'Cultural apes'. *E. Africa Journal* 6(6), 1969, p.7.
11 'Deviationism is inherent' (views on African Socialism). *E. Africa Journal* 1(1), 1964, pp.2-6.
12 'The East Africa we want, how about a conference?' *E. Africa Journal* 6(5), 1969, pp.7-8.
13 'East African Institute of Social and Cultural Affairs, Nairobi'. *Journal of Modern African Studies* 3(2), 1965, pp.283-5.
14 'Economic superannuation and political cleavage'. *E. Africa Journal* 7(12), 1970, p.3.
15 'The English-Swahili debate: an invitation'. *E. Africa Journal* 6(8), 1969, p.3.
16 'Evaluating East African writing'. *E. Africa Journal* 8(7), 1971, p.3.
17 'Freedom in bondage', Review of Denis Payne, *African Independence and Christian Freedom* (London: OUP, 1965); Bolaji Idown, *Towards an Indigenous Church* (London: OUP, 1965). *E. Africa Journal* 2(11), 1966, pp.38-9.
18 'From Chief to President'. *Atlas* 7 (January 1964), pp.24-8.
19 'From Chief to President', *Transition* 3(10), 1963, pp.26-30.
20 'From Wananchi to Wananje'. *E. Africa Journal* 8(8), 1971, p.2.
21 'The Garden of Eden and the Tower of Babel'. *E. Africa Journal* 9(6), 1972, pp.2-3.
22 'Ghana: the army and after'. *E. Africa Journal* 6(10), 1969, p.5.
23 'The good and the bad', Review of Pieter Lessing, *Only Hyenas Laugh* (London: Michael Joseph, 1964); David Hapgood, *Africa from Independence to Tomorrow* (N.Y.: Antheneum, 1965). *E. Africa Journal* 3(9), 1966, pp.39-41.
24 'Guerrilla tactics in economic planning'. *E. Africa Journal* 5(6), 1968, p.6.
25 'History and its sources', Review of D.F. McCall, *Africa in Time-Perspective: a discussion of historical reconstruction from unwritten sources* (Boston University Press, 1964); I. Schapera, ed., *Praise Poems of a Tswana Chief* (London: OUP, 1965); L. Harries, ed., *Swahili Prose Texts* (London: OUP, 1965); G. Barnett, *By the Lake* (Cambridge University Press, 1965). *E. Africa Journal* 2(9), 1966, pp.38-9.
26 'How have the mighty fallen?' *E. Africa Journal* 6(4), 1969, p.5.
27 'How Kenya became a blackman's country'. *Transition* 4(14) 1964, p.48.
28 'How not to create national unity'. *E. Africa Journal* 7(9), 1970, p.5.
29 K. Ingham, *A History of East Africa* (London: Longmans, 1962). *Uganda Journal* 26(2), 1962, pp.218-19.
30 'Intellectual smugglers in Africa', Review of Okot P'Bitek, *African Religions in Western Scholarship* (Nairobi: EALB, 1971). *E. Africa Journal* 8(12), 1971, pp.7-9.
31 'Inter-racial marriage: towards elimination of the superior or inferior complexes'. *E. Africa Journal* 5(9), 1968, pp.4-6.
32 'Introduction' (special issue on Mau Mau). *Kenya Historical Review* 5(2), 1977, pp.169-72.

33 J.M. Kariuki, *Mau Mau Detainee* (London: OUP, 1963). *Makerere Journal* 9 (March 1964), pp.85-6.

34 'Kenya elections'. *E. Africa Journal* 6(12), 1969, p.4.

35 'Kenya without Mboya'. *E. Africa Journal* 6(9), 1969, p.6.

36 M.S.M. Kiwanuka, *The Kingdom of Bunyoro Kitara – myth or reality?* (Kampala: Longmans, 1968). *E. Africa Journal* 6(10), 1969, pp.46-7.

37 'Land without thunder'. *E. Africa Journal* 7(5), 1970, pp.4-5.

38 'Men of the people and the second independence in Africa'. *E. Africa Journal* 8(6), 1971, pp.14-16.

39 'A national theatre'. *E. Africa Journal* 7(1), 1970, pp.4-5.

40 'The new breed in the civil service', Review of Richard Symonds, *The British and their Successors* (London: Faber and Faber, 1967). *E. Africa Journal* 4(5), 1967, pp.40-2.

41 'Nkrumah revisits Marx', Review of Kwame Nkrumah, *Consciencism* (London: Heinemann, 1964). *E. Africa Journal* 1(3), 1964, pp.29-32.

42 'OAU Summit venue and the Pan-African ideal'. *E Africa Journal* 8(5), 1971, p.3.

43 'Ojwang K'Ombudo: a rejoinder' – letter. *E. Africa Journal* 5(3), 1968, p.4.

44 G. Parrinder, *Religion in Africa* (Penguin, 1969). *African Historical Studies* 3(1), 1970, pp.182-3.

45 'The people around Lake Victoria', *Crane* (July 1962), pp.21-3.

46 'People in a corridor? What is African in terms of the 20th century?' *E. Africa Journal* 5(11), 1968, pp.9-12.

47 'Poetry and propriety'. *E. Africa Journal* 7(7), 1970, p.5.

48 'Politics and sport'. *E. Africa Journal* 9(8), 1972, p.3.

49 'Politics, culture and music in Central Kenya: a study of Mau Mau hymns, 1951-1956'. *Kenya Historical Review* 5(2), 1977, pp.275-86.

50 'Prestige, harambee projects and national development'. *E. Africa Journal* 8(11), 1971, p.2.

51 'Racial consciousness among Africans'. *E. Africa Journal* 2(1), 1965, pp.17-23.

52 ' "Reflection" and the University'. *E. Africa Journal* 7(11), 1970, p.3.

53 'Register of events', Review of M. Macpherson, *They Built for the Future: a chronicle of Makerere University College, 1922-1962* (Cambridge University Press, 1964). *E. Africa Journal* 2(2), 1965, pp.39-40.

54 'Reintroducing the African man into the world: traditionalism and socialism in African politics'. *E. Africa Journal* 4(8), Dec. 1967, pp.31-6.

55 'Rejection and affirmation', Review of E. Ashby, *African Universities and Western Tradition* (Oxford University Press, 1964). *E. Africa Journal* 2(2), 1965, p.39.

56 'Religion re-examined', Review of E.E. Evans-Pritchard, *Theories of Primitive Religion* (Oxford University Press, 1965). *E. Africa Journal* 3(3), 1966, pp.37-8.

57 Review of R.I. Rotberg and H.N. Chittick, eds., *East Africa and the Orient* (Africana Publishing Co., 1975). *Transafrican Journal of History* 5(2), 1976, pp.161-74.

58 Review of Ian Scott, *Tumbled House – the Congo at independence* (Oxford University Press, 1969). *E. Africa Journal* 6(9), 1969, pp.38-9.

59 'The silences in the old narratives or new trends in cultural history'. *Journal of E. African Research and Development* 12, 1982, pp.36-45.

60 'The style of politics in Uganda tomorrow'. *E. Africa Journal* 8(4), 1971, p.3.

61 'The supremacy of national interest'. *E. Africa Journal* 9(4), 1972, p.2.

62 'Sweet reasonableness in Southern Africa'. *E. Africa Journal* 7(2), 1970, p.3.

63 'Tanzania's decade of social dedication'. *E. Africa Journal* 8(9), 1971, pp.2-3.

64 'That Asian exodus: who's responsible?' *E. Africa Journal* 5(4), 1968, pp.5-8.

65 'Three decades of historical studies in East Africa, 1947-1977'. *Kenya Historical Review* 6 (1/2), 1978 (1980), pp.22-33.

66 'Through the glass, darkly – the two screens of a national image'. *E. Africa Journal* 5(10), 1968, pp.5-6.

67 'Tom Mboya: an appreciation'. *E. Africa Journal* 6(9), 1969, pp.9-13.
68 'Towards a history of Kenya'. *Kenya Historical Review* 4(1), 1976, pp.1-9.
69 'Towards a national system of University of Administration: the case of the University of Dar es Salaam'. *E. Africa Journal* 7(8), 1970, pp.5-6.
70 'Towards a revolution in agricultural education'. *E. Africa Journal* 7(5), 1968, pp.5-7.
71 'Traditional religion and the pre-colonial history of Africa – the example of the Padhola'. *Uganda Journal* 31(1), 1967, pp.111-16.
72 'Uganda moves to the left'. *E. Africa Journal* 7(6), 1970, pp.4-5.
73 'Unemployable graduates'. *E. Africa Journal* 9(10), 1972, pp.2-3.
74 'Unity by degrees'. *E. Africa Journal* 8(8), 1969, pp.6-7.
75 'University and society'. *E. Africa Journal* 7(4), 1970, pp.5-6.
76 'The University: its relevance and legitimacy to the community in East Africa'. *E. Africa Journal* 5(12), 1968, pp.7-10.
77 'An urgent need for effecting efficiency in low-level manpower'. *E. Africa Journal* 5(3), 1968, pp.7-8.
78 'Vagrants: what are they?' *E. Africa Journal* 6(3), 1969, pp.4-6.
79 'The white man's burden in Africa', Review of L.H. Gann and Peter Duigan, *Burden of Empire – an appraisal of Western colonialism in Africa South of the Sahara* (New York, 1967). *E. Africa Journal* 8(5), 1971, pp.13-15.
80 'Who's an East African?' *E. Africa Journal* 5(2), 1968, pp.5-8.
81 'Wildlife conservation and man'. *E. Africa Journal* 6(11), 1969, pp.3-4.
82 'Women in Kenya: the need for new organizational focus'. *E. Africa Journal* 8(3), 1971, pp.2-3.
83 'The youth: their problems in perspective'. *E. Africa Journal* 6(2), 1969, pp.11-12.

Index

representation, electoral 40, 50,
54, 73, 79, 86, 87, 88, 129
Reserve Foodstuffs Committee 150
rice production 114, 213
Rift Valley 8, 11, 14, 26, 41, 44,
62, 96; Province 131, 166, 167,
168, 216
road development 42, 50, 55, 112,
113, 158
Roho, Dini ya 103
rubber production 46, 48, 148
Rwanda 239, 240, 241

Savage, A. N. 191
Sande, Daniel 103
segregation, urban 86, 87, 135
Seko, Mobutu Seko 241
Selassie, Emperor Haile 232, 234
Senteu 16
Seroney, J. M. 208
sesame production 47, 49, 114,
115, 116, 119, 120, 122
settlers from Europe in Kenya 35,
39-43, 51, 55-6, 57, 60-2, 73,
88-9, 112, 113, 117, 133,
140, 146-55, 158, 159, 185,
198, 203, 204, 206, 210
Shaw, Timothy M. 219
Shikuku, Martin 208
Singh, Makhan 155, 165, 166, 215
sisal production 46, 48, 57, 79, 84,
91, 116, 132, 137, 139, 148,
210
slavery, (trade) 8, 10, 13, 17, 48
Socialism 217-43
society, social change 43-9, 58-66,
127, 129, 139-40, 151, 162,
190, 203-4; African 'petty-
bourgeoisie' 96-7, 98, 99, 104,
139, 140, 144, 145, 196
Society to Promote European
Immigration 40
soda ash production 138
soil erosion 128, 131, 160
Soldier Settlement Scheme 40, 41,
73, 74, 84, 112
Somali peoples 10, 29, 44, 45,
55, 124, 232
Somalia, Republic of 232, 233,
234, 235, 236, 237
Somaliland, Italian 45, 149
'squatters', African agriculture 27,
28, 48, 52, 53, 96, 105, 114,
122, 124-8, 131, 132, 133-5,
148, 159, 161
South Africa 77, 223
status, Kenya 66, 76, 81
stock rearing, livestock production
see agriculture
strikes 54, 139, 154, 164, 165,
166; see also discontent; labour
unrest

Sudan 237, 238, 239, 240
Sudanese peoples 9, 21
sugar production 56, 120, 139,
148, 211, 213
Swahili peoples and tribes 9, 13,
14, 17, 18, 21, 24, 48, 53, 55;
language use 24, 72
Swainson, Nicola 213
Swynnerton Plan 161, 190

Taita Hills Association (THA) 113,
184
Taita peoples and tribes 184
Tanganyika 91, 92, 117, 136, 161,
221
Tanzania 230-41
taxation 23, 29, 45, 46, 49-50, 58,
74, 79, 82, 85, 90, 116, 117,
129, 133, 184
tea production 57, 89, 94, 115,
124, 137, 210, 212
textiles 42, 152, 153, 211, 213
Thika 90, 96, 115, 132, 139, 195
Thuku, Harry 79, 80, 81, 98, 99,
101, 133, 140, 155, 183
tobacco production 57, 120, 121
trade 11, 13-14, 17, 18, 21, 27,
29, 44, 55-8, 61, 63, 64, 79,
94-5, 97, 104, 112, 123, 124,
130, 214
Transport and Allied Workers
Union (TAWU) 165, 167
tribalism 214-17
Tugen peoples and tribes 12, 124

Uasin Gishu 74, 75, 90;
District Council 159
Uganda 8, 21, 42, 54, 65, 77, 85,
87, 91, 92, 149, 183, 221, 230,
231, 232, 233, 234, 235, 236,
237, 238, 239, 240, 241
Uganda Protectorate 8, 18
Uganda railway 8, 9, 39, 42, 44,
60, 161
Ukamba Members Association
(UMA) 113, 129, 131, 133, 184
Ulalo, Odera 22
Union of Soviet Socialist Republics
(USSR) 175, 196, 228, 229, 234,
238
unions, unionism, trade 54, 55,
154, 155, 165, 166, 187; see
also individual unions
United Kingdom see Great Britain
United Nations Organization
(UNO) 157, 221, 223
United States of America (USA)
156, 174, 175, 176, 196, 212,
226, 229, 234, 237, 241, 242
urbanization 63-6, 86, 87, 135,
148, 163, 186

Vasey Report 165
Voi 56, 63

Wachira, K. K. 209
wages, wage rates 50, 81, 116,
154, 164, 182-4, 186
Waiyaki 18
Wakefield, E. B. 190
Wang'ombe 18
Wanga peoples 14, 17
Wanjau, Gakaara 209
War Council 40
wars:
First World 35, 40, 43, 45,
46, 49, 50, 54, 55, 57, 59,
88, 112, 114, 127, 132, 144,
146; Ethio-Somali 237, 242;
Morijo 16; Iloikop 14; Second
World War 113, 122, 144,
145-55, 156, 173, 174, 176,
196; Tanzania-Uganda 237
Waruhiu, Chief 168
wattle production 47, 57, 115,
120, 121, 122, 137
bark production 94, 121, 151
Waweru, Kabetu wa 7
Wedgwood, J. C. 77
Wedgwood, Josiah 85
West Germany 226, 229
Western Province 155, 167
wheat production 47, 94, 112,
116, 118
Wilson, Sir Samuel 92
Wilson Report 164
Winterton, Earl of 87
women, African, working 27, 47,
59, 163
Wood, Edward (later Viscount
Halifax) 78, 87
workers, working class, African 27,
53, 54, 61, 65, 73, 96, 105, 162,
164
Worthington Plan 159

Young Kavirondo Association 81-2,
101, 129, 130, 183 became
Kavirondo Taxpayers Welfare
Association qv
Young Kikuyu Association 79, 80,
102, 183 became East African
Association qv
Young Nyika Association (YNA)
113, 133

Zaire 239, 240
Zambia 232
Zanzibar 8, 9, 65, 76, 221
Zanzibari people 9, 10, 24,
trade 19